(Re)Constructing Communities in Europe, 1918–1968

This book offers a new perspective on the social history of twentieth-century Europe by investigating the ideals and ideas, the life worlds and ideologies that emerge behind the use of the concept of community. It explores a wide variety of actors, ranging from the tenants of London council estates to transnational cultural elites.

Stefan Couperus is Assistant Professor of European Politics and Society at the University of Groningen, the Netherlands.

Harm Kaal is Assistant Professor of Political History at Radboud University Nijmegen, the Netherlands.

Routledge Studies in Modern European History

For a full list of titles in this series, please visit www.routledge.com

29 **Hitler's Brudervolk**
   The Dutch and the Colonization of Occupied Eastern Europe, 1939–1945
   Geraldien von Frijtag Drabbe Künzel

30 **Alan S. Milward and Contemporary European History**
   Collected Academic Reviews
   Edited by Fernando Guirao and Frances M.B. Lynch

31 **Ireland's Great Famine and Popular Politics**
   Edited by Enda Delaney and Breandán Mac Suibhne

32 **Legacies of Violence in Contemporary Spain**
   Exhuming the Past, Understanding the Present
   Edited by Ofelia Ferrán and Lisa Hilbink

33 **The Problem of Democracy in Postwar Europe**
   Political Actors and the Formation of the Postwar Model of Democracy in France, West Germany and Italy
   Pepijn Corduwener

34 **Meanings and Values of Water in Russian Culture**
   Edited by Jane Costlow and Arja Rosenholm

35 **Italy and Its Eastern Border, 1866–2016**
   Marina Cattaruzza

36 **Franco-Israeli Relations, 1958–1967**
   Gadi Heimann

37 **(Re)Constructing Communities in Europe, 1918–1968**
   Senses of Belonging Below, Beyond and Within the Nation-State
   Edited by Stefan Couperus and Harm Kaal

(Re)Constructing Communities in Europe, 1918–1968
Senses of Belonging Below, Beyond and Within the Nation-State

Edited by Stefan Couperus
and Harm Kaal

NEW YORK AND LONDON

First published 2017
by Routledge
711 Third Avenue, New York, NY 10017

and by Routledge
2 Park Square, Milton Park, Abingdon, Oxon OX14 4RN

First issued in paperback 2018

Routledge is an imprint of the Taylor & Francis Group, an informa business

© 2017 Taylor & Francis

The right of the editors to be identified as the authors of the editorial material, and of the authors for their individual chapters, has been asserted in accordance with sections 77 and 78 of the Copyright, Designs and Patents Act 1988.

All rights reserved. No part of this book may be reprinted or reproduced or utilised in any form or by any electronic, mechanical, or other means, now known or hereafter invented, including photocopying and recording, or in any information storage or retrieval system, without permission in writing from the publishers.

Trademark notice: Product or corporate names may be trademarks or registered trademarks, and are used only for identification and explanation without intent to infringe.

Library of Congress Cataloging in Publication Data
A catalog record for this book has been requested.

ISBN 13: 978-1-138-32992-8 (pbk)
ISBN 13: 978-1-138-69228-2 (hbk)

Typeset in Sabon
by Apex CoVantage, LLC

Printed in the United Kingdom
by Henry Ling Limited

Contents

List of Figures ix
Acknowledgments xi

1 Introduction: (Re)Constructing Communities in Europe, 1918–68   1
STEFAN COUPERUS AND HARM KAAL

PART I
Urban Communities   17

2 Languages of Place and Belonging: Competing Conceptions of "Community" in Mid-Twentieth-Century Bermondsey, London   19
JON LAWRENCE

3 Rethinking the "Blueprint for Living Together": Community Planning and Sociology in Coventry, 1940–55   45
STEFAN COUPERUS

4 "Washing Away the Dirt of the War Years": History, Politics and the Reconstruction of Urban Communities in Post–World War II Helsinki   65
TANJA VAHTIKARI

PART II
Rural and Regional Communities   85

5 A Counter-Community between Regionalism and Nationalism: State-Building and the Vision of Modernisation in Interwar Romania   87
FLORIAN KÜHRER-WIELACH

6 Community Building and Expert Involvement with Reclaimed Lands in the Netherlands, 1930s–50s 108
LIESBETH VAN DE GRIFT

7 The Turn to Local Communities in Early Post-War West Germany: The Case of Hamburg, Lübeck and Bremen, 1945–65 130
JEREMY DEWAAL

PART III
Transnational Communities 151

8 Restoring the Republic of Letters: Romain Rolland, Stefan Zweig and Transnational Community Building in Europe, 1914–34 153
MARLEEN RENSEN

9 A Vatican Conspiracy? Internationalism, Catholicism and the Quest for European Unification, 1945–50 175
MAARTEN VAN DEN BOS

10 Piercing the Iron Curtain? Competing Visions of Transnational Expert Community and the Question of International Order after 1945 196
PHILLIP WAGNER

PART IV
Nation, Class and Religion 215

11 Reconstructing Post-War Political Communities: Class, Religion and Political Identity-Formation in the Netherlands, 1945–68 217
HARM KAAL

12 Dialogues on Religion in a "Socialist Society" under Construction: Marxist Social Scientists and Czech Protestants, 1940s–60s 238
ONDŘEJ MATĚJKA

13 Languages of "National Community" and Its "Others"
in Europe, 1918–68   260
STEFAN BERGER

Contributors   275
Index   277

Figures

2.1	Guinness Trust Buildings on Snowfields, Bermondsey (2013)	21
2.2	Bermondsey Election Special (1950), Southwark Public Library	35
3.1	Aerial view on the western part of Canley, Coventry, 1949. At the bottom workers hostels are sited. In the middle the steel BISF houses are laid out	52
3.2	Layout of the Thimbler Road residential unit, using pseudonym 'Braydon Road'	54
3.3	Original layout of the Tile Hill neighbourhood unit (1945)	57
4.1	'The Marching Military Reservists', a display in the historical procession staged as part of Helsinki's quadricentennial celebrations, 11 June 1950	70
4.2	'Population Growth', a display in the Helsinki Before and Today exhibition, June 1950	76
5.1	Map showing the borders of the Kingdom of Romania in 1920, the Romanian border of 1914 and the borders of various historical regions	91
6.1	Machine threshing. Combine harvesters in the Noordoostpolder, Netherlands, 8 August 1950	115
6.2	During the national holiday festivities, Queen Juliana speaks with a group of pioneers from the Noordoostpolder, carrying wheelbarrows and shovels	118
6.3	Housewife combing her daughter's hair, Ramsgat Noordoostpolder, 2 August 1951	121
7.1	Aerial view of Hamburg-Eilbek following bombing raids in June 1943	133
7.2	British in war-torn Bremen in April 1945	134
7.3	Lübeck after Allied bombing in March 1942	135
8.1	Romain Rolland on the balcony of his home (162, boulevard de Montparnasse, Paris), 1914	157
8.2	Stefan Zweig at his desk in his house in Salzburg about 1928	158

x *Figures*

9.1	The first meeting of the Association for Spiritual Renewal (May 1946). On the left is J.M.M. van der Ven	181
9.2	A Pax Christi hike near Altenberg, Germany (1953)	187
10.1	The Belgian section at the exhibition held during the 1946 IFHTP conference. The poster on the right represents the destruction committed by the German occupying forces and their shortcomings with regard to housing	203
11.1	In the 1946 campaign the PvdA issued posters aimed at different groups of voters, such as women, intellectuals, farmers and tradespeople. The caption at the top of this poster reads 'Labour, the source of all affluence', followed at the bottom by 'Also tradespeople vote for the Labour Party. At the service of the whole of the people'. Poster, 79.5 × 53.5 cm. Design: Studio Uschi Torens	222
11.2	Map showing the 'political orthodoxy of Catholic voters in the province of Noord-Brabant and Limburg 1956', printed in *De politieke keuze der Nederlandse katolieken*, a report published by KASKI in 1957. The map shows that political orthodoxy was relatively low in the mining areas of southern Limburg and in the urban areas of Tilburg, Breda, 's-Hertogenbosch and Eindhoven	226
12.1	In January 1969 Josef Lukl Hromádka attended a conference on East-West relations at VU University Amsterdam	240

Acknowledgments

(Re)Constructing Communities in Europe was the title of a conference hosted by the editors just before Christmas 2013 in the Soeterbeeck Study Center in Ravenstein: a former monastery that provided the appropriate surroundings and atmosphere for an intensive three-day academic discussion on the construction of communities. We would like to thank all participants and our keynote speakers Stefan Berger, Jon Lawrence and Rosemary Wakeman, who contributed greatly to the genesis of this volume.

(Re)Constructing Communities in Europe also brings together two research projects that were both funded by the Netherlands Organisation for Scientific Research. Harm Kaal's project deals with the emergence of a particular mode of mobilization and activation of grass-roots supporters of Dutch political parties. Methodologically, it leans heavily on a deconstructivist reading of political language in historical sources such as party propaganda and partisan discourse. The other project—executed by Stefan Couperus—centres on something completely different: the governance of urban planning in bombed out cities in Europe during the mid-twentieth century. This research adopts, to a large extent, a governmentality approach towards the ways in which urban life was forged before, during and after the bombings of the Second World War. At some point, discussing our mutual projects, we became aware of the fact that we were working with a shared set of historical categories that we were both attempting to deal with critically. Both projects address themes about burgeoning aspirations of social stability and coherence, and both projects distinguish a series of spheres or realms in which perceptions of social degeneration incited a responsiveness that ultimately found expression in a variety of ideas and proposals about social generation or re-generation, at least during the mid-twentieth century. Both projects, thus, in essence dealt with efforts to (re)construct communities.

We would like to thank the Netherlands Organisation for Scientific Research and Radboud University's International Office for funding our conference. Moreover, we are indebted to the anonymous reviewers for their helpful suggestions, to Jim Gibbons for his meticulous copy editing, and to

Max Novick and Jennifer Morrow for assisting in finalising our book proposal and getting it into print. Finally, we would like to thank all contributors to this volume for their patience, their willingness to meet deadlines and guidelines and their thoughtful comments. All remaining mistakes are of course our own.

1 Introduction
(Re)Constructing Communities in Europe, 1918–68

Stefan Couperus and Harm Kaal

The concept of community was at the heart of inter- and post-war discourses of reconstruction. The devastating effects of both World Wars offered plenty of ruined sites—literally and figuratively—on which new communities were to be constructed or projected, ranging from the highly exclusionary *Volksgemeinschaft* meant to underpin Hitler's Millennial Reich, to universalist and democratic notions of community epitomised by the establishment of the United Nations. The notion of community permeated plans for the rebuilding of ruined cities and the development of new, planned (sub)urban neighbourhoods, as well as efforts to maintain viable, cohesive and productive rural settlements amidst rapid urbanisation. Communities, whether in their imagined sense or through lived experience, were the social glue through which people tried to come to terms with the devastating experience of war, where they tried to heal their wounds or urge for the redemption of past injustices. Many panaceas for the perceived moral degeneration of humankind—due to the atrocities of war, anomie induced by the metropolis, the waning of religious values or any of the other alienating and disturbing effects of modernity—were informed by myriad notions of community.[1]

Historiography has mainly articulated the nation as a framework for community discourse and formation. Ever since Benedict Anderson's seminal study, the construction of communities has been presented as a national or even a nationalist historical undertaking.[2] In line with this predominant lens of inquiry, and in an attempt to reconcile the discursive and spatial dimensions of community, Charles S. Maier recently argued that 'a stable sense of community' emerges if a minimum degree of congruence exists between 'identity space'—a particular 'geography of alliance'—and 'decision space'—'the turf that seems to assure physical, economic and cultural security'.[3] As such, historiography has tended to confirm the spatial and discursive dimensions of community as being predominantly national. This applies in particular to the period between 1918 and the late 1960s, the timeframe under consideration in this volume. This period was held together by continual efforts to construct communities as an answer to the challenges of modernity in terms of class antagonism, political polarisation, social disruption and increasing state intervention. Legitimised by a host of sociological scholarship, for instance the work of Karl Mannheim, social planning was presented as the panacea for the 'crisis of liberalism and democracy' that had allegedly been key to interwar social fragmentation.[4]

In the late 1960s this collectivist discourse yielded to disaggregated and individualist attitudes towards the social in what Daniel Rodgers has coined the 'Age of Fracture'.[5] The German sociologist Ulrich Beck has convincingly shown that the late 1960s marked the end of what he termed the *Grossgruppengesellschaft*: a conceptualisation of society marked by 'big' social categories such as nation, class or religion.[6] In a similar vein, other authors have argued that, against the background of post-industrialism and post-materialism, the 1960s witnessed a shift from 'heavy' communities to 'communities lite', which they characterize as being dynamic, flexible, temporary and based on individual choice.[7]

In contrast to historiography predominantly oriented towards the nation-state, and in line with more recent inquiries into the *sub-* and *trans*-national sites of community construction, this volume presents a host of narratives that engage with scales, geographies and discourses that do not necessarily or exclusively articulate, confirm or produce national identities. This is not to say that the national is something to be denounced; it still serves as a trope or counterpoint in negotiating *decentred* conceptions of community.

This volume examines urban, rural, regional and transnational community building processes and relates these processes to one another, but it also looks at more functionalist community discourses in the realms of politics, religion, academia and literature from the end of the Great War up through the late 1960s. By adopting an actor-centred approach, the chapters bring to the fore a wide-ranging cast of actors, including intellectuals, artists, scholars, representatives of civil society, local administrators, politicians and ordinary citizens. These actors present us with a set of discursive and social practices from which the authors of this book distil the mechanisms, processes, social actions and interactions through which 'non-imagined' communities were constructed, mediated and made 'real'. Consequently, the analysis is not exclusively centred on the imaginaries of community. Articulated here as well are the lived experiences and social practices of community as they emerged and unfolded within specific spatial settings.

Thus, community (re)construction was not the sole result of state-controlled, impersonal, dirigist and top-down projects.[8] Different conceptions of community circulated, collided and were mediated discursively among officials and experts; social interventionism was challenged, thwarted or amended from within the administrative machinery, the expanding field of the (applied) social sciences and the 'communities' themselves.[9] Community, whether or not explicitly defined as a goal of interventionism, was not the product of a linear planning process. It was laboriously negotiated, not exclusively determined by administrative elites, and infused by the efforts of civil society, grass-roots initiatives and local customs.[10] Vernacular languages and imaginations existed alongside and contested state or expert conceptions of community.[11] As such, this collection of essays presents a series of cases where community was articulated or acted out at levels below, beyond and in interaction with the national framework of social thought and practice.

Community Thought since the Early Twentieth Century

From the end of the nineteenth century onwards, the prominence of the concept of community in modern European and North American history has inspired an expansive and ever-growing body of scholarship. Simplifications of Ferdinand Tönnies's highly influential dichotomy between *Gemeinschaft* and *Gesellschaft* remained strongly axiomatic in sociological thinking throughout the twentieth century. Renowned sociologists and socially minded thinkers such as Robert Park, John Dewey and Robert MacIver took this binary as the starting point of their explorations into the effects of modernisation, in its various guises, on the existence of communities.[12] Survey-based studies and participatory observation mapped communal life from the early twentieth century onwards. Research on the impact of urbanisation on existing social bonds flourished particularly in the field of urban studies. The negative effects of modernity on communal life, norms and values were downplayed in the famous Middletown studies conducted by Lynd and Lynd in the 1920s and 1930s, though in general, pessimism prevailed and *Gemeinschaft* lost ground to *Gesellschaft*.[13] In his influential article on 'urbanism as a way of life', published in 1938, Chicago School sociologist Louis Wirth stressed the impersonality of life in cities and argued that urbanisation hollowed out the communal ties fostered by the family and the neighbourhood.[14]

Similar accounts were still in vogue among urban sociologists in the 1960s.[15] In these studies community functioned as a concept both normative—needing to be strengthened and reinstated—and descriptive.[16] In the latter case, discussions centred on the key features of social bonds which qualified them as being essential to 'communities'. This resulted in a range of definitions of community and attempts to move from a descriptive take on the concept to a generic theory of community.[17] Communities were represented as essentially good, as inclusive entities that supported and facilitated social interaction. Promoting the reconstruction of communities thus seemed to be a 'good cause'; it would be hard to imagine how one would take a negative stance towards it.

The exclusionary mechanisms of community, however, had become very salient. As a result of Nazism and Soviet communism, the concept of community had been tainted by the ideological and totalitarian semantics it had acquired and its exclusionary tendencies and means. After all, the Nazi *Volksgemeinschaft* was constructed upon genocidal anti-Semitism. In *The Quest for Community*, published in 1953, the American conservative sociologist Robert Nisbet linked the rise of totalitarianism and the success of

Nazi *Volksgemeinschaft* propaganda with a yearning for community among rootless people. He saw these phenomena as a response to the suppression of pre-modern communities by the force of individualism and an ever-growing state apparatus. Paying tribute to Tocqueville, Nisbet called for a flourishing civil society to keep individualism and state rationalism in check.[18]

Alongside the predominant conceptions of national communities, community was considered as a sub- or trans-national category, too. Already during the interwar years intellectuals, politicians and members of civil society organisations had levelled scathing criticisms at nationalism. Associating distinct national communities with antagonism and exclusion, they looked for ways to embed these communities into a broader, inclusive international framework, a European community of some sort.[19] In this sense communities were thus perceived as social alliances that preferably had to remain *beyond* or *below* the framework of the nation-state, without the suggestion that national conceptions of community or biases towards them had become insignificant.

Below the national level, the planned reconstruction of Europe—after both World Wars—offered plenty of opportunities to implement new community schemes, for instance in (sub)urban neighbourhoods and new towns.[20] In the interwar period, many professionals and intellectuals defined the physical, social, cultural and economic substrates of envisaged urban communities.[21] Notably in the field of architecture and town planning, modernist conceptions of the social were undergirded by a firm belief that spatial preconditions could determine the tenor of human behaviour.[22] Technological advancements produced new instruments to survey, monitor and define 'social space' and to relate the social to the spatial.[23] From the late 1940s onwards, these technologies also assisted in the conducting of sociological surveys that provided ethnographic interpretations of communities, interlacing the concept with notions of family, class, neighbourhood and social behaviour.[24] Mass housing, to name another urban phenomenon taken up by scholarship on community, became a key realm for the investigation of community since the interwar period. As Kenny Cupers shows in his study on post-war housing in France, the matrix of physical, social and administrative planning—and social inquiry—fostered myriad sociological readings of community, which produced state-initiated 'life-size laboratories under the scrutiny of social-scientific experts'.[25]

Emerging simultaneously within the fields of rural and urban geography in the 1950s and 1960s were studies assessing the impact of modernisation on rural and urban communal life. Rural geographers, for instance, posited that urbanisation hollowed out rural communities, confronted as they were with declining service provisions, rising unemployment rates and population decline.[26] What these studies argued for, implicitly or explicitly, was state intervention. Through its planning apparatus the state could steer rural and urban (re)development in the 'right' direction, ensuring liveable communities both in cities and the countryside.

In the 1960s this approach was contested by a new generation of social and urban scholars. In her classic critique of the modernist urban planning paradigm of the post-war era, the American activist Jane Jacobs accused the elitist nexus of planners, politicians, builders and technocrats of having built cities without communities.[27] The 1970s saw a continuing rise of studies in which (urban) communal life was deconstructed and its exclusionary mechanisms highlighted. In *The Fall of Public Man* the American sociologist Richard Sennett argued that although communities were often perceived as 'bastions [. . .] against the depersonalization and alienation of urban life', they in fact reinforced depersonalisation and alienation through their mechanism of inclusion and exclusion and their 'celebration of the ghetto'.[28] Similar concerns are to be found in a range of studies on internal colonialism, 'the boomerang effect' of external colonialism, as Michel Foucault phrased it, which had brought back 'a whole series of colonial models' to the post-colonial West—and thus allowed for a number of new hegemonic, unequal divisions in society that produced segregated communities along the lines of class and ethnicity.[29] Recently, Carl Nightingale took up these ideas in a provocative study on segregation, in which he draws links between the emergence of segregated urban communities across the globe and segregation by ethnicity and race in the colonies.[30]

Up until the 1980s community had figured prominently in the social sciences, but now it was also catapulted to the centre of historical research. In 1978 and 1980 the American sociologist Craig Calhoun presented his musings over the concept and theory of community to an audience of historians in two papers published in *Social History*.[31] Calhoun argued for a structural approach to community by analysing it as a 'complex of social relationships' and not solely as a 'complex of ideas and sentiments'.[32] Historical research would, however, take a somewhat different turn. At nearly the same time three studies were published that exerted a huge impact on the study of communities. The American anthropologist Benedict Anderson famously introduced the concept of imagined communities in his 1983 study *Imagined Communities: Reflections on the Origin and Spread of Nationalism*. This seminal book introduced a heuristic conception of community that transcends exclusive associations of community with place, turf or territory. According to Anderson, national communities were constructed through acts of imagination, with people perceiving the nation as a 'deep horizontal comradeship'.[33] That same year, the British historians Eric Hobsbawm and Terence Ranger coined the concept of 'invented traditions', which was fruitfully applied to studying the construction of (national) communities around a shared culture.[34] Again in 1983 the Cambridge historian Gareth Stedman Jones published his seminal work on Chartism, *Languages of Class*.[35] Unlike Anderson, Hobsbawm and Ranger, Stedman Jones did not engage with nations and nationalism, but rather presented a new perspective on the construction of political communities by emphasising the capacity of language to unite people around a shared interpretation of the social. Taken together, these studies inspired an approach to communities as discursive and cultural constructions.

Within philosophy, in turn, a fierce debate developed between proponents of liberalism (ranging from John Rawls to, more recently, Will Kymlicka) and communitarianism (Michael Walzer, Amitai Etzioni and others), again vesting the term 'community' with a normative connotation.[36] The latter camp's criticism of liberalism was based on their fear of its moral consequences: they claimed that communities were an essential element of the good life. Following in the footsteps of Nisbet, the communities they promoted were mainly small-scale and grounded in direct interactions among its members as they took place in neighbourhoods and within the family. Kymlicka, in turn, has defended liberalism by contending that it acknowledges that individual values are linked with the wider community in which a person operates. Community, however, has no value of its own; it merely serves to contribute to liberal autonomy.[37] Recently, philosophers like Charles Taylor have argued for a combination of liberal and communitarian views, uniting an individual rights approach with an acknowledgment of the importance of a democratic political community.[38]

Finally, the field of historical studies recently witnessed an upsurge of transnational approaches to community. Again, the late Benedict Anderson proved the value of such an approach by laying bare the universal language of identity-formation and the mechanisms of inclusion and exclusion.[39] Other historians have probed modes of community formation from a transnational perspective, too. Pierre-Yves Saunier has been pivotal in unravelling transnational networks and groupings, starting with urban interchanges and, ultimately, coordinating—with Akira Iriye—the creation of a global overview of transnational endeavours and developments.[40] The work of Daniel Laqua, among others, has shown how, from the fin-de-siècle onwards, ideals and practices of trans-border collaboration developed into a transnational realm of communities dedicating themselves to science, peace, culture and social reform in perceived 'world capitals' such as Brussels.[41] Moreover, current scholarship addresses the local impacts of transnationalism, thus decentring the transnational interchanges and networks and looking at the way in which—and extent to which—transnational outlooks reverberated locally through agency and discourse in highly contextualised settings of social practices.[42]

Methodology and Outline of the Volume

Taking up this rich tradition of community scholarship, the authors in this volume present community as essentially a research category that centres on the contemplation and delineation of the social.

Communication is at community's core and, as such, community is always constructed and performed through language, attitudes and activities. Observing communities through the lens of discursive and social practices, as this volume sets out to do, implies that we do not treat the concept of community here as fixed and predefined. The term *community* is first and foremost used as a heuristic device, a marker that allows the pinpointing of community thought and practice in primary sources and literatures. Using the conceptions of community held by the historical actors as guidance, each chapter unearths particular instances of discursive and social practices of community.

First, community is approached from the perspective of the formation of identities and senses of belonging: communities were and are held together by continuously (re)negotiated social categories of class, race, gender, religion, culture, age and profession. These identities both emerged from below, as vernacular expressions of belonging to a particular community, but were also evident in elitist discourses of community. Second, community is related to territory in the sense that a community of people inhabits a particular geographical area: a region, a town, all the way down to the level of a neighbourhood or even a building block. The congruence of a social grouping with a particular place or turf has elicited myriad, particular, locally inscribed discourses of community. Third, communities are represented as a functionalist network, which is to say they are always groups of people sharing particular forms of knowledge, whether from participation in professional communities, or of having particular experiences (as with the survivors of bombed cities) or outlooks (as with members of religious groups).

This approach to the concept of community translates into the following set of questions that have guided this book. How did historical actors from a variety of social echelons conceive of the idea of community or community building? Which inclusionary and exclusionary claims accompanied the construction of communities? How did elitist efforts to construct communities interfere or interplay with bottom-up, vernacular understandings of selfhood and belonging? What impact did scientific knowledge production and dissemination have on conceptions of community? How did notions of place, and the importance of place as a site of belonging, interact with efforts to construct communities? Finally, how did people at a given moment negotiate and reflect upon the availability of multiple identities, linked to the presence of multiple communities?

The chapters in this volume, which cover Central and Western Europe, discuss one or several of these questions by applying a comparative perspective of some sort. Some chapters compare, contrast and deconstruct vernacular and established conceptions of community; others reflect on different conceptions of community among a range of social scientists or deliver an international comparison of the language of community in various distinct socio-political contexts. The first part of *(Re)constructing Communities in Europe* deals with community construction in cities: in the London neighbourhood of Bermondsey, the Finnish capital Helsinki and the bombed English city of Coventry. Jon Lawrence compares anthropological, political and vernacular understandings of communal life based on a case study of the London neighbourhood of Bermondsey in the mid-twentieth century. He shows that while social scientists doing fieldwork there were surprised to find that life in Bermondsey did not fit their theoretical notions of community, local Labour politicians successfully constructed a strong sense of community on the political level by creating an opposition between the hard-working people of Bermondsey and privileged outsiders. For much of the twentieth century, Lawrence argues, politics helped sustain a subtly distinctive, more inclusive politics of place, which operated above the level of the building, court or street. Although vernacular identification with place was generally more fine-grained and local, it often ran in tandem with politicians' broader, more inclusive rendition of local patriotism. Only when Labour's politics of place lost its pull in the 1960s did the internal social differences became more salient, and with it went narrower, more exclusionary interpretations of community.

The next chapter probes into the neighbourhood level. Based on a case study of Coventry, a city heavily bombarded by Luftwaffe air raids during World War II, Stefan Couperus unearths the local practices of community building in the 1940s and 1950s. He shows that the socio-spatial essentialisms that underpinned community thought among local administrators and urban planners became contested during the process of neighbourhood planning. New insights, stemming from empirical sociology, and an increasing awareness about the self-proclaimed wants and needs of dwellers altered the governance of community planning.

The reconstruction of urban communities viewed from the perspective of history and memory is at the heart of Tanja Vahtikari's chapter. Historical pageants, academic and popular history writing, films and exhibitions are approached as discursive practices through which a sense of belonging was constructed in post-war Helsinki. City authorities used historical narratives that reflected on the immediate and more distant past to construct an inclusive urban community ready to meet the challenges of the present. Through the celebrations of the city's quadricentennial in 1950 they transmitted an officially sanctioned and politicised version of its historically inspired urban community, but this was met by counter-narratives produced by those whose history was marginalized or ignored.

The second part of the volume consists of three chapters that are concerned with the regional or rural as sites for community construction. Florian Kührer-Wielach takes up the issue of the construction and persistence of regional identities against the background of the establishment of new nation-states in post–First World War Europe. He shows how Romanian Transylvanians, after their territory had been added to the Kingdom of Romania, fundamentally reconceptualised the notion of a Transylvanian community and negotiated their sense of belonging to this community with their membership in a new national community. Kührer-Wielach shows that the town of Alba Iulia played a vital role in the competition between regional and national senses of belonging. It simultaneously acted as a site for both the construction and maintenance of a distinct Transylvanian community and the construction of a new 'Greater' Romanian identity, which illustrates that place could be vested with different conflicting or competing senses of belonging at once.

Liesbeth van de Grift's chapter taps into the recent literature on the impact of the social sciences on legitimising and practicing colonial rule. Social scientific research helped to uncover the 'essence' and purity of communities, their customs and mechanisms, which were now turned into guidelines for the reconstruction of traditional, 'organic' communities set apart from modern communities constituted around the European colonial administrators and their families.[43] These narratives of community travelled back to Europe and materialised in projects of 'inner colonisation' such as the construction of new rural settlements, which are at the heart of van der Grift's research. State authorities became actively involved in the colonisation of new land, not only draining it, but also selecting colonists, building infrastructure, designing villages and monitoring the development of a settler community. In an analysis of practices of inner colonisation in the Netherlands van de Grift zooms in on two rural experts who perceived the construction of new rural communities as an antidote to the negative consequences of laissez-faire capitalism. Their plea for 'healthy' and productive rural communities tied in with existing anxieties about 'degeneration', fuelled by anti-urbanism, and reveals the importance of the social and political roles ascribed to the peasantry in the interwar years.

Jeremy DeWaal, in his chapter, investigates the identity space of local communities in post-war West Germany with a focus on the Hanseatic region in the north: the cities of Hamburg, Lübeck and Bremen. Turning away from a messianic national community as a source of personal redemption, in the early post-war years locals emphasized their local communities as sites of protection and orientation. DeWaal argues that citizens frequently described their local community as a site of 'life affirmation' and conflated their own fates with those of their home towns. Such discursive reconstructions of local community were neither top-down nor entirely grass-roots projects, but rather involved reciprocal cooperation from above and below. Following an era defined by exclusionary practices of community formation, many citizens reformulated local identities to encourage more permeable notions of community. DeWaal shows that emergent ideas such as 'Hanseatic democracy', 'Hanseatic world-openness' and 'Hanseatic tolerance', which underpinned popular conceptions of community, acted as discursive tools that influenced the cultural and political terms of community and its mechanisms of inclusion and exclusion.

The third part of the book moves towards the transnational, European level and deals with efforts to construct transnational communities based on shared cultural values, shared expertise and a common religion. In her chapter, Marleen Rensen moves beyond the level of the nation-state by analysing attempts to construct a European intellectual community in the spirit of the early modern notion of a 'Republic of Letters'. Zooming in on the ideas of Romain Rolland and Stefan Zweig, Rensen shows how artists and intellectuals in the interwar years sought to re-establish a cross-border community through the creation of associations and journals that fostered intellectual exchange on a European or worldwide scale. They identified the Republic of Letters with a community united around the triumph of reason and humanist values like tolerance, peace and justice. Their attempts to reconstruct such a Republic did materialize, but Rolland and Zweig had to acknowledge that a cultural notion of community also had political implications. Within their network, controversies emerged about the purpose and meaning of a transnational intellectual community, which soon resulted in the fragmentation of the Republic of Letters into separate communities.

Maarten van den Bos also adopts a transnational perspective, exploring the discursive construction of notions of community among Catholic intellectuals, clerics and politicians in the early post–Second World War years. They formed a broad network that discussed the role of religious doctrines and Catholic social teachings in the building of a peaceful post-war world. Van den Bos particularly tracks the conceptions of community formulated by leading intellectuals like the French philosopher Jacques Maritain and movements such as the Dutch Catholic Association for Spiritual Renewal, the French worker-priest movement and various national chapters of Pax Christi, and he shows how church authorities responded to their initiatives and ideas. Van den Bos argues that the various conceptions of community among European Catholics eventually met each other in support for some form of European unification—which helps to explain why the European project was often perceived to be a 'Vatican conspiracy'.

Phillip Wagner rounds out this part of the volume with an investigation of how international expert organisations sought to construct transnational professional communities following the end of the Second World War. Taking as a case study the International Federation for Housing and Town Planning (IFHTP)—the largest expert network for urban, regional and national planning in the North Atlantic world—Wagner tracks the negotiation and dissemination of different conceptualisations of a transnational professional community. These conceptions always carried certain implications for international order—for instance, whether it was imagined as an international or transnational structure, whether it would encompass different political regimes, and whether it was envisaged as a universalistic or pluralistic system. Visions of a transnational community therefore often created new ground for political conflict. The complex controversies of the post-war decade—the growing hostilities between East and West, the legacies of the war and the establishment of global institutions like the United Nations—led to a proliferation of competing ideas of transnational community and international order that emerged in tandem with post-war international conflicts.

The fourth and final part of the volume deals with communities formed around three key concepts of identity-formation: nation, class and religion. The chapters home in on the interplay between these concepts in processes of community construction and unearth their inclusionary and exclusionary mechanisms.

At the heart of Harm Kaal's chapter are the political discourses of community in Dutch party politics after the Second World War. Taking up the issue of the scientisation of the political, he explores the conceptions of political community among a range of social scientists who were involved in electoral research and tracks their impact on the language of politics. After the Second World War, all major parties started to make systematic use of research on social stratification and voting behaviour within the fields of sociology and the political sciences. Its findings provided them with clues about how to categorize the electorate and about the key characteristics of various groups in society. Kaal shows how parties struggled to respond to research that signalled the rise of the middle class and the secularisation of the electorate. From the late 1960s onwards, without disappearing completely, the notion of community as a framework through which political representation was achieved and discursively constructed in terms of a common identity, a shared culture and a common struggle for the realisation of a particular political agenda lost much of its force and so did the big social categories—in terms of class or religion—that had underpinned these conceptions of political communities.

In his chapter on Czechoslovakia Ondřej Matějka builds on recent studies on the role played by sociologists and ethnographers in post-war communist Europe, who, through their exploration of communal life, helped to construct the notion of a 'socialist society'.[44] Matejka adds religious identities to this perspective by discussing the clash between conceptualisations of community among leading members of Christian (mainly Protestant) churches and the communist state apparatus. Efforts of the former to re-affirm their right to exist in the new, post-war communist social order, and the reactions of their Communist adversaries, show the difficulties involved in putting a social communitarian utopia into practice.

In the final chapter of this volume Stefan Berger reads against the grain of most of the chapters. He argues that national community discourse was key to the emerging political language of post-war prosperity, peace and progress in post-war (Western) Europe, although it was also heavily contested. Berger maps different ways of constructing national communities, stressing the intersectionality of national identity with those articulated below and beyond the national framework. Languages of national community interacted with local, regional and transnational conceptions of community as well as with identities formed around class, religion, ethnicity and race.

Notes

1. Raphael, "Embedding," 51.
2. Anderson, *Imagined Communities*.
3. Maier, "Consigning," 816.
4. Mannheim, *Man and Society*; Mannheim, *Freedom*.
5. Rodgers, *The Age*, 3.

6. Beck, *Risikogesellschaft*, 116.
7. Duyvendak and Hurenkamp, eds, *Kiezen*.
8. Lebow, *Unfinished*; Etzemüller, "Strukturierter".
9. Klemek, *The Transatlantic Collapse*; Couperus, "Experimental Planning".
10. Sweeney, "Modernity"; Couperus, Lagendijk, and Van de Grift, "Experimental Spaces".
11. Lebow, *Unfinished*; Kuchenbuch, *Das Peckham-Experiment*.
12. Keller, *Community*, 42–45.
13. Lynd and Lynd, *Middletown*; Ibid., *Middletown in Transition*; see also Ware, *Greenwhich*; Warner and Lunt, *Social Life*.
14. Wirth, "Urbanism".
15. Stein, *Eclipse*.
16. Calhoun, "Community," 106.
17. Gillette, "Community"; Hollingshead, "Community"; Hillery, "Definitions"; Sjoberg, "Urban".
18. Nisbet, *Quest*.
19. Conway and Patel, eds, *Europeanization*; Hewitson and D'Auria, eds, *Europe*; Reijnen and Rensen, eds, *European*; see also the chapter by Marleen Rensen in this volume.
20. Wakeman, *Practicing* (currently in press). Clapson, *INTI*.
21. Heynickx and Avermaete, *Making a New World*.
22. Kuchenbuch, "Architecture"; Kuchenbuch, *Geordnete Gemeinschaft*; Henderson, *Building Culture*.
23. Haffner, *View*; Joyce, *Rule*; Kupers, "Mapping".
24. Gans, *Urban Villagers*. See the chapters by Jon Lawrence and Stefan Couperus in this volume.
25. Cupers, *Social Project*, xxii.
26. Kaal, "A Conceptual History," 536.
27. Jacobs, *Death*.
28. Sennett, *Fall*, 295.
29. Foucault, *Society*, 103; see also: Blauner, *Racial*.
30. Nightingale, *Segregation*.
31. Calhoun, "History"; Ibid., "Community".
32. Calhoun, "Community," 106.
33. Keller, *Community*, 6; Anderson, *Imagined Communities*, 7.
34. Hobsbawm and Ranger, eds, *Invention*; Stedman Jones, *Languages*.
35. Anderson, *Imagined Communities*.
36. Rawls, *A Theory*; Kymlicka, *Liberalism*; Walzer, *Toward*; Etzioni, *Spirit*.
37. Kymlicka, *Liberalism*.
38. Strath, "Community/Society".
39. Anderson, *Spectre*; Ibid., *Under Three Flags*.
40. Saunier, "Taking"; Saunier and Ewen, eds, *Another*; Iriye and Saunier, eds, *The Palgrave Dictionary*.
41. Laqua, *Age*.
42. Goebel, *Anti-Imperial Metropolis*; Kenny and Madgin, eds, *Cities*.
43. Cohn, *Colonialism*; Mantena, *Alibis*.
44. Brunnbauer, Kraft, and Schulze Wessel, eds, *Sociology*; Hann, Sárkány, and Skalník, eds, *Studying*.

Bibliography

Anderson, Benedict. *Imagined Communities: Reflections on the Origin and Spread of Nationalism*. London: Verso, 1983.

Anderson, Benedict. *The Spectre of Comparison*. London: Verso, 1998.
Anderson, Benedict. *Under Three Flags: Anarchism and the Anti-Colonial Imagination*. London: Verso, 2005.
Beck, Ulrich. *Risikogesellschaft. Auf dem Weg in eine andere Moderne*. Frankfurt am Main: Suhrkamp Verlag, 1986.
Blauner, Bob. *Racial Oppression in America*. New York: Harper & Row, 1972.
Brunnbauer, Ulf, Claudia Kraft, and Martin Schulze Wessel, eds. *Sociology and Ethnography in East-Central and South-East Europe: Scientific Self-Description in State-Socialist Countries*. München: Oldenbourg Verlag, 2008.
Calhoun, Craig. "History, Anthropology and the Study of Communities: Some Problems in Macfarlane's Proposal." *Social History* 3, no. 3 (1978): 363–73.
Calhoun, Craig. "Community: Toward a Variable Conceptualization for Comparative Research." *Social History* 5, no. 1 (1980): 105–29.
Calhoun, Craig. "Community without Propinquity Revisited: Communications Technology and the Transformation of the Urban Public Sphere." *Sociological Inquiry* 68, no. 3 (1998): 373–97.
Clapson, Mark. *Working-Class Suburb: Social Change on an English Council State, 1930–2010*. Manchester: Manchester University Press, 2012.
Cohn, Bernard S. *Colonialism and Its Forms of Knowledge: The British in India*. Princeton, NJ: Princeton University Press, 1996.
Conway, Martin and Kiran Klaus Patel, eds. *Europeanization in the Twentieth Century: Historical Approaches*. Basingstoke and New York: Palgrave Macmillan, 2010.
Couperus, Stefan. "Experimental Planning after the Blitz: Non-Governmental Planning Initiatives and Post-War Reconstruction in Coventry and Rotterdam, 1940–1955." *Journal of Modern European History* 13, no. 4 (2015): 516–33.
Couperus, Stefan, Liesbeth van de Grift, and Vincent Lagendijk. "Experimental Spaces: A Decentred Approach to Planning in High Modernity: Introduction." *Journal of Modern European History* 13, no. 4 (2015): 475–79.
Cupers, Kenny. *The Social Project: Housing Postwar France*. Minneapolis: The University of Minneapolis Press, 2014.
Cupers, Kenny. "Mapping and Making the Post-War Community." *Journal of Urban History* 2016 (forthcoming).
Duyvendak, Jan Willem and Menno Hurenkamp, eds. *Kiezen voor de kudde. Lichte gemeenschappen en de nieuwe meerderheid*. Amsterdam: Van Gennep, 2004.
Etzemüller, Thomas. "Strukturierter Raum—integrierte Gemeinschaft. Auf den Spuren des social engineering im Europa des 20. Jahrhunderts." In *Theorien und Experimente der Moderne. Europas Gesellschaften im 20. Jahrhundert*, edited by Lutz Raphael, 129–54. Cologne: Böhlau, 2012.
Etzioni, Amitai. *The Spirit of Community: Rights, Responsibilities, and the Communitarian Agenda*. New York: Crown Publishers, 1993.
Foucault, Michel. *Society Must Be Defended: Lectures at the Collège de France, 1975–76*. London: Allen Lane, 2003.
Gans, Herbert J. *The Urban Villagers: Group and Class in the Life of Italian-Americans*. New York: Free Press, 1962.
Gillette, John M. "Community Concepts." *Social Forces* 4, no. 4 (1926): 677–89.
Goebel, M. *Anti-Imperial Metropolis: Interwar Paris and the Seeds of Third-World Nationalism*. New York: Cambridge University Press, 2016.
Haffner, Jeanne. *The View from Above: The Science of Social Space*. Cambridge, MA: MIT Press, 2013.

Hann, Chris, Mihály Sárkány, and Peter Skalník, eds. *Studying Peoples in the People's Democracies: Socialist Era Anthropology in East-Central Europe.* Münster: LIT Verlag, 2005.
Henderson, Susan R. *Building Culture: Ernst May and the New Frankfurt am Main Initiative, 1926–1931.* New York: Peter Lang, 2013.
Heynickx, Rajesh and Tom Avermaete, eds. *Making a New World: Architecture and Communities in Interwar Europe.* Leuven: Leuven University Press, 2012.
Hillery, George A. "Definitions of Community: Areas of Agreement." *Rural Sociology* 20 (1955): 111–23.
Hobsbawm, Eric and Terence Ranger, eds. *The Invention of Tradition.* Cambridge: Cambridge University Press, 1983.
Hollingshead, August B. "Community Research: Development and Present Condition." *American Sociological Review* 13, no. 2 (1948): 136–46.
Iriye, Akira and Pierre-Yves Saunier, eds. *The Palgrave Dictionary of Transnational History.* Basingstoke and New York: Palgrave Macmillan, 2009.
Jacobs, Jane. *The Death and Life of Great American Cities.* New York: Random House, 1961.
Joyce, Patrick. *The Rule of Freedom: Liberalism and the City in Britain.* London: Verso, 2003.
Kaal, Harm. "A Conceptual History of Livability: Dutch Scientists, Politicians, Policy Makers and Citizens and the Quest for a Livable City." *City* 15, no. 5 (2011): 532–47.
Keller, Suzanne. *Community: Pursuing the Dream, Living the Reality.* Princeton, NJ: Princeton University Press, 2003.
Klemek, Christopher. *The Transatlantic Collapse of Urban Renewal: Postwar Urbanism from New York to Berlin.* Chicago: The University of Chicago Press, 2011.
Kuchenbuch, David. *Geordnete Gemeinschaft. Architekten als Sozialingenieure—Deutschland und Schweden im 20. Jahrhundert.* Bielefeld: Transcript, 2010.
Kuchenbuch, David. *Das Peckham-Experiment. Eine Mikro- und Wissensgeschichte des Londoner 'Pioneer Health Centre' im 20. Jahrhundert.* Cologne: Böhlau Verlag, 2014.
Kuchenbuch, David. "Architecture and Urban Planning as Social Engineering: Selective Transfers between Germany and Sweden in the 1930s and 1940s." *Journal of Contemporary History* 51, no. 1 (2016): 22–39.
Kymlicka, Will. *Liberalism, Community and Culture.* Oxford: Clarendon Press, 1989.
Laqua, Daniel. *The Age of Internationalism and Belgium, 1880–1930: Peace, Progress and Prestige.* Manchester: Manchester University Press, 2013.
Lebow, Katherine A. *Unfinished Utopia: Nowa Huta, Stalinism, and Polish Society, 1949–56.* Ithaca, NY: Cornell University Press, 2013.
Lynd, Robert S. and Helen M. Lynd. *Middletown in Transition: A Study in Cultural Conflicts.* New York: Harcourt, Brace, and Company, 1937.
Maier, Charles S. "Consigning the Twentieth Century to History: Alternative Narratives for the Modern Era." *The American Historical Review* 105, no. 3 (2000): 807–31.
Mannheim, Karl. *Man and Society in an Age of Reconstruction: Studies in Modern Social Structure.* New York: Harcourt, Brace & World, 1940.
Mannheim, Karl. *Freedom, Power, and Democratic Planning.* New York: Oxford University Press, 1950.

Mantena, Karuna. *Alibis of Empire: Henry Maine and the Ends of Liberal Imperialism*. Princeton, NJ: Princeton University Press, 2010.
Nightingale, Carl H. *Segregation: A Global History of Divided Cities*. Chicago: The University of Chicago Press, 2012.
Nisbet, Robert A. *The Quest for Community: A Study in the Ethics of Order and Freedom*. New York: Oxford University Press, 1953.
Raphael, Lutz. "Embedding the Human and Social Sciences in Western Societies, 1880–1980: Reflections on Trends and Methods of Current Research." In *Engineering Society: The Role of the Human and Social Sciences in Modern Societies, 1880–1980*, edited by Kerstin Brückweh et al., 41–56. Basingstoke: Palgrave Macmillan, 2012.
Rawls, John. *A Theory of Justice*. Cambridge, MA: Belknap Press of Harvard University Press, 1971.
Reijnen, Carlos and Marleen Rensen, eds. *European Encounters: Intellectual Exchange and the Rethinking of Europe 1914–1945*. Amsterdam: Rodopi, 2014.
Rodgers, Daniel T. *The Age of Fracture*. Cambridge, MA: The Belknap Press of Harvard University Press, 2011.
Saunier, Pierre-Yves. "Taking Up the Bet on Connections: A Municipal Contribution." *Contemporary European History* 11, no. 4 (2002): 507–28.
Saunier, Pierre-Yves and Shane Ewen, eds. *Another Global City: Historical Explorations Into the Transnational Municipal Movement, 1850–2000*. New York: Palgrave Macmillan, 2008.
Sennett, Richard. *The Fall of Public Man: The Forces Eroding Public Life and Burdening the Modern Psyche with Roles it Cannot Perform*. New York: Knopf, 1977.
Sjoberg, Gideon. "Urban Community Theory and Research: A Partial Evaluation." *The American Journal of Economics and Sociology* 14, no. 2 (1955): 199–206.
Stein, Maurice R. *The Eclipse of Community: An Interpretation of American Studies*. Princeton: Princeton University Press, 1960.
Stråth, B. "Community/Society: History of the Concept." In *International Encyclopedia of the Social & Behavioral Sciences*, edited by Neil J. Smelser and Paul B. Baltes, 2378–81. Oxford: Pergamon, 2001.
Sweeney, Dennis. "'Modernity' and the Making of Social Order in Twentieth-Century Europe." *Contemporary European History* 23, no. 2 (2014): 209–24.
Wakeman, Rosemary. *Practicing Utopia: An Intellectual History of the New Town Movement*. Chicago: The University of Chicago Press, 2016.
Walzer, Michael. *Toward a Global Civil Society*. Providence: Berghahn Books, 1995.
Wirth, Louis. "Urbanism as a Way of Life." *American Journal of Sociology* 44, no. 1 (1938): 1–24.

Part I
Urban Communities

2 Languages of Place and Belonging
Competing Conceptions of "Community" in Mid-Twentieth-Century Bermondsey, London

Jon Lawrence

Bermondsey, a riverside neighbourhood in South-East London, has often been identified as an unusually cohesive district characterised by a strong sense of place and 'community'; a popular local history pamphlet talks of 'the Bermondsey spirit'.[1] This strong sense of Bermondsey's distinctiveness is usually portrayed as arising from the district's relative isolation within the metropolis, supposedly reinforced by demographic stability, strong kinship networks and the homogeneity of its overwhelmingly working-class population. In *Bermondsey Story*, his 1949 biography of local socialist hero Alfred Salter, Fenner Brockway proclaimed that, '[n]ot one Londoner in thousands visits Bermondsey; its life is almost as self-contained as that of a provincial town.'[2] 'Nearly everyone who lived in Bermondsey worked in Bermondsey,' he explained, 'they knew each other at their job, they knew each other in their streets . . . In such a community local news and ideas spread quickly.'[3] Similarly, the sociologist Pearl Jephcott, writing in 1962, emphasised 'the stable, near-villagey character' of Bermondsey, arguing that its 'homogeneous character [derived] from a closely-knit social life and extensive kin relationships'.[4] According to Jephcott, the borough was 'solidly working-class in character, and possessed a strong sense of community'.[5] And in the 1970s, the American political scientist John E. Turner, in his study of Labour's doorstep politics in the capital, described Bermondsey as a 'tightly-knit community with a distinctive character' and as marked by 'sentiments of local loyalty and dignity among the people'.[6] Nor has this perception of Bermondsey been wholly undermined by the rapid social and cultural change of the late twentieth century. In the mid-2000s the social anthropologist Gillian Evans was still able to describe the district as 'akin to a typical English village occupied by a group of people closely tied to a particular location through a specific economic history and in-marrying links of kinship and residence'.[7]

It was this reputation for community cohesiveness which, in 1947, encouraged a large team of anthropologists from the London School of Economics to choose Bermondsey for their proposed study of English working-class kinship patterns. The American tradition of the community study had been slow to take root in Britain, where the 'social problem' paradigm continued to dominate social science down to the Second World War.[8] Organised by the New Zealand–born Raymond Firth, the team set out to establish whether tight-knit networks of kin relations underpinned the sense of 'community' that was believed to animate working-class districts such as Bermondsey.[9] Wartime celebration of the working-class Cockney as the epitome of the nation's defiance of the German bombing campaign fed a new-found interest in urban, working-class 'culture'.[10] But Firth and his team were unusual in having no strong political agenda and no connection with post-war efforts at reconstruction, unlike left intellectuals such as Ruth Glass, Charles Madge and Michael Young, who, in their different ways, all hoped that social research could help the post-war Labour Government realise its socialist ideals.[11] By contrast, Firth and his team relished the chance to work in a context where for once they did not have to fear being seen as representatives of an alien, colonial state power.[12]

Influenced by the communitarian social theory of Robert Morrison MacIver, as well as his own wartime experiences, Firth went into the field expecting to find that propinquity, reinforced by close kinship ties, generated a strong working-class sense of 'community'.[13]

Firth chose Bermondsey because it seemed to embody this ideal of tight-knit working-class community. In particular, he chose to study the Guinness Trust Buildings at Snowfields because they promised to offer a microcosm of the kin-based community system that interested him. There were known to be many long-term residents in the blocks, including many inter-related families.[14] But others on the team, notably the experienced Africanist Audrey Richards, were always more sceptical about the concept of 'community', and when the fieldwork offered little support for Firth's hypothesis about kin-based community feeling, he was happy to shift the project's focus to the reconstruction of working-class kinship networks.[15] His approach contrasts sharply with that of other British social scientists, such as Michael Young, who were more strongly committed to 'community' as a political ideal which could underpin a more decentralised, pluralist version of socialist reconstruction.[16]

From the outset Firth and his co-researchers were struck by the ease with which people felt able to ignore the supposed social obligations of kinship, let alone propinquity. In contrast to Michael Young and Peter Willmott in *Family and Kinship in East London*, their famous study of the East London borough of Bethnal Green, Firth concluded that kinship ties depended on 'emotional attachment' rather than any strong sense of familial obligation.[17] Aware of Michael Young's work from at least 1954, Firth sought to explain their divergent conclusions about the power of kin-based 'community' in working-class districts in terms of the different traditions of their two disciplines.[18] The sociologist, Firth argued, was 'apt to be surprised by the degree of patterning discernible in the kinship field when he turns his attention systematically to it', whereas the anthropologist was more struck by 'the degree of flexibility and personal choice' at play in comparison to

Languages of Place and Belonging 21

the 'highly formalised systems' encountered in non-Western societies (Firth himself worked mainly on Polynesia).[19]

Unusually, a large collection of field notes from this 1947 study, and from a follow-up study conducted between 1957 and 1959, survive with Firth's papers. Besides Firth's own field notebooks, the collection includes dozens of field reports from other researchers, detailed kinship histories of the main families studied, and two complete censuses of the tenants living in the six blocks of flats which formed the core of the two inquiries (these had been built by the Guinness Trust in the late 1890s and still stand on Snowfields, see Figure 2.1). This material provides strong support for Firth's conclusions about the limited and conditional nature of English kinship bonds. It also suggests that, whilst residents possessed a powerful sense of place and of belonging, communal interaction was more cautious and conditional than the researchers had originally supposed. Privacy was strongly guarded by almost everyone, and many residents had nothing to do with the communal life of the buildings, or even with their immediate neighbours.[20] Perhaps most strikingly, comparing the two censuses of the Guinness Buildings also suggests that there was much greater social flux in this part of Bermondsey than contemporary observers generally recognised. More than sixty per cent of the flats changed hands in the twelve years between the two studies. By

Figure 2.1 Guinness Trust Buildings on Snowfields, Bermondsey (2013).
Source: Photograph by the author.

the late 1950s many of those traced from the original study had mixed feelings about the changing character of both their immediate neighbourhood and Bermondsey. These respondents rehearsed a familiar narrative of declining 'community spirit', but crucially most also expressed a powerful desire to move out themselves. This was not simply a nostalgic lament for better times. Complaints about decline were mobilised specifically to justify moving on, even if this meant abandoning 'old Bermondsey'.

But if Bermondsey was not a closed, homogeneous district, despite widespread claims to the contrary, pride in its distinctiveness, and its reputation as a model of 'community', remained strong despite the considerable flux of the post-war era. It is this survival of an idealised sense of place—the imagined 'Bermondsey' of communitarian feeling and social homogeneity—which we need to find new tools to explain if it cannot simply be attributed to the area's unchanging character. This paper explores the discursive construction of 'community' by mapping the inter-connections and the disconnections between academic, vernacular and political languages of community in Bermondsey across the middle decades of the twentieth century. In doing so it argues that politics helped to develop a broad-based and relatively inclusive conception of community which complemented, rather than challenged, vernacular identification with place (identification that was often more localised and exclusive). But this is not all about political language—practice mattered too, particularly as enacted through the borough-wide social networks built up by the Bermondsey Labour Party.

The Anthropologists and "Community"

Firth's principal interest was kinship, and he had little to say about why Bermondsey should possess a strong and persistent reputation for community feeling if kinship bonds were weaker and more voluntaristic than he originally supposed.[21] Nor did he have much to say about what 'community' meant to local people—about how it was articulated in their testimony to researchers, or about the relationship between these 'vernacular' understandings of place and what we might call the formal 'politics of place'. But, crucially, his project's surviving field notes, when read alongside other sources such as the newspapers and political propaganda that circulated in Bermondsey, do allow us to address these vital questions.

From the outset Firth envisaged using the Bermondsey study to pioneer 'a sociological enquiry of a deeper nature than the ordinary social survey'.[22] This meant mobilising the techniques of anthropological fieldwork, including careful observations of material culture and behaviour, but it also meant favouring the 'deep interview' over formal questionnaires. Families were visited on multiple occasions, often for hours at a time, and the researchers, including Firth, happily allowed themselves to be drawn into facets of their subjects' social lives. Firth attended a family wedding, while younger members of the team, most of whom were post-graduates, accompanied residents to local pubs and became regulars at the Guinness Buildings' on-site Social Club, which held regular dances. Here they swapped imported jazz records and danced with residents who were young and single.[23]

Firth was convinced that his field team, which included researchers from Australia, Canada, South Africa, China, the United States, the Netherlands and Scotland alongside three fellow New Zealanders, were able to transcend the differences of class that might normally be thought to separate the university quarter of Bloomsbury from working-class Bermondsey by trading on what he termed their 'stranger-value' (just as the American post-graduate E. Wight Bakke had done in his important 1930s study of unemployment in nearby Greenwich).[24] Firth argued that the group's ethnic heterogeneity helped to ensure that they were ascribed a functional rather than class status by residents: 'We have been visitors from the University primarily.'[25]

We might object that London University was hardly a class-neutral institution, but there is ample evidence to suggest that researchers quickly established cordial, even intimate, relations with many residents of Snowfields Buildings. After a visit to the local Social Club with two of the young researchers, Audrey Richards commented on 'The marked change in attitude towards visitors from "over the river" that seems to have taken place since the war when I used to visit friends in this neighbourhood. There seemed to be little shyness, no deference, and little anticipation that we had come to "do good", or indeed surprise at our visit.'[26] Richards wondered if she was witnessing the 'break-down of class distinctions' in post-war Britain, but even if it was just the 'stranger-value' of her co-researchers, which she also registered, it seems evident that, from the outset, this was an unusually productive social-science encounter.

An early report talked of 'considerable community feeling and attachment to the building,' and in October 1947 Firth noted that,

> The tenants appear to form a more or less permanent community with strong ties in the Buildings. As a random example, when I knocked at the door of one man whom I wished to contact and got no answer I was told by his neighbour that he might be downstairs in the flat below with his grandmother.[27]

Although the bulk of their efforts would be devoted to collecting family trees and developing techniques for measuring the strength of kinship connections, the team also made notes on material culture, behaviour and social attitudes. They paid particular attention to communal activities. This was the rationale for going to Social Club dances, and they also attended the Parent Teacher Association at the nearby school, a discussion group run by the London County Council, the local football and darts clubs, and even the children's Christmas party. Indeed, Donald Munro, an outgoing young Canadian, helped collect pledges for the party door-to-door through November 1947, using the opportunity to help identify potential families for the study.[28] At the same time the researchers assiduously recorded what residents said about communal ties, although they gradually became less willing to accept their claims about communal feeling at face value. Attending a meeting of the Social Club committee in mid-November 1947, Kenneth Little acknowledged 'the "community" aspect of the situation' and the 'evident pride in being community conscious', but he nonetheless suspected that some of the men 'over-accentuated the strength of community feeling and this sense of exclusiveness'.[29]

Firth, in particular, felt that forced communalism within the buildings could actually divide families against their neighbours. Residents cleaned the communal parts of their building—stairwells, landings and bathrooms—by rota, leading to arguments because 'You always get someone that never does it'. Communal laundries were also a source of tension because of the severe consequence if a family missed its allotted wash day.[30] Firth was struck by the privatism of many families, particularly a couple he called Stanley and Sarah Ingles, whose testimony featured prominently in the published account of the study.[31] It was Mr Ingles who told him 'we keep ourselves to ourselves, and then we can't get into trouble', explaining 'The buildings are like a country village—anything happens everyone knows it—news travels'.[32] But Firth insisted that this privatism ran alongside, rather than against, 'strong recognition of the buildings as a community'. It was a consequence, Firth argued, of the close proximity of flat-living and the frequent need to breach conventional standards of respectability because of overcrowding (notably by using living rooms as makeshift bedrooms). In a short working paper on 'The Community,' Firth observed that, 'Pride in the conventional tidiness of the living room, and sense of independence make for a tendency to deny the home to visitors, even from within the buildings, except to close kin and when friendship has formed.'[33]

It seems doubtful whether the Ingles were quite as typical as Firth suggested. For one thing, no one else appears to have maintained a correspondence with him by letter (including sending Christmas cards), nor did anyone else invite him to a family wedding.[34] In addition, Stan Ingles had grown up outside Bermondsey, in nearby Camberwell, and his job was distinctly unusual: he was a labourer at Buckingham Palace. On the other hand, Mrs Ingles was local and had many kin in the Buildings.[35] Her mother still lived there (Sarah Ingles told Firth that her mother would be 'embarrassed' to be visited by his researchers because she only had a single room with a bed in it). Her maternal grandmother had been one of the original residents of the Buildings in 1898.[36]

But arguably what made the Ingles unusual was more their openness than their privatism. Others warned the researchers against knocking on doors at random in the blocks because people would resent the intrusion, and indeed the team met many residents who were reluctant to discuss family with strangers.[37] They also met people much more isolated from their neighbours than the Ingles, who were active in the local Parent Teacher Association and helped to organise the children's Christmas party. A 65-year-old widowed office cleaner had lost all contact with her extended family from the north of England, and had nothing to do with the social life of the Buildings. She told Richards, 'you have to keep yourself to yourself in a place like [this]. There would be quarrelling over sharing the sinks otherwise. As it is people wash up in their flats and carry out the dirty water.'[38] Similarly, Mrs Wood explained that she had not asked neighbours to borrow coal during the previous hard winter because she 'preferred to turn always "to her own", and not to strangers', even though her family lived at some distance.[39] But perhaps the most striking example of 'privatism' was a married engineer with two teenage sons who worked at Hackney Wick in North London, because 'he like[d] to have his work place away from his home.' Asked '[Don't you] like a drink with [your] mates', the man retorted: 'No . . . only [my] missus—"she's my mate".'[40]

But it was the team's primary focus on mapping family trees which led them to identify one of the most striking ways in which traditional practices had declined in mid-twentieth-century Bermondsey. As they collected the names of kin they were struck by a decisive break in family naming practices in the most recent generation. Well into the twentieth century local families had given their children the names of favourite relatives, and had generally maintained the traditional practice of giving first-born boys and girls their parent's name. But at some point around the Second World War, generations of Alberts and Adas, Freds and Lizzies gave way to a wave of unfamiliar names drawn from a much wider pool of cultural reference points. By the 1940s Bermondsey was awash with young Ronalds and Carols, Bryans and Patricias (Willmott and Young observed the same shift at roughly the same time in nearby Bethnal Green).[41] What was most striking about the new naming practices was the free rein given to an individualised language of taste, rather than one shaped predominantly by tradition and perceived communal expectations.[42] Barbara Ward noted that this break could be seen even in families, like the Dixons, which displayed a sharp sense of tradition and family history. Here generations of Alberts, Carries and Adas came to a halt in the 1940s: 'the present babies are called by quite different names e.g. Jonothon, Marrilyn (she quotes a relative saying "We mustn't call him John. It's got to be Jonothon, or there's trouble from his mother.")'[43]

In his work on naming practices in twentieth-century America, Stanley Lieberson has stressed how fashion can have its own internal, purely cultural dynamic, operating independent of any external socio-economic causes.[44] But, whilst this may well explain the relative popularity of different 'new' names in different decades, the break of a closed, family-centred tradition of naming, to an open system dominated by the dictates of individual taste smacks of deeper causes.[45] The pressure to conform to local custom was already in retreat—a retreat that would only accelerate over the succeeding decades.

Vernacular Languages of Place

The anthropologists' field notes also offer us insights into how local people conceptualised 'community', allowing us to explore the relationship between vernacular understandings of place and more overtly academic and political conceptualisations of 'community'. We have already heard some of these voices: in Mrs Dixon's sensitivity around naming, in comments about the avoidance of enforced communalism, and above all in that mantra of domestic privacy: 'we keep ourselves to ourselves' (which, contrary to the argument in *Family and Kinship*, was very definitely *not* the preserve of the new, supposedly socially isolating suburbs).[46] But the field notes also offer insights into residents' powerful identification with place: with the Guinness Buildings, with Bermondsey, and more broadly with coming from South London rather than 'over the water'. It is these overlapping forms of belonging—these concentric identities of place—that need to be unpicked if we want to develop an understanding of the vernacular meanings of 'community'. We need to acknowledge that the social dynamics of the interview may have shaped how people talked about place, but we learn much from deconstructing these socially charged exchanges.[47]

Starting first with the Buildings themselves, researchers noted the ubiquity with which residents spoke of 'our block'—i.e. block of flats—and 'our buildings', while the first thing to be said when introducing anyone new in pub or street was whether they lived (or did not live) in 'the Buildings'.[48] Similarly, the football club discussed how to look after 'our boys' when match-day injuries forced two of their players off work.[49] According to Barbara Ward, it was still considered a 'misfortune' for a family to have to leave the buildings, and she was assured that people did so only if their families got too large. Partly because the blocks lacked amenities, rents were significantly lower than those charged for council flats of a comparable size, and the Trust was generally seen as a good, if strict, landlord.[50] As one resident put it: 'We know when we are well off'.[51] Besides the tenants' Social Club and its various off-shoots such as the darts, football and debating clubs, in the 1940s residents also continued to go on regular organised charabanc trips, or 'Beanos', to the seaside. In 1948, one hundred residents were going to Margate for fifteen shillings per head (excluding drinks), paid in advance in weekly instalments.[52] 'Community' was something lived, rather than just spoken about, in 1940s Bermondsey, though of course by no means everybody participated in these activities. Less than a sixth of the residents went on the Margate Beano; perhaps predictably, Firth noted that the Ingles were among those that stayed behind.[53]

In fact not all the residents considered themselves fortunate to live in the Buildings even in 1947 (when the acute post-war housing shortage meant there were few alternatives available). In an early meeting with two long-time residents in the 'Rose' public house, Maurice Freedman, who would make his name as an anthropologist of China, noted their 'consciousness of

Languages of Place and Belonging 27

[the] antiquatedness of Snowfields—gas light, no private bathrooms, dinginess'.[54] Some were quite clear that they wanted to get out as soon as possible. Bill Buckley, a docker who had been born in the Buildings, denounced them as a 'slum' and declared his wish to move his family into a new, American-style 'prefab' where they would have their own bathroom instead of having to wash in a bowl on the kitchen table (prefabs were prefabricated houses which could be erected quickly to help relieve the post-war housing shortage).[55] As he spoke one son was eating supper while another tried to wash at the same table; Mrs Buckley interjected apologetically: 'It's been cleaned up once this evening.'[56] Although social anxiety about hosting an educated young Englishman may have played its part in this exchange, we know from the 1957 census of tenants that the Buckleys did move out of the Buildings, even though many of their relatives continued to live there.[57]

The project field notes also contain many examples of what Audrey Richards called the residents' overt 'pride in Bermondsey'.[58] Firth noted that, though they lived close to the border with Southwark, residents had a keen sense of Bermondsey as a distinct district, clearly distinguished from adjacent districts such as Camberwell, Southwark and the Borough. He observed how one of Stan Ingles' in-laws enthusiastically recited his knowledge of the borough's historical geography and legends, prompting Stan to declare: 'I don't know any of this—but then I was born in Camberwell.'[59] Richard Corbett (labourer) and his wife, 'both born in Bermondsey', told another interviewer that 'they would like to die and be buried there.'[60] John Wood, a docker who ran the local boxing and football clubs, emphasised the parochialism of the area with evident pride, insisting that many locals never left the borough, that 'any stranger would be spotted at once' and that 'we have all lived here all our lives' (it was this meeting which led Little to feel some locals 'over-accentuated' communal feeling).[61] Many residents were clearly aware that to come from Bermondsey was not socially neutral, and they sought to play up its positive, communitarian connotations. Some also sought to address its negative image head-on. At a darts match in the 'Rose', Bill Morris said he 'blamed the detective writers' for the 'tough' reputation of Bermondsey and neighbouring Southwark. He accepted that it 'used to be tough in his father's day,' but insisted that now the police no longer had to patrol in pairs and the dominant ethos of the area was one of 'sociability and friendliness'.[62]

Morris was clearly concerned to present his neighbourhood in a positive light, but he was also involved in a knowing engagement with outsiders' supposed preconceptions about the place he came from and, quite probably, about himself. This knowingness and concern with self-presentation was far from unique.[63] Firth noted that many residents had a keen sense of the difference between London's 'West End', what they termed 'over the water' or 'up there', and the predominantly working-class communities of inner South London. According to Firth, both the prices and the morals of the West End were imagined to be very different from 'down here'.[64] Discussing attitudes to daughters leaving home, Bill Buckley declared: 'University people are more loose in their morals than the poor class.'[65] Conversely, Dick Sexton told Barbara Ward, 'It's not like your part of the country, women have been in our pubs for years'.[66] At the same time, some residents clearly wanted to emphasise conformity to dominant stereotypes about life 'down here'. One simply implored Firth to 'say we're real cockneys,' while another told the Polynesia expert R. A. Scobie, another New Zealander, 'if you want to see the Londoner' visit the hop-picking in Kent, where every night still ended with a 'knees-up' in the local pub.[67] He appears to have considered Bermondsey's own street life to be too mundane to live up to the visitors' imagined sense of 'authentic' cockney culture.[68]

A similar motivation may explain why Dick Sexton assured Ward that the looming royal wedding between heir to the throne Princess Elizabeth and Philip Mountbatten would be the excuse for a 'real district pub party ("Like the Jubilee")' in Bermondsey.[69] In fact, when Audrey Richards went down to Snowfields to observe the celebrations she found that, in stark contrast to the West End, everything was deadly quiet. Finding the Snowfields Social Club completely empty and residents incredulous that she should expect 'anything special,' she made her way to a local pub. Here a repeat of the wedding ceremony was at least playing on the radio in a back room, but no one paid much attention, and there were no celebrations whatsoever. Richards was told that if she wanted a knees-up she'd have been better off coming down on Monday for the Social Club dance.[70]

The anthropologists were also interested to know whether Bermondsey's communal feeling spilled over into xenophobia and racism, whether it was as much about exclusion as belonging. Here their findings were inconclusive during the first, 1947–48 study. One family was praised for displaying 'no particular attitudes' towards their Chinese in-laws, but another was said to boast that all the surnames in the family tree were 'good old English names'.[71] But the researchers were certainly conscious of an undertow of ethnic exclusiveness. One young woman was clearly shocked to hear that Barbara Ward's job meant she had to 'sit next to a black man in Africa to take down his family tree' (though in fact she was a China expert), while a visit to the Social Club led Kenneth Little, already known for his pioneering work on race relations in Britain, to draw the general conclusion that 'the Jews and other "outsiders" are apparently looked on as less desirable, and this appears to apply more definitely to coloured people.' Intriguingly, he also noted that in local slang the term 'Irish' was used loosely to mean outsider, and more especially someone Jewish, despite the fact that a significant minority of residents were themselves of Irish descent.[72]

This strain of ethnic exclusiveness had apparently sharpened considerably by 1958, when LSE researchers returned to the Buildings. Re-interviewing residents they found many convinced that local community spirit had been all but obliterated by rapid social change, and especially by what they perceived as large-scale Irish immigration into the Buildings during the 1950s.

Mrs Warren complained that 'there were hardly any of the old families left', just a lot of 'strangers . . . and the best part of them are Irish.' However, her complaint was less about ethnic dilution, than about the transitory nature of the new population: 'they come & pay the rent O.K. but after 3 or 4 months they go back.'[73] Others complained that the Irish tenants were 'too "Clannish"', or that they overcrowded their flats, forcing the Trust to rehouse them, '& so they spread'.[74] Some tenants complained that the buildings' supervisor was 'too keen on the Irish'—'no one will be sorry to see him go'.[75]

This hostility to newcomers was largely the symptom of a broader malaise. As in Rosser and Harris's study of Swansea (1959–61), older residents complained of the general collapse of 'community', and many were clear that they would take the first opportunity to leave both the Buildings and Bermondsey if one arose.[76] Mrs Bower, the woman who complained about how the Irish 'spread' also lamented that 'the flats are not the same as they used to be—the clubs have all closed down'.[77] Mr Dyer, a warehouseman, concurred, telling his interviewer that there was now 'no boxing, no club for children, [the] club house [was] not used' and there were no longer any organised 'beanos'. He also complained of being 'very sad' that he no longer saw his family, explaining that 'the young couples have moved out of London to the New Towns & taken their parents with them'.[78] Mrs Bower's son was also 'waiting & hoping to move out' and wanted his mother to come too, though she was adamant that she would not leave Bermondsey.[79] In the Burford family the children were squabbling about how to look after their widowed mother because her youngest child, Ron, was planning to move out of London after his marriage in the summer. Mrs Burford was one of those who complained about the influx of Irish tenants and lamented the general decline of neighbourliness in the Buildings.[80]

This testimony also reminds us that many people willingly chose to leave the old working-class neighbourhoods of Victorian England in the postwar era—they were not simply the hapless victims of urban planners who failed to understand the importance of the 'sense of community' that had built up over generations in older urban districts.[81] In some senses residents' lament for the death of community helped to justify the decision to cut ties with place and people, which for some could be traced back two or more generations.[82] But change was by no means purely imagined. Using the two censuses of the Buildings compiled by the Guinness Trust in 1946 and 1958 we see clear evidence of the flux at play in post-war Bermondsey, despite its image as an isolated and unchanging 'traditional' community. Firstly, only two of the Social Club organisers mentioned in the 1947 study were still resident twelve years later, and they were now frail pensioners—all the others had either died or moved away.

Moreover, not only were almost two-thirds of 1958 tenants newcomers to the buildings in the previous twelve years, but in fact more than half of all tenants (fifty-three per cent) had been living *outside* Bermondsey prior to renting from the Trust. Almost all of these had moved from other parts of London.[83] And though only one person had come straight from Ireland, there was a noticeable cluster of new tenants with Irish surnames who had moved into the Buildings from various parts of North and North-west London such as Kilburn, North Kensington and East Finchley—districts strongly associated with post-war Irish migration. Among the new tenants, twenty-one per cent came from these districts, compared with less than three per cent among those already resident in the Buildings in 1946.

Finally, there had also been considerable change in the occupational profile of the tenants. There was almost a three-fold increase in the number of tenants in non-manual occupations (from just 4.2 per cent to 11.9) and a notable drop in the number of retired or otherwise unoccupied tenants (down from 26.8 per cent to 19.3 per cent). And though the proportion of tenants in manual occupations had barely changed (down from 69.1 to 68.8 per cent), there had been a distinct shift towards more skilled occupations. In 1947, 34.3 per cent of tenants had been unskilled workers; by 1958 this had fallen to 26.3 per cent.[84] Average real wages had also risen (by approximately fifteen per cent at constant prices).

But if Bermondsey appears to have been less static than is generally imagined, arguably what matters more is that myths of its distinct, communitarian and 'traditional' culture survived the social flux of the post-war era. This is why, in her recent ethnographic study of educational disadvantage among the district's white, working-class children, Gillian Evans was struck, as Firth had been sixty years earlier, by Bermondsey's village-like quality and its residents' powerful sense of pride in being 'real Bermondsey'.[85] Unlike Firth and his associates, Evans actually lived in Bermondsey, and her study is sensitive to the ways in which newcomers could be frozen out by those who proclaimed themselves 'born-and-bred Bermondsey'.[86] But if incomers can never become fully 'Bermondsey', they can and do acculturate—what Evans calls 'gettin' it' (she cites the example of an incomer who starts insisting that her children always have clean new clothes to wear for their after-school club).[87] Firth's 1947 unpublished paper on 'community' had observed something similar, with one of his interviewees apparently observing 'Bermondsey gets you' during a conversation about the difference between Bermondsey folk and other South Londoners.[88]

Evans emphasises the ways in which people can learn to be Bermondsey through imitation, but I would suggest that historically the discursive power of the idea of Bermondsey as a place apart—as a real 'community'—has been no less important. In contrast to Evans's 'real Bermondsey' we might call this 'discursive Bermondsey'. It doubtless helps that many of those who became disillusioned with this ideal—convinced that the district had lost its unique character—probably did end up leaving, taking their memories of an older, supposedly better Bermondsey with them. But for those who remained—and crucially also for many of those who moved into the borough from the 1950s—the story of Bermondsey as a different, more communal, sort of London represented a cultural resource through which a sense of belonging could be sustained and, to some extent, even acquired. It is to the political languages of community we now turn.

Political Languages of Place

It is important to recognise that many of the defining myths of Bermondsey have been shaped by its distinctive brand of community-based politics, and that the key figures in shaping that mythology have all been incomers. Alfred Salter, the borough's first Labour MP, grew up in leafy Blackheath and Lewisham before moving to the borough to live in its Settlement Mission and then set up in medical practice in the late 1890s. Bob Mellish, Labour MP for thirty-five years after the war, was an Irish docker's son from nearby Deptford who moved to the borough on marrying a 'Bermondsey girl' in 1938 (though they later moved south to leafier Lewisham).[89] Finally, Liberal Democrat Simon Hughes, who represented Bermondsey from 1983 to 2015, was born in Cheshire and grew up in Wales, but crucially lived in the borough continuously from 1981. In 2015, these men had represented the borough politically for eighty-nine of the previous ninety-one years. Each has his own place in the mythology of Bermondsey, but they have also played their part in *shaping* that mythology. For almost a century they reinforced Bermondsey people's sense that they, and their 'community', were different—more gregarious, more self-respecting, above all more communal than the average Londoner. But, for obvious reasons, the public discourse about 'being Bermondsey' articulated by these powerful outsiders has been less atavistic and exclusionary than the vernacular discourses of community that both Firth and Evans encountered on the streets of the borough. Arguably it is this public discourse of 'being Bermondsey' which has helped incomers to acculturate, in turn sustaining the idea of Bermondsey as a distinct, homogeneous 'community' despite the constant churn of metropolitan life that has operated even here.

Alfred Salter, the foremost pioneer of Labour politics in Bermondsey and its MP in 1922–23, and from 1924 until his retirement in 1945 (just months before he died), was a passionate advocate of a classless, humanitarian socialism. In public he presented himself as a man of strong principles who would never bend to the popular will—he made a virtue both of his unpopularity during the 1914–18 war, when he and many of his Independent Labour Party comrades had remained staunch pacifists, and of his lifelong commitment to teetotalism in a constituency with a pub on almost every corner. The Salter mythology was not about the good doctor being *like* his supporters, it was about him being *for* them, and *with* them—it was also about him *liking* them.

Salter's 1918 election address talked of how he had shunned 'a brilliant professional career' to 'live among the people' he loved, devoting his life to 'brightening . . . the lives of the working people.'[90] By 1929, when he had already won two elections, Labour propaganda had found a more down-to-earth tone to express the same sentiment. Salter was 'not an adventurer or a carpet-bagger who lives away in a comfortable suburb, who comes occasionally in his motor car . . . He is one of us. One of Our Own! He has stuck it here because he loves Bermondsey and wants to serve it.'[91] Or as he put it himself at the same election, 'I have lived amongst you for 32 years, sharing your joys and your sorrows, your interests and your intimacies . . . I have spoken my mind on the evils of the day regardless whether I made friends or enemies.'[92]

Labour politics in the Salter era was also about building up the civic pride of Bermondsey. In his 1949 biography, Brockway boldly asserted that 'Salter developed a Bermondsey civic pride'.[93] This is to ignore the powerful vernacular sense of place that Firth identified, and which existed outside politics. But it is clear that during four decades of uninterrupted municipal government from 1922, Labour cultivated a powerful sense of Bermondsey's shared communal struggle to overcome the scars of nineteenth-century urbanisation and industrialisation. Labour in Bermondsey built up a powerful, borough-wide network of councillors and street stewards which reached thousands of local people who had little or no contact with the labour movement's organised, industrial wing. At its peak, in the mid-1950s, more than five thousand local people were Labour Party members, paying weekly dues to the local street stewards whose job it was to keep an eye out for problems that the party might need to address.[94] Unlike Salter, most party activists were themselves working-class, and this helped to embed the party organisation in local neighbourhoods.

Together, party and unions provided what sociologist Mark Granovetter famously labelled the 'weak ties' capable of empowering strong, but localised and fragmented ties based on family and place.[95] In his classic article 'The strength of weak ties', Granovetter contrasted the ability of two working-class Boston suburbs to resist destructive, post-war urban redevelopment: the Italian West End and ship-building Charlestown. Both could boast a powerful sense of place and dense social networks based on family and friendship groups. But only in Charlestown were these strong, localised networks connected together by looser networks based on clubs, trade unions and other borough-wide social groupings, and it was only here that local people managed successfully to mobilise against the developers.[96] Similarly, in Bermondsey Labour was not responsible for creating a strong identification with place, but it did create the means by which these could be mobilised politically for the common good.

As elsewhere, Labour sought to improve the material lives of local people by building public facilities such as baths and wash-houses, and by providing modern homes to rent at affordable prices. But it also sought to nurture local civic pride—the distinctive 'spirit of Bermondsey'. It launched a widely heralded 'Beautification' campaign, in which trees were planted in the borough's drab streets and green spaces were created wherever an opportunity arose. Nor was this just another municipal programme. Rather it was a popular campaign in which local residents were mobilised into cultivating window boxes provided by the council, and, if they had one, also planting their front garden with plants grown by the council.[97] Alongside the construction of new public baths, wash-houses, medical facilities and model housing schemes, this initiative was part of a programme to create Bermondsey anew. It was a radical, transformative version of the politics of place. In 1934, celebrating the party's first twelve years in power, Salter predicted that in a dozen more years '[t]he drab sordidness of the old Bermondsey will have gone for ever, and the district will be illumined with touches of colour and beauty never known before.'[98] Earlier, in 1925, Salter had loftily proclaimed that he envisaged Bermondsey becoming the 'New Jerusalem, whose citizens shall have reason to feel pride in their common possessions, in their civil patriotism, in their public spirit, in the joint sharing of burdens, and their collective efforts to make happier the lot of every single dweller in their midst.'[99] Salter was an idealist, and his politics called for the transcendence of class, not its representation. As he explained in 1934, '[w]e do not want merely to ensure a rather more comfortable existence for "the working classes". We are out to abolish the working classes as such and to create a classless society'.[100]

In contrast to Salter's idealistic civic gospel of socialism, Bob Mellish, his successor, preached a more prosaic doctrine rooted in his own working-class upbringing and the harsh lessons this had taught him. The thirteenth of fourteen children, eight of whom died before they reached adulthood, Mellish's commitment to social justice was instinctive more than intellectual.[101] Unlike Salter, Mellish's claim to represent the people of Bermondsey rested on shared roots, shared values and shared language. Unlike Salter he was a union man, sponsored by the dockers' Transport and General Workers Union, and able to draw on the strong loyalties the union had built up across the borough since the 1890s. Indeed the union's local branches clearly worked hard behind the scenes to fix the candidate selection for Mellish both in 1946, when he became MP for Rotherhithe, and again in 1950 when he became MP for the new unified Bermondsey seat.[102] In his 1950 election address Mellish declared 'I am a very ordinary sort of person', while in the same contest a party Election Special proclaimed him to be '[o]f the people, for the people'.[103] Explaining devaluation in late 1949, Mellish projected the same characteristics on to his voters—they were 'the ordinary Bermondsey folk . . . the ordinary people who have suffered so much in the six years of war.'[104] In 1950 his wife Anne, who was described as a 'Bermondsey girl', addressed the 'women electors of Bermondsey,' telling them: 'I know something of the sincerity of my husband and of his loyalty to his "Own Folk" of Bermondsey.'[105] The following year Mellish adopted the tactic himself, opening his election address by boldly declaring: 'I can honestly claim to know what sort of people the Bermondsey folk are, as I have lived and worked amongst you all my life.'[106]

Most of the time Mellish preferred to address the people through inclusive idioms which left class loyalty implied rather than stated. He spoke of standing for 'the people', 'ordinary people,' or, in a more homely idiom, for 'Bermondsey folk'. Mellish was strongly influenced by Catholic social teachings with their emphasis on the defence of the family, locality and the common good. At the 1950 General Election, in the leaflet 'Of the People, for the People', Mellish declared that his vision of socialism 'consists not in Getting at all, but in Giving—Not in being Served, but in serving' (the words are those of the Scottish ethical socialist John Bruce Glasier). In the same appeal he explicitly juxtaposed 'the dignity of "The Family"' against 'the cry of "Profit Motive",' declaring, in a direct riposte to the Tories' election slogan 'Set the People free,' that 'the freedom that the People of Bermondsey want is from hunger and poverty.'[107]

But Mellish was not averse to playing on shared occupational and class identities. In November 1950, when the difficulties of the flagging Labour government were being exacerbated by unofficial strikes on the London docks, he went out of his way to stress 'the wonderful loyalty of the men towards their fellow workers and the extremely difficult nature of their work.' He was, after all, first and foremost a dockers' MP (and a docker's son and son-in-law to boot).[108] Labour was also happy to stir up bitter shared memories of the 1930s, and to give them an explicitly class-inflected twist by juxtaposing Bermondsey's suffering alongside stories of the excesses indulged in 'over the water'. In 1950, a local Labour leaflet recalled that while Bermondsey families had been 'forced to sell everything of value' in order to qualify for 'a meagre allowance of food' at the Bun House (the local term for the Poor Law workhouse), people up west had been dining at the Ritz on 'ten heavy courses of exhausting dimensions'.[109] Here Labour was feeding memories that were all too real for many Bermondsey families. At Snowfields, researchers were told about a woman in the Buildings 'said to have died of starvation' in the 1930s, and residents explicitly used the memory of such horrors to underline the transformation brought by full employment, higher wages and rationing during and after the war.[110]

Mellish was so confident of his direct and personal connection to his Bermondsey constituents that he could even afford to highlight how his role as their MP set him slightly apart. In 1948, he sought to explain recent cuts in the basic food ration by talking about how they impacted on his own wife and on 'the woman next door'. Thanks to the government's policy of 'FAIR SHARES FOR ALL,' he argued, it mattered not at all that 'I am an M.P. and able to give my wife more money each week than the dock worker who lives next door ... so far as basic foods are concerned we are equal. I should know because they both "moan" together'.[111] By this point Mellish was already considerably better off than most Bermondsey residents, and he had already moved out of the borough, but the story still cleverly conveyed the message that he and his wife were 'just like you'—neighbours to dock-workers and thus still 'ordinary folk'. His 1950 Election Newsletter made the same point visually, depicting Mellish sitting outside his fairly modest interwar semi, with his wife and three sons all dressed respectably but not expensively. 'Bob', the voters were told, was 'very much the family man' (see Figure 2.2).

Figure 2.2 Bermondsey Election Special (1950), Southwark Public Library.
Source: Reproduced by permission of the Southwark Labour Party.

But if identity politics mattered more to Mellish than Salter, he did not neglect the politics of place. This was why his wife was called a 'Bermondsey girl' and his agent, John R. Thomas, a 'Bermondsey boy'.[112] It was also why, in the 1960s, Mellish fought hard to resist plans for the abolition of Bermondsey council, and its absorption into a proposed new metropolitan super-Borough centred on, and, perhaps crucially, named after, nearby Southwark.[113] Mellish attacked the Tories for wanting to 'make the name of Bermondsey disappear' and declared his belief that 'the bulk of Bermondsey people love Bermondsey for what it is, for what it has achieved, and for the future it holds.'[114] The place belonged to its people, but the achievements Mellish had in mind were very much Labour's. He went on, 'The service given by Labour in Bermondsey is second to none . . . in almost every organisation in Bermondsey [you will find] Labour Party people giving their services to the people of Bermondsey. That is how I want it to stay.' Here Mellish was trying to do more than equate Labour with Bermondsey, presenting his party as integral to the borough's communal lifeblood; he was also hinting at fears that abolishing the Council, where Labour had enjoyed one hundred per cent representation for most of the previous thirty years, could fatally damage that connection.[115] In interviews conducted in the 1980s, after the wheels had come off the Bermondsey Labour machine, long-time party members recalled that 'The old ethos of the Bermondsey party was to become and be seen as part of the community itself, and not as a purely political party.'[116] Mellish had succeeded Salter as the party's figurehead, but its roots ran much deeper in the daily life of the borough. It was these roots, as much as the discursive strategies of its outsider MPs, that helped sustain the broad, inclusive community politics of Labour Bermondsey. Through its networks of trade unions, local-born councillors and activist street stewards, Labour bound together the local, face-to-face communities of street, court and building into a wider borough-wide network capable of mobilising in defence of its own interests. Granovetter's 'weak ties' of association turned the strong ties of family and friendship into a formidable political force.

After 1965, with Bermondsey merged into a new super-council six times its size, Labour politics lost this intimate, communal dimension. At the same time the local party became irreparably split between the old guard, still focused primarily on local issues and what Mellish termed 'service,' and a new generation of activists, most of whom were newcomers steeped in the radical, anti-capitalist politics of the sixties New Left. As the party tore itself apart, culminating in the notorious by-election of 1983, it would be a Liberal, Simon Hughes—like Salter also a young, professional incomer—who would reap the benefits with his own brand of local, community-centred politics. Labour's broad-based networks collapsed, but its discursive strategy lived on in the local 'pavement politics' that Liberals like Hughes had been championing since the early 1970s.

Conclusions

This chapter has explored how the concept of Bermondsey as a 'community' was constituted in discourse and behaviour across the middle decades of the twentieth century. I have deliberately side-stepped theoretical debates about what constitutes 'community' in order to explore what it meant to a range of different historical actors interacting in the same time and place. The anthropologists from the LSE went into the field with a powerful set of assumptions about working-class kinship and sociability, and they clearly expected to find a gregarious communal life on the streets and in the homes of Bermondsey. In practice they found kinship bonds to be highly variable, with few if any communal sanctions, beyond a little malicious gossip, for those who chose to ignore customary obligations to close kin.[117] As with naming, so with kin relations more broadly, personal taste was said to be the principal determinant of behaviour. They also found widespread dislike of enforced communalism within the Guinness Buildings, while communal activities from pubs and dances to seaside 'Beanos' were also shunned by a significant proportion of residents. Crucially, when they returned to the borough in 1958, the anthropologists also found that Bermondsey was considerably less static and unchanging than they had assumed. Not only were thousands leaving as rehousing progressed, but at the same time many people were moving into the borough from other parts of London.

Yet 'being Bermondsey' clearly carried powerful connotations for locals, including for people like Mr Ingles who had moved into the area from elsewhere. Given that those who proclaimed themselves 'born-and-bred Bermondsey' often maintained a highly exclusive attitude towards outsiders, even those who were fellow white, working-class Londoners, we need to look beyond simple models of 'community' as the day-to-day life of the street if we are to explain the particular cultural pull of the idea of Bermondsey as somewhere one could come to *belong*. For much of the twentieth century, it is suggested, politics helped sustain a subtly different, more inclusive, politics of place which operated above the level of the building, court or street. Salter and Mellish, and the powerful party machines they helped sustain, sought to cultivate an inclusive, visionary and communal understanding of Bermondsey. Their politics fed off vernacular suspicion of privileged London 'over the water', presenting the local Council's pioneering social programme as a shared achievement of local people, rather than the gift of benevolent reformers. In short, they mobilised strong group identities against powerful and wealthy outsiders in order to obscure internal differences and divisions that could easily have fractured this sense of Bermondsey as a viable political 'community'.

As Firth observed, most ordinary working people had little time for formal party politics even in Bermondsey, but they had nonetheless internalised a strong antipathy for Conservatism and identification with Labour.[118] Labour's discursive Bermondsey was defined negatively against London's privileged West End and positively through the celebration of a strong historical narrative the people's role in building a strong sense of civic identity and pride. Vernacular identification with place was generally more fine-grained and local, but it could run in tandem with politicians' broader, more inclusive, rendition of local patriotism. The abolition of the borough council and subsequent implosion of the local Labour Party destabilised this carefully constructed equilibrium; political and vernacular discourses of community could still come to intersect, but the basis of connection was weaker without the connecting ties of Salter's mass party and Mellish's trades union branches.

Notes

1. The author would like to thank the Leverhulme Trust for supporting this research with the award of a Major Research Fellowship, and the London School of Economics for permission to quote from the Papers of Sir Raymond Firth. Thanks are also due to the organisers and participants at the 'Re-constructing communities' conference and to Stephen Potter. Boast, *Story of Bermondsey*, 26–27.
2. Brockway, *Bermondsey Story*, 11.
3. Ibid., 36.
4. Jephcott, *Married Women*, 36, 62.
5. Ibid., 28.
6. Turner, *Labour's Doorstep*, 96–97.
7. Evans, *Educational Failure*, 20.
8. Savage, *Identities*; Lawrence, "Class".
9. "Kinship Survey London, Report of Committee Stage 2–23 Oct. 1947," 3, Firth 3/1/8, and "Problem: Study of Kinship Connections and Terminology in a Primarily Working-Class Community in London," Firth 3/1/13, file 2, Sir Raymond Firth Papers, LSE Library, London (hereafter cited as Firth Papers).
10. Jones, "Cockney"; Field, *Blood, Sweat, and Toil*, chap. 2.
11. Campsie, "Mass-Observation".
12. "An Inquiry into Contemporary Kinship," 3/1/8, Firth Papers, 7.
13. "Problem: Study of Kinship Connections and Terminology in a Primarily Working-Class Community in London" (Research note), no date, 3/1/13, file 2, Firth Papers; MacIver, *Community*.
14. "Census Dec. 1946," 3/2/8, Firth Papers; "Kinship Survey Report—23 Oct. 1947," 3/1/8, Firth Papers.
15. See "Bermondsey Kin Study Group Meeting, 28 Nov. 1947," 3/1/11, Firth Papers, where they first discuss the looming need to choose between a 'community study' and a 'kinship study', and Richards warns of the dangers of being accused of writing 'Just another community study'.
16. Butler, "Michael Young". See also Topalov, "Traditional Working-Class Neighborhoods".
17. Firth and Djamour, "Kinship in South Borough," 44.
18. "Mr Young's Anthropological Study of Bethnal Green—Discussion" [26 November 1954], 3/1/16, Firth Papers; Young, "Study of the Extended Family"; Young and Willmott, *Family and Kinship*.
19. Firth, ed, *Two Studies*, 16 (introduction).
20. Other studies drew similar conclusions, Bakke, *Unemployed Man*; Kuper, *Living in Towns*, esp. 42–82; University of Liverpool, *Neighbourhood and Community*; Gorer, *Exploring*, 52–63; Chapman, *The Home*, 68–70, 156–60.

Languages of Place and Belonging 39

21. "Bermondsey Kin Study Group Meeting, 28 Nov. 1947," 3/1/11, Firth Papers.
22. "Kinship Survey Report—23 Oct. 1947," 6, 3/1/8, Firth Papers.
23. "Club Reports," 1 and 12 December 1947 [Kaplan/Prins], 3/1/11, Firth Papers. See also, "Club Reports," 3 November 1947 [Munro] and 7 November 1947 [Munro/Prins], 3/1/11, Firth Papers.
24. "An Inquiry Into Contemporary Kinship," 3/1/8, Firth Papers, 2, 5–7; also "Initial Report" [December 1947], 3/1/12, Firth Papers, 1, 3, 6. Bakke, *Unemployed Man*.
25. "An Inquiry Into Contemporary Kinship," 3/1/8, Firth Papers, 7. Intriguingly, they were advised to say they were from 'London University' rather than from the LSE, "Kinship Survey London, Report of Committee Stage 2, 23 October 1947," 3/1/8, Firth Papers, 5–6.
26. A.I.R. [Richards] field-note, 17 November 1947 [untitled: on the Guinness Social Club], 3/1/11, Firth Papers, 1.
27. [Untitled Paper], 3/1/8, Firth Papers, 1 and "Kinship Survey London—23 Oct. 1947," 3/1/8, Firth Papers, 2.
28. "Club Reports," 30 October and 4 November 1947 [Munro], 3/1/11, Firth Papers.
29. "Social Club Report," 12 November 1947 [Little and Tien], 3/1/11, Firth Papers.
30. "Firth Field Notebook 1," 3/1/1, Firth Papers, 85; Firth and Djamour, "South Borough," 34.
31. Firth and Djamour, "South Borough," 34, 48–51. The 'Ingles' were one of three families that Firth visited multiple times through 1948 and 1949. Here, and throughout the paper, tenants' anonymity is preserved by the use of pseudonyms.
32. "Firth Field Notebook 1," 3/1/1, Firth Papers, 67 [also p. 58]; Firth and Djamour, "South Borough," 34.
33. "The Community," 3/2/1, Firth Papers. For similar observations about 1930s Greenwich, see Bakke, *Unemployed Man*, 153–54.
34. Christmas Card from the 'Ingles' to 'Dr Firth & Family', s.a. [1948?]; Wedding Invitation, 29 June 1948; 'Ingles' Family Wedding Photos [1948], all in 3/1/14, Firth Papers.
35. "Firth Field Notebook 1," 3/1/1, Firth Papers, 59–60; "Report Bermondsey, 11 May 1949," [Katherine Nelson], 3/1/14, Firth Papers, 2.
36. "Firth Field Notebook 1," 60 and 64; "Firth Field Notebook 2," 33 [17 February 1949], both in 3/1/1, Firth Papers. Sarah's mother died while Firth was still visiting the Ingles.
37. "Firth Field Notebook 1," 3/1/1, Firth Papers, 2 (interview with Social Club secretary, 19 October 1947), and 114 (Mrs Ingles reporting neighbours reasons for refusing help), 3/1/1, Firth Papers.
38. "'Nixon' Family History—14.XII.47," [Richards], 3/1/13, file1, Firth Papers. The notes say in "a place like G.T.B".
39. "Family Co-operation," 3/1/14, Firth Papers.
40. "Firth Field Notebook 1 [unpaginated]," 3/1/1, Firth Papers. Firth added, 'Seems to be solitary—eats lunch by himself in a corner'. He had lived in the Buildings since the early 1930s.
41. Young and Willmott, *Family and Kinship*, 25.
42. Firth and Djamour, "South Borough," 45. Also Young, "Extended Family," 112–13; Young and Willmott, *Family and Kinship*, 25.
43. "Naming," [Ward], 3/1/11, Firth Papers.
44. Lieberson and Bell, "Children's First Names"; Lieberson, *Matter of Taste*.
45. On the need for greater dialogue between family and academic history see Evans, "Secrets and Lies," 49–73; Light, *Common People*.

46. Young and Willmott, *Family and Kinship*, ch. 10 ("Keeping Themselves to Themselves"); Lawrence, "Inventing".
47. See Lawrence, "Social-Science Encounters". For awareness of these issues within the research team see "Football Club Report, 31.xi.47," [Munro & Littlejohn], 3/1/11; also "Attitudes to Survey," [22 January 1948], 3/1/4, Firth Papers, 1–2, where Little describes a resident as being conscious of "my higher educational etc. standing".
48. "Buildings," [Ward, 26 October 1947], 3/1/4, Firth Papers, 2.
49. "Football," [Munro, 31 October 1947], 3/1/11, Firth Papers (they paid compensation of 7s 6d for a day's lost wages and 30 shillings a week).
50. "Buildings," [Ward, 26 October 1947], 3/1/4, Firth Papers, 1; "Kinship Survey Report—23 Oct. 1947," 3/1/8, Firth Papers, 1; "Guinness Trust," [Freedman, 19 October 1947], 3/1/4; "Conditions for Securing or Transferring a Flat," 3/1/5, Firth Papers, 2–3.
51. "Buildings," [Ward, 26 October 1947], 3/1/4, Firth Papers, 1.
52. "Firth Field Notebook 2," [5 July 1948], 3/1/1, Firth Papers, 4; "Buildings," [Ward, 26 October 1947], 3/1/4, Firth Papers, 1; "'Glossop' Family Summary, 1959," 3/1/13 [File 1], Firth Papers.
53. "Firth Field Notebook 2," [5 July 1948], 3/1/1, Firth Papers, 4.
54. "Guinness Trust," [Feldman, 19 October 1947], 3/1/4, Firth Papers.
55. Vale, *Prefabs*.
56. Miscellaneous notes, 3/1/7, Firth Papers.
57. "'Buckley' Family Summary, 1959," 3/1/13, file 1, Firth Papers—his mother, three brothers, mother-in-law, brother-in-law and an uncle all lived in the Buildings (although Bill did not recognise in-laws as true relatives—family was about blood lines).
58. "Social Club Report," [Richards, 17 November 1947], 3/1/11, Firth Papers.
59. "Community," 3/2/1, Firth Papers.
60. "Structure of the Kin Universe," 3/1/5, Firth Papers.
61. "Social Club Report," [Little, 12 November 1947], 3/1/11, Firth Papers, 2.
62. "Darts Report," [Geddes, 28 October 1947], 3/1/11, Firth Papers. However, other residents still took pride in Bermondsey's 'tough' reputation, and especially in its strong boxing traditions, *Firth Field Notebook 1*, "Notes—on Preliminary Meetings," [19 October 1947], 3/1/1, Firth Papers, 11; "Boxing," [undated report], 3/1/4, Firth Papers.
63. See Bailey, "Bill Banks".
64. "Community," 3/2/1, Firth Papers.
65. "'Buckley' Family Report, 1948," 3/1/9, Firth Papers.
66. "Pubs Report," [Ward, 26 October 1947], 3/1/4, Firth Papers.
67. "Firth Field Notebook 2," [nd, 1949], Firth 3/1/1, 48; "Fruit & Hop-Picking," [Scobie, 12 November 1947], 3/1/4, Firth Papers.
68. See Jones, "Cockney".
69. "Weddings," [Ward], 3/1/11, Firth Papers.
70. "Social Club Royal Wedding," [Richards, 20 October 1947], 3/1/11, Firth Papers.
71. "Firth Field Notebook 1," 3/1/1, Firth Papers, 29 and 130. Firth reproduced this boast about surnames, arguing that names under-scored the 'surprising homogeneity' of the Buildings' population, Firth and Djamour, "South Borough," 35–36.
72. "Attitudes to Survey," [Ward, 7 October 1947], 3/1/4, Firth Papers, 1; "Social Club Report," [Little, 21 November 1947], 3/1/11, Firth Papers, 3. See Mills, *Difficult Folk?*, 132–47 and Little, *Negroes in Britain*.
73. "'Warren' Family Report," [11 November 1958], 3/1/13 [File 1], Firth Papers.

Languages of Place and Belonging 41

74. "'Goulden' Family Report," [22 January 1959]; "'Bower' Family Report," [14 November 1958], both 3/1/13 [File 1], Firth Papers.
75. "'Burford' Family Report," [28 January 1959], 3/1/13, file 1, Firth Papers; see also "'Goulden' Family Report," [22 January 1959], 3/1/13, file 1, Firth Papers where Mrs Goulden says 'He was all for the Irish . . . his wife was Irish'.
76. Rosser and Harris, *Family and Social Change*, 15–18, 265–68.
77. "'Bower' Family Report," [14 November 1958], Firth 3/1/13, file 1, Firth Papers.
78. "'Dixon' Family Report," [18 November 1958], Firth 3/1/13, file 1, Firth Papers.
79. "'Bower' Family Report," [14 November 1958], Firth 3/1/13, file 1, Firth Papers.
80. "'Burford' Family Report," [31 October 1958, 7 November 1958 & 28 January 1959], 3/1/13, file 1, Firth Papers. See also "'Goulden' Family Report," [2 December 1958], 3/1/13, file 1, Firth Papers.
81. Young and Willmott, *Family and Kinship*, 113.
82. Writing in the 1980s Wilmott and Young recognised that they had underestimated the importance of voluntary migration in their classic study of migration from 1950s Bethnal Green, Young and Willmott, *Family and Kinship*, xvii.
83. In their study of Bethnal Green, Young and Willmott found that 53 per cent of residents had been born in the borough, Ibid., 104.
84. Based on the modified Registrar General classifications used in Routh, *Occupation and Pay*, 221–25 (Appendix A).
85. Evans, *Educational Failure*, 17–22.
86. Ibid., 22.
87. Ibid., 39.
88. "Community," 3/2/1, Firth Papers.
89. Unlike most London dockers, Mellish's son would win a place at the University of Cambridge and Mellish would end his days as Baron Mellish of Bermondsey living in an impressive Georgian rectory in Sussex: Dalyell, "Mellish"; Turner, *Doorstep Politics*, 146–7.
90. "Alfred Salter Election Address, 1918," 1980/54 F/1, Bermondsey Labour Party Collection, Southwark Public Libraries, London (hereafter cited as BLPC, Southwark).
91. *Bermondsey Labour Magazine*, May 1929, 8.
92. Ibid., 3.
93. Brockway, *Bermondsey Story*, 17 (note).
94. Turner, *Doorstep Politics*, 158–59.
95. Granovetter, "Strength of Weak Ties".
96. Ibid., 1373–76.
97. Brockway, *Bermondsey Story*, 86–92; Goss, *Local Labour*, 25.
98. Bermondsey Labour Party, *12 Years of Labour Rule*, 4 (Salter's Foreword).
99. *Bermondsey Labour Magazine*, 22 October 1925, 1 (cited in Goss, *Local Labour*, 23).
100. Bermondsey Labour Party, *12 Years of Labour Rule*, 4.
101. Dalyell, "Mellish".
102. *Minute Book of the Executive and Management Committees of the Rotherhithe Labour Party*, 24 October 1946, 1980/54 A/1, BLPC, Southwark; "Bermondsey Labour Party", memo, 2 November 1948, CCO 1/7/3, CPA, Oxford.
103. "Mellish Election Address, 1950"; "Mellish: Of the People, for the People," [Bermondsey Election Special, 1950], 2, both 1980/54 F/5, BLPC, Southwark.
104. *Bermondsey Labour Magazine*, January/February 1949, 3–4; see also "Mellish: Of the People, for the People," 2, which talks of "his own folk in Bermondsey".

105. "Mellish Election Address, 1950".
106. "Mellish Election Address, 1951," Election Cuttings, PC 324, Southwark Public Library.
107. "Mellish: Of the People, for the People," 2; Goss, *Local Labour*, 47–48.
108. Goss, *Local Labour*, 46.
109. "Mellish: Of the People, for the People," 3 (quoting a 1930s advertisement for the Ritz).
110. "Darts Report," [Geddes, 28 October 1947], 3/1/11, Firth Papers; also Untitled Paper, 3/1/8, Firth Papers, 3: where "bitter memories of the depression" were said to explain "a general dislike of the Conservative Party".
111. Bob Mellish, "To the Women of Rotherhithe," *Rotherhithe Labour Magazine*, January 1948, 6.
112. "Mellish: Of the People, for the People," 2; "Labour's Three for the LCC," [1961], 1980/54/F/17, BLPC, Southwark.
113. On the broader political context of these changes see Goss, *Local Labour*, ch. 3, esp. 68–70.
114. "Labour's Three for the LCC," 1980/54/F/17, BLPC, Southwark.
115. Ibid.
116. Goss, *Local Labour*, 44.
117. For instance against a man who failed to attend his own mother's funeral, "'Scully' Family Report," 3/1/12, Firth Papers, 2; although J. K. Tien separately registered that local gossip claimed that this was because the man's father had married his mother's sister, "Interview with Mr 'Burford'," 3/1/12, Firth Papers.
118. "Politics" Report and "Notes on Interview with Mr 'Barrow'," 2, both 3/1/4, Firth Papers; Untitled Paper, 3/1/8, Firth Papers, 3.

Bibliography

Bailey, Peter. "Will the Real Bill Banks Please Stand Up?: Towards a Role Analysis of Mid-Victorian Working-Class Respectability." *Social History* 12 (1979): 336–53.

Bakke, E. Wight. *Unemployed Man: A Social Study*. London: Nisbet & Co, 1933.

Bermondsey Labour Party. *12 Years of Labour Rule on the Bermondsey Borough Council, 1922–1934: Labour's Magnificent Record*. London: Bermondsey Labour Party, 1934.

Boast, Mary. *The Story of Bermondsey*. [1978] London: Borough of Southwark, 2003.

Brockway, Fenner. *Bermondsey Story: The Life of Alfred Salter*. London: George Allen, 1949.

Butler, Lise. "Michael Young and the Institute of Community Studies: Family, Community and the Problems of the State." *Twentieth-Century British History* 26, no. 2 (2015): 203–24.

Campsie, Alex. "Mass-Observation, Left Intellectuals and the Politics of Everyday Life." *English Historical Review* 131 (Feb. 2016): 92–121.

Chapman, Chapman. *The Home and Social Status*. London: Routledge, 1955.

Dalyell, Tam. "Mellish, Robert Joseph, Baron Mellish (1913–1998)." In *Oxford Dictionary of National Biography*. Oxford: Oxford University Press, 2004.

Evans, Gillian. *Educational Failure and Working Class White Children in Britain*. Basingstoke: Palgrave Macmillan, 2006.

Evans, Tanya. "Secrets and Lies: The Radical Potential of Family History." *History Workshop Journal* 71 (2011): 49–73.

Field, Geoffrey G. *Blood, Sweat, and Toil: Remaking the British Working Class, 1939–1945*. Oxford: Oxford University Press, 2011.
Firth, Raymond, ed. *Two Studies of Kinship in London*. London: Athlone Press, 1956.
Firth, Raymond and Judith Djamour. "Kinship in South Borough." In *Two Studies of Kinship in London*, edited by Raymond Firth, 33–66. London: Athlone Press, 1956.
Gorer, Geoffrey. *Exploring English Character*. London: Cresset Press, 1955.
Goss, Sue. *Local Labour and Local Government: A Study of Changing Interests, Politics and Policy in Southwark, 1919 to 1982*. Edinburgh: Edinburgh University Press, 1988.
Granovetter, Mark S. "The Strength of Weak Ties." *American Journal of Sociology* 78 (1973): 1360–80.
Jephcott, Pearl. *Married Women Working*. London: George Allen, 1962.
Jones, Gareth Stedman. "The Cockney and the Nation." In *Metropolis: London: Histories and Representations Since 1800*, edited by David Feldman and Gareth Stedman Jones, 272–324. London: Routledge, 1989.
Kuper, Leo, ed. *Living in Towns: Selected Research Papers in Urban Sociology*. London: Cresset Press, 1953.
Lawrence, Jon. "Class, 'Affluence' and the Study of Everyday Life in Britain, c.1930–1964." *Cultural and Social History* 10 (2013): 273–99.
Lawrence, Jon. "Social-Science Encounters and the Negotiation of Difference in Early 1960s England." *History Workshop Journal* 77 (2014): 215–39.
Lawrence, Jon. "Inventing the 'Traditional Working Class': A Re-Analysis of Interview Notes from Young and Willmott's *Family and Kinship in East London*." *Historical Journal* 59 (2016) 567–593.
Lieberson, Stanley. *A Matter of Taste: How Names, Fashion and Culture Change*. New Haven, CN: Yale University Press, 2000.
Lieberson, Stanley and Eleanor O. Bell. "Children's First Names: An Empirical Study of Social Taste." *American Journal of Sociology* 98 (1992): 511–54.
Light, Alison. *Common People: The History of an English Family*. London: Fig Tree, 2014.
Little, K.L. *Negroes in Britain: A Study of Racial Relations in English Society*. London: Kegan Paul, 1947.
MacIver, Robert M. *Community: A Sociological Study: Being an Attempt to Set Out the Nature and Fundamental Laws of Social Life*. London: Macmillan, 1917.
Mills, David. *Difficult Folk? A Political History of Social Anthropology*. New York and Oxford: Berghahn Books, 2008.
Rosser, Colin and Christopher Harris. *The Family and Social Change: A Study of Family and Kinship in a South Wales Town*. London: Routledge, 1965.
Routh, Guy. *Occupation and Pay in Great Britain, 1906–79*. London: Macmillan, 1980.
Savage, Mike. *Identities and Social Change in Britain Since 1940: The Politics of Method*. Oxford: OUP, 2010.
Topalov, Christian. "Traditional Working-Class Neighborhoods: An Inquiry Into the Emergence of a Sociological Model in the 1950s and 1960s." *Osiris* 18 (2003): 212–33.
Turner, John E. *Labour's Doorstep Politics in London*. London: Macmillan, 1978.

University of Liverpool. *Neighbourhood and Community: An Enquiry Into Social Relationships on Housing Estates in Liverpool and Sheffield.* Liverpool: University of Liverpool Press, 1954.

Vale, Brenda. *Prefabs: The History of the UK Temporary Housing Programme.* London: Routledge, 1995.

Young, Michael. "A Study of the Extended Family in East London." PhD diss., University of London, 1955.

Young, Michael and Peter Willmott. *Family and Kinship in East London.* [1957] London: Penguin, 1986.

3 Rethinking the "Blueprint for Living Together"
Community Planning and Sociology in Coventry, 1940–55

Stefan Couperus

Introduction[1]

The notion that urban communities could be created through the spatial arrangement of dwellings and amenities was deeply entrenched in the thinking and practice of British urban planning in the late interwar period through the 1940s. In 1944, the Study Group of the Ministry of Town and Country Planning argued that urban planners had to (re)create a 'sense of neighbourhood' through their spatial interventions.[2] Allegedly this 'sense' had been lost due to the irresistible process of urban aggrandizement during the late nineteenth and early twentieth centuries, and particularly during the economic hardship of the 1930s. And now, as the war approached its end, the task of generating 'community spirit' through spatial planning was considered to be particularly urgent for Britain's bombed-out cities. As these cities were about to undergo their physical, economic and social reconstruction, British planning authorities, administrators and scholars aimed to achieve a malleable 'social balance' so that 'community spirit' would emerge improved and redeveloped in the post-war era.

The so-called Dudley Committee reported in 1944 on how dwellings had to be planned internally, but it also presented new standards for the layout of new residential districts, conceived as neighbourhood units having ten thousand inhabitants and two primary schools.[3] The committee's plan adopted the neighbourhood unit principle designed by the American planner Clarence Perry in 1929 but rested on a much stronger belief in creating desired patterns of social behaviour through spatial arrangements.[4]

The Dudley Report and the *Housing Manual* of 1944 derived from it, expressed the government's ambition to create mixed, socially balanced neighbourhoods. Urban Britain's post-war neighbourhoods were to be inhabited by 'families belonging to different ranges of income groups' and households 'differing in experience and outlook as well as size'.[5] The architectural historian Nicholas Bullock concludes that a 'new orthodoxy' for residential development was established along these lines in the mid-1940s.[6] Socially, this orthodoxy sought to remove class boundaries and promote community spirit; spatially, it amounted to what opponents dubbed physical or environmental determinism in urban planning.[7]

In a recent analysis, the historian James Greenhalgh explains the intricate and perceived causal relationship between spatial design and the desired amelioration of 'community spirit', referring to 'a never-existent community past' that had informed post-war British neighbourhood planning as a whole.[8] The neighbourhood unit was championed by the Labour government of Clement Attlee as the planning tool that allowed for the design of social interactions through spatial arrangement. Or as George Herbert summarised the matter in 1963: 'The basic function of the neighbourhood unit, its raison d'etre, is to provide a physical environment which will regenerate and maintain primary, face-to-face, social contacts and associations within the city.'[9] Essentially, the arrangement of urban space was conceived to be a primary determinant of social relatedness.

In the processes of physical reconstruction and the planning of new residential neighbourhoods, the local authorities in bombed-out cities such as Birmingham, Hull, Plymouth, Manchester, Southampton, London and Coventry were quick to adopt the national directives and standards for dwellings and residential neighbourhoods. Case studies on community planning in these cities suggest that the planners' language 'indicates some confusion over what exactly community was'.[10]

A similar conclusion can easily be transposed to what happened in Coventry, the case study in this chapter. Here, the physical determinism that spoke from the neighbourhood planning schemes of the 1940s became increasingly contested both by municipal authorities and by other local groups. Studies of Coventry's post-war redevelopment and its local government at the time (Labour-led since 1937) have already pointed at shifting alliances and beliefs in neighbourhood planning and reconstruction politics.[11] However, adopting a perspective oriented towards community thought, one can see that the city's post-war planning history discloses how a complex governance nexus of sociological empiricism, popular input and administrative self-critique generated a move away from the belief in social malleability through spatial design in late 1940s and early 1950s, well before neighbourhood unit schemes were subjected to widely shared objections in urbanist, sociological and political thought.[12]

This chapter shows how a sociological survey, conducted against the backdrop of increasing discontent with the governance of planning in general, intervened in community and neighbourhood planning in post-war Coventry. By using primary sources and texts related to the city's neighbourhood planning schemes, it unearths how the knowledge regime of the neighbourhood unit was permeated by alternative understandings of community as an object of planning and policy. Empirical sociology was key in this process as it fundamentally questioned the social and spatial premises of the neighbourhood unit and, ultimately, altered the governance of urban planning in Coventry in the early 1950s. This reading of Coventry's experience adds to recent understandings of the decline of the neighbourhood unit principle in British post-war planning.[13] However, rather than delineating the fundamental criticisms of the neighbourhood unit principle by urbanists and administrators in the 1950s, this chapter centres on its local adaptation in Coventry and the way that the orthodoxy of community promotion through optimal spatial planning became subject to well-informed alterations.

Coventry is a relevant case study in at least three respects. First, the city gained an iconic status as a site of post-war reconstruction in public debate, in professional publications and the popular press, and in policy discussions nationally and internationally. Second, envisioned as an industrial powerhouse for post-war Britain, its reconstruction was imbued with a sense of urgency and national significance. Third, Coventry presented itself—and was presented by governmental actors—as a showcase of a newly emergent post-war affluence and as a locale showing progress for working-class families. As such, community and neighbourhood planning in Coventry generated publicity beyond the confines of its local government and debates around urban affairs.

The Governance of Planning in Post-War Coventry

On 14 November 1940, Coventry endured one of Battle of Britain's heaviest air bombardments. Because the city was a key centre of Britain's war industry and thus attracted large numbers of migrant workers, its resurrection was a priority for the national government. Whereas industry was up and running a few weeks after the Luftwaffe raid, housing shortages remained a pressing issue throughout the reconstruction process, even through the late 1950s. Local authorities had already anticipated a programme of urban renewal even before the outbreak of war, appointing the modernist architect Donald Gibson in 1937 to serve as the City Architect and head of a new municipal architecture and planning department. The bombardment's devastation allowed Gibson and his team to extend the city's planning agenda from piecemeal slum clearance and suburban extension in the late 1930s to a full redesign of the destroyed inner city, and, somewhat later, its surrounding neighbourhoods, in many cases newly planned. Gibson's team produced a radical scheme for the city's inner core, a highly modernist design revolving around an eye-catching shopping precinct.[14]

Working within the city's firmly established Labour-dominated political culture, local authorities sought to extend post-war reconstruction to the urban fabric as a whole.[15] Voicing the national Labour rhetoric of bold and comprehensive planning, the Coventry Corporation presented plans for extended municipal ownership (e.g., taxis, theatres, leisure facilities), new neighbourhood units and a range of short- and long-term housing solutions. As such, Coventry matched Clement Attlee's post-war aspirations of planning 'from the ground up'.[16]

Nationally, Labour's planning agenda met with increased criticism, ideologically and practically. Accusations of 'socialist authoritarianism' and the perceived preference of bureaucratic planning routines over democratic decision-making amounted to the fundamental criticism that British planning was 'inefficient, unjust and undemocratic'.[17] Recent studies, however, made the gulf between popular demands and Labour's alleged etatist planning model more nuanced.[18]

Despite Labour's dominance in Coventry's post-war urban governance the political and public agenda became increasingly prone to change and amendment, as historical inquiries have shown.[19] This changing attitude was partly fostered by legal reform: regulations in the Town and Country Planning Act of November 1944 obliged local authorities to consult local interest groups before submitting a planning scheme for approval to the national government.[20] Other studies have revealed a number of vernacular and social narratives of post-war reconstruction politics that alter the popular image of Coventry as an impermeable Labour bulwark.[21]

However, relatively little historical analysis is devoted to the shift towards a more self-critical, inclusive mode of urban governance and planning politics in Coventry from the late 1940s onwards, especially concerning neighbourhood planning.[22] Informed by the 'physical determinism' of neighbourhood planning in the Dudley Report, Coventry, and in particular Gibson's planning department, initially presented neighbourhood unit plans in which housing, amenities and public buildings were arithmetically laid out in space—on paper at least. The Coventry Corporation designed grand schemes for neighbourhoods such as Tile Hill, Bell Green and Canley, to name but a few, which obtained national status as award-winning examples of optimal neighbourhood planning.[23]

From the late 1940s onwards, however, there was a growing awareness within the municipal fabric that the social impact of implemented planning schemes had not been sufficiently understood or acknowledged, particularly with regard to newly planned neighbourhoods in the making—or, in the case of Canley, already inhabited. A letter from Coventry's planning department to the city council solicitor argued that planning was 'still largely in its infancy'. Moreover, the letter continued, planning standards had mostly been 'worked out on a national basis' and did not 'necessarily apply in individual towns'.[24] As such, Coventry did not fit the general planning template that had been devised nationally and was a case in its own right because:

> (a) the population composition is so very different from the national average, the bias being strongly on younger age groups and (b) the size of the city as between (1) a large market town with a well defined community life and (2) a very large city such as Birmingham or Leeds which become split up into quite definite community groups.[25]

Within the City Council, similar concerns about Coventry's idiosyncratic nature (e.g., its great share of migrant workers, its high-tech engineering industries and working-class dominance) came to the fore. Knowledge about planning's social effects in Coventry was lacking; a sociological survey, it was agreed, was necessary to fill this gap.

Municipal officials and councillors were not the only parties to urge a sociological survey. Their advocacy fitted in a larger pattern of perceived discrepancies between Labour's visions on mixed-class, planned communities and the post-war social realities of working-class Coventry. According to the historian Nick Tiratsoo a 'gulf [. . .] had arisen between popular attitudes and Labour aspirations'.[26] This gulf became apparent too, when the planning of community centres—pivotal institutions in the municipality's neighbourhood schemes—was broached. The voluntary sector immediately claimed its share, particularly with regard to the short-term planned community centres, for which the municipality received a $75,000 gift from the British War Relief Society, an organisation based in the United States.

A range of local associations demanded to be consulted and involved in decision-making.[27] The Guild of Citizens, an association of civil defence workers, citizens and shopkeepers engaged in the reconstruction process, wrote that it wanted to have a say in the layout and location of community centres.[28] The Community Centre Committee invited a number of organisations for a first meeting, but kept on receiving requests for involvement in the planning of community centres throughout the city. A 'number of organisations in the Bell Green District', one of the planned neighbourhoods, collectively addressed the town clerk and asked for substantial influence in the project, ominously stressing that 'unless the co-operation and interests of the local citizens is secured before the building is erected, the work of the Centre will be restricted and hampered from the start'.[29] Although community centre activity and membership never reached high levels in Coventry in the late 1940s and 1950s—the social clubs proved more popular in many neighbourhoods—the allocation and building of community centres attracted much attention from the voluntary sector.[30]

Probably the most publicized affair involved Labour's plan to extend municipal ownership into the realms of leisure and cultural facilities, similar to plans for Birmingham and Scunthorpe.[31] The new Coventry Corporation Bill of 1947 stated that the municipality would create all sorts of entertainment facilities and acquire—or build—the necessary buildings. Due to protests from local interests groups such as the Coventry Chamber of Commerce, the City Council promised to hold a referendum on the matter in early 1948. The outcome was a blow to Labour's municipal commerce plans: whereas district heating, the creation of smokeless zones, a washing delivery service and one municipal theatre were accepted by the voters, plans for municipal taxi services, hotels and entertainment provision were rejected by approximately two-thirds of the votes.[32]

Such clashes were a clear reminder for local authorities to include other social representatives in governmental affairs. Consensus emerged over the increasing visibility of a double deficit in Coventry's neighbourhood planning: the absence of citizen participation in neighbourhood planning and the mounting knowledge deficiency in urban governance about the social effects of planning. With regard to the former, the municipality increasingly resorted to consultation in urban governance with other interested parties outside its own administrative circles. In May 1949, for instance, the town clerk contacted a wide range of interest groups and cultural associations to ask them about their ideas of providing for entertainment facilities in the new inner city.[33]

However, with regard to the understanding of the social effects of planning schemes, it was less obvious what immediate action could be taken, and whether such action was even attainable. This issue dealt with the epistemology of neighbourhood planning and the politicized belief in it. To address the matter, the municipality invited a research group from the University of Birmingham, led by business professor P. Sargant Florence and the poet, sociologist and co-founder of Mass Observation, Charles Madge, to conduct a sociological survey. The research group branded its task as an empirical, practical inquiry into 'the relation of planning to the behaviour of individuals, families and groups' by means of 'the sociologists' microscope' of 'intensive case-study, interview and observation'.[34]

The Coventry request for a sociological inquiry by an external party was not exceptional. A recent study has shown that planning frequently adopted social science methodologies, in particular the social survey, in the 1940s.[35] Especially during the early and mid-1940s, the understanding of public needs and demands and local demographics was considered to be instrumental to urban planning and reconstruction. An avalanche of surveys, conducted by agencies, public and private, local and national, brought forward a variety of social issues ranging from post-blitz trauma, community life, family affairs and the use of amenities and services.[36]

However, the conclusions of recent historiography that the heyday of consultation through survey in post-war British planning had already faded away by the end of the 1940s does not seem generally to apply. The observation that 'the discourses around the importance of surveys for democratization died away' in the late 1940s does not account for the Coventry case study at the very least.[37] In fact, the late 1940s and early 1950s witnessed a growing awareness about popular consent and participation in Coventry. This increased consciousness aligned with emerging governance clusters made up of local authorities, commercial interest groups and professionals in the 1950s, as Peter Shapely argues, but this development does not imply that aspirations to 'democratise' community planning had faded.[38] On the contrary, the sociological survey in Coventry, as will be shown in the rest of the chapter, catapulted a highly critical notion of 'planning for people', as the survey's director Madge dubbed it, back into the urban governance matrix of post-war Coventry.[39]

The Sociological Survey in Canley

The conducting of social surveys had been instrumental to urban policy-making in Britain since the early twentieth century when Coventry put in its order for sociological research. However, both the City Council and the research group itself were aiming at something different than what had been achieved by the usual social surveys, which had already been done extensively in Coventry, for instance by Mass Observation after the blitz in 1940 and by the municipal planning department over the course of the 1940s. The adjective 'sociological' pointed to a new aspiration. In particular one of the main investigators, the South African–born sociologist Leo Kuper, continuously emphasised the main, fundamental research question that extended beyond the questionnaires and observations of the typical social survey: does the neighbourhood unit plan promote community development? Kuper, trained as a lawyer and hired to teach sociology at the University of Birmingham, became a key figure in the Coventry survey, regularly communicating his preliminary findings to local planning officials. After the publication of the survey's final results in 1953, Kuper returned briefly to South Africa and ultimately settled at the University of California, Los Angeles, becoming a renowned scholar in the field of racism and genocide studies.[40]

Kuper selected as a case study the district of Canley, just south-west of the inner city (see Figure 3.1). Already hosting some large industries, most notably the Standard Motor Company (which had moved all of its production to the district in 1935), Canley was a working-class residential extension onto which some planned estates were projected as part of a slum clearance rehousing scheme in the late 1930s.[41] Some brick family houses had been constructed, but the outbreak of war and concomitant material scarcities thwarted the building of the planned estates. During wartime prefabricated brick 'shelter houses' were built, but from late 1941 onwards many of them lacked the planned second floor.[42] As elsewhere in Britain, the idea of using different materials in dwellings, and of using prefabricated houses, became attractive to Coventry's planning and housing authorities.[43]

Canley became a laboratory for such housing experiments, its prefabricated steel units placed within the larger neighbourhood estate so that they completely changed the estate's layout as it had been planned in the late 1930s. On 29 October 1945, alderman G. E. Hodgkinson opened two 'trial houses' of the so-called BISF (British Iron and Steel Federation) type.[44] The press were keen to pick up the propaganda surrounding Coventry's new 'dream houses':

> The houses are all-electric and he saw how the problem of providing 'shadowless' lighting everywhere for the benefit of the housewife has been overcome. Throughout the houses are interchangeable plug points so that any light or appliance can be plugged in anywhere, and there are no trailing flexes to trip over. The kitchen equipment, in addition to cooker, waterheater and refrigerator, includes complete home laundry facilities.[45]

Newspaper advertisements lured the needy people of Coventry into 'the house with hope's windows'.[46] However, due to labour shortages and costly logistics

Figure 3.1 Aerial view on the western part of Canley, Coventry, 1949. At the bottom workers hostels are sited. In the middle the steel BISF houses are laid out.

Source: Britain From Above (EAW024755). ©Historic England. Licensor canmore.org.uk

it took much longer than expected for the steel houses to be completed. The national government promised Coventry two thousand steel BISF houses but ultimately only 506 were completed, almost all of them in Canley.[47]

In November 1948, when the survey began, the residential unit at Thimbler Road was entirely built and all ninety steel houses were inhabited (see Figure 3.2). Kuper selected this site for his pilot survey, as the entire Canley estate would be too vast for him to conduct his research. The survey was designed 'to throw light primarily on problems of neighbourhood planning [. . .] We will analyse the behaviour of individual families within this [the Thimbler Road residential unit, SC] ecological framework and enquire how the functions of the family are carried out, and satisfaction derived, within the house, in the immediate locality, in the wider neighbourhood or local area, and in the town as a whole'.[48]

As such, the sociological survey engaged with the neighbourhood unit principle, but it claimed to do so primarily from the social perspective, rather than from a spatial-design point of view. Kuper, in most of his preliminary reports and final conclusions, published under the title "Blueprint for Living Together" as part of a series of research papers in 1953, regularly emphasised the allegedly groundbreaking and distinctive character of what he was doing in Canley. But surely, Kuper was not the only sociologist or planner to denounce the socio-spatial assumptions behind the neighbourhood unit as presented in the Dudley Report.

The renowned British architect Charles Reilly, for instance, had gained a strong reputation as someone whose planning was based on the 'Community Principle of Neighbourhood Unit'.[49] Departing from the Dudley prescriptions, Reilly presented a smaller-scale and citizen-centred alternative reflecting the wish to foster 'neighbourliness' rather than 'community spirit'.[50] Kuper, however, concluded that although Reilly's scale was indeed different from that of the Dudley template, his plan, too, adhered to 'a theory of environmental determinism, linked to a number of assumptions as to the motivation of human behaviour'.[51] Whether it was the 'service unit' of the accepted neighbourhood schemes or the 'neighbourly unit' of Reilly, human interaction, in both cases, was seen as an outcome and not as a starting point of planning.

Kuper remained sceptical even towards the well-known case of Middlesbrough, where the sociologist Ruth Glass provided the social basis for Max Lock's planning scheme.[52] To him such surveys did not fundamentally question the social epistemology of the neighbourhood unit, and therefore such research needed to be supplemented with 'deep-level studies of residential units [. . .] in the context of social relations of the families'.[53] As such, Kuper proposed a different, more prominent and, above all, continuous role for social scientists in town planning in general. In the words of an admirer of Kuper's survey, sociologists were needed in planning practices to secure 'active participation of civilized intellects on the endless search for clarification, statement, and restatement, as required to maintain the delicate balance between security and liberty, stability and social change'.[54]

Methodologically, Kuper did not necessarily resort to highly innovative tools. The Thimbler Road survey involved interviews and observations made over a considerable period of time. What he did do distinctively was to not adopt the categories of neighbourhood unit thinking, such as the use of particular amenities, preferably those provided by public authorities, the use of public green space or the demarcation of social behaviour in a pre-defined space, i.e., the residential unit. Kuper, by contrast, allowed his respondents to determine the social categories of their daily lives.

Consequently, Kuper's findings were not what the Coventry authorities were expecting. One key outcome of the survey was a perceived lack of privacy and quietness. The steel houses were noisy; adjacent living rooms, separated only by a thin steel wall, became shared echo spaces. 'It's terrible, you can hear everything', one woman told Kuper, as did many others.[55] Moreover, the respondents almost unanimously complained that their families were visible to other neighbours, whether they were inside or outside the house.

Kuper showed that a persistent demand for privacy existed among the working-class residents of Thimbler Road, doing away with the dominant conception that privacy was only a typical middle- or higher-class value. The establishment of privacy, which was to many extents irreconcilable with the creation of communal spaces, was a crucial matter in neighbourhood planning, the survey concluded. Even if housing shortages urged economical building at the expense of residents' privacy, the 'sparing use of very intimate clusters of houses' should be respected at all costs.[56]

In more general terms, the research made clear that the social habits and the idiosyncrasies of each family were in fact driving most of the demands about housing and neighbourhood facilities. The imagined mixed-class communities of the post-war urban planning schemes were not simply created

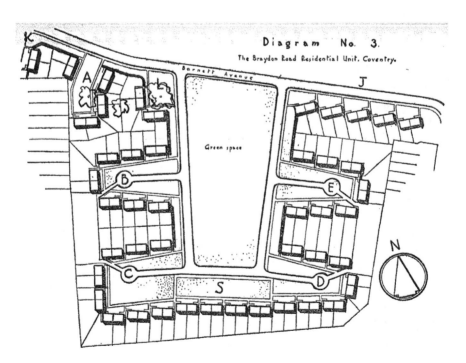

Figure 3.2 Layout of the Thimbler Road residential unit, using pseudonym 'Braydon Road'.

Source: Kuper, *Living in Towns*, 21.

by social imperatives produced by the spatial arrangements of dwellings and amenities. Kuper's conclusion presented an inverted rationale: rather than preconceived socio-spatial templates, planning should take as its point of departure a variety of preferences about living space, neighbourliness, privacy, association and services.

In addition to the demands for privacy, Kuper's report also presented worrying conclusions with regard to amenities. Many planned amenities had not yet been completed in Canley, which, despite the completion of many BISF houses, was still a neighbourhood in the making. However, from the questionnaires and interviews it had become clear that most inhabitants of the Thimbler Road estate did not seem to mind that much. In fact, Kuper concluded, 'They adjusted more readily to the inadequacies of the neighbourhood services than to the dissatisfaction with the immediate living area'.[57] People easily moved beyond the borders of the Canley estate for shopping or leisure activities, prompting Kuper to conclude that 'arguments for a small scale neighbourhood unit and clear definition of the area, as determinants of community life, have very little cogency'.[58]

Even the institutions that had been prioritised by the municipality, such as the Canley Community Centre, attracted far fewer people than privately organised social clubs, even if the premises of such social clubs were at a greater distance. As such, 'the Social Club was more effective than the Community Centre as a means of stimulating social life'.[59] The local pub, the Dolphin Inn, the *Coventry Standard* reported, served as a *de facto* community centre as well. It was considered 'a true home of the people', providing associational life and leisure time for nearly four thousand people.[60] Kuper referred to the same phenomenon more generically: 'The basis of community structure may be found also in the informal, diffuse, self-expressive interaction of residents.'[61] The sociological survey's conclusions thus cut through most of the assumptions of Coventry's neighbourhood planning policy. But what impact did these findings have on this policy?

Impact: From Determinism to Experiment

The sociological survey in Coventry provoked a discourse in which sociologists and planners did not seem to appreciate each other's take on community. Kuper wrote in his final report:

> [T]own-planners do operate with a theory of physical determinism [. . .] They rely on their control of the physical environment to promote community or neighbourhood spirit by two means: first, the clear demarcation of an area with spatial barriers, such as railway lines, parks and highways, on the assumption that the physical unity will engender in the residents a perception of social unity, the feeling that they belong together; and second, the arrangement of houses, and the siting of service units, so as to increase opportunity for acquaintance between the residents.[62]

Conversely, a critical review in *The Town Planning Review* argued that Kuper was rather ignorant about the alleged roots of British town planning in Patrick Geddes's social biology and acknowledged need for civic consultation: 'It has not been your reviewer's experience that public officials are entirely ignorant of human needs'.[63]

In essence, the sociological survey in Coventry contested a perceived 'physical determinism' among planners that was reflected in neighbourhood planning policies. The Coventry authorities took Kuper's accusations seriously. In December 1951, after a series of preliminary reports as the research was being conducted, the final report of Kuper's research in Canley was submitted to the Town Planning Department. However, already during the preparation of the Development Plan, a plan to be submitted by all local authorities according to the Town and Country Planning Act of 1947, tentative findings and conclusions from the survey had been taken into account.

The Coventry Development Plan of 1951 presented a much less fixed conception of neighbourhood planning than the Dudley Report had. It proposed 'a modified "neighbourhood" principle' varying in population size from five thousand to more than twenty thousand residents. No longer were any clear physical boundaries prescribed. Declaring indebtedness to the sociological survey's preliminary findings, the Development Plan concluded straightforwardly 'that the neighbourhood principle contributes little to the actual neighbourliness of people within the unit'.[64] Therefore the neighbourhood unit is 'an economic and physical unit rather than a sociological one'. The creation of 'neighbourhood spirit' would be only 'an additional advantage' and no longer a key constituent of neighbourhood planning.[65] This was a clear scaling-down of the planners' ambitions on account of Kuper's findings.

The survey's first results came too late to have an impact on the planning department's designs for Tile Hill, the first British residential unit to be presented as a 'neighbourhood unit' (see Figure 3.3).[66] Largely designed by the City Architect Gibson, Tile Hill provided homes for nine thousand families and included all the amenities necessary to be a 'self-contained township'.[67] Tile Hill would become one of the showcases and official examples of neighbourhood planning in Britain, winning the ministerial Housing Medal in 1950 and being praised as 'second to none in the whole of England'.[68] However, while confirming most of the spatial prescriptions of the Dudley Report and the *Housing Manual*, not a single hint of 'physical determinism' was to be found in the Tile Hill references in the Development Plan of 1951. As such, Kuper's sociological survey had clearly intervened in ongoing neighbourhood planning projects in Coventry too, albeit predominantly discursively in the case of Tile Hill.

Stretching far beyond the negation of community building through spatial design, Kuper put forth a set of clear suggestions about popular involvement in planning more generally. Coventry's voluntary associations should be involved in the execution of the Development Plan, whereas elected representatives at the neighbourhood level should have a say in the provision

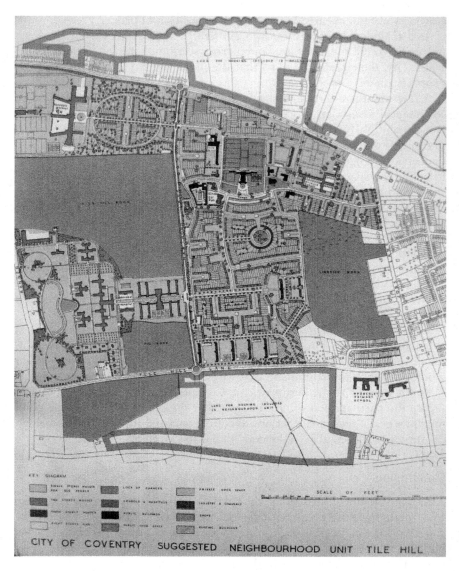

Figure 3.3 Original layout of the Tile Hill neighbourhood unit (1945).
Source: Coventry Corporation, *Future Coventry*, 26.

of particular amenities. Finally, applicants for the housing list should be asked how they wanted their house to be arranged internally.[69] Kuper's most powerful and overarching effect, then, was 'to shift the emphasis from the physical determinism of the expert bureaucratic plan to the activities of the residents themselves'.[70]

Kuper's far-reaching suggestions had already found appreciation beyond Coventry in Hull in early 1950. A local association of property owners contrasted their local authorities' 'too autocratic' attitude to Coventry's 'serious endeavours' to 'ascertain from a cross-section of the inhabitants of the whole city, their preferences, so that the planning may be on the lines the people want'.[71]

A few months after Kuper had published his findings in a collection of sociological essays, an official of the Coventry Architectural and Planning Department, W. Burns, reflected on the survey in *The Town Planning Review*, the journal that had been rather critical of Kuper's research. The rhetoric was diametrically opposed to that of the earlier planning discourse in the 1940s. It lacked the space-centred conception of neighbourhood communities and socio-cultural homogeneity. Burns wrote: 'We are planning for people, not for a homogeneous mass of something that can be moulded to our satisfaction. People have diverse requirements and they have different attitudes to life, different aspirations and different sets of values'.[72] The author acknowledged the significance of varieties in background, occupation and preferences of families for urban planning and went as far as to say that 'the Dudley type of neighbourhood unit should be used only as a single model and not as a universal one'.[73] Moreover, he argued, 'it is doubtful whether it is relevant today, to seek "social balance" by mixing income groups'.[74]

This was a radical move away from the neighbourhood unit principal as advocated in the Dudley Report and as applied in many towns and cities throughout Britain: 'The most important departure should be in our whole approach to planning, in that we should regard it as experimental'.[75] A major part of the experiment, the Coventry official concluded, was to secure the participation of citizens, whether organised or not, 'in the planning process as a whole'.[76] Serving as the citizens' mouthpiece, the sociological survey had been able to do exactly that in Coventry.

Conclusion

After the wartime destructions, the spatial and social imperatives of British town planning were projected onto the immediate future of Coventry. The city's working-class families would experience lives of prosperity in a newly built urban environment, which would ensure jobs, shops, leisure facilities, amenities and high-quality housing, all cemented together by a reinvigorated community spirit. As of the early 1940s, reconstruction schemes extended from the inner city to the urban fabric as a whole, reflecting a nationwide orthodoxy (at least among planning and administrative elites) of community planning through the layout of clearly articulated neighbourhood units. Modernist spatial designs, ranging from the layout of entire districts to the organisation of interiors in dwellings, were informed by a widely shared belief in shaping social relations through the arrangement of buildings, green space, infrastructure and amenities.

As the immediate needs of post-blitz survival policies yielded to a more reflective attitude towards the reciprocal relationship between citizens and authorities, the mid- and late-1940s witnessed instances when the governance of planning became ever more inclusive: interest groups were consulted, citizens participated in a referendum and awareness grew about the limitations and problems of *dirigiste* planning and government. In this context the request for a sociological survey, which was then conducted by Kuper, proved to be a crucial step in community and neighbourhood planning in Coventry. What at first glance might seem as one of many contributions to the emerging field of empirical urban sociology and neighbourhood research in post-war Britain, was in fact a key intervention in the governance of planning there.

In the short run, Kuper's findings pointed out biases toward working-class values and virtues that were embedded in neighbourhood planning and housing designs. The inhabitants of Thimbler Road in the working-class estate of Canley did not want communal spaces and intimacy: they wanted privacy, a conclusion that also came to the fore in sociological research conducted elsewhere in Britain a few years later.[77] Moreover, respondents to the survey found planned facilities and amenities to be much less important than had been predicted in local policy recommendations. Their social practices did not coincide with community promotion as imagined by the 'service'-centred spatial layouts in neighbourhood unit planning. As such, it is worth pointing out Leo Kuper's agency as a sociologist: he adopted a fundamentally different take on community life than Coventry's planners had. Again, his proposed shift from 'the physical determinism of the expert bureaucratic plan' to 'the activities of the residents themselves' was diametrically opposed to what municipal officials had been promoting since the late 1930s.[78] Kuper's intervention, set against the backdrop of obligatory consultation due to the Town and Country Planning Act of 1944 and a reflective attitude among Coventry officials such as W. Burns, proved highly influential in shaping Coventry's epistemology of community.

In the longer run, however, it remains questionable whether the sociological survey's generic conclusion of institutionalising citizens' participation in planning worked out. Whereas the Coventry Corporation and planning officials, as a result of the survey, explicitly denounced physical or environmental determinism in neighbourhood planning, there was hardly any substantive institutional reform concerning popular participation in the governance of planning in the 1950s.

In line with recent studies on the role and significance of non-state actors in wartime and post-war planning and reconstruction, this analysis shows that competing and colliding conceptions of the social were instrumental to the way that British cities developed from the 1940s onwards. In particular, it discloses how persistent understandings of community, as part of spatial planning policies, became contested due to interventions from outside the planning apparatus. In the case of Coventry, it was Kuper's empirical

60 *Stefan Couperus*

sociology that urged local officials to reconsider the basic assumptions of British neighbourhood planning from the late 1940s onwards. However, research on the changing knowledge regimes and policy epistemologies might reveal a much more kaleidoscopic history of community thought—and practice—in post-war urban planning in Britain and beyond.

Notes

1. The research for this article has been made possible by a grant of the Dutch Organisation for Scientific Research (NWO). I want to thank Ruth Cherrington and Stephen Milder for their critical comments and suggestions on draft versions of this chapter.
2. Cited in: University of Liverpool, *Neighbourhood and Community*, 135.
3. Great Britain Central Housing Advisory Committee, *Design of Dwellings*, 472–73.
4. On this see: Greenhalgh, "Consuming Communities".
5. Cited in: Burns, "The Coventry Sociological Survey," 136.
6. Bullock, *Building the Post-War World*, 164.
7. Lawhon, "The Neighborhood Unit".
8. Greenhalgh, "Consuming Communities," 17.
9. Cowan, "Planning to the People".
10. Greenhalgh, "Consuming Communities," 7.
11. Tiratsoo, *Reconstruction*; Hubbard, "Contesting the Modern City"; Johnson-Marshall, *Coventry*; Couperus, "Experimental Planning"; Procter, "The Privatisation"; Mason and Tiratsoo, "People".
12. On the institutionalisation of sociological working-class community research in Britain and elsewhere in the mid-1950s, see: Butler, "Michael Young"; Topalov, "'Traditional'".
13. Fielding, Thompson, and Tiratsoo, "*England Arise!*," 103–6; Clapson, *Working-Class Suburb*.
14. Walford, "Architecture in Tension".
15. Tiratsoo, *Reconstruction*, 46–52.
16. Daunton, *Wealth and Welfare*, 594; Morgan, *Britain Since 1945*, 232.
17. Cited in: Tiratsoo, "New Vistas," 137.
18. Tiratsoo, "Reconstruction"; Larkham and Lilley, "Exhibiting the City"; Larkham and Lilley, "Plans, Planners and City Images"; Larkham, "Selling the Future City"; Lilley, "On Display".
19. Tiratsoo, *Reconstruction*.
20. Mason and Tiratsoo, "People," 103.
21. Ichihashi, "Working-Class"; Hubbard, Faire, and Lilley, "Contesting the Modern City"; Lilley, "Conceptions and Perceptions"; Hubbard, Faire, and Lilley, "Remembering Post-War Reconstruction"; Goebel, "Commemorative Cosmopolis".
22. Nick Tiratsoo makes a brief reference to this episode in Coventry's neighbourhood planning. See: Tiratsoo, *Reconstruction*, 57 and 91.
23. Bullock, *Building the Post-War World*, 238; Richardson, *Twentieth-Century Coventry*, 226–28.
24. Letter from Planning Department to Mr. J. Besserman (Town Clerk Department), 1 June 1949, Coventry History Centre (hereafter cited as CHC), CCA/3/1/9874.
25. Ibid.
26. Tiratsoo, *Reconstruction*, 51.
27. USA British War Relief Society gift of $75,000 for erection of Community Centres in Coventry, CHC, CCA/3/1/10522.

28. Letter from Guild of Citizens, Leon Griffiths (secretary) to Town Clerk CHC, 2 October 1944, CCA/3/1/10522/21. On the Guild of Citizens see: Richardson, *Twentieth-Century Coventry*, 93.
29. Letter from a number of 'organisations in the Bell Green District' to Town Clerk, 21 April 1945, CHC, CCA/3/1/10522/24.
30. On this see: Cherrington, *Not Just Beer*; Ichihachi, "Working-Class," 200–4 and 305–8.
31. *Western Morning News*, 10 April 1948.
32. Ichihachi, "Working-Class," 217.
33. Ibid., 214.
34. Kuper, *Living in Towns*, ix.
35. Cowan, "Democracy," 58–65.
36. Among others: Mass Observation, Wartime Social Survey, Nuffield College Social Reconstruction Survey, Women's Advisory Housing Council Survey, Stepney Reconstruction Group, National Council for Social Service Survey Unit.
37. Cowan, "Democracy," 83.
38. Shapely, "Governance"; Shapely, "Civic Pride"; Cowan, "Democracy," 135.
39. Madge, "Planning for People," 131.
40. Charny, "In Memoriam".
41. Richardson, *Twentieth-Century Coventry*, 221.
42. *Minutes Housing Committee*, 11 December 1941, CHC, CCA; *Midland Daily Telegraph*, 19 April 1940.
43. Vale, *Prefabs*, 56 and 102.
44. *Birmingham Daily Post*, 30 October 1945.
45. Ibid.
46. Ibid.
47. Tiratsoo, Reconstruction, 37; Bulmer, Bales, and Sklar, *Social Survey*; Hinton, *Mass Observers*; Shaw, "Experimentation," 37; *Coventry Evening Telegraph*, 25 August 1947.
48. The Canley Pilot Study, 2, CHC, CCA/3/1/9874/5.
49. Stadler, *Induction*, 302.
50. Richmond, *Marketing Modernisms*, 177–98.
51. Kuper, *Living in Towns*, 174.
52. Glass, *Social Background*; Lock, *County Borough*.
53. Kuper, *Living in Towns*, 167.
54. Junker, "Book Review," 513–14.
55. Kuper, *Living in Towns*, 13.
56. Ibid., 167–68.
57. Ibid., 166.
58. Ibid., 175.
59. Ibid., 174.
60. *Coventry Standard*, 26 November 1949.
61. Kuper, *Living in Towns*, 175.
62. Ibid., 8.
63. Dennis Chapman. *Town Planning Review*, 25, no. 4 (January 1955) 286-288, 287.
64. The Coventry Development Plan 1951, 113, CHC, no inventory.
65. Ibid.
66. Walford, "Architecture in Tension," 157.
67. Cited in: Kynaston, *Family Britain*, 58.
68. Cited in: Bullock, *Building the Post-War World*, 238.
69. Report on the Braydon Road Residential Unit, CHC, no inventory.
70. Cited in: Tiratsoo, *Reconstruction*, 57.
71. *Hull Daily Mail*, 22 February 1950.

72. Burns, "The Coventry Sociological Survey," 130.
73. Ibid., 133.
74. Ibid., 138.
75. Ibid., 134.
76. Ibid., 146.
77. Tiratsoo, *Reconstruction*, 89; See Jon Lawrence's chapter in this volume, note 20.
78. Cited in: Tiratsoo, *Reconstruction*, 57.

Bibliography

Bullock, Nicholas. *Building the Post-War World: Modern Architecture and Reconstruction in Britain*. London: Routledge, 2002.

Bulmer, Martin, Kevin Bales, and Kathryn Kish Sklar. *The Social Survey in Historical Perspective, 1880–1940*. Cambridge: Cambridge University Press, 1991.

Burns, W. "The Coventry Sociological Survey: Results and Interpretation." *Town Planning Review* 25, no. 2 (1954): 128–48.

Butler, Lise. "Michael Young and the Institute of Community Studies: Family, Community and the Problems of the State." *Twentieth-Century British History* 26, no. 2 (2015): 203–24.

Charny, Israel W. "In Memoriam: Professor Leo Kuper." *Holocaust and Genocide Studies* 8, no. 3 (1994): 446–47.

Cherrington, Ruth. *Not Just Beer and Bingo! A Social History of Working Men's Clubs*. [S.l.] Authorhouse, 2012.

Clapson, Mark. *Working-Class Suburb: Social Change on an English Council Estate, 1930–2010*. Manchester: Manchester University Press, 2012.

Couperus, Stefan. "Experimental Planning after the Blitz: Non-Governmental Planning Initiatives and Post-War Reconstruction in Coventry and Rotterdam, 1940–1955." *Journal of Modern European History* 13, no. 4 (2015): 516–33.

Coventry Corporation. *The Future Coventry: Some Proposals and Suggestions for the Physical Reconstruction and Planning of the City of Coventry*. Coventry: Coventry Corporation, 1945.

Cowan, Susanne Elizabeth. "Democracy, Technocracy and Publicity: Public Consultation and British Planning, 1939–1951." PhD diss., University of California, 2010.

Daunton, M.J. *Wealth and Welfare: An Economic and Social History of Britain, 1851–1951*. Oxford: Oxford University Press, 2007.

Fielding, Steven, Peter Thompson, and Nick Tiratsoo. *England Arise! The Labour Party and Popular Politics in 1940s Britain*. Manchester: Manchester University Press, 1995.

Glass, Ruth. *The Social Background of a Plan: A Study of Middlesbrough*. London: Routledge & Paul, 1948.

Goebel, Stefan. "Commemorative Cosmopolis: Transnational Networks of Remembrance in Post-War Coventry." In *Cities Into Battlefields: Metropolitan Scenarios, Experiences and Commemorations of Total War*, edited by Stefan Goebel and Derek Keene, 163–84. Farnham: Ashgate, 2011.

Great Britain Central Housing Advisory Committee and Great Britain Ministry of Housing and Local Government. *Design of Dwellings: Report of the Design of Dwellings Subcommittee of the Central Housing Advisory Committee Appointed by the Minister of Health and Report of a Study Group of the Ministry of Town* and *Country Planning on Site Planning and Layout in Relation to Housing*. London: H.M.S.O., 1944.

Greenhalgh, J. "Consuming Communities: The Neighbourhood Unit and the Role of Retail Spaces on British Housing Estates, 1944–1958." *Urban History* 43, no. 1 (2016): 158–74.

Hinton, James. *The Mass Observers: A History, 1937–1949*. Oxford: Oxford University Press, 2013.

Hubbard, P., L. Faire, and K. Lilley. "Remembering Post-War Reconstruction: Modernism and City Planning in Coventry, 1940–1962." *Planning History* 24, no. 1 (2002): 7–20.

Hubbard, Phil, Lucy Faire, and Keith Lilley. "Contesting the Modern City: Reconstruction and Everyday Life in Post-War Coventry." *Planning Perspectives* 18, no. 4 (2003): 377–97.

Ichihashi, Hideo. "Working–Class Leisure in English Towns 1945–1960, with Special Reference to Coventry and Bolton." PhD diss., University of Warwick, 1994.

Johnson–Marshall, Percy. "Coventry: Test Case of Planning." *Official Architecture and Planning* 21, no. 5 (1958): 225–26.

Junker, Buford H. "Book Review: Living in Towns." *American Journal of Sociology* 60, no. 5 (1955): 513–14.

Kuper, Leo. *Living in Towns: Selected Research Papers in Urban Sociology of the Faculty of Commerce and Social Science, University of Birmingham*. London: Cresset Press, 1953.

Kynaston, David. *Family Britain, 1951–57*. London: Bloomsbury, 2009.

Larkham, P. and K. Lilley. "Exhibiting the City: Planning Ideas and Public Involvement in Wartime and Early Post-War Britain." *Town Planning Review* 83, no. 6 (2012): 647–68.

Larkham, P.J. "Selling the Future City: Images in UK Post-War Reconstruction Plans." In *Man–Made Future: Planning, Education and Design in Mid-Twentieth–Century Britain*, edited by Iain Boyd White, 99–120. London: Routledge, 2007.

Larkham, Peter J. and Keith D. Lilley. "Plans, Planners and City Images: Place Promotion and Civic Boosterism in British Reconstruction Planning." *Urban History* 30, no. 2 (2003): 183–205.

Lilley, K. "On Display: Planning Exhibitions as Civic Propaganda or Public Consultation?" *Planning History* 25, no. 4 (2003): 3–8.

Lilley, K. D. "Conceptions and Perceptions of Urban Futures in Early Post-War Britain: Some Everyday Experiences of the Rebuilding of Coventry, 1944–62." In *Man–Made Future: Planning, Education and Design in Mid-Twentieth–Century Britain*, edited by Iain Boyd White, 145–56. London: Routledge, 2007.

Lloyd Lawhon, L. "The Neighborhood Unit: Physical Design or Physical Determinism?" *Journal of Planning History* 8, no. 2 (2009): 111–32.

Lock, Max. *The County Borough of Middlesbrough Survey and Plan*. Yorkshire: Middlesbrough Corporation, 1946.

Madge, Charles. "Planning for People." *Town Planning Review* 21, no. 2 (1950): 131–44.

Mason, Tony and Nick Tiratsoo. "People, Politics and Planning: The Reconstruction of Coventry's City Centre, 1940–53." In *Rebuilding Europe's Bombed Cities*, edited by Jeffrey M. Diefendorf, 94–113. London: Macmillan, 1990.

Morgan, Kenneth O. *Britain Since 1945 the People's Peace*. Oxford: Oxford University Press, 2001.

Procter, Ian. "The Privatisation of Working-Class Life: A Dissenting View." *The British Journal of Sociology* 41, no. 2 (1990): 157–80.

Richardson, Kenneth. *Twentieth-Century Coventry*. London: Macmillan, 1972.

Richmond, Peter. *Marketing Modernisms the Architecture and Influence of Charles Reilly*. Liverpool: Liverpool University Press, 2001.

Shapely, Peter. "Civic Pride and Redevelopment in the Post-War British City." *Urban History* 39, no. 2 (2012): 310–28.

Shapely, Peter. "Governance in the Post-War City: Historical Reflections on Public-Private Partnerships in the UK." *International Journal of Urban and Regional Research* 37, no. 4 (2013): 1288–1304.

Shaw, Sarah Helen. "Experimentation and Innovation in Coventry 1938–1995." MA diss., Keele University, 1993.

Stadler, Friedrich. *Induction and Deduction in the Sciences*. Dordrecht: Kluwer Academic Publishers, 2004.

Tiratsoo, Nick. *Reconstruction, Affluence, and Labour Politics: Coventry, 1945–60*. London: Routledge, 1990.

Tiratsoo, Nick. "New Vistas: The Labour Party, Citizenship and the Built Environment in the 1940s." In *The Right to Belong: Citizenship and National Identity in Britain, 1930–1960*, edited by Richard Weight and Abigail Beach, 136–56. London: I.B. Tauris, 1998.

Tiratsoo, Nick. "The Reconstruction of Blitzed British Cities, 1945–55: Myths and Reality." *Contemporary British History* 14, no. 1 (2000): 27–44.

Topalov, Christian. "Traditional Working-Class Neighborhoods: An Inquiry Into the Emergence of a Sociological Model in the 1950s and 1960s." *Osiris* 18 (2003): 212–33.

University of Liverpool and University of Sheffield. *Neighbourhood and Community; An Enquiry Into Social Relationships on Housing Estates in Liverpool and Sheffield*. Liverpool: University Press of Liverpool, 1954.

Vale, Brenda. *Prefabs: The History of the UK Temporary Housing Programme*. London: Spon Press, 1995.

Walford, Sarah Helen. "Architecture in Tension: An Examination of the Position of the Architect in the Private and Public Sectors, Focusing on the Training and Careers of Sir Basis Spence (1907–1976) and Sir Donald Gibson (1908–1991)." PhD diss., University of Warwick, 2009.

4 "Washing Away the Dirt of the War Years"
History, Politics and the Reconstruction of Urban Communities in Post–World War II Helsinki

Tanja Vahtikari

Introduction

Unlike many other European cities, Helsinki was not reduced to rubble in the Second World War. Even though it was bombed heavily by the Soviets, especially in February 1944, the human casualties and material damage caused by the air raids were relatively limited.[1] Despite the modest scale of physical destruction during the war, reconstruction—in its material, psychological and discursive senses—became a major part of Helsinki's post-war life. In Helsinki, as in other cities in the aftermath of the war, modernisation prompted a complex response: modernity was celebrated even in the presence of considerable nostalgia towards the actual or imagined past. Reconstruction historiography, however, rarely discusses this engagement with the past by urban citizens after the war.[2] Furthermore, in recent years there has been a burgeoning interest among historians in acts of 'writing the nation.'[3] The significance of local representations of history is, however, often reduced to something to be understood primarily within the framework of the construction of a national community.[4] While agreeing that overlapping local and urban histories played an important part in localising national memory and identity, this chapter will show their parallel uses in creating a sense of localism, which ties in with the approach adopted by Jeremy DeWaal elsewhere in this volume.[5] The existing research on the uses of the past deserves enrichment in the consideration of the writing, consumption and performance of *urban* history, especially during the post-war period. Using Helsinki as an example, this chapter examines the significance of history in reviving and readjusting the idea of urban community after the long war and within the framework of the new post-war situation.

As for its theoretical underpinnings, this chapter builds on the understanding of memory studies and critical heritage studies on the fundamental connection linking memory, place, community and identity. Heritage and memory at any given time are active contemporary cultural relationships that facilitate shared identities by situating collectives within meaningful historical sequences.[6] They are also essentially about a sense of place, providing a geographical sense of belonging but also allowing us 'to negotiate a sense of social "place" or class/community identity.'[7] Furthermore, memory and community are inherently political and contested, as they always belong to *someone*—which often means the exclusion of somebody else.[8] The plural 'communities' in this chapter's title points to the obvious fact that in post-war Helsinki, despite the shared experience among its residents of urban life in the recent war and subsequent peace, urban community was imagined in various and sometimes contradictory ways: along public-private and official-vernacular divides, and in terms of class, which acted as a potent mechanism of inclusion and exclusion in the construction of urban community. In this chapter, the historically oriented community discourse in Helsinki is viewed both as a conscious strategy on the part of the municipal government, which aimed to transmit an officially sanctioned version of the city's history and civic identity, and as an indication of a sense of belonging, or alienation, on the part of Helsinki's citizens.

In 1950, Helsinki extensively celebrated its four-hundredth anniversary, which involved wide-ranging reflections, explicit and implicit, on the city's past, present and future. By no means was this a phenomenon unique to Helsinki. Other European cities—Oslo (1950), Nuremberg (1950), Zürich (1951), St Petersburg (1953) and Stockholm (1953), just to mention a few—engaged in similar festive commemorative performances. Helsinki's jubilee programme was spread out over the entire year and featured a wide array of events: a ceremonial city council meeting; historical, art and industrial exhibitions; a historical pageant; inauguration of new monuments; publication of professional and popular histories; the organisation of neighbourhood festivities; and so forth. This diversity of historical representations allows for a multifaceted study of the uses of the past. Therefore, this chapter's analysis is based on a diverse collection of sources, including official city government documents, speeches by leading politicians and historians, newspaper articles, history books, photographs, letters written on behalf of local firms and associations, and citizens' reminiscences. Before exploring the narratives of the urban past and of communal and spatial belonging in greater detail, the following section briefly places Helsinki in its post-war context.

Presence of the War in Post-War Helsinki

The war's hostilities ended in Helsinki, as in all of southern Finland, in September 1944.[9] Helsinki shared the post-war experiences of loss, displacement and shortages suffered by most European cities, but, importantly, it did not experience unconditional defeat, occupation or violence. Like only London and Moscow among the capitals of the European nations waging war, Helsinki did not endure foreign occupation at any time from 1939 to 1945, and this had important consequences for Finnish memory culture related to the war.[10] A reminder of the war and the harsh terms of the 1944

Moscow Armistice was the presence of the Allied Control Commission in the capital from September 1944 until the signing of the Paris Peace Treaty in 1947. The 240-member commission, led by Andrei Ždanov, was dominated by the Soviet Union. The encounters between the citizens and the commission members were limited, especially in the beginning. The commission's interpreter, Stefan Smirnov, recalled in his memoirs how on his first walk through the streets of Helsinki people would change sides as he passed, 'avoiding him as if he were a leper.'[11] During the first months following the armistice many Finns wondered whether the cessation of hostilities was only temporary and war would break out again.

The armistice agreement legalised the Finnish Communist Party, which had been banned since 1930, and outlawed those organisations considered to be fascist and paramilitary by the Soviets.[12] In line with a new 'political realism' in foreign policy towards the Soviet Union, the most pronounced anti-Soviet statements were censored, while the war and Finland's participation in it began to receive more criticism. Despite such discontinuities, it should be noted that there were important continuities in Finnish society extending from the pre-war to the post-war eras, most importantly at the level of state bureaucracy and the political system: Finland remained a parliamentary democracy governed by a broad coalition.[13]

Helsinki's party landscape was likewise marked by simultaneous expressions of continuity and discontinuity. While in the 1945 municipal elections the new Communist-led party, the People's Democratic Union of Finland (SKDL), became the largest group in the City Council (taking fifteen seats out of fifty-nine) and was joined by the Social Democratic Party of Finland (eleven seats) in a leftist coalition, centre-right groups (thirty-three seats) maintained their majority. The role of the extreme left in municipal politics diminished as a result of the elections of 1947 and 1950, which was also the case in national politics, as the Social Democrats left the coalition with the SKDL and found common political ground with the centre-right parties.[14] These political shifts and the complex post-war reality of Finland's position in the Cold War, together with Helsinki's rapid post-war growth, make the questions of which pasts were displayed and which messages were conveyed especially worth exploring. The questions posed about the past, and the supposed answers that history offered, emerged from the city's contemporary situation.

Survival Narratives: Coming to Terms with the Experiences of War

> Insofar as the festivities in the context of the city's four-hundred-year anniversary can even temporarily help to relieve the anxiety and gloominess that so greatly mark our time, and insofar as they create for the inhabitants of Helsinki a comforting sense of community, they have been successful and worth their cost. A small portion of optimism and hope cannot harm

anyone. Instead, the jubilee may become enduringly useful if it can even slightly lighten the dark atmosphere we are living in. Perhaps the jubilee can do that, if it turns the attention of the people of Helsinki towards the history of the city.[15]

These reflections, quoted from an editorial published in the Swedish-language newspaper *Nya Pressen*, justified the mounting of the four-hundred-year jubilee festivities during times of economic scarcity: the communal celebration could help to relieve the dark mood of the time and spur optimism about a better future among Helsinki's citizens. The editorial writer highlighted the healing capacity of community in difficult times. Like many other writers of the period, he suggested that a comforting sense of community and optimism could be fostered if citizens were encouraged to consider, and celebrate, their urban past.

What the editorial in *Nya Pressen* perhaps especially had in mind were the positive events in the city's history: royal visits, the building of the Fortress of Finland beginning in the 1740s, Helsinki becoming the country's capital in 1812 and the subsequent redesign of the city centre by the German architect Carl Ludvig Engel. All these events did indeed form an important part of the version of the local past presented through the jubilee festivities, and thus the gazes of Helsinki's residents were directed towards a nostalgic vision of the past. During the celebration, however, professional historians, the press and members of the city government also invited citizens to reflect upon previous wars and other disasters the city had experienced. In their writings, they portrayed the recurring destructions as a key narrative thread and an element of continuity in Helsinki's history.[16] The same held true for the most popular event of the quadricentennial celebration, the historical pageant. Because of its nature as a performance and a spectacle traversing urban space, the pageant provided a very selective reading of Helsinki's past. Among its thirty-five historical displays, six depicted disasters: the Great Northern War (given two displays), the Plague of 1710, the Great Fire of 1808, the Finnish War and the recent Winter War of 1939.[17]

The hardships of earlier generations and their strategies of survival were commemorated not just for the sake of recreating the past. Rather, as with any act of heritage or memory, they served a purpose in the present. As part of the overall narrative of post-war survival, representations of previous disasters worked to justify the sacrifices made during the most recent conflict.[18] The stories often unfolded along similar lines: in the beginning, the focus was on the hardships of earlier generations, sometimes in direct comparison to the loss of lives and homes in the Second World War.[19] 'Ruins' and 'ashes' were frequently used discursive elements. Given the relatively few ruins in Helsinki after the Second World War (most of which had quickly been removed or repaired, in any case), 'ruin' served as a metaphor for the universal experience of 'the pity of the war'.[20] After describing the disaster, the story then continued by expressing admiration for the will and

"Washing Away the Dirt of the War Years" 69

resilience of earlier generations in rebuilding their urban community. Ruin was a metaphor for community reconstruction: 'One would think that many of these events would have suffocated all the life in the city, especially when history has witnessed the demise of even bigger cities in such times. But they did not; life persisted even in the ruins. The city rose again, with a new appearance.'[21] Past instances of reconstruction provided exemplars for present and future reconstruction, which was to be modernist and undertaken in an optimistic spirit. As noted by one Helsinki newspaper columnist: 'If we, the people of Helsinki, did not have the examples from the past as to how to overcome difficult times, we would not look to the future with the same confidence.'[22] The tale of community survival presented by the city government, professional historians and the bourgeois and social-democratic press was very much a narrative of community unity: Helsinki residents had always made it through their hardships as a coherent community. Their shared experience of war and other hardships were essential in cementing this imagined community, which was always coherent and always resilient.

Often these survival lessons from previous disasters drew inspiration from a distant past. Not surprisingly, the Civil War of 1918, still fresh in the memory of many in Helsinki as a highly controversial, divisive experience (though less polarising in the post-war period than in the interwar years),[23] was not presented as a model for post-war community survival. In 1918 Helsinki had been a site of the final battles between the Whites and the Reds. Historian Eino E. Suolahti, in his popular history of Helsinki published in 1950, briefly discussed the part played by the city in the conflict; this short narrative, however, located the responsibility for the war outside the urban community.[24] Obviously, more distant conflicts had their ambiguities, but being further back in time they offered more favourable symbols for feelings of community unity.[25] To use Jan Assmann's categories of collective memory, more distant conflicts were no longer within the scope of communicative memory, relying on contemporary witnessing, but had become part of a more distant cultural memory that indicated a shared certainty about the past.[26]

Overlapping Spatial and Commemorative Relations

As with the Civil War, there was no mention in the historical pageant of the policy of Russification prior to Finland's independence or the recent presence of the Allied Control Commission in the city.[27] This is not to say that the recent past was altogether silenced: nine out of thirty-five history displays dealt with events dating from the 1870s onwards. The recent war was among them, although not the more controversial Continuation War. The Winter War in turn was commemorated in a subtle but effective way: in the programme, in which the displays were usually described in a paragraph or two, the Winter War apparently needed no explanation—simply stating the year 1939 was deemed sufficient. In the pageant itself, the war scene was

70 *Tanja Vahtikari*

represented by a nameless group of military reservists displaying no visible symbols of heroism, honours or masculinity (see Figure 4.1). In this way, the pageant contributed to the post-war production of imagery of the Finnish soldier as a modest and dutiful hero and a victim.[28] It also allowed the Finnish war effort to be interpreted as that of a nation dragged against its will into conflict by great powers.

Public memory in post-war Helsinki was thus associated with the wider politics of war memory in Finnish society. In post-war Finland, up until the end of the Cold War, the state's memory culture was, if not completely silent about the Second World War, then at least very selective about what it acknowledged and commemorated. 'Official memory' was adapted to the realpolitik of Finnish-Soviet relations. Historical interpretations, presented

Figure 4.1 'The Marching Military Reservists', a display in the historical procession staged as part of Helsinki's quadricentennial celebrations, 11 June 1950.
Source: Helsinki City Museum.

in public by state representatives and produced by professional historians, abandoned the earlier, openly nationalist narratives of the past. But the other two sources of memory production in society, the private/family sphere and the wider public sphere, were much more vocal about the war, and thus worked against any 'imposed silences' in Finnish post-war society.[29] Cities provided convenient arenas below the official state level for the commemoration of the war—as can be seen in post-war Helsinki, where national and local meanings associated with the war coexisted.

Take, for example, the memorial graveyards or 'Heroes' Cemeteries', more than six hundred of which were founded around the country. These places became important sites of war memory. During the war, whenever possible, the Finnish military brought the bodies of fallen soldiers back to their home parishes for burial. As noted by historian Ville Kivimäki, in the memorial graveyards 'different layers of war memories mould into one: personal losses are given collective meaning, national history acquires a local character and "the sacrifice for the nation" was personalized by the names inscribed on the gravestones.'[30] Perhaps the most prominent place of nationwide mourning was, and still is, Hietaniemi Cemetery in Helsinki. In 1950, the historian Eino E. Suolahti wrote about the destruction of the war, the sacrifices made by the urban community and Hietaniemi Cemetery as a place for collective remembrance: 'The Hietaniemi memorial graveyard makes up a part of Helsinki's most immortal history. From the marble headstones one can count the sacrifice the capital had to make during the war [. . .] They portray for succeeding generations just how total and destructive the recently ended world war has been for us.'[31] Here, too, the different layers of war memories merged into a single trope, but not only for the sake of the nation and national unity—the memorial graveyards, as Suolahti's writing shows, were equally used to reconstruct a sense of cohesion for the urban community and its memory. The 'deep, horizontal comradeship' through which the national community is conceived, as pointed out by Benedict Anderson,[32] shows itself here to have equal relevance with regard to subnational levels of community.

Even the funeral in February 1951 of the widely honoured Second World War hero, marshal and president (1944–46) of Finland, C.G.E. Mannerheim, often viewed only through the national lens, can be seen in light of the different and coexisting levels of memory and community. In addition to being a major patriotic ceremony, the memorial service also exerted a unifying effect for the people of Helsinki: shop owners in the city centre decorated their shop windows, and around one hundred thousand people gathered in the streets to take part in the huge funeral procession traversing the city.[33] When, in 2004, the Finnish Literature Society solicited Helsinki reminiscences to collect in a publication, several respondents mentioned the funeral as a key communal event in the city's post-war period.[34] Moreover, for the national and urban communities alike, the funeral acted as a rite of passage—like the four-hundred-year jubilee a year earlier and the Olympics a year later—in the transition from the immediate post-war era to the period of 'normalcy'.

The urban community, although the primary community imagined via Helsinki's four-hundred-year jubilee, needed to be positioned in relation to the conceptualisation of the national community at the time. The availability of multiple identities when narrating the local past, some working to 'localise' national identity and memory,[35] others being conscious expressions of localism, and some even stretching beyond the nation, becomes evident in the following excerpt from the official programme leaflet for the historical pageant:

> In the history of our capital, up to the present, our nation's developmental phases are portrayed in a concentrated form. Even if the annals of Helsinki cannot tell the story of Farmer Paavo [the rural landowning peasant], they still reflect the images of the pioneers of our land and thought. Even the characteristic *sisu* [persistence] of the Finnish people has had the chance to find its form in the developing urban community. Helsinki, even though younger than Stockholm and Copenhagen, has experienced several different cultural periods during its four centuries, seen many societal changes and shifts of power [. . .] As a harbour city Helsinki has, to its benefit, received cultural influences in all ages which have travelled a far shorter distance than one would expect just by looking at a map. But it is from the hinterland, from the great wilderness and lakes that the city has gained living vigour, which gradually has become one with its own life form.[36]

The character of Farmer Paavo, created by the Finnish national poet Johan Ludvig Runeberg (1804–1877), deserves a closer look. After Finland won independence in 1917, the country's national community was strongly associated in the interwar period with rural landscapes and peasant traditions and values, which were often idealised. As noted by historian Antero Holmila, Farmer Paavo, a peaceful agrarian character, was a frequent symbol for reconstruction in post-war Finland, which was still predominantly agrarian.[37] In the poem named for him (1830), Farmer Paavo experiences severe hardships while cultivating his crops but never loses his determination or faith. For Helsinki, Farmer Paavo also served as a symbol for starting again and for the difficult reconstruction effort: the settler spirit could also be found in the developing capital. In this sense, the Farmer Paavo rhetoric linked Helsinki to a community ideal that was traditional and based in the countryside. However, one can discern a simultaneous need to dissociate the urban community from the agrarian national narrative. In the characteristic Finnish rural-urban dichotomy, Helsinki represented the urban other for rural Finns, and the opposition cut both ways: post-war Helsinki could not and did not want to tell the story of Farmer Paavo. The four-hundred-year jubilee made a conscious plea for urban culture and urban history, something that was considered highly important by the professional historians helping to organise the events.[38] When referring to Helsinki's long-term cultural influences, the urban community was imagined to extend beyond the limits of the nation. In addition, references to other Nordic capitals, their pasts, presents and futures, and the strong existing bonds among them,[39] placed Helsinki discursively within the framework of the transnational Nordic conceptualisation of community, *Norden*, a politically successful, supra-national identity that one finds in all Nordic countries after the Second World War.[40]

History as a Guide to Post-War Urban Growth

In Helsinki, as in many other European cities, the war was followed by rapid urban growth. Population growth was fueled by a high birthrate and migration from other parts of the country, and also by the resettlement of evacuees from areas that Finland had ceded to the Soviet Union under the terms of the armistice agreement—most importantly Finnish Karelia, located on the border of Finland and Russia. By the summer of 1945 Helsinki had received around twenty-five thousand Karelian evacuees, who came from the city of Vyborg and from smaller rural communities. Another important push for post-war urban growth was a programme of massive land annexation, planned before the war but realised only in 1946, which increased the city area over fivefold from its earlier 30-km2 area. The population of Helsinki grew almost overnight by over fifty thousand to three hundred forty thousand in 1946.[41] Thus, after the war Helsinki received many new people to whom the city and its urban lifestyle were foreign. Moreover, many of the annexed rural or semi-urban areas still retained distinctive local identities. In the process, Helsinki's sense of place changed significantly.

While there was not, in post-war Finland, the same abandonment of the idea of national community as Jeremy DeWaal sketches for West Germany elsewhere in this volume, it seems warranted to argue that local communities in Finland exerted a strong appeal as emotional spaces of home and social orientation. In part, this resulted from the renewal of Finnish associational life after the war. As noted, organisations that the Soviets considered fascist and paramilitary were forbidden. As a result, the strong patriotic sentiments associated with these organisations dwindled.[42] In post-war Helsinki the influx of new residents further strengthened local Heimat work, which manifested itself in two settings. On the one hand, the newcomers to Helsinki, in Heimat societies such as the Society of Helsinki Karelians (*Helsingin Karjalaiset*), preserved the sense of community and traditions associated with their former homes. On the other hand, the immediate post-war period saw a proliferation of neighbourhood associations for new and old neighbourhoods alike. Whereas the Heimat societies imagined a counter-community oriented towards the past and outside the urban community in Helsinki, the neighbourhood associations, though they reflected upon the local past, fostered a notion of community oriented towards the growing city of the future. As Stefan Couperus discusses elsewhere in this volume with regard to Coventry in Helsinki, too, decentralisation was understood to be important to the restoration of the urban community.

At the same time, Helsinki's city government aspired to construct a new sense of community in relation to the capital for the city's new residents. There was indeed a strong political and social impetus in Finnish post-war society to resettle and reintegrate the Karelian evacuees as quickly as possible into their new communities. This process, however, turned out to be more complicated than expected. Many Karelian evacuees felt alienated in their new local communities.[43] Some wondered, in line with a long-established sociological concern about community life in impersonal big cities, whether there could even be a genuine sense of community in metropolitan Helsinki. Novelist and historian Maila Talvio concluded that metropolitan life and communal sentiments were not in conflict. Again the common experience of war, placed in relation to an older conflict, was used as a marker for true communal belonging:

> [The inhabitants of Helsinki] have experienced the horrors of modern warfare [. . .] They have seen the bombs fall and they have trembled in fear for their home. They have stood there where for three centuries the church and the cemetery stood and where the flames of [the Great Northern] War destroyed everything so that the birds did not have a limb to sit on; and here at the most central part of Helsinki, the Senate Square, they have seen the most precious and beautiful building in Finland on fire after the night's air raid. Urbanites, whose love for their homesteads built of brick and mortar never can be fully understood by anybody from the countryside, felt deep agony when they saw the smoking ruins of the university's main building. The old citizens wept that morning, at the sight [. . .] They loved Helsinki.[44]

Sociologist and historian Heikki Waris was somewhat more doubtful about the possibility of building a metropolitan collective identity. Yet if local history was taught early enough to children in schools, 'even the fast expanding metropolis could become near and personal to its new generations.'[45] In the post-war years, schoolchildren in Helsinki were engaged in the historically motivated construction of Heimat, for example, by means of organised writing and drawing competitions. Already in the 1930s, the Helsinki Society had acknowledged the importance of a metropolitan pedagogy when it published a series of schoolbooks to be used in the teaching of history and geography in Helsinki schools, and for chidren to use independently when exploring the city. In the 1950s, the book intended for the elementary school level was modified to respond to the 'great changes' in the post-war era; according to its foreword, 'Helsinki cannot be a mere habitat with no character, where one arrives and lives without any feelings of attachment.'[46]

In this book, siblings Anneli and Timo, after moving to Helsinki from the countryside, get to know their new place of residence bit by bit thanks to the help of their Helsinki-born cousin Kari. In various arenas of public memory, the urban past was accorded the pedagogical role of educating good citizens and creating 'a sense of responsibility for the city and for future generations.'[47] How many citizens used these books in the intended way remains unclear; a reminiscence by a Karelian evacuee, born in 1929, however, shows that at least some did. On weekends this teenage girl and her mother would 'study Helsinki' with the help of a Helsinki guidebook. They memorised street names and made trips to unfamiliar neighbourhoods.[48] What is visible is the desire of these Karelian evacuees to become full members of the urban community.

History was to be a guide, not just to post-war survival but also to post-war urban growth. To construct of a sense of community in Helsinki, it was important to stress the city's inclusive nature by showing that the urban community had been able to incorporate new citizens coming from elsewhere while maintaining its own distinct identity. The past, especially the recent past, was testimony to this process.[49] A community attached to and informed about its past was also perceived as providing a counterweight to the disturbing effects of high modernisation. History, responded to by the community, helped citizens to manage the changes Helsinki was experiencing.[50] In post-war Finnish society, modernism in urban planning and as an overall societal mindset gained a very prominent position. Helsinki, as the capital city, was an important showcase for the nation's modern image. Although modernist urban renewal in Helsinki was actualised on a broader scale only from the mid-1950s onwards, the ethos of change was already present during the immediate post-war years. Embracing a sense of historical community was meant to assure the city's residents that the municipal government and urban planners were able to control—and explain—the ongoing transformation that was intended to improve the community. Top-down community discourse served to legitimize the materialised and future interventions in the urban fabric. Undoubtedly, the rhetoric of community was also a means of self-affirmation for the ruling elite with regard to the decisions that they had made.[51]

At the same time, the various historical narratives loudly declared that constant change was at the heart of the history of Helsinki. According to historian Eino Suolahti, instead of displaying the stagnation typical of small towns, Helsinki's development had, right from the beginning, been dynamic and 'dramatic'.[52] Continuous and linear civic development was a recurring theme. Helsinki's history as an evolutionary narrative of continuous change was especially prominent in the framework of the historical exhibition of 1950, which, like the historical pageant, was popular among citzens.[53] In the exhibition, the city's development was given visual form through maps, charts and statistics, portraying Helsinki's geographic, population and industrial growth (see Figure 4.2). As presented to the visitor, Helsinki's past served as a means to promote an indisputably future-oriented vision of a

Figure 4.2 'Population Growth', a display in the Helsinki Before and Today exhibition, June 1950.
Source: Helsinki City Museum (Photographer: A. Pietinen).

growing, modernising city. In a similar vein, the final scenes of the historical pageant were devoted to introducing various municipal institutions, such as the fire department and the social welfare system, in the past and in the present. The message was clear: Helsinki today is a modern city that takes good care of its old and new inhabitants; there had been great progress because of municipal interventions; the past remains meaningful in the present. The same future-oriented vision of a modernising city can be seen in the organisation of the pageant in urban space. The fact that it ended in the Olympic Stadium, the recently erected symbol of modern Helsinki and Finland, crystallised, in space, the continuum from past to future. Thus, reflecting on the past underscored the striking modernity of the present city.[54] The modernist conception of community and its historically inspired counterpart were two sides of the same coin.

Whose Past? Whose Community?

Helsinki's four-hundred-year jubilee, like many other similar festivities, had a strong paternalistic orientation.[55] It was an attempt by the social and political elite to articulate their sense of an inclusive, singular community. There were conservative, anti-modern and traditionalist concerns involved.

Professional historians played a major role in the discursive construction of community: they provided new, up-to-date interpretations of Helsinki's history and controlled the overall narrative presented through the jubilee. The post-war years thus strike us as a period when Helsinki took more conscious control of its history, which had previously been left in the hands of volunteer associations. It was, precisely, after the war that the city took the initiative to finalise an official version of its history. The first three volumes of the multi-volume *History of the City of Helsinki* were published in 1950. The historical pageant provided another thorough summary of the city's past by professional historians and city officials. Through their expert status, historians were credited as visionary mediators between the past and the future of the post-war urban community. Citizens, for their part, were not consulted about which histories should be told. Furthermore, more spontaneous, grass-roots-level activities initiated by the citizens themselves did not become part of the official jubilee programme, which remained controlled from above.

Still, processes of communication taking place in institutional settings, such as the 1950 jubilee, should not be regarded as one-sided, directed only from above and towards passive audiences by active professionals and organisers. Rather, here we see consumption and production intermingling.[56] First, even though it is difficult to track down individual citizens' readings of history, it is obvious that when residents consumed the various history products, they interpreted the narratives presented as they saw fit. Second, citizens themselves took voluntary and active part in the collective performances of the past. This kind of engagement was visible in the way they welcomed the various events and participated in them. On 11 June 1950, nearly one hundred fifty thousand Helsinki residents gathered on the city streets and in the Olympic Stadium to welcome the pageant, while around one thousand people took part in it as actors. Engaging communities through heritage is a major concern among heritage professionals today; the manner in which the past was brought alive, and was felt to be alive, by the citizens participating in the historical pageant in 1950 shows a similar, even though significantly earlier, sort of communal engagement through the past.

The active involvement of citizens in collective performances of the past could also be seen in various neighbourhood and associational events organised by citizens within the framework of the official quadricentennial celebrations, and even in the letters and postcards sent by local firms, associations and individuals that congratulated Helsinki or announced participation in the planned events.[57] Urban historian Simon Gunn argues, with regard to the civic parades and processions in British cities in the later Victorian period, that participation in them 'represented a claim to citizenship and to a public voice' in the city.[58] The 1950 historical pageant in Helsinki can be analysed along similar lines: taking part in the narrative of successive generations building the city conferred a claim to both urban memory and present citizenship, and thus to membership in the urban community.

With regard to the previously discussed example of memorial graveyards, it is clear that even though not everyone wanted to belong to this community of remembrance and comradeship, nor shared its symbols, the many ritual commemorations and events that took place at the memorial graveyards had wide resonance among the Finnish (and Helsinki) population.[59] The community of war remembrance was constructed from above by professional historians and politicians tasked with creating such remembrance. However, through repeated visits, rituals and face-to-face interactions, this community was also experienced and performed from below.

Judging from the wide participation of citizens in the events organised within the framework of the 1950 jubilee, many citizens indeed wanted to perform the past and community along the lines proposed by the city government. Still, notions of community and history had very different connotations for many citizens, especially working-class people. For example, in the 1940s, memory of the Civil War was still divided into two separate realms: the 'White' history and the 'Red' oral history.[60] Since class was an obvious dividing line in Finnish society, the following paragraphs will elaborate on the conceptualisation of urban community in post-war Helsinki from the perspective of class.

The Social Democrats were generally sympathetic towards the four-hundred-year anniversary celebration, and for the most part consented to the historical narratives articulated in association with it. They also shared the educational mission of the jubilee. The Social Democratic newspaper, *Suomen Sosiaalidemokraatti*, took an active part in the celebration's success, both beforehand and afterwards. For instance, it advised its readers to properly study the history of Helsinki before attending the historical exhibition and the pageant.[61] Moreover, the Social Democrats themselves were not excluded from the imagined urban community as it was shaped through the 1950 jubilee. One of the two lectures given in the City Council's jubilee meeting on 12 June 1950 discussed the growing influence of the working class in the urban community.[62] Notably, most of the scenes in the historical pageant that focused on contemporary history also dealt with workers' history. These scenes included the display of workers participating in the May Day parade of 1898, the demand for universal suffrage in 1905 and the construction of the new Workers' House in Helsinki, the 'Granite Castle', in 1906. The presentation of the Workers' House was especially symbolic. According to the Social Democratic newspaper: 'the Workers' House in Helsinki passed before us reminding us of the time when that house, already having witnessed so many fates over the years, was built by workers' cooperation.'[63] In this building the revolution had started. At the end of the Civil War, it had been seriously damaged by German troops entering the city. The pageant's final display brought before the urban audience a wide collection of workers association and trade union flags. In April 1940 the Ministry of the Interior had lifted a prohibition on red (Social Democratic) flags, which had been considered to be symbols of the enemy in the interwar years.⁶⁴ In 1950, red flags were included, without hesitation, in what was in essence a bourgeois celebration. The inclusive representation of working-class identity—in its moderate version—was congruent with the political constitution of the City Council in the post-war era, with its significant leftist presence. By underlining Social Democratic narratives, it was also, and perhaps more importantly, congruent with the anti-communist links between the centre-right parties and the Social Democratic Party in the political life of the capital.

At the same time, it should be pointed out that there were different emphases in conservative and Social Democratic constellations of memory and in their notions of urban community. For example, whereas the conservative newspapers treated the Winter War scene in the historical pageant with patriotic enthusiasm,⁶⁵ the Social Democratic newspaper reported on it rather laconically, stating, in the voice of one spectator: 'that is how it was.'⁶⁶ In addition, the newspaper made a clear distinction between the main celebration in the city centre and the celebration 'north of the long bridge', which was the traditional workers' area in Helsinki, thus suggesting that the community there had its own distinct narratives and ways of celebrating.⁶⁷

In post-war Helsinki, many social groups relied on the past in their visions of the future, and these different interpretations sometimes conflicted with each other. In fact the extreme left contested—and politicised—the very idea of the four-hundred-year anniversary. Soon after the main festivities had ended, the Communist members of the City Council protested to the city government about the war scene in the historical pageant.⁶⁸ In line with the general extreme-left reading of the Finnish Second World War experience, in which Soviet aggression did not play any role,⁶⁹ the Communist council members declared the Winter War scene to be anti-Soviet propaganda. Articles published in *Vapaa Sana*, the Communist newspaper, depicted the jubilee as a parade of bourgeois power that found no resonance among the working-class people who were living in slumlike conditions in the capital's hinterlands. Current rule was equated with the history of Helsinki under Swedish rule; conversely, it was felt that the historical representation had put too little emphasis on the city's industrialisation and development during the Russian period.⁷⁰ *Vapaa Sana* also constructed a counter-narrative to the four-hundred-year anniversary celebration in Helsinki: namely, it told of the fiftieth anniversary festivities of the Communist women's organisation, which took place in the city of Tampere at the same time. While the celebration in Helsinki could not move working-class souls, the commemoration in Tampere was a truly communal event, so the Communist newspaper claimed.⁷¹ The extreme left thus positioned itself outside the boundaries of the urban community set by the city government. Nowhere was this more evident than in the publication, in the Communist newspaper on the day of the main celebration, of scenarios imagining what would happen if Helsinki, should there be a new war, were hit by a nuclear bomb.⁷²

Conclusion

Constructing a coherent continuum from the past through the present and into the future was an important priority for post-war discourses of reconstruction and community—for the sake of nostalgia, of creating a sense of place and belonging, and of modernity itself. In a situation marked by social and political uncertainty, economic scarcity and rapid urban growth, Helsinki's post-war city govenment feared that community spirit would be lacking. As elsewhere in Europe, there was a political and social need for the re-establishment of urban community and memory, which in Helsinki culminated in the four-hundred-year jubilee organised in 1950. Effective community discourse was founded against the background of Helsinki residents' shared experiences of war and of post-war urban growth and transformation.

The four-hundred-year jubilee transmitted an officially sanctioned, politicised version of a historically inspired urban community, aiming to include as large a part of Helsinki's citizenry as possible.[73] The elite's discursive construction of urban community built upon history had a conservative undertone, as it favoured romantic notions of an enduring and safe community. In the historical context, present political uncertainties and social injustices could be left uncommented upon. Thus, as the Helsinki example shows, historical narratives, even though they serve as political instruments to promote an inclusive sense of citizenship, often simultaneously possess an exclusive character. At the same time, it should be noted that history was equally commented upon when it was used to radically redefine ideas of community, as was the case with the extreme left. Popular historical representations were met with counter-narratives: some, like the extreme left's, surfaced in public, while others stayed within the walls of private homes.

With regard to place, urban community was constructed in relation to 'several places and multiple experiental dimensions':[74] the expanding metropolis as a whole, the old and new neighbourhoods that each possessed distinctive identities, the areas north and south of the 'long bridge' that traditionally divided the workers' and non-workers' areas, the city centre and the outskirts, and the Karelian lost spaces now existing only in memory. Urban community was also constantly negotiated in relation to national narratives. Often the city was seen to complement the national community; one can sometimes detect, however, a certain uneasiness in how these two were married. Still, the discursive construction of urban community that historical representations fostered shows itself primarily to be a community built on human associations. The often-used metaphor of ruin indicated that the city provides a home even when it lies in ruins.

Notes

1. This chapter was written as part of my postdoctoral research funded by the Academy of Finland (project number SA 138551). In the three massive aerial bombardments of February 1944, only four per cent of the nearly seventeen

"Washing Away the Dirt of the War Years" 81

thousand bombs that were dropped on Helsinki hit their targets. One hundred fifty people were killed and around three hundred fifty were injured. Six per cent of the city's building stock was destroyed or damaged. This low rate of destruction was the result of an effective air defence. Helminen and Lukander, *Helsingin suurpommitukset*, 252–3.
2. Pendlebury, Erten, and Larkham, *Alternative Visions*; Whyte, *Man-Made Future*.
3. An important contribution is, for example, Berger and Lorenz, *Nationalizing the Past*.
4. On localisation of national history in the Nordic framework, see Aronsson et al., "Nordic National Histories," 272.
5. For a similar argument in the context of historical pageantry in post-war Britain, see Freeman, "Splendid Display," 427.
6. See, for example, Harrison, *Heritage: Critical Approaches*; Aronsson and Gradén, "Introduction," 14; Thiessen, *Eingebrannt ins Gedächtnis*.
7. Smith, *Uses of Heritage*, 75.
8. Ibid.; Waterton and Smith, "The Recognition," 8.
9. Finns tend to perceive their country's participation in the Second World War as involving three connected but separate wars: the Winter War, fought against the Soviet invasion from November 1939 to March 1940; the Continuation War, fought again against the Soviet Union starting in June 1941, but this time alongside Nazi Germany as an officially unallied 'brother-in-arms'; and the Lapland War, fought against Germany in northern Finland from September 1944 to April 1945 to drive the remaining German troops out of the country. For an overview in English of Finland in the Second World War, see Kinnunen and Kivimäki, *Finland in World War II*.
10. Kivimäki, "Between Defeat," 484–85.
11. Smirnov, *Tornin*, 30.
12. Besides the genuinely fascist organisations, the most notable national organisations abolished in 1944–45 were the Civil Guards, the women's Lotta Svärd organisation and the Finnish soldiers' and war veterans' organisations, all of which also had an important social function. Meinander, *Tasavallan tiellä*, 87.
13. Kinnunen and Jokisipilä, "Shifting Images," 439; Kivimäki, "Between Defeat," 484.
14. Kolbe, "Helsinki kasvaa," 510–11.
15. Quoted in *Uusi Suomi*, 10 June 1950. All translations are by the author unless indicated otherwise.
16. See, for example, *Kertomus Helsingin kaupungin kunnallishallinnosta* 1950, I, 12; Eino E. Suolahti, *Helsingin neljä vuosisataa* (Helsinki: Otava, 1949).
17. *Helsingin kaupungin 400-vuotisjuhlat. Ohjelma 11.6.1950* (hereafter referred to as Programme Leaflet).
18. See also Holmila, "Jälleenrakentamisen narratiivit".
19. *Suomen Kuvalehti* 40/1944, 1136–37.
20. Judt, *Post-War*, 16.
21. *Suomen Sosiaalidemokraatti*, 11 June 1950.
22. *Hufvudstadsbladet*, 11 June 1950.
23. Tepora, "Changing Perceptions of 1918".
24. Suolahti, *Helsingin neljä vuosisataa*, 323–25.
25. See also Holmila, "Jälleenrakentamisen narratiivit," 8–9.
26. Assmann, "Collective Memory," 125–33.
27. Programme Leaflet.
28. Kemppainen, "Kuolema, isänmaa ja kansalainen," 235.
29. Kinnunen and Jokisipilä, "Shifting Images," 437–39.
30. Kivimäki, "Between Defeat," 485.
31. Suolahti, *Helsingin neljä vuosisataa*, 325.
32. Anderson, *Imagined Communities*, 7.

33. *Helsingin Sanomat*, 2–5 February 1951.
34. Reminiscence collection Helsinki—Stadini (Helsinki—My City), collected between 12 June–15 October 2004, male, born 5 November 1940; female born 9 November 1941; female born 11 January 1941. Folklore archives of the Finnish Literature Society (hereafter cited as SKS, KRA).
35. Aronsson et al., "Nordic National Histories," 272.
36. Programme Leaflet.
37. Holmila, "Jälleenrakentamisen narratiivit," 8.
38. Historial pageant, counter-proposal by R.R. Papers of the 400 Years Jubilee Committee, 262:2, Helsinki City Archives (hereafter cited as HCA).
39. *Helsingin Sanomat*, 7 May 1950.
40. Kolbe, "Symbols," 383.
41. Kolbe, "Helsinki kasvaa," 63–68.
42. Turunen, *Suomalainen kotiseutuliike*, 15–20.
43. Raninen-Siiskonen, "Karjalaisen siirtoväen," 127.
44. Maila Talvio, "Helsinki kotiseutuna," *Kotiseutu* 3–4 (1950): 468.
45. Heikki Waris, "Suurkaupungin kotiseutuharrastus," in *Kauppiaiden ja merenkulkijain Helsinki* (Helsinki: Helsinki-Seura, 1954), 7–10.
46. Eero Salola, *Helsinkiä oppimassa* (Helsinki: Otava, 1957).
47. *Helsingin kaupungin historia* I, 1950, 5.
48. Helsinki–Stadini, female, born 30 September 1929, SKS, KRA.
49. Eino E. Suolahti to the Helsinki Society, 15 February 1948, Jubilee Committee, 262:2, HCA.
50. See also Freeman, "Splendid Display," 444, 453.
51. See Waterton and Smith, "The Recognition," 8.
52. Eino E. Suolahti, "Helsingin historian dramaattisuus," *Valvoja* 5 (1950): 147–52.
53. *Suomen Sosiaalidemokraatti*, 7 May 1950.
54. See also Kervanto Nevanlinna, *Kadonneen kaupungin*, 147–48.
55. Kolbe, "Helsinki kasvaa," 93–94.
56. Aronsson and Gradén, "Introduction," 14.
57. For a collection of letters and postcards see Jubilee Committee, 262:3, HCA.
58. Gunn, "Analysing Behaviour," 193.
59. Kivimäki, "Between Defeat," 485–87.
60. Peltonen, "Sisällisodan muistaminen," 467.
61. *Suomen Sosiaalidemokraatti*, 7 June 1950.
62. Ibid., 13 June 1950.
63. Ibid., 12 June 1950.
64. Tepora, "Changing Perceptions," 372.
65. *Uusi Suomi*, 12 June 1950.
66. *Suomen Sosiaalidemokraatti*, 12 June 1950.
67. Ibid.
68. *Helsinki City Council*, 29 June 1950. City Council Minutes of 1950, 427, HCA.
69. Tepora, "Changing Perceptions," 385.
70. *Vapaa Sana*, 11 June 1950.
71. Ibid., 11 and 13 June 1950.
72. Ibid., 11 June 1950.
73. Freeman, "Splendid Display," 426.
74. Kuusisto-Arponen, "The Politics of Identity," 196.

Bibliography

Anderson, Benedict. *Imagined Communities: Reflections on the Origin and Spread of Nationalism*. Revised edition. London: Verso, 2006.

Aronsson, Peter, Narve Fulsås, Pertti Haapala, and Bernard Eric Jensen. "Nordic National Histories." In *The Contested Nation: Ethnicity, Class, Religion and Gender in National Histories*, edited by Stefan Berger and Chris Lorenz, 256–82. Basingstoke: Palgrave Macmillan, 2008.

Aronsson, Peter and Lizette Gradén. "Introduction: Performing Nordic Heritage— Institutional Preservation and Popular Practices." In *Performing Nordic Heritage: Everyday Practices and Institutional Culture*, edited by Peter Aronsson and Lizette Gradén, 1–26. Franham: Ashgate, 2013.

Assmann, Jan. "Collective Memory and Cultural Identity." *New German Critique* 65 (1995): 125–33.

Berger, Stefan and Chris Lorenz, eds. *Nationalizing the Past: Historians as Nation Builders in Modern Europe*. Basingstoke: Palgrave Macmillan, 2010.

Freeman, Mark. "Splendid Display; Pompous Spectacle: Historical Pageants in Twentieth-Century Britain." *Social History* 38, no. 4 (2013): 423–55.

Gunn, Simon. "Analysing Behaviour as Performance." In *Research Methods for History*, edited by Simon Gunn and Lucy Fair, 184–200. Edinburgh: Edinburgh University Press, 2012.

Harrison, Rodney. *Heritage: Critical Approaches*. New York: Routledge, 2013.

Helminen, Martti and Aslak Lukander. *Helsingin suurpommitukset helmikuussa 1944*. Helsinki: WSOY, 2004.

Holmila, Antero. "Jälleenrakentamisen narratiivit ja niiden muotoutuminen Suomen lehdistössä 1944–1945." *Elore* 15, no. 2 (2008): 1–20.

Judt, Tony. *Post-War. A History of Europe Since 1945*. London: Vintage, 2010.

Kemppainen, Ilona. "Kuolema, isänmaa ja kansalainen toisen maailmansodan aikaisessa Suomessa." In *Ihminen sodassa*, edited by Tiina Kinnunen and Ville Kivimäki, 229–41. Helsinki: Minerva, 2006.

Kervanto Nevanlinna, Anja. *Kadonneen kaupungin jäljillä. Teollisuusyhteiskunnan muutoksia Helsingin historiallisessa ytimessä*. Helsinki: Finnish Literature Society, 2002.

Kinnunen, Tiina and Markku Jokisipilä. "Shifting Images of 'Our Wars': Finnish Memory Culture of World War II." In *Finland in World War II: History, Memory, Interpretations*, edited by Tiina Kinnunen and Ville Kivimäki, 435–82. Leiden: Brill, 2012.

Kinnunen, Tiina and Ville Kivimäki, eds. *Finland in World War II: History, Memory, Interpretations*. Leiden: Brill, 2012.

Kivimäki, Ville. "Between Defeat and Victory: Finnish Memory Culture of the Second World War." *Scandinavian Journal of History* 37, no. 4 (2012): 482–504.

Kolbe, Laura. "Helsinki kasvaa suurkaupungiksi. Julkisuus, politiikka, hallinto ja kansalaiset 1945–2000." In *Helsingin historia vuodesta 1945*, vol. 3, edited by Laura Kolbe and Heikki Helin, 10–511. Edita: Helsingin kaupunki, 2002.

Kolbe, Laura. "Symbols of Civic Pride, National History or European Tradition? City Halls in Scandinavian Capital Cities." *Urban History* 35, no. 3 (2008): 382–413.

Kuusisto-Arponen, Anna-Kaisa. "The Politics of Identity and Visuality: The Case of Finnish War Children." In *Images in Use: Towards the Critical Analysis of Visual Communication*, edited by Matteo Stocchetti and Karin Kukkonen, 181–98. Amsterdam: John Benjamins Publishing Company, 2011.

Meinander, Henrik. *Tasavallan tiellä: Suomi kansalaissodasta 2000-luvulle*. Translated by Paula Autio. Helsinki: Schildts & Söderströms, 2012.

Peltonen, Ulla-Maija. "Sisällissodan muistaminen." In *Sisällissodan pikkujättiläinen*, edited by Pertti Haapala and Tuomas Hoppu, 464–73. Helsinki: WSOY, 2010.

Pendlebury, John, Erdem Erten, and Peter Larkham, eds. *Alternative Visions of Post-War Reconstruction: Creating the Modern Townscape.* London: Routledge, 2015.
Raninen-Siiskonen, Tarja. "Karjalaisen siirtoväen sopeutuminen tutkimuksen kohteena." In *Karjala-kuvaa rakentamassa*, edited by Pekka Suutari, 122–55. Helsinki: Finnish Literature Society, 2013.
Smirnov, Stefan. *Tornin miehet.* Helsinki: Tammi, 1995.
Smith, Laurajane. *Uses of Heritage.* New York: Routledge, 2006.
Tepora, Tuomas. "Changing Perceptions of 1918: World War II and the Post-War Rise of the Left." In *The Finnish Civic War 1918: History, Memory, Legacy*, edited by Tuomas Tepora and Aapo Roselius, 364–400. Leiden and Boston: Brill, 2014.
Thiessen, Malte. *Eingebrannt ins Gedächtnis. Hamburgs Gedenken an Luftkrieg und Kriegsende 1943 bis 2005.* Hamburg: Dölling und Galitz Verlag, 2007.
Turunen, Harri. *Suomalainen kotiseutuliike 1945–2000.* Helsinki: Finnish Literature Society, 2004.
Waterton, Emma and Laurajane Smith. "The Regognition of and Misregognition of Community Heritage." *International Journal of Heritage Studies* 16, no. 1–2 (2010): 4–15.
Whyte, Iain Boyd, ed. *Man-Made Future: Planning, Education and Design in Mid-Twentieth-Century Britain.* New York: Routledge, 2007.

Part II
Rural and Regional Communities

5 A Counter-Community between Regionalism and Nationalism

State-Building and the Vision of Modernisation in Interwar Romania

Florian Kührer-Wielach

On 1 December 1918, in the Transylvanian town of Alba Iulia, a 'National Assembly' of the Hungarian Romanians declared independence from Hungarian rule and the union of their (shared) territories with the Kingdom of Romania. The nascent 'Greater Romania' was intended not only to unite the Romanians facing marginalisation and assimilation in Hungary but also to support their political, economic and social advancement in a national context. In their proclamation of annexation, the political leaders of the Transylvanian Romanians underscored their vision of a modern, democratic society based on the 'Western' model.

The 'Transylvanian model' proclaimed in Alba Iulia was envisaged as the matrix for the 'Greater Romanian' integration process—the unification of culturally and politically very diverse territories with the 'Old Kingdom' of Romania, the so-called Regat. But about a year and a half after the declaration of annexation, it was already apparent that the integration process amounted rather to the assimilation of the 'new areas' by the 'old' feudal system and its political elites in Bucharest. At this point the Transylvanian Romanian opinion leaders began to mobilise the population of their political 'home base'—the territories that had passed to Romania from Hungary in 1918—against the government. And so Transylvanian Romanian regionalism was born as a political phenomenon: the borders between the territories in which Romanians lived on both sides of the Carpathians, borders that had been dismantled after the First World War by the Paris Peace Conference in 1919–20, were symbolically re-established in discourse, and the Transylvanian population—until 1918 a people under Habsburg rule—was indiscriminately declared a *counter-community*. Such a declaration showed the Transylvanian politicians attempting to gather their supporters and generate momentum to achieve power in Romania. They offered a vision of a more democratic and Western-oriented answer to the question of how to achieve Romania's 'catch-up modernisation'. This discursively generated community was intended to drive home a 'Transylvanian alternative' to Bucharest's political establishment and to contest the alleged assimilation and uniformisation of the entire state territory by way of a mass movement. At times they met with great success: in 1928, for example, the

Transylvanian Romanian–led National Peasants' Party (*Partidul Național Țărănesc*) came to power and as the governing party dominated political life in Romania for several years.

The process of uniting territories that had formerly been Habsburg-Cisleithanian (Bukovina), Habsburg-Transleithanian (Transylvania, the Banat, Partium) or Russian (Bessarabia) with what had been the relatively small Kingdom of Romania (Old Kingdom, *vechiul Regat*) led to profound ideological and real-world political ruptures in 'Greater Romanian' society before it could become fully formed. However, Romanian historiography, and in its wake general societal discourse, has described this transition as a smooth process that enjoyed the support of all Romanians in national concord.[1]

This chapter seeks to look behind the façade of this national masternarrative by analysing the integration process from an 'ethno-regional' perspective. To this end, it examines the political discourse after the First World War of the Transylvanian Romanian elite, who aimed to create a counter-community in order to distance itself from the entrenched political establishment. The unique aspect of this focus is its emphasis not on a 'classical' conflict *between* ethnicities or nations, but rather on a process of *intra*-national diversification and group formation: what initially appeared to be a short-term, easily solved integration problem for a nation forming a state—the Romanians in the ethnic sense—ultimately proved to be a massive collision of diverse cultural and historical worlds, promoted in the sphere of discourse and fought out in the arena of politics, a battle between the allegedly superior civilisation of the 'Habsburg heirs' and the 'Balkanised' centralists.

This analysis focuses on the discourse strategies of the Transylvanian Romanian political elite, which aimed to create a strong identification with its regional culture and history on the basis of a sometimes highly radical political regionalism in order to distance itself from 'Greater Romanian' society. Which circumstances enabled Transylvanian Romanian regionalism to triumph after the First World War? And which 'cultural and psychological material' was used by its actors to construct a sense of community and belonging among Transylvanian Romanians?[2]

After some methodological considerations and a brief introduction to the history of the region in the Central European context, I will describe the connection between institutional centralisation (administration, cultural institutions, the Church, etc.) and the emergence of community-making regionalist discourses: namely, the re-establishment of former borders via discourse and the reception of this regionalist concept by its opponents, and the transition from an *ethno-regional* to a *trans-regional* community on the basis of the canon of values proclaimed by the Romanian Transylvanian National Assembly on 1 December 1918. The empirical section concludes with an outline of the central role played by the town of Alba Iulia as a place of both discourse and performance, as it served government and opposition alike as a venue for political demonstrations.

Shaping Communities and Political Entrepreneurship

According to Rogers Brubaker, whose observations on 'groups' and 'groupness' form the methodological basis of this study, categories such as 'race', 'ethnicity' or 'nation' cannot be considered to represent 'discrete, sharply differentiated, internally homogenous and externally bounded groups'.[3] 'Regionality', on the other hand, probably due to its semantic relation to the idea of 'locality', is often perceived as a less imaginary, more 'grounded' and more stable concept, since it can refer to a more tightly defined territorial space (of origin).[4] Rejecting this assumption, this study is informed by the theory that the establishment of discursive demarcation and the 'evocation' of regional-societal cohesion take place on the same performative level as the creation of ethnic, national or 'racial' communities: 'Transylvanian-Romanians' are hence the result of spatial, cultural, social and political categorisation achieved via discourse. The 'reality' of 'regionality' and regional identification is not dependent on the existence of 'regions' 'as the imagery of discrete, concrete, tangible, bounded and enduring' entities, but should rather be conceptualised 'in relational, processual, dynamic, eventful and disaggregated terms: [. . .] practical categories, cultural idioms, cognitive schemas, discursive frames, organizational routines, institutional forms, political projects and contingent events'.[5]

Therefore, the discursive formation to be analysed was a result of the intersection of 'people, geographical places, and historical change'.[6] After 1918, a small group of 'ethno-political entrepreneurs',[7] which despite its size possessed strong leadership and was extremely influential well beyond the war years, was able to develop the Romanian National Party of Transylvania and the Banat (*Partidul Național Român din Transilvania și Banat*), founded in 1881,[8] into a powerful collective movement that over the course of the 1920s became a significant actor in Greater Romanian politics. After 1918 and the move from the Hungarian to the Romanian state, the members of this 'ethno-party'[9] became 'regionalist entrepreneurs' and then, from the mid-1920s onwards, 'trans-regionalist entrepreneurs'; their rhetoric centred, implicitly and explicitly, on the proclamation of the Transylvanian town Alba Iulia as the core of a democratic concept that offered an alternative to the ideas of the 'centralists' ruling in Bucharest, whose politics they criticised as clientelist, outdated and feudal.

Transylvanian periodicals written in Romanian in the interwar period are the source material for this study. Reproducing in compact form the statements of regional political actors—including opponents of the National Party and its representatives—these publications presented these regionalist sentiments to local literate elite functionaries (priests, teachers, officials). Such multiplying and mobilizing support made possible the reification of a regional community largely consisting of villagers and farm workers, people with very little school education and political awareness. Community thus became an 'event':

> Shifting attention from groups to groupness and treating groupness as variable and contingent rather than fixed and given [. . .] allows us to

take account of—and, potentially, to account for—phases of extraordinary cohesion and moments of intensely felt collective solidarity, without implicitly treating high levels of groupness as constant, enduring or definitionally present. It allows us to treat groupness as an *event*, as something that 'happens', as E.P. Thompson famously said about class.[10]

In the case of the Transylvanian Romanians, this 'event' is situated very precisely by the portrayal of Alba Iulia as the spiritual centre of the ethno-regional community, in which the town is positioned as a kind of 'counter-capital' to Bucharest. This (implicit) attribution enabled Transylvanian politicians to give Alba Iulia a wider appeal that extended even to other marginalised groups in 'Greater Romania'.

Moreover, this phenomenon of 'co-regionalism'—as an expression of solidarity, which subsequently led even to the formation of coalitions between opinion leaders from different regions in Romania—can be observed in the evolution of the Transylvanian opposition from the 1920s onwards. In the years following the First World War, a two-camp system developed. On one side, there was the National Party and the Peasants' Party as representatives of the new provinces and the rural population in general; on the other, there was the 'Bucharest establishment', the (only nominally) Liberal Party and the People's Party (*Partidul Popular*). For the National Party this division meant that the Romanians of Transylvania now had an alternative model to traditional ethno-regionally oriented political representation. The Peasants' Party offered a 'left-wing' alternative marked with social revolutionary tendencies, so voters did not have to resort to electing Socialist or Social Democratic parties. The Liberal Party, on the other hand, despite its (contrary to its name) conservative programme and authoritarian leanings, was able to win over sections of the elites from the Transylvanian Orthodox Church who felt threatened by the politicians of the National Party belonging to the (Catholic) United Church. Furthermore, the People's Party had been the refuge of disaffected National Party politicians since 1920.[11] To counter the loss of importance that went hand in hand with such defections, the regionalist actors strove to expand the counter-community to include people in all the newly annexed territories of 'Greater Romania' and certain target groups in the Regat with the help of the unifying democratic and 'occidental' ideals of 1 December 1918. The expanding opposition movement thus spread beyond its regional boundaries and became a transregional 'community of Alba Iulia'.

Transylvania and the Transylvanian Romanians

As the term *ethno-regionalism* suggests, the political movement that forms the focus of this study is based on the creation of a connection between a group of people and a territory: we are concerned with people considered to belong to the ethnic group of Romanians from the region known as Transylvania. It is relatively simple to designate someone as belonging to such a group (precisely because it is an imaginary process); an act of 'declaration' suffices (for example in a census, a document or, conclusively, by way of personal testimonial). More ambiguous, however, is the spatial demarcation of a regional concept like 'Transylvania', whose existence, while not contested, is not acknowledged by definitive borders drawn on a map; the *Ausgleich* of 1867 between Vienna and Budapest saw what had hitherto been the Grand Duchy of Transylvania (*Großfürstentum*) pass into Hungary's centralist system of counties, whereupon it lost its independence as a political entity. The unitary Hungarian state put increasing pressure on its non-Hungarian subjects—in Transylvania primarily Romanians, Germans and Jews—to assimilate, which led to growing alienation between these 'nationalities' and the Hungarian state.[12] From this point on, 'Transylvania' existed only as a concept of discourse; it was no longer an administrative entity.[13]

Figure 5.1 Map showing the borders of the Kingdom of Romania in 1920, the Romanian border of 1914 and the borders of various historical regions.

Source: Institut für deutsche Kultur und Geschichte Südosteuropas an der Ludwig-Maximilians-Universität München.

As outlined above, on 1 December 1918 a Romanian national assembly in Alba Iulia declared, it is claimed before one hundred thousand people, 'the union of these Romanians, and all the territories inhabited by them, with Romania', in a measure passed by 1,228 deputies.[14] This included the 'historical' Transylvania (*Ardeal* in Romanian), the Banat to its south and Partium, a strip to the west and north of the historical Transylvania. Ardeal, the Banat and Partium were more or less subsumed under the concept of Transylvania in Romanian discourse after 1918; politicians were concerned less with a precise territorial demarcation than with a distinction between 'this side of' and 'beyond' the Carpathians.[15]

The historical 'core' of Transylvania—the plateau in the Carpathian arc—nevertheless remained at the heart of Transylvanian regionalism. It was here that Romanian historians located the ancient 'birthplace' of the Romanian nation; without Transylvania, a Romanian state striving for completeness did not make sense. It was here that the Dacian people built their capital and the Romans established a province. The national master-narrative traces the ethno-genesis of the Romanians back to the 'mixing' of both 'peoples'—from this perspective the Romanians are the product of a two-thousand-year 'Daco-Romanian continuity' in this area.[16]

Among the pre-war political leadership of the Romanians in Hungary—that is, those from the extended region of Transylvania (Ardeal, the Banat and Partium)—there were very different ideas on how to deal with 'foreign rule'; these leaders showed relatively little solidarity with one another and in terms of religion were divided among Orthodox and (United) Catholic adherents. Despite these unfavourable circumstances, the National Party, even forbidden at times, acted as the representative of all Romanians in Hungary or even the entire Habsburg Empire.[17] The divisions within the party, which was ultimately more of an ethnic collective movement without a clearly defined ideological profile, were alleviated, if not entirely overcome, by a new generation of politicians, foremost among them Iuliu Maniu and Alexandru Vaida-Voievod, two members of the United Church who led the party at the turn of the century.[18] With the exception of a few members who distanced themselves from the party after 1918, Transylvanian Romanian politicians before and after the First World War were the advocates, supporters and ultimately the beneficiaries of Romanian solidarity within the Habsburg monarchy. The outstanding representative of the significantly smaller group of 'centralists' among the Transylvanian Romanians was Octavian Goga, who before 1918 had aggressively advocated the unification of Hungarian territories inhabited by Romanians into a common Romanian nation-state.[19]

The Nascence of 'Greater Romania'

The collapse of the Ottoman and Habsburg empires and the change of political systems in Germany and Russia during and after the First World War made possible the foundation of several states in East-Central and Southeastern Europe which, despite having many citizens who did not belong to the 'state-bearing' nation, considered themselves 'nation-states'. Particular beneficiaries were Czechoslovakia, the State of Slovenes, Croats and Serbs (later Yugoslavia) and the Kingdom of Romania. After the declaration of the 'Union' in Alba Iulia—which was also declared in Bukovina (separated from the 'Austrian' part of the Habsburg Empire)[20] and Bessarabia (separated from Russia),[21] but without the confident proclamation and mass assembly—the country doubled in size and now called itself, half officially, 'Greater Romania'. The territory grew from 138,000 to 295,049 square kilometres, the population from 7.9 million (in 1915) to 14.7 million (in 1919).[22] By 1930 it had reached 18 million.[23] The areas separated from Hungary constituted, then, around a third of the state's territory and population. Even if the union of these areas with 'Greater Romania' was nominally complete, the process of institutional and psychological unification was only beginning. On the *countrywide* level, the government in Bucharest launched an all-embracing process of institutional unification and centralisation: government administration, schooling, the legal system were to be united and—in the eyes of the dominant Liberal Party—unified. The big question now became: which region and culture would have the greatest influence on the new society that was to be formed? Fights broke out over positions of political influence, key posts in state and society and the cultural orientation of, among other institutions, government administration, schooling, theatres and churches, and of remembrance politics in general.

At the same time, a comprehensive 'Romanisation'[24] began in all the newly annexed territories: government administration and educational and cultural institutions were to be prised out of the hands of the ethnicities that had ruled previously—in Transylvania mainly the Hungarians—and taken over by Romanians. Behind this transformation on the basis of national arguments stood the hope for social advancement; the Romanian 'class' was inclined to 'conquer' all the areas where they had previously been excluded.[25]

After its reorganisation, the regional administration of Transylvania was occupied almost exclusively by members of the National Party.[26] The administrative centre was based in Sibiu (ultimately Alba Iulia was deemed to be too far from the core of regional power structures); what was initially a provisional 'governing council' headed by Iuliu Maniu ultimately amounted to a fully functioning administrative entity.[27] According to the idea of decentralism as formulated in Alba Iulia, the administrative integration into 'Greater Romania' was not to be carried out without respect for the established structures and needs in their region. In other words, 'Romanisation' was acceptable as long as only the *Transylvanian* Romanians could benefit from it.

Since Alexandru Vaida-Voievod's appointment as prime minister in Bucharest in 1919, the National Party had been the leading party not only in the region, but also nationwide. It had won the new state's first elections in

November 1919 even though it had stood only in formerly Hungarian areas. A coalition of various regional parties and other smaller opposition groups from 'Old Romania' appeared to offer the greatest hope for a population completely shaken by the war.[28] At this point, everything seemed to point to a 'takeover' of Romanian politics by the Transylvanian Romanian elites.

However, contrary to their assumption that Transylvanian dominance on the regional and national levels would endure, this government made up of prevalently regional parties collapsed quite soon, in March 1920.[29] The new prime minister, Alexandru Averescu, the leader of the People's Party, dissolved the regional governmental structures with the help of a royal decree.[30] From this point on, the administration experienced uninterrupted centralisation, which entailed integration into the Old Kingdom's system in line with the conception laid out in the 1866 constitution.[31]

A Counter-Community between Regionalism and Nationalism

The National Party's efforts to expand its political home base did not end with the dissolution of the regional government, although this act attempted to radically disempower Transylvanian politicians. In fact, such actions provided the basis for a new kind of regionalism—expressed in an oppositional discourse that stressed the feeling of regional togetherness, centred on the notion of a community of Transylvanians. Iuliu Maniu, the uncontested leader of the National Party, explained which role he envisaged for his party at the first party congress after its double loss of power: 'This National Party is itself a synthesis of the Romanian people beyond the Carpathians'.[32] As becomes clear in Maniu's speech, his National Party, forced to bend to the new circumstances, was in a phase of transition, but it was to continue to serve as a melting pot for all Transylvanian Romanians. The government's centralism, which increasingly made the 'new Romanians' feel 'colonised', offered a welcome opportunity for it to do so.

The driving force behind the administrative centralisation was the National Liberal Party (*Partidul Național Liberal*), headed by Ion I.C. Brătianu, which dominated the political scene for most of the interwar period.[33] Ruling uninterruptedly from 1922 to 1926 with an absolute majority, it could put the most important reforms into practice. The main measures it implemented were the introduction of the new constitution in 1923, followed by reform of the administration (1925) and reorganisation of the electoral law (1926).[34]

The dominant topos in the regionalist discourse of the Transylvanian Romanians was the call for a *decentralisation* of the state's administrative structure. The pressure of centralisation applied by Bucharest went hand in hand with the arrival in Transylvania of an increasing number of administration officials, teachers and even politicians from the Regat. The intra-state, intra-national but also trans-regional feeling of *Überfremdung* (foreign infiltration) was first expressed by the pugnacious and eloquent Vaida-Voievod when he introduced the slogan 'Transylvania to the Transylvanians' or 'Transylvania for the Transylvanians' into the political discourse.[35]

A decentralised state—the term 'federal' was not used, since it induced too much 'fear of collapse'[36]—seemed to offer the perfect protection from direct political seizure by the 'centre'; national 'mental' unity, strived for by all political camps, along with administrative unification, did not demand 'administrative uniformity',[37] the representatives of the National Party argued. A 'province' possessed special historical rights[38] and should have the opportunity to develop freely in a regional context according its own desires and needs.[39] It should not be forgotten, the *Gazeta Transilvaniei* wrote in 1922, that Transylvanians were an 'entire people' with a certain level of civilisation and special cultural and administrative traditions. *Chemarea Tinerimei Române*, the newspaper of the party's youth, went a little further in its definition and described the region as a living organism, likening it to a cell consisting of an 'ensemble of convictions, customs, collective wishes, prevailing needs and shared interests', which should also be reflected in a country's administration.[40]

But who were these 'Transylvanians' whose community was invoked in the political speeches and polemical writings of the regionalist actors? Since the National Party pursued a clear goal of creating a counter-community as a means of distancing itself from those in power in Bucharest, one could not be said to 'belong' to the community solely on the basis of Transylvanian 'provenance'. The demarcation as Transylvanian, particularly when aimed at collective self-assurance, had to take place in manifold ways. I will explore this complex discourse on the question of common ground and differences between the Romanians 'this side of' the Carpathians and those 'beyond' the mountains in the newspapers and magazines of the 1920s and 1930s in order to trace this process of ethno-regional self-attribution, trans-ethnic depictions of 'the other' and the ambitions of demarcation they served.

The National Party's proponents produced *historical arguments* which referred to special characteristics of the region and hence the Romanians who lived there. In seeking out comparisons marked by an East-West dichotomy, the National Party and its supporters in newspapers and magazines would raid—quite selectively—virtually any historical epoch: the Transylvanians' geographical location in the Carpathians allowed them to attribute a well-developed and 'pure' Daco-Roman heritage to the group.[41] Moreover, the regionalist discourse often recalled historical periods in which it was universally assumed that the Transylvanians had existed as a (relatively) independent political entity, particularly in the phase before the region's integration into the Habsburg Empire in the late eighteenth century. Referring to this heritage, Vaida-Voievod criticised the poor treatment of the 'new provinces' by the Bucharest government, which he claimed was preventing the regional administration of Transylvania, and pointed to the 'independence' of Transylvania in previous centuries: anyone who had read a history book knew that God had created the Transylvanian territory as a 'single geographical entity', as it had been 'under the Dacians and always' had been.[42]

The treatment of the Habsburg heritage, on the other hand, was very ambivalent. On the one hand, there had been few positive references since 1918 in public discourse regarding the period of Habsburg rule. In particular, the time after the *Ausgleich* of 1867 was depicted as a period of national oppression and increasing pressure to assimilate. Nevertheless, the collective memory of Hungarian oppression and the political fight for national emancipation in the context of the monarchy served as a strong—negative—identification model for the National Party's clientele; the political leaders saw the group they represented as being former victims of an outdated system who had been under the yoke of Habsburg-Hungary, in the 'claws of the Habsburg eagle'.[43]

At the same time, however, it was precisely the impact of Habsburg rule on the region and its inhabitants that provided National Party politicians with arguments that emphasised the superiority of the Transylvanians over the 'Regatists' (*regățeni*[44]); it was the increased cultural contact through the connection to Vienna in the seventeenth and eighteenth centuries that had allowed the Romanians of Transylvania to develop a culture of scholarship. Participation in the Habsburg system had also enabled Transylvanians to place themselves in a tradition of modernisation and democracy unknown to the feudal principalities of Moldavia and Walachia that were united to form the Regat in 1859: 'They are poorer and less modern'.[45] The claim of being able to draw on a well-developed democratic tradition was an argument put forward in the service of both the National Party's fight for the democratisation of Austria-Hungary and the relatively participatory ordinances of the two 'Romanian' churches under Habsburg rule, the Orthodox and the United.[46]

The historical perspective is closely connected to the argumentation on questions concerning *mentality* and its regional differences. In their attempts to describe the special nature of the region, both the self-portraits and foreign depictions of the Transylvanian Romanians' 'specific character' tend to reduce the Transylvanians to a set of characteristics that were seen as clichés of 'Western' or even 'German' culture.[47] George Șerban, for example, writing for *Societatea de Mâine*, a magazine close to the National Party, sought to express the specific mentality of his region with the idea of the 'Transylvanian Romanian soul', which was characterised by an 'organised spirit', a supra-confessional 'religious spirit' and a high degree of national self-awareness.[48] Even a leading intellectual like the philologist and sometime rector of Cluj University, Sextil Pușcariu, was not averse to ascribing to the Transylvanian Romanians a more hard-working nature and greater organisational ability[49] than their 'brothers'[50] in the Regat. Even before the war, when Transylvanian Romanians were working already 'beyond the Carpathians' in Bucharest, they showed a special seriousness, perceptiveness and honesty.[51] The Brașov publicist Ioan Bran-Lemeny was one such

Transylvanian who had settled in the Regat at the beginning of the First World War and had volunteered there for the Romanian army. Correspondingly committed to striking a balance between the 'Old Romania' and the 'New Romania', he attempted to characterise the Romanians on the different sides of the Carpathians using 'humoralism' (!). He, too, recognised barely two years after the formation of the new state that the toughest internal front was the 'cultural, moral and social' differences between the Regat and Transylvania. For Bran-Lemeny the difference was mainly a question of the 'methods, tactics and temperament' of the opposing factions; the Transylvanians were less clever, more ponderous and often grumpier than people from the Regat. This was due to the 'yoke' endured by the Transylvanian Romanians. At the same time, however, he considered them to be more advanced as a civilisation and living in a 'more solid' environment, which had made them taciturn, deliberate, more profound, more prudent, more tenacious and more consistent people. These characteristics pointed to a 'bilious', *melancholy* temperament—presumably because the Transylvanians had more Dacian blood in them. The joviality and frivolity of the people from the Regat showed that they were more 'sanguine'.[52]

Identification models for the Transylvanian Romanians, with their emphasis on their 'Westernness' and their belonging to modern civilisation, were particularly effective when they openly exercised *discrimination* against people from the Regat. A high degree of alterity was intended to improve the National Party's political and identity models for its clientele. At times very effective, denigrating the Regat was thus an integral strategy of regionalist Transylvanian discourse; the culture beyond the Carpathians was described as outdated, undemocratic and degenerate[53] in order to further the idea of an East-West cultural divide, to the point of 'intellectual antagonism between Regatians and Transylvanians'.[54]

The spectrum of demarcation through discourse combined a polemic against the actions and attitudes of Bucharest politicians in relation to specific events with a fundamental criticism of the prevailing 'morals' of the Regat. For instance, the *Gazeta Transilvaniei* wrote that the 'politicos' and their 'pseudo-culture' was 'without morals'.[55] This criticism of the political culture was generally combined with a mode of orientalism, the areas beyond the Carpathians being depicted as belonging to an outdated, authoritarian, 'Eastern' culture. The regionalists saw the Liberals as fighting with 'fire and the sword' for a coerced unification of the country, which they wished to rule like a Turkish province.[56] 'Byzantinism' became, as in other European discourses, a synonym for clientelism or nepotism, political shiftiness, subservience and manipulation.[57] Concerns about potential regional orientalism were largely expressed through talk of an impending 'Balkanisation' of Transylvania: unification had been achieved by 'Balkan means', complained the *Gazeta Transilvaniei* in May 1920;[58] two years later it considered the 'Balkanisation of Transylvania' to be well under way and excused its own regionalism as a means to an end in the face of this process of acculturation.[59]

In this nightmarish vision painted by the regionalist politicians and their supporters in the press, this *Überfremdung* was the cause of the increasing subjugation of the entire region by the 'centre'. Speaking at a party congress in 1931, Vaida-Voievod noted that the Transylvanian Romanians were no longer the 'slaves of master Tizsa' (the former Hungarian prime minister) but regretted that they were now 'slaves of master Brătianu', something they had not realised in 1918.[60] The media close to the party were not averse to comparing their fate with that of 'African colonies'[61]—the Transylvanians had to be liberated.

The aim of constructing a counter-community in opposition to the ruling political establishment meant that the region's generally very clear *ethnic* borders became more permeable in the discourse; the formerly oppressed Transylvanian Romanians were not to become oppressors of the non-Romanian ethnic groups, as Vaida-Voievod stressed in 1921 to the displeasure of the region's radical nationalists.[62]

The 'renegade' Transylvanian Octavian Goga, who along with the People's Party he supported was one of the main opponents of the National Party, saw regionalist ambitions as posing a threat to national and state cohesion, which was already shaky; the 'spirit of demarcation', which amounted to the frenetic defence of local values, could be found everywhere, in 'Cluj, in Bucharest, in the parliament, in the buffet car [sic!] etc.'. He simply could not understand why the Transylvanian Romanians insisted on clinging to 'yesterday's geography'.[63]

The accusations levelled at the National Party by the Liberals, Goga and the group of other 'renegade Transylvanians' around him all centred on a 'dynastic attitude', either latent or explicit. For these renegades, politicians like Maniu and Vaida-Voievod were ghosts of the past, 'revenants of loyalty to the Habsburgs'.[64]

In contrast to the 'subjugation' of the Hungarian Romanians, the centralist discourse of the Regat stressed the longer tradition of political and national freedom in the Kingdom of Romania and the related opportunities for cultural development. Because of Hungarian dominance, the Transylvanian Romanians lacked tradition, which explained the region's poor contribution to 'Greater Romania'.[65] As a response to the accusation of feudalist attitudes in the Regat, they saw in Transylvanian subordination a high degree of backwardness; the Transylvanians were still suffering from 'tribal organisation', a political primitivism that explained why the 'new Romanians' were so hostile, wrote Radu Dragnea in Goga's militant paper *Țara Noastră*. He argued that Maniu was acting like an Oriental potentate who felt regional solidarity was under threat.[66]

A further paradigmatic aspect of the 'centralist' counter-discourse is the recognition that the region's multicultural character, the 'hybrid mixed culture' that had served as 'intellectual fodder' for the Transylvanian Romanian elite before 1918, was finally coming to an end.[67] Regionalism was born of this 'atmosphere of [national] foreignness', with the effect that there was ultimately greater 'spiritual kinship' among representatives of the various political movements *in* the Regat than *between* a 'regional leader from Transylvania' and any politician from the Old Kingdom.[68]

Localising the Community: 'Alba Iulia'

Alba Iulia was not only the perfect and ultimately the uniquely appropriate place to hold the national assembly on 1 December 1918 but also the suitable *lieu* to discursively and performatively concentrate all the hopes for change and social advancement harboured by the Transylvanian Romanians. All the other larger centres in Transylvania were associated with 'other ethnicities' (particularly the region's big city, Cluj, which was dominated by Hungarians) and/or controlled by one of the two 'Romanian' confessions. (The 'German' Sibiu was also the seat of the Orthodox metropolitan, and Blaj, while associated with the Revolution of 1848–49, was the centre of the United Church.[69]) That left Alba Iulia, which with its historical and Habsburg connections could symbolise both tradition and renewal: the *historic ensemble* of Alba Iulia's stronghold symbolised the regime that the Romanians had deposed, but also referred to the positive Central European cultural legacy of Transylvania and its population. The Baroque-style ensemble, built in the eighteenth century under Emperor Karl VI, was chosen in order to base the new Romanian society on this Occidental relief: Alba Iulia embodied and 'localised' what the Transylvanian Romanian elite believed Romanian society needed to become—a society that was tolerant of minorities but oriented towards Central Europe and led by the Transylvanian Romanians.

'Alba Iulia' became a conceptual reference point in the dichotomous transformation discourse between the 'old' and 'new' Romania; for instance, the debate about the Romanian constitution was initiated by the intention to merely revise the 1866 constitution in order to adapt it to the 'new events'[70] that Alba Iulia represented. For the politicians of the National Party, 'Alba Iulia' represented not just a 'suggestion' but rather a fundamental programme that had to be realised in the 'Greater Romanian' context. Ultimately, however, the mid-nineteenth-century constitution of the Kingdom of Romania was merely updated—this was the greatest defeat of the 'community of Alba Iulia'. The Transylvanian German *Kronstädter Zeitung* summarised the main criticisms shortly before the final decision in 1923:[71] the constitution did not do as much for workers' rights, national minorities, women, the religion sects and the freedom of education as had been intended by the 'final and just treaty' of Alba Iulia.[72]

'Alba Iulia' also stood for solidarity beyond ideological, ethnic and confessional boundaries (depending on which arguments were required); when the Peasants' Party was amalgamated with the National Party in 1926, 'Alba Iulia' was the lowest common denominator uniting what were at times very different ideological approaches adopted by the two parties. Moreover, 'Alba Iulia' was something on which Romanian Transylvanians and non-Romanian minorities (in the ethnic sense) could agree; the Germans and the Hungarians, too, demanded the realisation of the 'declaration' of 1 December 1918. For those who opposed the nascent confessionalism of the two 'Romanian' churches, the events of Alba Iulia were the zenith of trans-confessional, national unity: the United Church had recognised the national council formed in Alba Iulia 'hand in hand with their Orthodox brothers', wrote a contemporary author on the relationship between the two confessions immediately after 1918.[73]

But 'Alba Iulia' was not only a textual and contextual reference point, a discursive place of political 'pilgrimage'. It also regularly served as a site of assembly and mobilisation for the National Party; it was here that in probably the worst hour of its history, in May 1920, shortly after its fall from regional and national power, its members met to revise the party programme. Exactly eight years later, a mass rally in Alba Iulia heralded its entry into government, culminating in Maniu's minister-presidency. Before an alleged crowd of one hundred thousand supporters (a figure that should probably be understood as symbolic; one hundred thousand Romanians were also said to have assembled there in 1918), it was demanded that the exiled Karl von Hohenzollern-Sigmaringen, who had been forced to abdicate in 1926, be brought back and proclaimed king. An emotional oath united the masses in the aim not to rest until the government had resigned. The rally—something of a reenactment of the events ten years earlier—became an evocative turning point for the National Peasants' Party.[74]

At the same time, the 'centralists' considered the increasing discursive-symbolic and physical dominance of Alba Iulia to be dangerous, as it continued to develop into a counter-centre to Bucharest. The influential politician and historian Nicolae Iorga was forced to respond to the assembly in the spring of 1928 by saying it would be a 'big mistake' if the regionalists tried to shift the centre of 'Greater Romania's' political interests to a provincial town. Any action had to be oriented towards the capital Bucharest, since this was a principle of national unity.[75] Averescu thus wished in 1930 that the events of 1918 could be put to bed; the Transylvanian leaders should finally understand that Alba Iulia had decided only the *annexation* of Transylvania, not the *union* of the Romanian people in one state.[76]

Alba Iulia was, however, too valuable an instrument to be left entirely to the Transylvanians. Hence the 'centralists' regularly attempted to hijack the site and the positive emotions associated with it. A striking example of such appropriation was the celebrations marking the coronation of the royal couple Ferdinand and Maria in the autumn of 1922, which took place not only in Bucharest but in Alba Iulia, too. Since King Ferdinand supported the government against the wishes of the opposition, leading opposition politicians refused to take part in the celebrations staged by the Liberals and in so doing put to the test the reciprocal loyalty between the dynasty and Transylvanians.[77]

As outlined above, the National Party felt compelled by the consolidation of the Romanian state and the subsequent transformation of the political

A Counter-Community between Regionalism and Nationalism 101

situation to expand its activities from its historical 'core electorate territory' to 'Greater Romania' as a whole. The foundation for this expansion was the solidarity that had existed between the various 'new Romanian' areas since the founding of 'Greater Romania', in particular between the inhabitants of those areas who considered themselves to be of Romanian ethnicity; having welcomed national unity in principle, they all felt duped and exploited by the 'centre'. The political activists of the annexed territories thus shared the values postulated in Alba Iulia, even if—or indeed because—circumstances had meant that their own regional declarations of annexation had been less programmatic and less confident. The *Gazeta Ardealului* reported in 1921 that following the Transylvanian model of 'Transylvania to the Transylvanians', similar slogans were becoming widespread in the Banat, Bukovina and Bessarabia—the Banat to the Banatians, Bukovina to the Bukovinians, Bessarabia to the Bessarabians.[78]

In 1922 the National Party moved its seat to Bucharest in order to shake off its reputation as a regional party for Transylvania.[79] Following several amalgamations with smaller parties it landed its great coup in 1926: a merger with its closest ally among the opposition parties, the Peasants' Party. The newly formed party, the National Peasants' Party, dominated by Transylvanians, proclaimed a 'new regionalism' and promised its programme would do away with Romania's decayed political morality—'injustices, irregularities and dishonesty'—which they considered a consequence of the war. Even the leader of the former Peasants' Party, now the deputy leader of the National Peasants' Party, Ion Mihalache, born and raised in Walachia, made it clear that the battle cry 'Regatism' was only directed at people of ill will. He distinguished—paradigmatically for the new orientation of the regionalists—not between the regions but on the basis of moral criteria: 'Regatians, Transylvanians and the others should join one another, but Regatism should disappear'.[80]

The metaphors of demarcation began to penetrate, then, the East-West dichotomy, especially when the emphasis was to be placed on the differences between the 'good' local, autochthonous peasants and the mercantile, 'slave-owning' urbanites. The comparison with mobile mercantile groups transported the fear of *Überfremdung*: urban culture, particularly that of Bucharest, was being ruined by non-Romanians—Jews, Greeks, Armenians, Levantines, Venetians and 'Greco-Bulgarians'. The decadent 'salon culture' of the capital was turning its inhabitants into effeminate and godless people.[81]

Thus the rhetoric of trans-regional solidarity reached new heights, since the National Peasants' Party was active and agitating throughout Romania. At party assemblies in all the important cities of 'Greater Romania' its representatives announced a new kind of politics that would finally take into consideration the provinces' regional needs: Transylvanians, Bessarabians and Bukovinians had been deemed a 'destructive element', but soon only the human qualities of the individual would count, wrote *Românul* in 1927.[82]

The Transylvanian Romanian politicians considered themselves, as usual, to be playing a pioneering role.

Thus a community created by a discourse of *ethno-regional* demarcation criteria became a *trans-regional* counter-community. Its common point of reference was 'Alba Iulia'. The main aim of the trans-regionalist actors was to rule in Bucharest. If an end was put to the 'centralizing oligarchy' and the collaboration between the 'bankers from the Regat' and the 'crooks' from the annexed provinces, and the provinces' true representatives ruled, then there would no longer be any reason to be a regionalist, wrote *Chemarea* in the spring of 1928.[83]

Conclusion

In late 1928 the National Peasants' Party did indeed come to power after the resignation of the Liberal government. It formed the cabinet until 1933, with a hiatus in 1931–32. Despite its success, political regionalism in the government remained an ephemeral phenomenon. The National Peasants' Party fell from power after only a few years when the effects of the Great Depression increasingly turned violent in the streets—as in Germany and many other European countries, hopes for modernisation and democratic ideals did not necessarily go hand in hand. Thus the political project of turning the whole of Romania into a 'community of Alba Iulia' came to nothing. The phase 'of extraordinary cohesion', the moment 'of intensely felt collective solidarity',[84] as Brubaker terms such periods of intensified feelings of togetherness, swiftly came to an end when actions were to follow words.

In 1933 the Liberal Party returned to power, while large sections of the population increasingly turned to authoritarian ideologies. Regionalisms did not disappear from political discourse completely, but they were without meaning in the subsequent years of practised centralism and increased nationalism—which would again play an important role, including in Communist Romania from the 1960s onwards. 'Alba Iulia' was shorn of its modernising and democratic connotations and transformed into a purely national symbol standing for the unity of Romania. December 1 has been Romania's official national holiday since 1991.

This study has interpreted regionalism as a political phenomenon that, combining regional and ethno-national tendencies, stood in opposition to a hostile state that was supposed to be its 'own'. The discursive creation of what was initially an ethno-regional and then a trans-regional counter-community in opposition to the centralist political establishment ruling this state thus also served as a means of dealing with contingency, as an outlet for the expression of disappointment with the sluggish integration process and the (overly optimistic) expectations that went with it. The conscious evocation of 'Alba Iulia', which stood for unity beyond political, confessional or indeed ethnic boundaries, was intended to promote cohesion in order to substantially shape the development of a 'Greater Romanian' society.

A Counter-Community between Regionalism and Nationalism 103

If we compare the Transylvanian and the 'centralist' discourses, it is striking that the arguments and the concrete accusations are extremely similar. Both are ultimately concerned with the question of who has 'purer' blood, who can look back on a longer tradition of freedom and who represents the model of a modern society. In this case, the feeling of *Überfremdung* was not caused by ethnic or linguistic differences, but was based on social and economic criteria in an *intra*-ethnic context. In contrast to Jeremy de Waal's findings on 'local communities' in the Federal Republic of Germany, which emphasise the long-term efficacy of local identification models, in the case of Romania the model of strong regional identification was without significance. This is clearly due to the different degrees of success of the measures taken by the two states in their respective post-war years; while West Germany created an 'economic miracle' that was partly sustained by local self-images, in the case of Romania, just as democracy and modernisation on the basis of federal principles were on the upswing, the country fell, together with large parts of the rest of the world, into the Great Depression.

To this day, regionalist sentiments are present in the political discourse of the Transylvanian Romanians. At times this is latent, at other times quite obvious. The orientalisation of the 'other' beyond the Carpathians, the depravity of urban society as represented by Bucharest, but also, more pragmatically, the siphoning off of taxpayers' money that will never 'flow back' are constant themes, even if all this has yet to be exploited in a party-political context. The roots of these political argumentation strategies, as well as the cultural and historical awareness created by them, can be traced back, as this chapter has demonstrated, to the first decade of the interwar years.

Notes

1. Turda, "Transilvania post-comunistă," 35–42.
2. Brubaker, "Ethnicity," 171.
3. Ibid., 164.
4. See Haslinger, "Selbstbild," 28; Ther, "Zwischenräume," xvi; Ploch, "Handlungslandschaft," 122–57.
5. Brubaker, "Ethnicity," 166–68.
6. Applegate, "Europe of Regions," 1180.
7. Brubaker, "Ethnicity," 167.
8. Hitchins, *Rumania*, 204–5.
9. Before 1918 it limited itself to representing people of Romanian nationality within the Habsburg Empire—making monopolistic claims to their various political and ideological views, however. The Transylvanian Social-Democratic Party remained a marginal phenomenon both before and after the First World War.
10. Brubaker, "Ethnicity," 168.
11. Kührer-Wielach, *Siebenbürgen ohne Siebenbürger*, 166–70.
12. Gogolák, *Nationalitätengesetze*, 1223.
13. Kührer-Wielach, "Siebenbürgen," passim.

14. Constantinescu, *Unification*, 262–63.
15. To this day, the respective terms for the three most widely spoken languages in the Carpathian arc, Romanian, Hungarian and German (*Ardeal, Erdély* and *Siebenbürgen*), refer as a rule to the historical Transylvania, an area defined in the Middle Ages by estate borders between the Carpathian arc and the Apuseni Mountains.
16. Boia, *Mythos*, 108–16.
17. Volkmer, *Siebenbürgische Frage*, 49–54.
18. Hitchins, *Nation*, 163.
19. Boia, *Germanophile*, 70.
20. Hausleitner, *Rumänisierung*, 100–1.
21. Lasch, "Großrumänien," 288.
22. *Istoria Romanilor*, vol. 8, 32.
23. Manuilă, *Recensământul*, xlvi.
24. Livezeanu, *Regionalism*; Suveica, *Basarabia*; Hausleitner, *Rumänisierung*; Kührer-Wielach, *Siebenbürgen ohne Siebenbürger*.
25. Kührer-Wielach, *Siebenbürgen ohne Siebenbürger*, 83–84.
26. Scurtu, *Din viața politică,* passim.
27. Galea, *Formarea*, 40.
28. *Istoria Românilor*, vol. 8, 247–48.
29. Brown, "Movement," 468.
30. *Istoria Românilor*, vol. 8, 250.
31. Boila, "Verfassung," 327.
32. "Un nou interview cu d-l I. Maniu," *Gazeta Transilvaniei*, 3 April 1920.
33. *Istoria Românilor*, vol. 8, 221–23.
34. Ibid., 253–55.
35. E.g. "Problema ardelenească," *Gazeta Ardealului*, 20 November 1921.
36. Goga, "Schwarzenberg," 98.
37. "Problema regiunii în noua reforma administrative," *Chemarea Tinerimei Române*, 21 April 1929.
38. Ghiulea, "Regionalismul," 48.
39. "Suntem regionaliști?," *Chemarea Tinerimei Române*, 12 February 1928.
40. "Reformă administrativă și regionalism," *Chemarea Tinerimei Române*, 14 April 1929.
41. "Două concepții," *Gazeta Transilvaniei*, 24 March 1920.
42. "Congresul provincial al partidului național-țărănesc din Ardeal și Banat," *Chemarea Tinerimei Române*, 30 March 1932.
43. "Cei din urmă legionary," *Românul*, 17 December 1919.
44. "Între regățeni și ardeleni," *Chemarea Tinerimei Române*, 23 June 1929.
45. "Să cedăm reciproc," *Clujul Românesc*, 4 February 1924.
46. Dan, "Ardealul," 201; "Separatism și regionalism," *Gazeta Transilvaniei*, 30 April 1920.
47. "Separatism și regionalism," *Gazeta Transilvaniei*, 30 April 1920.
48. Șerban, "Sufletul," 798.
49. Pușcariu, "Regionalism," 85.
50. "Lupta între frați," *Gazeta Transilvaniei*, 27 April 1920.
51. Ghiulea, "Regionalismul," 49.
52. "Mijloace, tactică, temperament," *Gazeta Transilvaniei*, 29 June 1920.
53. "Un nou regionalism," *Românul*, 5 June 1927; "Partidul național față de proiectul Constituției liberale," *Gazeta Transilvaniei*, 28 February 1923; "La M.S. Regele e nădejdea noastră . . .," *Gazeta Transilvaniei*, 9 May 1920.
54. "Între regățeni și ardeleni," *Chemarea Tinerimei Române*, 23 June 1929.
55. "Două concepții," *Gazeta Transilvaniei*, 24 March 1920.

56. "La M. S. Regele e nădejdea noastră . . .," *Gazeta Transilvaniei*, 9 May 1920; Averescu, "Pete urâte," 271; "Centralismul administrativ," *Gazeta Transilvaniei*, 19 July 1925.
57. "Die Verwaltungsreform," *Kronstädter Zeitung*, 28 December 1920; "Cameleonul dela Ciucea," *Chemarea Tinerimei Române*, 21 May 1926; "Die Zeit wird kommen . . .," *Kronstädter Zeitung*, 26 October 1930; "Să desbrăcam haina bizantinismului," *Gazeta Transilvaniei*, 22 March 1931.
58. "La M. S. Regele e nădejdea noastră . . .," *Gazeta Transilvaniei*, 9 May 1920.
59. "S'a balcanizat și Ardealul," *Gazeta Transilvaniei*, 14 February 1922.
60. "Grandioasa manifestație populară din Alba-Iulia," *Gazeta Transilvaniei*, 4 November 1931.
61. Averescu, "Pete urâte," 271.
62. "Un nou access regionalst al d-lui Al. Vaida," *Gazeta Ardealului*, 20 November 1921; Goga, "Ardealul," 35.
63. Goga, "Regionalismul," 41.
64. Anon, "Un document . . .," 386.
65. Dan, "Ardealul," 201.
66. Dragnea, "Formarea," 45–6.
67. Moldovan, "Ardelenii," 144.
68. Goga, "Regionalismul," 43.
69. Kührer-Wielach, "Alba Iulia," passim.
70. "Lămuriri pentru ardeleni: o nouă constituție," *Gazeta Ardealului*, 4 September 1921.
71. "Die neue Verfassung Rumäniens," *Kronstädter Zeitung*, 21 March 1923.
72. "Die Nationalpartei und der Verfassungsentwurf," *Kronstädter Zeitung*, 28 February 1923.
73. "Problema religioasă," *Gazeta Transilvaniei*, 5 September 1926.
74. "Proclamarea adunării naționale," *Românul*, 13 May 1928; Beer, *Entwicklung*, vol. 1, 223.
75. "D. N. Iorga și adunarea dela Alba-Iulia," *Clujul Românesc*, 1 April 1928.
76. Ibid., 273.
77. *Istoria Românilor*, vol. 8, 253.
78. "Formule nefericite," *Gazeta Ardealului*, 15 September 1921.
79. Scurtu, *Viața*, 22–23.
80. "Un nou regionalism," *Românul*, 5 June 1927.
81. "La M. S. Regele e nădejdea noastră . . .," *Gazeta Transilvaniei*, 9 May 1920.
82. "Un nou regionalism," *Românul*, 5 June 1927.
83. "Suntem regionaliști?," *Chemarea Tinerimei Române*, 1 April 1928.
84. Brubaker, "Ethnicity," 168.

Bibliography

Anon. "Un document . . ." *Țara Noastră* 4, no. 12 (1923): 385–86.

Applegate, Celia. "A Europe of Regions: Reflections on the Historiography of Sub-National Places in Modern Times." *The American Historical Review* 104 (1999): 1157–82.

Averescu, Alexandru. "Pete urâte, pe o pagină frumoasă." *Țara Noastră* 10, no. 7 (1930): 265–73.

Beer, Klaus P. *Zur Entwicklung des Parteien- und Parlamentssystems in Rumänien. 1928–1933: Die Zeit der national-bäuerlichen Regierungen*, Vol. 1. Frankfurt/M., Bern: Peter Lang Verlag, 1983.

Boia, Lucian. *Geschichte und Mythos. Über die Gegenwart des Vergangenen in der rumänischen Gesellschaft*. Cologne, Vienna and Weimar: Böhlau, 2003.

Boia, Lucian. *Die Germanophilen: Die rumänische Elite zu Beginn des Ersten Weltkrieges*. Berlin: Frank & Timme, 2014.

Boila, Romulus. "Die Verfassung und Verwaltung Rumäniens seit dem Weltkriege." *Jahrbuch des öffentlichen Rechts der Gegenwart* 18 (1930): 324–54.

Brown, Victoria F. "The Movement for Reform in Rumania after World War I: The Parliamentary Bloc Government of 1919–1920." *Slavic Review* 38 (1979): 456–72.

Brubaker, Rogers. "Ethnicity without Groups." *Archives Européennes de Sociologie* 43, no. 2 (2002): 163–89.

Constantinescu, Miron and Ştefan Pascu. *Unification of the Romanian National State: The Union of Transylvania with Old Romania*. Bucharest: Publishing House of the Academy of the Socialist Republic of Romania, 1971.

Dan., N. "Ardealul şi cultura românească." *Societatea de Mâine* 6, no. 12–13 (1929): 201–2.

Dragnea, Radu. "Formarea criticismului în Ardeal." *Ţara Noastră* 6, no. 2 (1925): 44–47.

Galea, Aurel. *Formarea şi activitatea Consiliului Dirigent al Transilvaniei, Banatului şi ţinuturilor româneşti din Ungaria: 2 decembrie 1918–10 aprilie 1920*, Vol. 1. Târgu-Mureş: Editura Tipomur, 1996.

Ghiulea, Nicolae. "Iar regionalismul." *Societatea de Mâine* 4, no. 4 (1927): 48–49.

Goga, Octavian. "Regionalismul." *Ţara Noastră* 3, no. 2 (1922): 41–44.

Goga, Octavian. "Ardealul şi politică partidului naţional." *Ţara Noastră* 6, no. 2 (1925): 33–42.

Goga, Octavian. "Dela principele Schwarzenberg la d. Aurel Dobrescu." *Ţara Noastră* 10, no. 3 (1930): 97–99.

Gogolák, Ludwig. "Ungarns Nationalitätengesetze und das Problem des magyarischen National- und Zentralstaates." In *Die Habsburgermonarchie. 1848–1918: vol. 3: Die Völker des Reiches*, edited by Adam Wandruszka and Peter Urbanitsch, 1207–1303. Vienna: Verlag der Österreichischen Akademie der Wissenschaften, 1980.

Haslinger, Peter and Klaus Holz. "Selbstbild und Territorium. Dimensionen von Identität und Alterität." In *Regionale und nationale Identitäten: Wechselwirkungen und Spannungsfelder im Zeitalter moderner Staatlichkeit*, edited by Peter Haslinger, 15–38. Würzburg: Ergon, 2000.

Hausleitner, Mariana. *Die Rumänisierung der Bukowina: Die Durchsetzung des nationalstaatlichen Anspruchs Großrumäniens 1918–1944*. München: Oldenbourg, 2001.

Hitchins, Keith. *Rumania. 1866–1947*. Oxford: Clarendon Press, 1994.

Hitchins, Keith. *A Nation Affirmed: The Romanian National Movement in Transylvania, 1860–1914*. Bucharest: The Encyclopedic Publishing House, 1999.

Kührer-Wielach, Florian. "Alba Iulia." In *Religiöse Erinnerungsorte in Ostmitteleuropa: Konstitution und Konkurrenz im nationen- und epochenübergreifenden Zugriff*, edited by Joachim Bahlke, Thomas Wünsch, and Stephan Rohdewald, 13–19. Berlin: De Gruyter Akademie Verlag, 2013.

Kührer-Wielach, Florian. *Siebenbürgen ohne Siebenbürger. Zentralstaatliche Integration und politischer Regionalismus nach dem Ersten Weltkrieg*. München: De Gruyter Oldenbourg, 2014.

Kührer-Wielach, Florian. "Siebenbürgen als administrative Einheit und diskursives Konzept." In *Das Südosteuropa der Regionen*, edited by Michael Metzeltin and Oliver Jens Schmitt, 349–410. Vienna: Verlag der Österreichischen Akademie der Wissenschaften, 2015.

Lasch, Katja. "Die Entstehung Großrumäniens." *Zeitschrift für Siebenbürgische Landeskunde* 27 (2004): 176–94.

Livezeanu, Irina. *Cultural Politics in Greater Romania: Regionalism, Nation Building and Ethnic Struggle: 1918–1930*. Ithaca and London: Cornell University Press, 1995.

Manuilă, Sabin, ed. *Recensământul general al populației României din 29 Decemvrie 1930. vol. II and vol. III*. Bucharest: Institutul central de statistică, 1938.

Moldovan, Valer. "Ardelenii și limba franceză." *Societatea de Mâine* 8, no. 6–7 (1931): 143–45.

Ploch, Beatrice and Heinz Schilling. "Region als Handlungslandschaft: Überlokale Orientierung als Dispositiv und kulturelle Praxis. Hessen als Beispiel." In *Die Wiederkehr des Regionalen: Über neue Formen kultureller Identität*, edited by Rolf Lindner, 122–57. Frankfurt/Main and New York: Campus, 1994.

Pușcariu, Sextil. "Regionalism Constructive." *Societatea de Mâine* 2, no. 6 (1925): 83–86.

România Intregită. 1918–1940. vol. 8 of Istoria Romanilor. Edited by Academia Română. Bucharest: Editura Enciclopedică, 2003.

Scurtu, Ioan. *Din viața politică a României. 1926–1947: Studiu critic privind istoria Partidului Național-Țărănesc*. Bucharest: Editura Științifică și Enciclopedică, 1983.

Șerban, George. "Sufletul Ardelenesc." *Societatea de Mâine* 3, no. 51–52 (1926): 798.

Suveica, Svetlana. *Basarabia în primul deceniu interbelic (1918–1928): modernizare prin reforme*. Chișinău: Pontos, 2010.

Ther, Philipp. "Sprachliche, kulturelle und ethnische 'Zwischenräume' als Zugang zu einer transnationalen Geschichte Europas." In *Regionale Bewegungen und Regionalismen in europäischen Zwischenräumen seit der Mitte des 19. Jahrhunderts*, edited by Philipp Ther and Holm Sundhaussen, ix–xxix. Marburg: Verlag Herder Institut, 2003.

Turda, Marius. "Transilvania în România post-comunistă." *Sfera Politicii* 80 (2000): 35–42.

Volkmer, Gerald. *Die Siebenbürgische Frage (1878–1900): Der Einfluss der rumänischen Nationalbewegung auf die diplomatischen Beziehungen zwischen Österreich-Ungarn und Rumänien*. Cologne, Weimar and Vienna: Böhlau, 2004.

6 Community Building and Expert Involvement with Reclaimed Lands in the Netherlands, 1930s–50s

Liesbeth van de Grift

Introduction[1]

In the interwar period, the rural world became a site of social, economic and political planning and intervention. The situation in the countryside and the plight of its inhabitants had been a political concern since the end of the nineteenth century, raising doubts about the purportedly beneficial effects of laissez-faire capitalism. The Great War and the economic crisis of the 1930s reinforced pleas for increased state interference and led to an extension of state responsibilities into the social and economic spheres. National governments and international organisations launched inquiries into rural life and working conditions with a view to reforming the countryside. After World War I, the post-war need to secure food production and to protect contested border areas, as well as the extension of the vote, resulted in a myriad of schemes aimed at modernising agriculture and regenerating rural societies.

In these years, modern statecraft became increasingly imbued with the rationality of science. Emerging scholarly disciplines such as rural sociology, agricultural economics and spatial planning took a central role in defining problems and solutions and setting the political agenda, thus contributing to a 'scientisation of the social': the application of the social sciences to solve social problems.[2]

In the Netherlands, social scientists were especially involved in thinking about ways to improve rural welfare. The rise and institutionalisation of the discipline of social geography—the direct forerunner of sociology in the Netherlands—was strongly linked to a groundbreaking reclamation project, the Zuiderzee Works.[3] In 1918, the Dutch parliament agreed to a major hydraulic scheme aimed at creating 200,000 hectares of arable land by draining part of the Zuiderzee, a North Sea inlet, and turning what remained into a freshwater lake. Between 1930 and 1968 four polders were created: Wieringermeer (1930), Noordoostpolder (1942), Oostelijk Flevoland (1957) and Zuidelijk Flevoland (1968). The reclamation project's importance to the emerging discipline of social geography is evident in a remark by Sjoerd Groenman, one of the founding fathers of Dutch sociology: 'The reclamation of new arable land when applied on a not too limited scale results in new human settlements and community building [*groepsvorming*]. Here, sociology with its primary interest in collective forms of life finds its subject in the making'.[4]

Farmers and their families flocked from different parts of the country to the newly drained lands. The colonisation of 'new' land offered social scientists an opportunity to gather data and gain insight into the process of community building. In addition, social geographers played an important role in the development of policies aimed at community organisation on the new land, for which they used their theoretical knowledge. Gain was mutual: the state, active in more fields than ever before, needed experts able to produce relevant knowledge and help make policy; social scientists, for their part, used this vacuum to strengthen their position as experts and develop applied sociology into an established scholarly discipline.

The period from the 1930s to the 1950s saw the emergence and heyday of state planning in the Wieringermeer and Noordoostpolder projects. In these years the first generation of Dutch sociologists established themselves as 'experts' and through their research and advisory work strongly influenced state policies aimed at developing rural communities on reclaimed lands. Three social geographers considered to be the founding fathers of Dutch sociology, Henri Nicolaas ter Veen, Sjoerd Groenman and Evert Willem Hofstee, were of central importance in this respect. Whereas ter Veen exerted a strong influence on the settlement of the Wieringermeer in the 1930s, Groenman and Hofstee carried out most of their work during later stages of the reclamation project, in the 1940s and 1950s. This chapter discusses their work and examines the changing discourses and practices of rural planning in the Netherlands in the interwar and immediate post-war periods. It will do so, first, by analysing the experts' notions of what a 'community' entails and the extent to which they reflected upon the problematic nature of this concept. A second aspect to be addressed is the process of community building and the question as to which methods and instruments may facilitate such efforts. Lastly, the respective roles ascribed to sociologists and the people they plan for will be discussed. As will become clear from this chapter, the ideas and practices of the early Dutch rural sociologists were characterised by a paradox: on reclaimed lands, an organic peasant community was to emerge—but one that was constructed from scratch by means of science and technology.

Social Engineering in Europe and the Netherlands

The planning of new communities on reclaimed lands in the Netherlands presents a clear case of 'social engineering', i.e., scientifically founded attempts to govern and influence social behaviour. For a long time, social engineering tended to be associated with the violent practices of totalitarian regimes. After the Second World War, Western democracies were quick to 'forget' that their own attempts to perfect society through social planning had shared common roots with the initiatives of authoritarian states.[5] From the 1980s onwards, a group of scholars, among them Detlev Peukert and Zygmunt Bauman, argued that social engineering is a characteristic feature of the modern interventionist state.[6] Still, even after these works were published, the primary focus has remained the exclusionist nature of authoritarian state planning.[7] In recent years, historians have added important nuances to this picture by including in their analyses cases of social planning that occurred within a liberal-democratic context. Their work has revealed that social engineering became a widespread and transnational practice throughout Europe after the First World War and remained so until the beginning of the 1960s.[8] Even when the outcomes of 'democratic social engineering' were often much less radical than the effects of social planning in the Third Reich or the Soviet Union, the dangers of transgressing legal boundaries and fostering social exclusion were always inherently present.[9]

'Social engineering' is a fuzzy concept, often used but hardly ever defined. Some historical actors described themselves as 'social engineers, measuring the forces within society in order to construct on the basis of the knowledge thus gained', but such self-identification has not been very frequent.[10] Scholars, when using the concept for analytical purposes, do not often provide a clear definition or distinguish it from similar terms such as 'social planning', 'social technology' and 'planned society'.[11]

The historian Thomas Etzemüller has recently probed the various aspects that defined the specific discourse and practices of social engineering that emerged and developed between 1918 and the beginning of the 1960s. The central actors involved in social engineering understood themselves as 'experts', whose 'rational' solutions for the 'problems' they conceptualised were grounded in empirical observations. The population (rather than individuals) was their unit of study; instead of imposing blueprint models, they emphasised the need for learning processes that would teach the people to discipline themselves. The essential conception undergirding their interventions was Ferdinand Tönnies's axiom of *Gemeinschaft* and *Gesellschaft*; the reconstruction of communities—'community' being an organic social system that is territorially defined and governed by informal relationships—remained their central aim throughout.[12] In that sense, there was no genuine break in 1945: social experts continued their efforts to reconstruct communities far into the 1950s, until a younger generation of social scientists increasingly came to criticise these ideas and interventions in the 1960s.

In general, the 'scientisation of the social' in the Netherlands reflected a European trend, even if in certain respects important differences were manifested as well. From the end of the nineteenth century, (new) professionals such as engineers, architects, medical doctors and social workers gained prominence by conceptualising social problems, setting the political agenda and providing solutions to the dilemmas they identified. Compared with other European countries such as Sweden and Germany, where social planning really took off in the interwar years and was considered a remedy for many social problems, Dutch liberal-confessional governments were generally reluctant to have the state intervene in the social sphere. This attitude would change after the end of the Second World War, when governing coalitions were dominated by Social Democrats and Catholics generally in favour of increased responsibilities for the state, and their governance ultimately amounted to the establishment of the post-war welfare state. Still, under exceptional circumstances such as the First World War, which gave rise to far-reaching policies to regulate economy, trade and food distribution, economic crisis and the development of 'new' land, opportunities did arise in the interwar period to experiment with new forms of state intervention, the legitimacy of which was grounded in expert knowledge.

The establishment of the social sciences followed a similar trend; only after the Second World War would professorial chairs and departments of the social sciences be established, whereas in Germany, France and the United States this was already occurring in the first half of the twentieth century.[13] The general recognition of the social sciences and their contribution to society derived from the belief that academic schooling was necessary for civil servants newly charged with social policymaking in an emerging welfare state.[14] As mentioned, the first Dutch sociologists were in fact social geographers, trained during the interwar period and appointed professors in the years after World War II. Their work has been described as 'empirical sociology', as their objective was to gather factual information that provided insight into social processes such as community building. Numerous studies were published that inquired into the effects of modernisation on geographically defined (and often rural) communities.[15]

Historians have assessed the relevance of the work of early Dutch sociologists in different ways. However, they have agreed on two points: their relative lack of international orientation and theoretical underpinnings of the early discipline of socio-geography.[16] Jacques van Doorn, representative of the new 'modern sociology' in the 1960s, was particularly severe in his judgement when he described the work of his academic forebears as the product of immature scientific interpretations lacking theoretical foundations and concluded that rather than making a contribution, their work had actually hampered the professionalisation of the social sciences.[17] Other historians have been less harsh and have argued that the early sociological work cannot reductively be called merely an 'immature empirical forerunner of sociology' because, when judged on their own terms, the works of the early rural sociologists contained valuable insights into social processes in the countryside.[18]

The early Dutch sociologists worked within a socioeconomic context that preoccupied them. Their concerns centred on the harmful effects of industrialisation and urbanisation. The importance of the countryside as an economic and social factor had been decreasing from the end of the nineteenth century. In 1947, the share of the population that made a living in the agrarian industry amounted to approximately twenty per cent of the total Dutch working population.[19] Moreover, the distinction between urban and rural areas became blurred as an 'urban lifestyle' pervaded the countryside. In particular, the weak viability of small family farms was a source of grave concern.[20] The early Dutch sociologists shared a worldview that may at first glance be described as conservative. The rationale for their recommendations lay in the recognition that in the face of society's impersonal forces, it was imperative to restore the institutions of community and family.[21] This focus on community building persisted, perhaps even intensified, in the postwar years. Yet whereas their outlook on the state of Dutch (rural) culture at first seems culturally pessimistic, their ambition to shape and modernise social structures, and their belief that the social sciences offered the means to do this, defy this characterisation. Their conviction that their role was of central importance during a time when profound socioeconomic changes were dissolving existing structures was reflected in their contributions to the social planning efforts that followed the reclamation of the Zuiderzee.

The Zuiderzee Works

The Zuiderzee was a North Sea inlet that frequently flooded surrounding regions. Since the mid-nineteenth century there had been plans to close off the unruly inlet by constructing a dam, turning it into a freshwater lake and reclaiming land through the creation of polders,[22] but these initiatives had never been implemented because of doubts about their practicability and financial viability. By 1918, the prospects for such a scheme had improved. The First World War, throughout which the Netherlands maintained neutral status, led to food shortages and hunger among the population. The need to increase agricultural production and secure food supplies became urgent, and the state took the lead in regulating food distribution and agricultural exports. The extension of state responsibilities into the social and economic spheres during the war years made bold state-led projects more acceptable and seem more feasible to the public. The final impetus for the approval of the Zuiderzee initiative came from a storm surge in 1916, which caused severe damage. In July 1918, the Dutch parliament agreed to the government's proposal to embark upon the ambitious reclamation project.

The Zuiderzee Works, designed by Minister of Transport and Water Management Cornelis Lely, a civil engineer, were to create an additional 200,000 hectares of arable land for the country. The draining of land would increase agricultural production, a goal eagerly sought during a time when hunger and war had underlined the importance of food security. Moreover, the closing off of the Zuiderzee would create a freshwater reservoir, improve drainage, diminish the risk of flooding and connect the two northern parts of the country by means of a 32-kilometre dam. Finally, and most importantly from the view of the social scientists involved in this scheme, the creation of arable land would provide Dutch peasants with an opportunity to start their own farms, at a time when the lack of available land had been driving farmers' sons into the cities or across the Atlantic. The reclamation of land would allow social scientists—or so they believed—to construct rural communities from scratch.

It was not only the imaginations of social scientists that were captivated by the seemingly unlimited possibilities offered by the new land. Politicians, representatives of interest groups, public intellectuals, lobbyists and scientists projected their conceptions of an ideal community onto the newly created polders. As a result, in the 1920s the creation of the Wieringermeer and the subsequent organisation of the land and the settlement of farmers provoked heated debate related to questions concerning the precise role of the state, the system of property relations to be introduced, the selection of inhabitants and the administrative organisation of the new territory.[23] These debates continued into the 1930s, when the villages were constructed, the farms issued and the area populated.

The Involvement of Social Scientists

Henri Nicolaas ter Veen, lecturer in social geography who was appointed to the chair of social geography at the University of Amsterdam in 1933, put his mark on the public debate about the Wieringermeer and played a crucial role in the ensuing decision- and policymaking processes. In 1925, ter Veen completed his dissertation, which was to have a decisive influence on the public debate. In his work, entitled *The Haarlemmermeer as an Area of Colonisation*, the social geographer analyses the reclamation of the Haarlemmermeer that had been carried out in the mid-nineteenth century. This project, he argued, was typical of the nineteenth-century night watchman state: upon draining the lake, state authorities left the actual organisation of the new land to private agents. His dissertation was a strong plea for the state's increased involvement in the reclamation projects that were planned at the time of his writing. His numerous articles from the 1920s and 1930s expressed his views about various issues surrounding the colonisation of new land, such as the appropriate system of landownership, form of governance and selection of farmers, all of which needed the input of social scientists.

Ter Veen's main contribution to Dutch sociology lies in his incessant efforts to have social geography recognised as an applied science of great significance to policymakers. In 1936 he founded the Foundation for Population Research in the Reclaimed Zuiderzee Polders (Stichting voor Bevolkingsonderzoek in de Drooggelegde Zuiderzeepolders) with the aim of collecting and studying data about the new inhabitants that was relevant to a variety of disciplines, such as anthropology, psychology, genetics, phonetics, dialects, 'social hygiene', rural economy, folklore, social geography and law. Four years later, he went on to establish the Institute for Social Research on the Dutch People (Instituut voor Sociaal Onderzoek van het

Nederlandse Volk—ISONEVO). Many of ter Veen's students would end up working as social experts in the service of governing bodies, such as the agencies responsible for the Zuiderzee Works.[24]

The clearest sign of the widespread recognition of ter Veen's work was his appointment as secretary to the State Commission set up in 1926. Composed of representatives from a range of political parties and agricultural organisations, the so-called Vissering Commission, named after its president, the liberal bank president Gerard Vissering, was charged with reporting on the granting of reclaimed land. The commission's report, published in 1930, clearly bears ter Veen's stamp and denotes a shift in thinking about the role and responsibilities of the state. This shift was manifest in the commission's recommendation to the state not to sell the land to private agents immediately upon draining it, but instead to act as landowner and prepare the land for settlement.[25] The agricultural crisis, land speculation and the weak position of tenant farmers had caused a majority of commission members to seriously doubt the beneficial effects of laissez-faire capitalism and propose a regulatory role for the state instead.

The Zuiderzee Works continued to inspire members of the first generation of social scientists after the Second World War. During the war, the authorities of the German occupation had agreed to continue the reclamation project, sharing with the Dutch a preference to increase agricultural production and create new farmsteads. Sjoerd Groenman and Evert Willem Hofstee, who both were appointed chairs of sociology after the end of the war, shared with ter Veen a background in social geography and an interest in rural communities. Following ter Veen's example, they became involved in the drafting of social policy as well: Groenman served as researcher to the government agency responsible for the reclamation project in the 1940s and would later become director of ISONEVO. Similarly, Hofstee worked as an advisor to the governing agencies responsible for the Zuiderzee Works before taking his chair at Wageningen Agricultural University. In the 1940s and 1950s, both produced work that was specifically related to the settlement of reclaimed land as well as books and articles that dealt with community building, rural welfare and social planning more generally.

The New Rural Community

The work of these three social scientists was strongly informed by Ferdinand Tönnies's conceptual pair, 'community' and 'society'. As a result of processes of modernisation, traditional rural communities, territorially defined and governed by personal relationships, were gradually disappearing; an urbanised lifestyle increasingly prevailed in the countryside. Their work reveals an ambivalent attitude towards these changes: on the one hand, they recognised this process as a fact; there could be no return to a past condition in history, hence longing for this condition was of no use. On the other hand, they were unwilling to yield to these changes without attempting to channel

Community Building and Expert Involvement 115

them in a direction that they deemed desirable. The reclaimed lands offered an opportunity to do this. The social scientists came to pursue a paradoxical aim: they wanted to *construct* an *organic* peasant community on reclaimed lands, which inevitably implied that it would be created artificially, by means of scientific methods and with expert help.

The new rural community would be composed of farmers who were future-oriented, well-educated and innovative—hardly a description of a traditional peasant farmer. A central role was ascribed to the farmers' wives, who were to be hard-working, prudent and thrifty and whose support and contributions to the establishment of new farms were considered important factors for their success. Farming communities were not to be made up of settlers largely from one part of the country, because a significant concentration of people from a particular area would encourage sustained ties to their former region and hinder the emergence of a new community. Schools were to play an important part; unlike in other parts of the country, where schools were strictly organised along confessional (Catholic, Protestant) lines, the schools on reclaimed lands were of a general 'Christian' nature and were to function as institutions where a sense of place and belonging was fostered among children and youth. Another sign of the modern character of the communities to be constructed manifested itself in opportunities for social mobility, as ter Veen, from a modest background himself, was keen

Figure 6.1 Machine threshing. Combine harvesters in the Noordoostpolder, Netherlands, 8 August 1950.

Source: National Archives, Spaarnestad Collection, Pim Stuifbergen.

to emphasise. The state remained owner of the land; the lease system introduced there allowed qualified farmers' sons who lacked capital to apply for available farmsteads. This particular conception of community, encompassing conservative and progressive features alike, reveals a tension that is inherent in the work and self-understanding of social geographers from the 1930s to the 1950s.

Whereas the notion of community was frequently used in the entire period under study, reflection upon the exact definition and nature of 'community' as a concept enters the work of social scientists only in the 1950s. Ter Veen's work is typical of early Dutch social geography in its lack of reflection on theory and concepts. He uses the concepts of community and society interchangeably, without defining them—although his frequent references to 'society' to describe the collective of pioneers emerging in the polders is striking when compared to the persistent references to 'community' by his colleagues in the post-war years.[26] From the mid-1950s onwards, an increasing awareness of the potentially problematic nature of the concept of community as defined by Tönnies can be observed among sociologists. Jakob Kruijt, professor of sociology in Utrecht, took the lead when he delivered a lecture in 1955, in which he discussed the analytical value of the axiomatic *Gemeinschaft* and *Gesellschaft* opposition and its frequent use by Dutch scholars. In his view, Tönnies had not only romanticised peasant communities of the past, but had also failed to recognise the intimate nature of the modern family, which—more so than in the past—was based on affection rather than economic motives. He addressed the uncritical adoption of the community concept by Dutch sociologists. Such use, he believed, illustrated that the discipline of sociology was still young and its internationalisation had only just begun: the various meanings and connotations attributed to concepts transferred to and used in different national contexts had not yet been sufficiently acknowledged by their users.[27]

Others social scientists followed suit, albeit somewhat ambivalently. The observable general pattern is an increase in reflection on the concept of community, even as 'community' continued to be used as both an analytical category and an ideal to be realised. Sjoerd Groenman endorsed Kruijt's criticism in 1955 and sought an explanation for the frequent sloppy application of the concept by scholars, who 'for their own practical purposes' simply selected a few of the many features that made up the concept as originally defined by Tönnies. At other occasions, he warned of its normative and romantic connotations: 'We [. . .] think too quickly [when referring to community] of a social system that is supposedly ideal and may fill us with nostalgia'.[28] Hofstee, too, was very critical of attempts to restore supposedly ideal peasant communities from the past.[29]

At the same time, it turned out to be difficult, if not impossible, to think beyond the community-society dichotomy. Speaking about the settlement of reclaimed lands, Hofstee expressed the view that a *modern* rural community should come to fruition there. The process he envisioned on reclaimed lands was one in which the 'masses' peopling reclaimed lands would gradually develop into a tight-knit 'community' with its own more or less uniform behavioural pattern and social codes.[30] In 1953, Groenman continued to regard community, conceived as a spatially bounded network characterised by personal relationships and shared traditions—even when these still needed to be created—as the ultimate objective of internal colonisation. He observed that in the initial stages, a *'Gesellschaft'* (using the German term) emerged on reclaimed lands. In this phase, apart from the *'Gemeinschaft'* of the family, no other organic social entity (*natuurlijk verband*) existed. The sociologist expected this to change in the course of time: 'Time will allow for the emergence of a "Gemeinschaft" in the new area'.[31] Although he expressed these views in 1953, two years before Kruijt's explicit criticism, his continued use of the analytical category becomes manifest in an article about the meaning of time and space in sociology, in which Groenman used the German term *Gemeinschaft* without further specification.[32] Somewhat ironically, this piece was published in the same journal issue of 1955 that also carried his endorsement of Kruijt's plea for a more critical attitude.

Constructing the New Rural Community

From the 1930s through the 1950s, the general aim remained the construction of a modern rural community that would serve as an example to the rest of the country. The question, then, was how to develop a strong collective of productive farmers, held together by informal ties and a shared innovative mentality. The respective answers to this question reveal a significant change from the interwar to the post-war period. In the 1920s and 1930s, ter Veen was of paramount importance in the development of ideas that strongly informed state practices of social planning in the Wieringermeer, the first area to be reclaimed from the Zuiderzee in 1930. Both Groenman and Hofstee would come to question the validity of his assumptions and the lack of empirical evidence in his work after 1945. What is striking, however, is that the selection procedure designed to choose the most qualified farmers in the interwar period remained in place during the post-war years, without, it seems, much contestation. Key to that procedure were biologist notions and the selection of farmers on the basis of individual traits such as professional experience, education, physical state and personality.

In his 1925 dissertation, ter Veen not only offered a historical analysis of the results of an earlier reclamation project, but also used the occasion to present recommendations with regard to future reclamation projects.[33] His work, which became an important point of reference in the public debate on the colonisation of the Wieringermeer, exhibits clear Social Darwinist tendencies. Central to the analysis was natural selection: a 'struggle for survival', in which only the 'fittest' were able to endure, had grown out of the extremely difficult circumstances encountered by the settlers of the Haarlemmermeer in the mid-nineteenth century. As a result, only the most hardy, strong-willed farmers and their families managed to adapt themselves to the harsh circumstances on the reclaimed land, whereas 'weaker' ones gave up and left. The result was the emergence of a productive farming community, endowed with an entrepreneurial and innovative spirit. Due to the loss of (human) capital, however, this process was costly, inhumane and inefficient. So as not to endure these costs, ter Veen proposed that the modern state take upon itself a 'rational' selection procedure, which would avoid the 'inefficient' loss of human and financial capital characterising the Haarlemmermeer settlement but would bring about the same result: the founding of a modern rural community.

The impact of ter Veen's ideas on policymaking becomes clear from the paragraphs on the selection of settlers in the report of the State Commission published in 1930, which served as a basis for later government policy. Social assistance by the state, it argued, hampered 'spontaneous social selection'; for that reason, selection ought to be organised by the state before land was colonised.[34] These ideas were put into practice: in the 1930s a procedure was developed to select candidate-farmers and give them the opportunity to start their own farms. The selection was based on physical,

Figure 6.2 During the national holiday festivities, Queen Juliana speaks with a group of pioneers from the Noordoostpolder, carrying wheelbarrows and shovels.

Source: National Archives, Spaarnestad Collection, ANP.

mental, professional and educational criteria; the size of the farm and area awarded reflected the supposed qualities of the applicant.[35] This procedure was refined in the post-war years and used to select new settlers for the Noordoostpolder.[36]

After the Second World War, however, social scientists began to question the scientific value of theories that until then had generally been assumed to be true and had informed social policy. The criticism was mainly directed against two views: migration leads to negative effects, and the individual traits of migrants are decisive in determining the nature of the developing community. Hofstee in particular criticised the theory of 'selective migration', which was based on the notion that migrants are generally more valuable than the average individual of the group from which they originate. As a result, their departure produces a negative effect on the group of people left behind. This view is reflected in ter Veen's work. Hofstee argued that it is typical of early Dutch sociology to simply take this assumption for granted without having any empirical basis for doing so. He then goes on to present empirical findings from his own and others' research that do not corroborate the theory. In his view, the spatial distribution of different kinds of opportunities, rather than the individual qualities of migrants, is of decisive influence:

> If intelligence, an enterprising spirit, the desire for adventure, and similar qualities often said to be associated with the propensity to emigrate really influenced it decisively, it would be difficult to understand why the rural population—prudent, more bound by tradition, certainly not above the rest of the population in intelligence—should be so heavily represented among migrants.[37]

The view became prevalent among social scientists that in addition to migrants' mental and physical characteristics, other clusters of factors, mostly informed by communal notions, determine the quality of settler communities. According to Hofstee, the 'cultural ideal' of the *group* determines the nature of the new community. Should migrants be in the process of developing a new cultural ideal, 'they will carry this new cultural ideal with them, and they will be able to realise it more quickly and in a purer form than was possible in the old country [or region]', where efforts at such fundamental changes would be hampered by existing structures. On the other hand, should migrants cherish a static 'cultural ideal', they will import their traditional ways and institutions to the new land, where these will perpetuate themselves.[38] Criticising ter Veen and other theorists for emphasising merely one explanatory factor, Groenman proposed that a variety of factors needed to be identified to understand the process of community building. Factors that in his view influence the nature of the community-in-the-making include the physical environment, the physical and mental qualities of individual migrants and groups of colonists as well as their 'culture' in a broader sense, which he called 'spiritual and material cultural heritage'.[39] It is important to note that whereas Groenman found fault with ter Veen's Darwinist analytical framework, he continued to regard physical and mental qualities as important factors. This goes to show that the 'biologist paradigm' continued to exert its influence in the post-war years, as also becomes clear from the selection procedure for the reclamation settlements.

Strikingly, even when the value attached to certain sociological theories had changed over time and scholars were incorporating new insights into their work, the practice of selecting candidate-farmers to settle on reclaimed land remained basically unchanged.[40] Whereas the Wieringermeer proved an experimental garden in this respect, the colonisation of the Noordoostpolder allowed for the selection procedure to be elaborated and perfected. The official charged to oversee this process, Bram van Lindenbergh, would later explain that the importance attached to community building increased significantly over the course of years: whereas in the first polder agricultural planning was prioritised over community building, in the second polder community building came first.[41]

Looking back, van Lindenbergh noted that the 'suitability' of individual farmers was decisive for their selection. Even when it was impossible to define exactly what 'suitability' entailed, the inspectors, through their training and years of experience, grew to recognise whether 'people had the ability—as it is so nicely put—to contribute to community building in the new polder'.[42] Exceptional circumstances, such as the Great Storm Surge of 1953 and the post-war policies of land consolidation, at times allowed for the selection of a disproportionally large share of farmers from a particular part of the country, but even then an attempt was made to apply the prevailing criteria. In practice, matters could become refractory, however. The discrepancy between the experts' ideals and reality became evident when the selection committee's aim of attracting 'modern and rational' farmers and its wish to involve farmers' wives in the interviews clashed with the orthodox Protestant views of farmers from the southern region of Walcheren, who were expected to migrate to the Noordoostpolder after the storm surge of 1953. For them, the involvement of women in decision-making proved a bridge too far.[43]

Ter Veen, Hofstee and Groenman were all closely involved in the drafting of the selection procedure and the setting of its criteria.[44] Despite changing scholarly views, the selection practice consistently emphasised the individual qualifications of candidate-farmers. Hofstee's work offers an explanation of this paradoxical state of affairs. While in the 1930s farmers were screened on the basis of their individual qualities with the aim of selecting the most educated, experienced, 'rational' and 'modern' candidates to construct a new rural community, post-war social geography held that the nature of the group, rather than individual qualities, should prove decisive. To realise the objective of a modern rural community, it was imperative to select those farmers who shared a 'modern cultural ideal'. Whether a candidate-farmer had internalised this ideal could be determined on the basis of several

Figure 6.3 Housewife combing her daughter's hair, Ramsgat Noordoostpolder, 2 August 1951.

Source: National Archives, Spaarnestad Collection, Wout van de Hoef.

criteria: his level of education, the way he had managed his farm, the qualities of his wife and his physical and mental qualities.

In short, the selection procedure and its criteria remained the same, even if their underlying rationale had changed. As Hofstee noted in retrospect, the selection for the Wieringermeer settlement had been carried out properly; experts had applied the right criteria—without recognising at the time that these were in fact expressions of the 'modern cultural ideal'.[45]

Exactly what the modern rural community entailed remained somewhat unclear, yet Hofstee was very clear about what it was *not*. His plea for a new rural culture should not, he emphasised, be understood as an attempt to hold on to the old. At the other extreme, the adoption of urban ways of life, as could be observed in the countryside, should also be avoided. Writing in 1954, Hofstee concluded that the rural world found itself in a transitional stage: 'The old has lost its foundations and finds itself in a state of increasing erosion, yet the fundamental adoption, the creation of right and new forms of life [in the countryside] has not yet been realised'. Hofstee expected change to come from rural women. Their associations could foster the revitalisation of rural culture; because of their relative short institutional history, these organisations were hotbeds for new ideas.[46]

Throughout his academic career, Hofstee continued to combine a culturally pessimistic view on the dissolution of communities and the hope that something new and valuable could be constructed on the remains of the past. In his retirement speech in 1981, this leitmotif returned when he warned that the modern emphasis on Enlightenment ideals of freedom and equality had come at the expense of fraternity, in the sense of one's responsibility for fellow human beings and one's embeddedness in a shared system of norms and values. The value placed on freedom and equality had produced a process of 'hyper-individualisation'. Still, he believed or hoped that a spontaneous, bottom-up movement might counter this trend.[47]

The Social Scientist as Expert

Ter Veen, Hofstee and Groenman agreed that the contribution of social geographers lay in their collection of empirical data on the process of community building among new settlers and the impact of the reclamation project on surrounding municipalities. The knowledge and recommendations they produced were used to formulate policy; often they were involved in the policymaking and implementation processes as well. They perceived themselves to be neutral, objective scientists, the executors of objectives provided by others, such as politicians and governing authorities. As Groenman noted, 'To him [the social scientist] the principles and objectives [of community organisation] are mere givens. He does not judge them in his capacity as sociologist; he merely accepts them'.[48]

In an attempt to remove potential doubts centred on the revolutionary undertones of social planning, they emphasised the gradual nature of their interventions. As ter Veen noted about the new role of the state in 1940, when state planning had assumed radically violent forms in other parts of Europe: '[The state's] objective is no other than to create order where it had dissolved or threatened to dissolve. Instead of revolutionary purposes, it aims at preservation'.[49] Groenman underlined a similar ambition to reinforce existing social structures rather than remake society altogether, as exemplified by the system of property relations introduced on reclaimed lands. Apparently, proposals were presented for more far-reaching initiatives, such as the establishment of a health centre based on the example of the Peckham Health Centre. This Pioneer Health Centre was an experiment initiated in the same period that was geared towards bottom-up community organisation, based on the assumption that once left to themselves and offered a wide range of facilities, people who were selected from local neighbourhoods would begin to spontaneously organise in a creative, meaningful way.[50] Such radical experiments, Groenman concluded, lacked a sufficient base of support in the Netherlands.[51]

The Dutch sociologists' discourse on social planning reveals an important change from the interwar to the post-war period that concerns their methodology and toolkit. Again, whereas ter Veen hardly reflected on meta-issues and simply took it for granted that qualified social scientists and civil servants could select the best farmers, Groenman's work reveals the gradual adoption of a new approach that would become prevalent in the 1960s. Referring to Karl Mannheim's *Man and Society in an Age of Reconstruction* (enlarged English edition, 1940), Groenman distinguishes between top-down and piecemeal community organisation, which correspond to different stages in the progressive development of social planning. In the first stage, direct methods were used to influence individuals' behaviour; in the next stage experts came to prefer indirect forms of social influence produced by certain social patterns and networks within society that induce individuals to modify their behaviour.[52] Groenman also underlined the necessity of planning-by-doing rather than defining a blueprint beforehand, another expression of the change from top-down planning to forms of social engineering that ascribed more importance to interaction, feedback mechanisms and self-governance. As Groenman noted, 'The goal cannot be separated from the social situation, in which the action takes place'. In his view, the goal was in part determined *by* the process, which encompassed among other things an investigation into the wishes of the population and the feasibility of proposed objectives; conversely, the process itself *became* the goal, as popular participation and collaboration could foster social cohesion and community building, provided that there was no suspicion of top-down interference.[53]

The Objects of Planning

This brings us to the role of the people who were targets of social planning. In theory, the tasks were clearly defined: even if experts were increasingly willing to take account of the wishes of the people in the post-war period, at the end of the day these people were supposed to follow the guidelines laid out by the experts. In practice, friction arose as soon as the perceived interests of the state, social planners and the planned communities did not correspond with one another. The Wieringermeer offers an exemplary case of such a situation: selected colonists, governed by a technocratic directorate, were denied political representation at the local administrative level. They only temporarily accepted the experts' justification that a state of exception existed for the new land. The directorate's reasoning—only when a socially cohesive 'community' has come into being can we grant the new inhabitants political influence; until then, we have to create the preconditions for such a community to emerge—sparked a backlash, as a substantial number of citizens organised themselves and filed a petition to be granted suffrage at the local level.

Several media outlets, politicians, public intellectuals and state bodies supported their cause. This case reveals that it was not so much the temporary suspension of political rights per se that produced resistance, but rather the prolonged period in which this exceptional situation persisted and was justified by reference to the need for community building. What the collective effort of Wieringermeer colonists made unequivocally clear to contemporaries was that some form of community had unmistakably come into existence in the ten years that had passed since land had been reclaimed. Ter Veen sympathised with their cause, as he, too, felt that a sufficient degree of community life had emerged by that time.[54] But the rationale for the temporary abolition of political rights remained uncontested: similar technocratic bodies were established in the other polders as well, and only after these areas were integrated into the state's municipal structure would new inhabitants regain their political rights.

As we have already seen, the wishes of the population and their participation in the planning process were taken more seriously after the Second World War. Under the umbrella of 'community organisation', people were asked to express their wishes in polls and to become members of neighbourhood councils. Important publications such as Murray Ross's *Community Organization* and the 1955 UN report 'Social Progress through Community Development' articulated the same position: the population's active participation is a fundamental aspect of community organisation.[55]

Groenman took a somewhat ambivalent stance towards these new views. He underlined the importance of popular participation and agreed that only by involving people in the planning process could lasting effects be realised and social cohesion increased. However, should the people refuse to cooperate, experts should take the lead and help them out of their state of 'lethargy': 'If we were to make community organisation dependent on the cooperation of the population, [earlier mentioned] programs in Egypt or South Italy could just as well be terminated or else they would proceed very slowly'.[56]

Conclusion

In the 1970s the economic crisis undermined belief in the perfectibility of society through science and planning. In the previous decade, a new generation of scholars had already begun to criticise the technocratic and elitist attitude of social experts and had called for more bottom-up initiatives and increased popular participation. This chapter has shown that important changes in the discourse of social planning can already be observed in the immediate post-war period. The reclamation of the Wieringermeer in the interwar years allowed for growing state intervention in new fields and the involvement of social experts, more so than had ever been possible on the 'old' land. After 1945, social planning and the 'scientisation of the social' entered a new stage in terms of scale and methods, as is exemplified by the colonisation of the Noordoostpolder. In the interwar years, ter Veen's scholarly and practical contribution to community building in the Wieringermeer had been informed by Social Darwinist ideas and lacked any reflection on concepts and theories. He assumed a priori that a direct causal relation existed between the mental and physical qualities of individual colonists and the quality of the community that they built together. In the 1950s, social scientists such as Hofstee and Groenman began to criticise the lack of empirical foundations and theoretical underpinnings in the work of earlier sociologists, and their uncritical use of value-laden concepts such as 'community'. They emphasised that multiple factors determined the process of community building and gradually began to incorporate new ideas about the desirability of popular input into social planning practices.

At the same time, several notions that had predominated among social scientists in the interwar period continued to exert influence until the end of the 1950s. Ter Veen, Hofstee and Groenman, social geographers appointed by the state to work in advisory and research positions, all shared the similar objective of constructing a modern rural community on reclaimed lands, an aim that reconciled modern means and technologies with a large degree of social cohesion and the persistence of informal relationships. They were wary of the perceived effects of industrialisation and urbanisation, the dissolution of traditional communities among them, yet they realised that a return to the past was impossible and undesirable. They grew increasingly critical of the concept of 'community' when used in Tönnies's sense to express a nostalgic longing for some prior state in the past, but continued to perceive a modern community to be the ideal to be achieved. The hybrid nature of post-war conceptions of community building was manifested in other ways as well. The Social Darwinism of ter Veen was rejected after 1945, but the biologist paradigm—the idea that the physical and mental qualities of individual farmers shape the quality of the community—continued to exercise influence, even when the impact of social factors was recognised as well. And whereas popular participation was gradually taken more seriously, the work of these social scientists—both on paper and in practice—reveals an unconditional belief in the expert as an objective authority. A clear sign that this belief was accepted more broadly as well is evident in the top-down selection policies for colonists and the technocratic governance that were introduced by the government in the 1930s and maintained in the post-war years.

Notes

1. The research for this article has been made possible by a grant from the Netherlands Organization of Scientific Research. A draft version of this chapter was presented at the Rural History Conference in Girona, 2015. The author would like to thank the editors of the volume for their comments on an earlier version.
2. Raphael, "Die Verwissenschaftlichung des Sozialen"; see also: Raphael, "Embedding the Human and Social Sciences".
3. On the early work of Dutch sociologists, see also the chapter by Harm Kaal in this volume.
4. S.J. Groenman, *Kolonisatie op nieuw land* (Assen: Van Gorcum & Comp., 1953), 7.
5. Roseman, "National Socialism".
6. Peukert, *Volksgenossen*; Bauman, *Modernity*.
7. Cf. Scott, *Seeing Like a State*.
8. Etzemüller, *Die Romantik*; Kuchenbuch, *Geordnete Gemeinschaft*; Couperus, Van de Grift, and Lagendijk, "Experimental Spaces".
9. Broberg and Roll-Hansen, *Eugenics*; Van de Grift, "On New Land".
10. These are the words of Henri Nicolaas ter Veen as recollected by one of his students. Hagoort, "Sociale wetenschappen," 38.
11. Etzemüller, "Social Engineering," 20.
12. Ibid., 20–31.
13. Van Peype, "Ontwikkeling van de sociologie," 24. See also Harm Kaal's chapter elsewhere in this volume.
14. Gastelaars, *Een geregeld leven*, 124.
15. See for instance: Evert Willem Hofstee, *Het Oldambt: een sociografie* (Groningen: Wolters, 1937); Sjoerd Groenman, *Staphorst: sociografie van een gesloten gemeenschap* (Meppel: Stenvert, 1947).
16. Van Doorn, *Beeld en betekenis*; Gastelaars, *Een geregeld leven*; van Peype, "Ontwikkeling van de sociologie"; Van Heerikhuizen and Wilterdink, "Conservatisme en sociologie"; Biervliet, Bun, and Köbben, "Biologisme". On the rise and the establishment of the social sciences in the Netherlands, see also: Jonker, *De sociologische verleiding*.
17. Van Doorn, *Beeld en betekenis*, 16, 41.
18. Gastelaars, *Een geregeld leven*, 67.
19. E.W. Hofstee, *Rural Life and Rural Welfare in the Netherlands* (The Hague: Government Printing and Publishing Office, 1957), 10. This report, written for the Food and Agriculture Organisation of the United Nations, provides a general overview of the rural welfare situation in the Netherlands.
20. Karel, *De maakbare boer*, 84–91.
21. Gastelaars, *Een geregeld leven*, 74–75.
22. Polders are tracts of lowland that are surrounded by dikes. Water is drained from these areas and transported to surrounding canals.
23. Van de Grift, "On New Land".
24. Hagoort, "Sociale wetenschappen," 38.
25. *Verslag der Commissie inzake het bestudeeren van de uitgifte der Zuiderzeegronden ingesteld bij besluit van den minister van waterstaat d.d. 24 december 1926* (The Hague: Ter Algemeene Landsdrukkerij, 1930).

26. Henri Nicolaas ter Veen, "Op nieuw land een nieuwe maatschappij: het Zuiderzeeprobleem," *Mensch en Maatschappij* 6, no. 4 (1930): 313–29.
27. J.P. Kruijt, "Gemeenschap als sociologisch begrip. Een kritiek op Tönnies," *Mededelingen der Koninklijke Nederlandse Akademie der Wetenschappen* 18 (1955): 59–84.
28. Sjoerd Groenman, "Kanttekeningen," *Mens en maatschappij* 30 (1955): 236; Sjoerd Groenman, *Sociale opbouw op territoriale grondslag (community organization)* (Nederlandse Bond voor Sociaal-Cultureel Vormingswerk, 1960 [1957]).
29. Evert Willem Hofstee, "De selectie van kolonisten en de ontwikkeling van de plattelandscultuur in de IJsselmeerpolders," in *Langs gewonnen velden. Facetten van Smedings werk* (Wageningen: H. Veenman en Zonen, 1954): 291–92, 294.
30. Hofstee, "De selectie van kolonisten," 289.
31. Sjoerd Groenman, *Kolonisatie op nieuw land* (Assen: Van Gorcum, 1953), 30.
32. Sjoerd Groenman, "Het begrippenpaar tijd en ruimte in de sociologie," *Mens en maatschappij* 30 (1955) 157–69.
33. Van de Grift, "On New Land".
34. *Verslag der Commissie inzake het bestudeeren van de uitgifte der Zuiderzeegronden*, 78.
35. Lindenbergh, "Het algemene uitgifteplan".
36. Van Dissel, *59 jaar eigengereide doeners*, 147–9; Vriend, *Het nieuwe land*.
37. Evert Willem Hofstee, *Some Remarks on Selective Migration* (The Hague: Nijhoff, 1952), 13.
38. Ibid., 20.
39. Groenman, *Kolonisatie op nieuw land*, 22–28, 40–41.
40. Interview with Bram van Lindenbergh by Dirk Jan Wolffram, accessed 19 October 2015, http://www.flevolandsgeheugen.nl/5381/nl/a-g-lindenbergh-vertelt-over-het-begrip.
41. Ibid., http://www.flevolandsgeheugen.nl/5333/nl/a-g-lindenbergh-vertelt-over-de-selectie-van.
42. Ibid., http://www.flevolandsgeheugen.nl/5340/nl/de-selectie-van-pachters-in-de-nop.
43. Ibid., http://www.flevolandsgeheugen.nl/5376/nl/a-g-lindenbergh-vertelt-over-de-walcherse-boeren.
44. Ibid., http://www.flevolandsgeheugen.nl/5340/nl/de-selectie-van-pachters-in-de-nop.
45. Hofstee, "De selectie van kolonisten," 286.
46. Ibid., 293–94.
47. Evert Willem Hofstee, "Vrijheid, gelijkheid en eenzaamheid," *Universiteit en Hogeschool* 27, no. 4 (1981): 240–43.
48. Groenman, *Sociale opbouw*, 8.
49. H.N. ter Veen, "De maatschappelijke achtergrond van sociale zorg en sociale planmatigheid," in *Van aardrijkskunde tot sociale wetenschap. Keur uit verspreide geschriften*, ed. H.N. ter Veen (Amsterdam: Uitgeverij H.J. Paris, 1950), 252. This article first appeared in *Mens en Maatschappij* in 1940.
50. Kuchenbuch, *Das Peckham-Experiment*.
51. Groenman, *Kolonisatie op nieuw land*, 94. For a similar experiment that failed to take off in the Netherlands, see: Couperus, "Experimental Planning".
52. Groenman, *Kolonisatie op nieuw land*, 4.
53. Ibid., 31.
54. See for a detailed analysis: Van de Grift, "On New Land".
55. *Social Progress through Community Development* (New York: United Nationals Bureau of Social Affairs, 1955); Murray G. Ross, *Community Organization: Theory and Principles* (New York: Harper, 1955).
56. Groenman, *Sociale opbouw*, 33.

Bibliography

Bauman, Zygmunt. *Modernity and the Holocaust*. Cambridge and Malden: Polity Press, 1989.

Biervliet, H., B. Bun, and A.J.F. Köbben. "Biologisme, racisme en eugenetiek in de antropologie en sociologie in de jaren dertig." In *Toen en thans. De sociale wetenschappen in de jaren dertig en nu*, edited by Frank Bovenkerk et al., 208–35. Baarn: Amboboeken, 1978.

Broberg, Gunnar and Nils Roll-Hansen, eds. *Eugenics and the Welfare State: Sterilization Policy in Denmark, Sweden, Norway, and Finland*. East Lansing: Michigan State University Press, 1996.

Couperus, Stefan. "Experimental Planning after the Blitz: Non-Governmental Planning Initiatives and Post-War Reconstruction in Coventry and Rotterdam, 1940–1955." *Journal of Modern European History* 13, no. 4 (2015): 516–33.

Couperus, Stefan, Liesbeth van de Grift, and Vincent Lagendijk. "Experimental Spaces: A Decentred Approach to Planning in High Modernity." *Journal of Modern European History* 13, no. 4 (2015): 475–79.

Dissel, A.C.M. van. *59 jaar eigengereide doeners in Flevoland, Noordoostpolder en Wieringermeer: Rijksdienst voor de IJsselmeerpolders 1930–1989*. Lelystad: Walburg Pers, 1991.

Doorn, J.A.A. van. *Beeld en betekenis van de Nederlandse sociologie*. Utrecht: Bijleveld, 1964.

Etzemüller, Thomas. "Social engineering als Verhaltenslehre des kühlen Kopfes. Eine einleitende Skizze." In *Die Ordnung der Moderne. Social Engineering im 20. Jahrhundert*, edited by Thomas Etzemüller, 11–39. Bielefeld: Transcript, 2009.

Etzemüller, Thomas. *Die Romantik der Rationalität. Alva & Gunnar Myrdal— Social Engineering in Schweden*. Bielefeld: Transcript, 2010.

Gastelaars, Marja. *Een geregeld leven. Sociologie en sociale politiek in Nederland, 1925–1968*. Amsterdam: SUA, 1985.

Grift, Liesbeth van de. "On New Land a New Society: Internal Colonisation in the Netherlands, 1918–1940." *Contemporary European History* 22, no. 4 (2013): 609–26.

Hagoort, Peter. "Sociale wetenschappen op het kruispunt van binnenweg en heirbaan; sociale wetenschappen in het interbellum." *Grafiet* 1 (1981/1982): 14–71.

Heerikhuizen, Bart van and Nicolaas Arie Wilterdink. "Conservatisme en sociologie in de jaren dertig." In *Toen en thans. De sociale wetenschappen in de jaren dertig en nu*, edited by Frank Bovenkerk et al., 119–31. Baarn: Amboboeken, 1978.

Jonker, Ed. *De sociologische verleiding. Sociologie, sociaal-democratie en de welvaartsstaat*. Groningen: Wolters-Noordhoff, 1988.

Karel, Erwin. *De maakbare boer. Streekverbetering als instrument van het Nederlandse landbouwbeleid 1953–1970*. Groningen and Wageningen: Nederlands Agronomisch Historisch Instituut, 2005.

Kuchenbuch, David. *Geordnete Gemeinschaft. Architekten als Sozialingenieure— Deutschland und Schweden im 20. Jahrhundert*. Bielefeld: Transcript, 2010.

Kuchenbuch, David. *Das Peckham–Experiment. Eine Mikro- und Wissensgeschichte des Londoner 'Pioneer Health Centre' im 20. Jahrhundert*. Cologne: Böhlau Verlag, 2014.

Lindenbergh, A.G. "Het algemene uitgifteplan." In *Wording en opbouw van de Noordoostpolder. Deel 3: de inrichting en ontwikkeling van het landbouwgebied,* edited by J.H. van Kampen et al. Lelystad: Rijksdienst voor de IJsselmeerpolders, 1988.

Peukert, Detlev. *Volksgenossen und Gemeinschaftsfremde: Anpassung, Ausmerze und Aufbegehren unter dem Nationalsozialismus*. Cologne: Bund–Verlag, 1982.

Peype, D.C.J. van. "Ontwikkeling van de sociologie in Nederland." In *Sociologie in Nederland*, edited by L. Rademaker, 22–60. Deventer: Van Loghum Slaterus, 1979.

Raphael, Lutz. "Die Verwissenschaftlichung des Sozialen als methodische und konzeptionelle Herausforderung für eine Sozialgeschichte des 20. Jahrhunderts." *Geschichte und Gesellschaft* 22 (1996): 165–93.

Raphael, Lutz. "Embedding the Human and Social Sciences in Western Societies, 1880–1980: Reflections on Trends and Methods of Current Research." In *Engineering Society: The Role of the Human and Social Sciences in Modern Societies, 1880–1980*, edited by Kerstin Brückweh et al., 41–56. Basingstoke: Palgrave Macmillan, 2012.

Roseman, Mark. "National Socialism and Modernisation." In *Fascist Italy and Nazi Germany: Comparisons and Contrasts*, edited by Richard Bessel, 197–229. Cambridge: Cambridge University Press, 1996.

Scott, James C. *Seeing Like a State: How Certain Schemes to Improve the Human Condition Have Failed*. New Haven and London: Yale University Press, 1998.

Vriend, Eva. *Het nieuwe land. Het verhaal van een polder die perfect moest zijn*. Amsterdam: Uitgeverij Balans, 2012.

7 The Turn to Local Communities in Early Post-War West Germany

The Case of Hamburg, Lübeck and Bremen, 1945–65

Jeremy DeWaal

In 1945, Arthur Dickens, a Yorkshireman in the British Royal Artillery, took up a post as press supervisor in the Baltic town of Lübeck, a city for which he developed an odd local enthusiasm.[1] Taking regular nightly walks through the town ruins, he recorded his nocturnal ruminations on the local landscape, writing in his diary in July 1945 of his deep affection for Lübeck.[2] His position as press supervisor exposed him to the writings of local enthusiasts that proliferated in ruined German cities, which reminded him of the Yorkshire regionalists he knew from his youth. Dickens reacted positively to the turn to the local that took place in the ruins and saw it as anything but narrow, close-minded or reminiscent of Nazism, recording in his diary:

> No man whose heart lies truly in his local history can, I like to hope, be utterly lost, and whatever one thinks of political regionalism in Germany, these local cults must at all cost be encouraged; apart from their intrinsic mental worth, they are the basis of a truer and better patriotism, as opposed to a state-engineered Chauvinism[3].

Dickens' argument is stunning not in terms of its uniqueness, but in how it reflected popular German discourses on the crucial role of local communities in building a new post-war order.

While Nazi Germany promoted a vision of messianic national community as the ultimate guarantor of future life, in the ruins of early post-war cities, a broad localist turn occurred. Localism is typified by an emphasis on the locality as a site of meaning, community, cultural particularity and decentralisation, while its political context can be ideologically variant. The early post-war localist turn, I argue, reshaped the spatial imaginary in ways that deeply influenced both culture and politics and ultimately redounded to the benefit of post-war democratisation. Instead of looking for redemption from the national community, local citizens imagined restored civilian lives within their local communities—a development crucial to post-war cultural demobilisation. The turn to local community can be seen above all in the profuse appeal to *Heimat* sentiment in the rubble years. Heimat, a unique German term, refers to a sense of belonging in local and regional places of home.[4] Desires for Heimat reached unprecedented heights amidst the ruins. Facing trauma, pervasive destruction, dislocation and loss of locally situated personal pasts, local Heimat emerged as a site of imagined protection, restored community and a geography in which citizens could bridge across rupture and build new civilian lives.

While the national idea was burdened, citizens further took advantage of localities as sources of alternative identities and reshaped ideas of local tradition to forge identification with a new democratic system and *rapprochement* with former enemies. Though historians have overlooked the phenomenon, localists and regionalists throughout the Federal Republic reconfigured local historical memory and reinvented traditions to fashion notions of 'democracy', 'republicanism', 'world-openness' and/or 'tolerance' as local values. In the German Southwest, for example, regionalists fashioned ideas such as 'Swabian democracy' and 'Badenese world-openness', while citizens in places like Cologne underscored 'democracy', 'world-openness' and national reconciliation as values rooted in local community. Citizens throughout West Germany further articulated the importance of orientation to local community in establishing a decentralized democracy. Though such identifications did not suddenly turn Germans into adept practitioners of democracy, neither did they contribute to coming to grips with crimes of the recent past; they did, however, prove crucial in forging conceptual identifications with a new democratic system and post-war order.

While these developments can be found in scores of localities and regions, this study will focus on the cases of the coastal Hanseatic cities of Lübeck, Hamburg and Bremen, which well illustrate both the use of flexible local identities and emphasis on reconstructed home towns as geographies of life after death. It will trace particularly the reformulation and growing popular advocacy of ideas of Hanseatic 'world-openness', 'democracy' and 'tolerance' as local values. Of course, Hanseaten had long identified with the position of their cities within a global network of trade. They also had long pre-war histories of local independence. But while these cities had very unique profiles and histories, what proves most interesting is not their deviation from other localities in West Germany, but rather how they marshalled unique cultures and histories to fashion similar local value claims.

In focusing on the role of local communities and identities in post-war reconstruction, this work addresses an area in much need of further scholarly attention. Significant work has been done on the cultural history of physical reconstruction and on desires to maintain local identities and memory in the landscapes of rebuilt cities.[5] But local identities were more than just objects of reconstruction and bore much significance beyond questions of physical rebuilding. They represented vital tools, particularly in the German case, through which citizens imagined new post-war private lives and forged crucial identification with a new post-war order. The rubble world was filled with discussions on how re-establishing 'Heimat' was essential both to repairing torn life narratives and establishing a new political system. In spite of the prevalence of such popular discussions, histories of post-war West Germany have neglected the extent to which local places of home and local communities acted as centre points of cultural-political reconstruction. Historians have likewise overlooked the extent of early democratic identifications and the role of localities in facilitating them.[6] Admittedly, histories of federalism have noted the role of localism and regionalism in post-war Germany.[7] Celia Applegate's study of the Heimat concept has also pointed out how it was one of the few community concepts not tainted after 1945.[8] Such findings, however, have not prevented scores of subsequent scholars from repeating the myth of Heimat and localism as tainted after 1945. Much work, in short, remains to be done to uncover the role of the local communities as vital tools in the broader project of post-war reconstruction—particularly in its identificational, personal and cultural aspects.

Local communities were, in contrast to the nation, embedded within more personally experienced spaces. At the same time, they were also imagined communities that were shaped discursively. This chapter therefore probes local community as a discursive proscriptive construction super-imposed onto diverse networks of social solidarities and fragmentations. In turn, rather than seeing emergent ideas such as 'Hanseatic democracy', 'Hanseatic world-openness', and 'Hanseatic tolerance' as broadly descriptive and corresponding to experience, it views them as discursive tools used to influence the cultural and political terms of community and its mechanisms of inclusion and exclusion. Behind these ideals remained ongoing pitfalls, divisions and exclusions. These ideas about local community, however, had broad resonance and were not simply the project of a small elite. They were promoted interchangeably by a range of actors including lay localists, Heimat societies, writers and intellectuals, as well as local politicians.

This chapter will first examine the cognitive and emotional turn to home towns and local communities as manifested in the local cultural reawakening and efforts to patch together dislocated and shattered communities. It will then turn to articulations of local community as essential to democracy and parallel discourses on 'world-openness', 'democracy' and 'tolerance' as local values. *Hanseaten* used ideas of world-openness to reject former nationalist narratives of their cities as nodes of German power, propagating instead a notion of their harbour communities as internationalist, peaceful intermediaries between Germany and the world. Progressive local enthusiasts further used notions of world-openness and tolerance to encourage embrace of outsiders.

While representative of phenomenon in West Germany, the turn to local community in the three cities at least partly reflected broader European trends. Of course, the combination of burdened national identity, the challenge of identifying with a very different political system and the free availability of alternative sources of identity certainly made West German cities unique. While cities in the Eastern bloc witnessed the imposition of official socialist narratives of place, other Western countries like Britain, France, Belgium and the Netherlands had neither significantly burdened national identities nor the same pressing need to construct radically new political identifications.[9] While the German context may be more unique in the sheer extent to which locals reformulated local identities to adjust to a very different political system, war-torn citizens across Europe shared the belief that reconstruction of local community proved vital to establishing new post-war orders. Countries across Western and Eastern Europe experienced many of the same conditions that informed preoccupation with local communities, including the destruction of home towns, the shattering of local communities through dislocation and death and experiences of rupture most deeply felt in lost local places of home. Much evidence suggests a similar preoccupation with reconstructing local communities throughout war-torn Europe.

Rebuilding Local Communities from the Ashes

The post-war turn to local communities can scarcely be understood without reference to its feared loss. Unlike after World War I, home towns had become sites of utter devastation. As Hanseatic citizens returned to survey the rubble of their home towns, they had to first convince themselves that their 'Heimat' was not on its deathbed. As citizens experienced rubble landscapes, disappeared sites of past lives and ruptured communities, they turned to the local community idea in response to its perceived loss. Hamburg was the hardest hit, with bombings in 1943 leading nine hundred thousand of its 1.7 million inhabitants to flee, with forty-one thousand locals perishing in the raids and forty-four thousand Hamburg soldiers dying on the front (see Figure 7.1).[10]

Figure 7.1 Aerial view of Hamburg-Eilbek following bombing raids in June 1943.
Source: Imperial War Museums, London, CL 3400.

Bremen, nestled on the Weser River, lost thirty-six per cent of its population and fifty to sixty per cent of its inhabitable structures, with the cities buried in 8.7 million cubic meters of rubble (see Figure 7.2).[11] Finally, Lübeck, after a large bombing raid in 1942, had been twenty per cent destroyed, with sixteen per cent of buildings completely destroyed and 41.4 per cent lightly damaged, leaving ten per cent of the city homeless (see Figure 7.3). Lübeck was spared from later bombings by becoming a Red Cross hub.[12] Its position near the Soviet zone, however, brought its own challenges. East German expellees, driven from their native regions, sought to push beyond the Soviet zone, many arriving in the new border city. In the early years, ninety thousand expellees flooded Lübeck, nearly doubling its population.[13] All the Hanseatic cities faced widespread death, dislocation and straining circumstances, with citizens living on a daily diet of around one thousand calories.

Figure 7.2 British in war-torn Bremen in April 1945.
Source: Imperial War Museums, London, BU 4434.

Figure 7.3 Lübeck after Allied bombing in March 1942.
Source: Bundesarchiv, Koblenz, Bild 146–1977–047–16, CC-BY-SA 3.0.

Their inhabitants all expressed fears that local community and Heimat had been permanently lost.

But the cities soon witnessed an astonishing cascade of returning citizens, often defying the materially irrational nature of premature return. The sheer volume of return sparked a crisis in Hamburg. Of the nine hundred thousand Hamburgers who evacuated in 1943, six hundred fifteen thousand returned within only a few years to a city still covered in forty-three million square meters of rubble, with the British quickly blocking further entry.[14] Returning citizens recounted not national slogans and the redemption of national community. Instead, they expressed their desires for local community and home town. In April 1946, the *Hamburger Echo* reported on how the 'storm to the Heimat' crashed into allied relocation restrictions. The article cited a representative letter from a female evacuee who wrote, 'I must, as a Hamburger, be allowed to again live in Hamburg . . . I have spent my entire life there until 1943 . . . I want to, and must go back to my Heimat.' The newspaper reported that thousands of Hamburger felt the same.[15] Local newspapers continually reported that evacuees wrote to them in droves of their desires to return to their Heimat. When locals did return, they faced the daunting task of finding a place to live and found their sense of lost Heimat all the more heightened.[16] In 1946, a citizen who lived in the rubble for years recounted how a Hamburg soldier returned home after six years to find a former personal landscape turned into a 'city of ruins' that left him grasping for familiar places.[17] Another local wrote how, prior to seeing the rubble, he was not aware that local landscapes held such personal significance for him.[18] Rather than reflecting on abstract national community, returning citizens were faced with the destroyed local places of past personal life and how to address their loss.

In Lübeck and Bremen, the same spectre of lost local community was apparent. Lübecker, whose city suffered less destruction, noted a turn to local Heimat sentiment in response to its feared loss. In 1948, the head of the Lübeck Society for *Heimatschutz* wrote that widespread belief that Lübeck was on its deathbed triggered a surge of interest in local Heimat and reconstruction.[19] The city witnessed a wave of foundings and re-foundings of localist Heimat societies and publications. These included the *Verein für Heimatschutz, Natur und Heimat*, the very Heimat-engaged *Gesellschaft zur Beförderung Gemeinnütziger Tätigkeit*, the *Plattdütsche Volksgill to Lübeck* and the *Vaterstädtische Vereinigung*, founded in 1949, which included Thomas and Heinrich Mann among its members.[20] New or re-established Heimat periodicals included the *Lübeckische Blätter, Vaterstädtische Blätter, Zeitschrift des Vereins für Lübeckische Geschichte* and *Der Wagen*. Heimat associations did not hold monopoly on local culture, but did much to jump-start a local cultural renaissance that helped compensate for destroyed local landscapes. Lübecker noted how the war's destruction of *Heimatgut* (material anchors of Heimat) informed the subsequent local cultural revival. Re-awakening traditions like the Lübeck city festival, they argued, would help make up for losses in the familiar built environment of Heimat.[21] Heimat societies and publications proliferated in Hamburg and Bremen to an equal degree. By 1946, the Hamburg mayor, Max Brauer, addressing the sad state of their 'Heimat', noted that their 'glowing love' of Hamburg had reached greater heights than in times of the city's 'blossoming'. Hamburg, he believed, 'bleeding from a thousand wounds' needed this local sentiment to rebuild, strengthen community and fight for their local independence.[22] Eighty miles to the west, Brauer's fellow mayor in Bremen, Theodor Spitta, similarly recounted a growing localist spirit amidst the rubble, where Bremen's 'Polis spirit' fuelled rebuilding.[23] Spitta's description conveyed a notion of their localism as emerging from local 'democracy', while equating their tradition with the ancient Greek *polis*. City quarters also emerged as strong sites of Heimat sentiment, achieving a prominence that surpassed city quarter feeling prior to the bombings.[24] On an even more intimate level, small groups of localists regularly met in 'Heimat evenings' to foster community and face the challenges of the rubble world together.[25]

Though all three Hanseatic cities had strong pre-war local traditions, parallel turns to local geographies of home can be found throughout the ruins of post-war Germany. Whether it be a Konstanz archivist noting how Heimat feeling had become 'all the more valuable' in the ruins than it had been in peace time or a Cologne city report from 1945–46 recording the 'wild growing' Heimat enthusiasm that gripped the rubble, home towns emerged as crucial sites of reconstructing torn communities.[26] As the South Baden state president argued in 1946, after the disaster of war, they could begin anew by 'holding together' within the smaller circle of their 'Heimat'.[27] Hanseatic citizens, though having very different traditions and living hundreds of kilometres to the north, very much shared these sentiments.

'It Is Our Will to Exist': Local Heimat as a Site of Life-Affirmation

Singular focus on an abstract national community hardly seemed to offer the promise of a new beginning. While Nazism valorised sacrifice of individual life for abstract national glory, in the ruins, citizens associated emphasis on grandiose national community with death like never before. The nation had been eliminated as an actor and could no longer redeem exhausted citizens. As Mark Roseman argues, nationalist politics made little sense as the 'realities of power were against it'.[28] Reconstructing local communities, by contrast appeared to offer visions of peaceful civilian lives. Like many other Germans, Hanseaten increasingly described their *local* places of home as 'life-affirming'. Richard Bessel and other historians have raised the question of how war-torn citizens after 1945 created a sense of 'life after death'.[29] Local communities and local Heimat, I argue, were the primary geographies in which life after death was pursued. Reconstructing the local world was, to use the words of Hamburg mayor Paul Nevermann, doing away with 'mountains of death!'[30] Wilhelm Kaisen recalled Bremen's reconstruction in the same vein, asserting that local rebuilding represented the 'triumph of life over destruction'.[31] As the Hamburg author, Wolfgang Borchert, wrote in 1948, for him and Hamburg citizens, their rubble city was more than a 'pile of stones'. It represented their 'will to exist'; not just their desire to live 'anywhere or somehow'—'but to live here'. Borchert's prose recounts tableaux of Hamburg civilian life which may strike the contemporary ear as mundane: screeching street cars, ship sirens and seeing factory chimneys, the Alster Lake and gray-red rooftops, and feeling sea winds.[32] The prospect of such everyday life on a local stage resonated deeply with the early post-war psyche. Lines like Borchert's, in turn, found public resonance. Mayor Brauer repeated them, insisting that Hamburg was more than a harbour, economy or place of work. It was a 'life community' and a 'humanitarian community'. By clearing the rubble and maintaining local community, he believed Hamburger demonstrated their 'will to live'.[33]

Given its association with life-affirmation, local Heimat sentiment fuelled popular reconstruction fervour. The Bremer citizen Hans Kasten, in a poem on Bremen's reconstruction recounted with intensity how a 'life stream' still flowed the city, which he argued, demonstrated throughout its history the ability to pull itself out of the ashes. He ardently called on the community to rebuild, inspired by local tradition.[34] By evoking historical memories of his city rising from past disasters, Kasten reflected broader trends in historical memory in the rubble. Convincing themselves that their local community was a source of life after death required not simply idealistic memories of better times; it entailed drudging up the cities' worst historical moments. In Hamburg, locals emphasized historic destructions, plagues and disasters, including the 1842 Hamburg fire and how their 'Hanseatic spirit' pulled them through.[35] The same can be seen in Lübeck. An article in the *Vaterstädtische Blätter*, for example, emphasized 'the six historic destructions of Lübeck' from 1149 to 1945. After 1945, they undertook the 'sixth rebuilding'.[36] Beyond the Hanseatic cities, in rubble cities from Magdeburg to Cologne, locals similarly evoked destructive local histories, from the Thirty Years War to the Black Plague, to insist on reconstruction as a local tradition.[37] These historical memories transfigured reconstruction into a local tradition in the Hanseatic cities as they did elsewhere. Moreover, just as Hamburger viewed their city as their 'will to exist', local enthusiasts in places like Cologne reflected on how citizens in the rubble were filled with 'Heimat love' and a 'life-affirming optimism' that fuelled local reconstruction.[38] Hanseatic citizens' view of home town as a life-affirming geography, in short, followed a broader trend.

Hanseatic Democracy, World-Openness and Tolerance

In turning to local worlds to imagine new civilian lives, Hanseaten were not simply sticking their heads into local sands. Reflecting on broader issues, many citizens from both above and below re-shaped local identities to forge identification with a new democracy and international *rapprochement*. They further elucidated how rootedness in local communities was vital to democracy. While vast geographic spaces and communities are often viewed as those with the greatest potential to be progressive and modern, localists in the Hanseatic cities articulated how local rootedness was both harmonious with modernity and essential for democracy. Indeed, they often saw absence of local community as the essence of dictatorships, which, rather than respecting local rootedness, uprooted peoples for purposes of mass geopolitics. Comprehensible realms of community, early post-war localists frequently argued, were further needed as forums of democratic participation.

Articulations of a locally rooted democratic modernism can be found in all three cities and in localities throughout the Federal Republic, but let us consider in detail the example of Lübeck and its largest localist society, the *Vaterstädtische Vereinigung* (1949). Their society publication was filled with elaborations on the importance of local community to democracy, with their society emphasizing both devotion to Heimat and promoting democratic governance.[39] By tending to local traditions, forging local unity and strengthening neighbourly connections, they believed they could promote a 'new understanding of the world'. This meant fighting forces they claimed threatened democracy: 'massification', 'technocracy' and 'nihilism'—presumable by-products of a dark strain of modernity.[40] Society members continually re-iterated that comprehensible community was a *sine qua non* for democracy. Localities, they argued, acted as schools of democratic participation that gave everyday citizens political responsibilities.⁴¹ They further wrote of how emphasis on their local world contributed to federalized, de-centred ideas of nationhood. The society president, for example, drew on Hanseatic history to argue for a federalized 'German future from a Hanseatic spirit' instead of a Prussian-Nazi tradition that he argued subverted individualism. 'Connection to Heimat' in a 'Hanseatic-Lübeck disposition' seemingly provided the antidote.⁴² Identical theories of local rootedness as essential for democracy can be found throughout West Germany. Localists from the Southwest to the Rhineland argued that democracy was best realized within the reach of the 'Heimat-like parliament' with absence of local rootedness creating 'helplessness and passivity' which resulted in dictatorship.⁴³

Beyond emphasizing local communities as essential for democracy, citizens further promoted notions of democracy as a specifically Hanseatic value. Historians continue to debate the extent of the cities' 'democratic' histories.⁴⁴ Whatever the historical matter contained, reconfigured historical memory facilitated new identifications. Discourses in the rubble cities contained prolific considerations of how their local tradition could be useful for democratization and European unification. Already in 1947, one newspaper approvingly wrote of how locals in the Hanseatic cities were talking incessantly about the 'Hanseatic spirit' and its force in reconstruction.⁴⁵ Localists like the Lübecker, Hans Wittmack, were representative of this phenomenon in arguing for the use of local traditions to prop up a German and European federalism:

> It is the Hanseatic spirit which once encompassed all of Europe that must be reawakened. Hanseatic spirit is more than simply the spirit of a single city, whether it be as large and world-open and bold as Hamburg. Hanseatic spirit was a federalist spirit that filled an entire league of cities. It could, today, act as a model.⁴⁶

Lay localists like Wittmack were hardly alone in this view. In 1948, mayor Brauer addressed the Hamburger *Bürgerschaft*, calling for a federalist nation in which Hamburg would 'interweave' their local democratic traditions and encouraging Hamburgers to profess their allegiance to their city's 'healthful republican and democratic traditions'.⁴⁷ Brauer's colleague on the Weser, Wilhelm Kaisen also marshalled local history to forge identities rooted in Hanseatic republicanism, democracy and federalism. During his twenty-year tenure, the SPD (Sozialdemokratische Partei Deutschlands) mayor argued for local democratic decentralization and Bremer independence.⁴⁸ Bremen, he believed, must remain a free Hanseatic city for the sake of its republican principles, position in world trade and importance to having a federalist nation and a 'federalist Europe'.⁴⁹ Such narratives of Hanseatic democracy proved useful in efforts to maintain their local independence, with the Nazis having eliminated hundreds of years of local independence in Bremen and Lübeck. While the American occupiers restored Bremen's federal statehood, Lübecker pressed for a popular vote on the issue throughout the 1950s.

While ideas of Hanseatic democracy proved useful in the independence issue, it hardly explains the idea's emergence, particularly given that West German localists not facing the same issue fashioned similar local identity tenets, from 'Swabian-Alemannic democracy' to 'Colognian democracy'.[50] The phenomenon was ultimately more about attempts to affiliate local identities with a new post-war order.

Along with reformulation of local historical memories, citizens further re-invented local traditions to promote democracy and internationalism as local values. A range of traditions prove illustrative, including Hamburg's re-invention of its harbour birthday, used after 1945 to promote locally rooted ideas of world-openness and international *rapprochement*. Beyond the Hanseatic cities, locals in cities like Cologne similarly re-invented local ritual traditions and depicted them as embodying local values of democracy, tolerance and world-openness.[51] One of the most telling examples in the Hanseatic cities, however, was the re-awakening and re-invention of Lübeck's *Volks- und Erinnerungsfest*. The tradition was first celebrated in Lübeck by the 1848 revolutionaries and, until 1870, was rooted in desire for German unity and enthusiasm for the local constitution. Between 1870 and 1914, the tradition morphed into a nationalist and militarist celebration, shedding democratic undertones, with the Nazis later seeking to obliterate memory of 1848 altogether, depicting it as 'ancient Germanic' festival.[52] Amidst the post-war local cultural renaissance, both lay Heimat societies and the city government cooperated in reviving the tradition, which they stripped of nationalist elements, reawakening instead remembrance of 1848 and constitutional democracy. Perhaps due to fears that sharp-shooting events, held since 1848, would counter the message of local democracy and anti-militarism, they were not revived.[53] At the peak of the tradition's revival, its organizing committee couched the festival as an opportunity to build solidarity with expellees and as a tradition that memorialized the democratic 1848 revolutions and their democratic constitution.[54] In the ensuing years, diverse interpretations of the tradition were dominated by ideas of it as a deeply democratic tradition that honoured Lübeck's constitution and the freedom-seeking of 1848.[55]

Advocation of democracy as a local value paralleled promotion of Hanseatic world-openness as assisting in international *rapprochement*. Ideals of localist world-openness highlighted the transnational significance of local identificational reconstruction. Almost immediately after 1945, local enthusiasts and politicians jointly articulated the international ameliorating influence of Hanseatic world-openness. In May 1945, Rudolf Petersen, a Hamburg tradesman who had just become mayor, addressed war-torn citizens by drawing on their Hanseatic history of trade and international contact. While the Nazis defined the city as a hub of expansionary German power, Petersen defined it as one of 'connection of international peoples' and as a door of reconciliation between Germany and the outside world. Their history, he further argued, made them a 'mediator' between Germany and the Anglo-Saxon world and notions of freedom.[56] These principles would be enshrined in the city constitution, which cited Hamburg's duty to be 'in the spirit of peace, a mediator between all people and lands of the globe'.[57] Such a narrative of local community overwrote nationalist and national socialist spatial narratives of the cities as exit points of expansionary German power.

A continuous trope of local identity rather than a new one best illustrates post-war changes in ideas of localness: the representation of their cities (particularly Hamburg) as being 'gates to the world'. The term existed since at least the nineteenth century. Yet, being a 'gate to the world' bore different meanings in different times. Was the gate for exit, entrance, or both? In Nazi propaganda, it was the gate through which national power exited onto a global stage. After 1945, the concept, as used in popular Heimat publications like the *Hamburger Journal*, was a gate of 'openness' and 'breadth' rooted in international mutuality, cooperation and a 'willingness to give and to receive'.[58] The popular appeal of such local self-definitions is reflected in the deluge of early post-war Heimat publications. In Bernard Meyer-Marwitz's *Hamburg, Heimat am Strom* from 1947, for example, he wrote that the city knew 'no boundaries' and stood 'at the gate of infinity, open to all five continents and the seven seas'.[59] The local author Ernst Schnabel described Hamburg as the world contained within a local nutshell, while his fellow Heimat enthusiast in Bremen, Hermann Tardel, cited two components of the Bremer: the first revolving around house, family, city and state, and the second looking into the distance of foreign countries.[60] The Hamburg philosopher Hans Driesch similarly wrote that being a Hamburger combined both 'particularism and world citizenship'.[61] This re-definition of localities in border and maritime regions had parallels elsewhere. Just as Hanseatic citizens inverted nationalist narratives, so too did Rhinelanders abandon notions of themselves as 'watches on the Rhine', defining themselves instead as a world-open 'bridge' to the West.[62] Similarly, in the South-west, regionalists abandoned notions of their region as a fortress of Germanness. In advocating for the creation of differently bordered federal states, regionalists competed over which particular regional state vision would act as the better 'bridge' to the West.[63]

Appealing to Hanseatic world-openness to identify with international reconciliation was largely a cognitive task. Applying such local values to outsiders on the local stage took practising tolerance and openness to a different level entirely. Ideas of local world-openness and tolerance hardly transformed their local communities into utopias of acceptance. Nor did democratic identities make them adept practioners of democracy. Rather, these tenets of local identity represented tools that more inclusively inclined localists wielded to both promote conceptual identification with democracy and to mitigate select exclusionary mechanisms of community formation. The most prominent group of outsiders that early post-war locals faced was East German expellees, whose arrival in large numbers shocked Hanseatic citizens. Hamburg became home to three hundred twenty-seven thousand, making up 18.8 per cent of the population, with 8.6 per cent of Bremen's population made up of expellees.[64] Neither witnessed the tidal wave that hit Lübeck, which had a population of two hundred forty thousand residents, ninety thousand of whom were expellees.[65] Lübeckers feared that the outsider influx would extinguish their local community. A Heimat society which later became a strident voice of expellee inclusion, the *Vaterstädtische Vereinigung* cited both physical destruction and expellee influx as motivating their founding. Years later an expellee himself would sit at the head of the localist society.[66]

So what of 'Hanseatic tolerance' vis-à-vis such outsiders? How, after an era defined by exclusionary community formation practices did locals seek to fashion more permeable and inclusive reconstructed communities? Research for Hamburg and Bremen has illustrated the many challenges and exclusions that expellees faced during the early years when competition for resources was most pervasive.[67] After the shock of expellee influx subsided and competition for scant resources relented, however, many progressive localists countered local rejection of newcomers by depicting expellee embrace and integration as a performance of Hanseatic world-openness and tolerance. At expellee gatherings in the Hanseatic cities, many native Hanseaten drew on local historical memories of outsider influx into their cities to argue for integration as a tenet of local identity.[68] The *Vaterstädtische Vereinigung*, after brief fears over expellee influx, quickly emphasized integration, inclusion of expellees in local traditions and giving expellees a new sense of Heimat. By the early 1950s, the society re-iterated how it aimed to tend to the Heimat sentiment of both old and new residents and how all could become members.[69] Some Heimat society members even bragged about the viability of their city by pointing to expellee influx.[70]

Amidst the challenges of integration, goodwill toward the expellees also came from other localist societies, such as the *Verein für Heimatschutz in Lübeck*. The expellees, the society president argued in 1946, 'will bear their loss much easier when they have a feeling of belonging in Lübeck'. The primary goal of his society, he argued, was to promote attachment to Heimat, which for many was a 'new Heimat'.[71] The Lübeck Senator Hans Ewers similarly held up as a Lübecker tradition the capability to make outsiders feel as 'eager Lübecker' shortly after they set foot in the city. Lübeck, he believed, had a secret 'power of attraction'.[72] Other Lübecker localists argued for use of their city's revived ritual traditions to integrate outsiders and give them a 'connection to their new Heimat'.[73]

Such examples should not be equated with a rosy and smooth path to integration, nor should they lead us to overlook strong Western hostilities vis-à-vis the expellees. Counter examples could be readily found and conceptual identification with world-openness and tolerance did not equate to adept practice of inclusion. Localist groups, like the 'Society of Born Hamburger' continued exclusionary practices, allowing neither native women nor men born outside of Hamburg to join.[74] Women's exclusion reflected a misogynist and classist strain of Hanseatic tradition which viewed the successful businessman as the truest Hanseat. The society lexicon was filled not with words like world-openness, but rather with terms like *Quidjes*, local dialect for 'the non-Hamburger'. The society, founded amidst outsider influx amidst late nineteenth-century urbanization, saw itself in the post-war period as again protecting local culture against outsiders.[75]

Despite the persistence of exclusionary practices, popular identification with local tolerance and world-openness encouraged more inclusive ideas of community. The resonance of such ideas can be seen throughout the deluge of early post-war localist publications, which included reflections like those of a 1955 *Bremer Heimatchronik*, which argued:

> It is a an essential criteria of all true living communities with promising futures that they attract into their orbit those people who have come from the outside and impress and instil in them their natures without completely divesting them of the unique characteristics that they bring with them.[76]

Localists like the author of the *Heimatchronik* did not see the turn to Heimat as incompatible with embracing outsiders and internationalist orientations; they saw them instead as mutually re-enforcing. Localists beyond the Hanseatic cities did the same, including Rhinelanders who evoked Roman histories and histories of outsider influx to argue for embrace of Italian immigrants as harmonious with local tradition.[77]

Such attempts to reconstruct community along more inclusive lines extended beyond the early post-war years. In the late 1960s and afterwards, figures like the Jewish SPD mayor, Herbert Weichmann, frequently promoted ideas of Hamburger tolerance, freedom, republicanism and liberalism.[78] Such tropes could also be used to argue for integration of new foreign immigrants, who often faced significant exclusion. One contemporary Hamburg philosopher has emphasized Hamburg's localness as defined by its embrace of other nationalities.[79] Other outsider groups have insisted that local openness should mean acceptance of their group. Hamburg's gay population in the early years of gay liberation, for example, appealed to ideas of Hamburg's world-openness.[80] While the strength of exclusionary community formation practices should not be underestimated, in the contemporary cities, ideas of Hanseatic tolerance and world-openness remain useful tools in the progressive arsenal. The tropes of local identity that emerged from early post-war reconstruction, in short, had dynamic afterlives and their subsequent reformulations are worthy of continued attention.

Conclusion

In the wake of destruction, dislocation, the submersion of everyday private life into global struggle and the discrediting of nationalism, local communities came to the fore as crucial sites of reconstruction in early West Germany. This process proved central to the abandonment of a grandiose vision of national community as a redemptive force—a shift that informed cultural demobilization and had important ramifications for culture and politics. Local places of home represented geographies where citizens imagined 'life-affirming' civilian existences and found flexible sources of identity that facilitated identification with a new system. Emphasis on 'Hanseatic democracy' and 'Hanseatic republicanism' strengthened identification with both the post-war search for democracy and Western *rapprochement*. Following an era defined by exclusionary practices of community formation, many citizens further reformulated local identities to encourage more permeable notions of community. Of course, claims to democracy, world-openness and tolerance as local traditions should not be mistaken as descriptive. They neither helped Germans come to grips with their complicity in the crimes or the recent past, nor did they do away with exclusionary and undemocratic practices. Rather, they represented proscriptive utterances, significant in how they facilitated conceptual identifications with democracy and more open forms of community formation and in how they could be reformulated by subsequent generations.

The cities offer but one example of how alternative sources of identity beyond the nation could prove useful in post-war eras of reconstruction. We see a similar phenomenon in Kührer-Wielach's chapter on interwar Transylvania and in Vahtikari's chapter on post-war Helsinki. Much evidence, moreover, suggests a similar preoccupation throughout war-torn Europe with reconstructing local communities and saving local culture and uniqueness. Experiences, however, still differed along national and state lines, as Mark Mazower has pointed out.[81] West Germany's defeated and occupied status, the burdens of national identities and the requirement to rapidly adapt to a new system made localities uniquely suited as sites of identificational reformulations. In Britain, France, the Netherlands and Belgium, by contrast, the nation stood out more prominently as a community of reconstruction.[82] At the same time, as we see in Stefan Couperus's chapter, urban planners, governors and citizens in Britain strongly emphasised the need to reconstruct local communities as sites of belonging and bearers of urban citizenship and democracy. Looking at ravaged eastern German cities, we see a similar obsession with local communities, though citizens were limited in their ability to publically articulate and re-shape local identities.[83] Even in Soviet cities, we find local efforts to saving local traditions in a way that could thwart centralised national reconstruction plans.[84]

Though those beyond Germany rarely faced the same identificational challenges, war-torn Europeans broadly shared experiences of local communities ripped apart through destruction, dislocation and death. Many Europeans faced flattened local landscapes that represented not only material monuments of local culture, history and identity, but also deeply meaningful sites of personal life narratives. The resulting feared loss of local community, tradition and personal geographies of home together formed a common thread that transcended state and national borders, with many post-war citizens deeply preoccupied with repairing local communities as a crucial task of post-war reconstruction.

Notes

1. The author would like to thank Helmut Walser Smith and Celia Applegate for their feedback on this project, as well as participants of the Greifswald conference on *Hansische Identitäten* and the Nijmegen conference on Reconstructing Communities.
2. Arthur Dickens, diary entry, 31 July 1945, in Dickens, *Lübeck*, 30–32.
3. Dickens, diary entry, 9 July 1945, in Ibid., 29.
4. Much previous work on the Heimat concept has depicted its post-war history as simply about repressing the past. See Knoch, *Das Erbe*, and Confino, *Germany*. Alon Confino, whose approach reduces Heimat to a mere strategy of imagining nation, neglects how Heimat after 1945 centred around a ruptured relationship between individual and lost local places of home. Looking at tourism to get at post-war Heimat, he argues that it was simply about depicting the nation as 'victim'.
5. See Wagner-Kyora, *Wiederaufbau*; Clapson and Larkham, *Blitz*; Diefendorf, *Wake of the War*; Durth and Gutschow, *Träume in Trümmern*; Gutschow and Düwel, *Fortgewischt*.
6. Much work on post-war cultural-political reconstruction, by contrast, has focused on the national and state levels and on elite actors. See Moeller, *West Germany*; Jackson, *Civilizing the Enemy*; Niethammer, *Deutschland danach*. For works on German democratization that downplay early democratic identifications, see Jarausch, *Die Umkehr*; Herbert, *Wandlungsprozesse*; Benz, *Auftrag Demokratie*.
7. For contrasting interpretations of localist contributions to post-war federalism as democratic versus 'anti-modern', see Heil, *Gemeinden*, and Huhn, *Lernen aus der Geschichte?*
8. Applegate, *Nation of Provincials*.
9. This is not to say that locals throughout Western Europe did not reformulate local identities for other purposes—particularly amidst radical changes in the local built environment.
10. Heitmann, *Ende des Zweiten Weltkrieges*, 22; Tormin, *Schwere Weg*, 39–41.
11. Wedermeier, "Vorwort," 7; Schwarzwälder, *Geschichte*, 599.
12. Meyer, "Vom Ersten Weltkrieg," 724–28.
13. Luise Klinsmann, "Kulturpolitik und Kulturpflege Lübecks," *Vaterstädtische Blätter* 9, no. 5 (May 1958): 3.
14. Tormin, *Schwere Weg*, 39–41.
15. "Drang zur Heimat," *Hamburger Echo*, 10 April 1946. All translations are by the author unless indicated otherwise.
16. "Heimatlos in der eigenen Heimat," *Hamburger Echo*, 30 October 1946.
17. "Zwischen Schutt und Ruinen," *Hamburger Echo*, 20 April 1946.
18. "Im Grimm," *Hamburger Echo*, 4 February 1947.
19. Jahresbericht 1948/49, Verein für Heimatschutz, nr. 9, 05.4-085, Archiv der Hansestadt Lübeck (hereafter cited as AHL).
20. 30 Jahre Vaterstädtische, Vaterstädtische Vereinigung, nr. 5, 05.4-81, AHL.
21. "Um unser altes traditionelles Lübecker Volksfest," *Vaterstädtische Blätter* 4, no. 7 (July 1953): 1.
22. Max Brauer, "Rede in der Sitzung der Hamburger Bürgerschaft am 22. November 1946," in *Nüchternen Sinnes*, ed. Brauer, 24–25.

23. Theodor Spitta, "Ansprache an Professor Carl Jacob Burckhardt am 1 Februar 1952," in 'Keine andere Rücksicht,' Spitta, 121.
24. Thiessen, *Eingebrannt*, 223.
25. "Stimmen der Heimat," *Hamburger Echo*, 17 April 1946.
26. Feger, *Konstanz*, 11; Statistischen Amt der Stadt Köln, *Verwaltungsbericht*, 50–55.
27. Leo Wohleb, "Rede vor den Delegierten der Landestagung der Badischen Christlich-Sozialen Volkspartei, 24 February 1946," in *Humanist*, eds. Ludwig-Weinacht and Maier, 171.
28. Roseman, "Defeat and Stability," 263.
29. Bessel and Schumann, *Life after Death*.
30. Paul Nevermann, "Ein Eigenes Gedicht," in *Metaller*, ed. Nevermann, 48.
31. Grundsteinlegung der Synagoge am Freitag, den 29 Janr. 1960, Archiv Wilhelm Kaisen, 7,97/0, nr. 11, vol.11 (1960), Staatsarchiv der Hansestadt Bremen (hereafter cited as StAHB).
32. Wolfgang Borchert, "In Hamburg," in *Lieder*, ed. Neumann, 77.
33. Max Brauer, "Ansprache zum Überseetag auf dem Werftgelände von Blohm & Voß am 7. Mai 1952," in *Nüchternen Sinnes*, ed. Brauer, 243.
34. Hans Kasten, "An Bremen: Mai 1945," in *Bremen*, ed. Kasten, 30.
35. Thiessen, *Eingebrannt*.
36. "Lübecks dunkle Tage," *Vaterstädtische Blätter* 5, no. 6 (June 1954): 5–6.
37. Arnold, *Allied Air War*, 61–67; Hoßdorf and Firmenich-Richartz, "Et Gespens om Schötzefeß," in *Rheinische Puppenspiele*, ed. Amt für kölnisches Volkstum, 64.
38. Klersch, *Volkstum*, 26–28.
39. Gerhard Boldt, Speech, 24 April 1969, Vaterstädtische Vereinigung, 05.4–81, nr.1, AHL.
40. "Eine Doppelaufgabe der 'Vaterstädtischen'," *Vaterstädtische Blätter* 6, no. 10 (October 1955): 2; Hans Wittmack, "Unter uns," *Vaterstädtische Blätter* 7, no. 3 (March 1956): 2.
41. "Gemeindefreiheit-Schlüssel zur wahren Demokratie," *Vaterstädtische Blätter* 8, no. 4 (April 1957): 1–2.
42. Hans Wittmack, "Deutsche Zukunft aus hansischem Geist," *Vaterstädtische Blätter* 6 (June 1965): 1.
43. Joseph Klersch, "Volkstum und Volkstumspflege," in *Heimatchronik*, ed. Klersch, 82; Walter von Cube, "Um die Selbständigkeit des Landes Baden," in *Vom See bis an des Maines Strand*, ed. Arbeitsgemeinschaft der Badener, Bundesministerium für Angelegenheiten des Bundesrates und der Länder (B144), inv.nr. 253, Bundesarchiv-Koblenz.
44. See Schramm, *Hamburg*; Evans, *Death in Hamburg*; Hohendahl, *Patriotism*; and Jenkins, *Provincial Modernity*.
45. "Geschichte als Lehrmeisterin," *Westfalenpost*, 7 June 1947, Hansischer Geschichtsverein, 05.4–30, nr. 438, AHL.
46. Hans Wittmack, "Hat Lübeck noch genug geistige Substanz?," *Lübeckische Blätter* 92/116, no. 4 (18 February 1956): 42–43.
47. Max Brauer, "Zur Verfassung der Freien und Hansestadt Hamburg," in *Nüchternen Sinnes*, ed. Brauer, 57–63.
48. Wilhelm Kaisen, "Gefahren für Bremen," *Weser-Kurier*, 12 January 1946, reprinted in *Occupation*, ed. Staatsarchiv Bremen, 30–31.
49. Wesen und Geist einer Hansestadt, 7 March 1953, 1–4, Archiv Wilhelm Kaisen, 7,97/0, nr.4, vol.4, (1953) StAHB.
50. Feger, *Schwäbisch-Alemannische Demokratie*; DeWaal, "The Reinvention of Tradition".
51. DeWaal, "The Reinvention of Tradition".
52. Jaacks, *Lübecker Volks- und Erinnerungsfest*, 15–26, 37–38, 47–69, 137–39, 158–64.

The Turn to Local Communities 147

53. Ibid., 82–90, 128–31, 166.
54. Volksfestkomitee Lübeck, *Lübecker Volksfest 1957*, "Zum Geleit," and Conrad Neckels, "'Hurra, Schiebenscheeten!' Das Lübecker Volksfest entsteht wieder im alten Glanz," Vaterstädtische Vereinigung von 1949, 05.4–81, nr. 45, AHL.
55. Jaacks, 10–11.
56. Antrittsrede des Hamburger Bürgermeisters Rudolf Petersen, 16 Mai 1945, 131–1 II Senatskanzlei I, nr.2798, StAHH.
57. Drexlius and Weber, *Verfassung*, 1.
58. Untitled, *Hamburger Journal* 1, no. 1 (December 1953): I.
59. Meyer-Marwitz, *Hamburg*, 5.
60. Tardel, *Bremen*, 8.
61. Hans Driesch, "Lebenserinnerungen," in *Hamburg*, ed. Thomsen, 159.
62. Pünder, *Rhein und Europa*; Jürgen Brügger, "Das Kölner Domjubiläum 1948," in *Köln*, ed. Dülffer, 219–23; Karl Arnold, "Heimat und Jugend," *Alt-Köln* 8, no. 9 (September 1954): 33.
63. Among other examples, see Heimatbund Badenerland, *Baden*.
64. "Bevölkerungsbewegung 1956 in Hamburg," *Monatschrift: Verein geborener Hamburger* 60, no. 1 (February 1957): 2; Aschenbeck, *Bremen hat Zuzugssperre*, 11.
65. "Das neue Gesicht der alten Stadt," *Vaterstädtische Blätter* 1 (June 1950): 2; "Lübeck 1960derne Großstadt mit hansischer Tradition," *Lübeckische Blätter*, 1 January 1967.
66. "30 Jahre der 'Vaterstädtischen'. Die 'Vaterstädtische' am Scheidewege," *Vaterstädtische Blätter* 17, no. 4/5 (April/May 1966): 1, Vaterstädtische Vereinigung, 05.4–81, AHL.
67. Esenwein-Rothe, *Eingliederung*, 108–40.
68. Edgar Engelhard, "Tag der Deutschen Heimat," 12 September 1953, 131–1 II, nr. 1243, StAHH; Ansprache von Bürgermeister Max Brauer anläßlich der Eröffnung der Ostdeutschen Heimatwoche, 135–1 VI, Staatliche Pressestelle VI., nr. 341, StAHH; "Begrüssung zum Tag der Heimat," "Tag der Heimat Hamburg 1966," "Heimat, Vaterland, Europa," "Tag der Heimat im Jahr der Menschenrechte," "Wahrer Friede wurzelt in Gerechtigkeit," 131–1 II, nr. 1243, StAHH; Schier, *Aufnahme und Eingliederung*, 11, 258–65.
69. "Wie hören wir des Volkes Stimme?," *Vaterstädtische Blätter* 2, no. 10 (October 1951): 3; "Zum Geleit," *Vaterstädtische Blätter* 1, no. 1 (June 1950): 1.
70. ". . . durch künstliche Atmung erhalten," *Vaterstädtische Blätter* 5, no. 10 (October 1954): 1.
71. "Heimatschutz vor neuen Aufgaben," 31 July 1946, 05.4–085, nr. 16, Verein für Heimatschutz, AHL.
72. Hans Ewers, "Stadtgemeinde oder Stadtstaat?" *Lübeckische Blätter* 15 (April 1956): 85–87.
73. "Fangen wir an!," *Vaterstädtische Blätter* 3, no. 8 (August 1952): 1. "Um unser altes traditionelles Lübecker Volksfest," *Vaterstädtische Blätter* 7, no. 4 (July 1953): 2; Paul Brockhaus, "Ein Neues Lübecker Volksfest," *Lübeckische Blätter* 88, no. 8 (27 April 1952): 77–79.
74. "Hamburg-Tor zur Welt," *Vün Düt un Dat un Allerwat ut Hamborg* 68, no. 7 (July 1965): 11; "Tradition und Gegenwart," *Monatschrift: Verein geborener Hamburger* 60, no. 3 (April 1957): 1; "Unser 70 jähriges Vereins," *Vün Düt un Dat un Allerwat ut Hamborg* (February 1967): 4.
75. "Unser 70 jähriges Vereins—ABC," *Vün Düt un Dat un Allerwat ut Hamborg* (May 1967): 4, Adolf Heitmann, "Die Bedeutung unserer Zeitschrift," *Monatschrift: Verein geborener Hamburger* 60, no. 10 (November 1957): 1, "Heimotleev mut lüchten as ne hevenshoge Flamm . . .," *Vün Düt un Dat un Allerwat ut Hamborg* (September 1961): 5, "Hamburgisches Wesen muß bewahrt bleiben," *Hamburger Abendblatt*, 11 January 1957, 731–8, Zeitungsausschnittsammlung A 507, StAHH.

76. Prüser, *Heimatchronik*, 247.
77. Adam Wrede, "Um die Erhaltung Kölner Eigenart," *Alt-Köln* 2, no. 3 (March 1948): 9–10; Flecken, *Gestaltung der Heimat*, 15–16.
78. Herbert Weichmann, "Erklärung vor der Bürgerschaft am 16 Juni 1965, Zur Eröffnung des Hamburg Centrums am 20. September 1966, Zur Matthiae-Mahlzeit im Rathaus am 23 Februar 1968, Das Liberale Hamburg, and Auf dem Boden der Demokratie," in Weichmann, *Freiheit und Pflicht*, ed. Vogel, 7, 82, 98, 112–13, 123, 154, 181.
79. Hans-Dieter Loose, "Vor der Geschichte besser dastehen," in Italiaander, *Vielvölkerstadt*, 7–12.
80. Voigt and Weinrich, *Hamburg ahoi*, 3, 6.
81. Mazower, "Reconstruction," 28.
82. Edgerton, "War, Reconstruction," 29–46; Conway, "The Making," 303. For differences in the meaning and terms of reconstructing in East-Central Europe, see Case, "Reconstruction in East-Central Europe," 71–102.
83. Arnold, *The Allied Air War*.
84. Qualls, *Ruins to Reconstruction*.

Bibliography

Applegate, Celia. *A Nation of Provincials: The German Idea of Heimat*. Berkeley, CA: University of California Press, 1990.

Arnold, Jörg. *The Allied Air War and Urban Memory: The Legacy of Strategic Bombing in Germany*. Cambridge: Cambridge University Press, 2011.

Aschenbeck, Nils. *Bremen hat Zuzugssperre. Vertriebene und Flüchtlinge nach dem Krieg in Bremen*. Bremen: Temmen, 1998.

Benz, Wolfgang. *Auftrag Demokratie: die Gründungsgeschichte der Bundesrepublik und die Entstehung der DDR 1945–1949*. Berlin: Metropol, 2009.

Bessel, Richard and Dirk Schumann, eds. *Life after Death: Approaches to a Cultural and Social History of Europe during the 1940s and 1950s*. Cambridge: Cambridge University Press, 2003.

Brauer, Max. *Nüchternen Sinnes und Heissen Herzens. Reden und Ansprachen*. Hamburg: Auerdruck, 1956.

Case, Holly. "Reconstruction in East-Central Europe: Clearing the Rubble of Cold War Politics." *Past and Present* Supplement 6 (2011): 71–102.

Clapson, Mark and Peter Larkham, eds. *The Blitz and Its Legacy: Wartime Destruction to Post-War Reconstruction*. Farnham: Ashgate, 2013.

Confino, Alon. *Germany as a Culture of Remembrance: Promises and Limits of Writing History*. Chapel Hill, NC: University of North Carolina University Press, 2006.

Conway, Martin. "The Making of Democratic Stability." In *Creative Crises of Democracy*, edited by Joris Gijsenbergh et al., 291–308. Brussels: Peter Lang, 2012.

DeWaal, Jeremy. "The Reinvention of Tradition: Form, Meaning, and Local Identity in Modern Cologne Carnival." *Central European History* 46 (2013): 495–532.

Dickens, Geoffrey. *Lübeck 1945. Tagebuchauszüge von Arthur Geoffrey Dickens*. Edited by Gerhard Meyer. Lübeck: Schmidt-Römhild, 1986.

Diefendorf, Jeffry M. *In the Wake of the War: The Reconstruction of German Cities after World War II*. Oxford: Oxford University Press, 1993.

Drexlius, Wilhelm and Renatus Weber, eds. *Die Verfassung der Freien und Hansestadt Hamburg vom 6. Juni 1952*. Berlin: Gruyter, 1972.

Dülffer, Jost, ed. *Köln in den 50er Jahren. Zwischen Tradition und Modernisierung*. Cologne: SH-Verlag, 2001.

Durth, Werner and Niels Gutschow. *Träume in Trümmern. Stadtplanung 1940–1950*. Munich: Taschenbuch, 1993.

Edgerton, David. "War, Reconstruction, Ad the Nationalization of Britain, 1939–1951." *Past and Present* Supplement 6 (2011): 29–46.

Esenwein-Rothe, Ingeborg. *Die Eingliederung der Flüchtlinge in die Stadtstaaten Bremen und Hamburg*. Berlin: Duncker & Humblot, 1955.

Evans, Richard. *Death in Hamburg: Society and Politics in the Cholera Years, 1830–1910*. Oxford: Clarendon, 1987.

Feger, Otto. *Schwäbisch-Alemannische Demokratie. Aufruf und Programm*. Konstanz: Weller, 1946.

Feger, Otto. *Konstanz. Aus der Vergangenheit einer alten Stadt*. Konstanz: Weller, 1947.

Flecken, Adolf. *Gestaltung der Heimat nach rheinischer Eigenart*. Neuss: Gesellschaft für Buchdruckerei, 1966.

Gutschow, Niels and Jörn Düwel. *Fortgewischt sind alle überflüssigen Zutaten. Hamburg 1943. Zerstörung und Städtebau*. Berlin: Lukas, 2008.

Heil, Peter. *Gemeinden sind Wichtiger als Staaten: Idee und Wirklichkeit des kommunalen Neuanfangs in Rheinland-Pfalz, 1945–1947*. Mainz: Hase & Koehler, 1997.

Heimatbund, Badenerland, ed. *Baden als Bundesland*. Waldkirch: Waldkircher, 1955.

Heitmann, Jan. *Das Ende des Zweiten Weltkrieges in Hamburg*. Frankfurt: Peter Lang, 1990.

Herbert, Ulrich, ed. *Wandlungsprozesse in Westdeutschland. Belastung, Integration und Liberalisierung, 1945–1980*. Göttingen: Wallstein, 2002.

Hohendahl, Peter Uwe, ed. *Patriotism, Cosmopolitanism and National Culture: Public Culture in Hamburg 1700–1933*. Amsterdam: Rodopi, 1994.

Huhn, Jochem. *Lernen aus der Geschichte? Historische Argumente in der westdeutschen Föderalismusdiskussion 1945–1949*. Melsungen: Kasseler Forschungen, 1990.

Italiaander, Rolf. *Vielvölkerstadt. Hamburg und seine Nationaltäten*. Düsseldorf: Droste, 1986.

Jaacks, Gisela. *Das Lübecker Volks- und Erinnerungsfest*. Hamburg: Museum für Hamburgische Geschichte, 1971.

Jackson, Patrick Thadeus. *Civilizing the Enemy: German Reconstruction and the Invention of the West*. Ann Arbor, MI: University of Michigan Press, 2006.

Jarausch, Konrad. *Die Umkehr. Deutsche Wandlungen, 1945–1995*. Munich: Deutsche Verlags-Anstalt, 2004.

Jenkins, Jennifer. *Provincial Modernity: Local Culture and Liberal Politics in Fin-de-Siècle Hamburg*. Ithaca, NY: Cornell University Press, 2003.

Kasten, Hans, ed. *Bremen in der Dichtung*. Bremen: Bremer Schlüssel, 1946.

Klersch, Joseph, ed. *Heimatchronik des Landkreises Köln*. Cologne: Archiv für Deutsche Heimatpflege, 1954.

Klersch, Joseph. *Volkstum und Volksleben in Köln*. Cologne: Bachem, 1965.

Knoch, Habbo, ed. *Das Erbe der Provinz. Heimatkultur und Geschichtspolitik nach 1945*. Göttingen: Wallstein, 2001.

Mazower, Mark. "Reconstruction: The Historiographical Issues." *Past and Present* Supplement 6 (2011): 17–28.

Meyer, Gerhard. "Vom Ersten Weltkrieg bis 1985." In *Lübeckische Geschichte*, edited by Antjekathrin Graßmann, 724–28. Lübeck: Schmidt-Römhild, 1988.

Meyer-Marwitz, Bernard, ed. *Hamburg Heimat am Strom*. Hamburg: Hamburgische Bücherei, 1947.

Moeller, Robert, ed. *West Germany under Construction: Politics, Society, and Culture in the Adenauer Era*. Ann Arbor, MI: University of Michigan Press, 1997.
Neumann, Paul, ed. *Lieder und Sprüche auf Hamburg*. Hamburg: Hans Christians, 1960.
Nevermann, Paul. *Metaller-Bürgermeister–Mieterpräsident*. Cologne: Deutschen Mieterbundes, 1977.
Niethammer, Lutz. *Deutschland danach. Postfaschistische Gesellschaft und nationales Gedächtnis*. Bonn: Dietz, 1999.
Prüser, Friedrich. *Heimatchronik der Freien und Hansestadt Bremen*. Cologne: Archiv für Deutsche Heimatpflege, 1955.
Pünder, Hermann, ed. *Der Rhein und Europa*. Cologne: Bachem, 1947.
Qualls, Karl. *From Ruins to Reconstruction: Urban Identity in Soviet Sevastopol after World War II*. Ithaca: Cornell University Press, 2010.
Roseman, Mark. "Defeat and Stability: 1918, 1945 and 1989 in Germany." In *Three Postwar Eras in Comparison: Western Europe, 1918–1945–1989*, edited by Carl Levy and Mark Roseman, 257–75. Basingstroke: Palgrave, 2002.
Schier, Siegfried. *Die Aufnahme und Eingliederung von Flüchtlingen und Vertriebenen in der Hansestadt Lübeck*. Lübeck: Schmidt-Römhild, 1982.
Schramm, Percy. *Hamburg. Ein Sonderfall in der Geschichte Deutschlands*. Hamburg: Hans Christians, 1964.
Schwarzwälder, Herbert. *Geschichte der Freien Hansestadt Bremen*, Vol. 4. Hamburg: Hans Christians, 1985.
Spitta, Theodor. *Keine andere Rücksicht als die auf das Gemeine Beste. Briefe und Reden*. Bonn: Bouvier, 1997.
Staatsarchiv, Bremen, ed. *Occupation, Enclave, State. Die Wiederbegründung des Landes Bremen nach dem Zweiten Weltkrieg. Dokumente zu Politik und Alltag*. Bremen: Staatsarchiv Bremen, 2007.
Statistischen, Amt der Stadt Köln. *Verwaltungsbericht der Stadt Köln, 1945/47*. Cologne, 1947.
Tardel, Hermann, ed. *Bremen im Sprichwort, Reim und Volkslied*. Bremen: Bremer Schlüssel, 1947.
Thiessen, Malthe. *Eingebrannt ins Gedächtnis. Hamburgs Gedenken an Luftkrieg und Kriegsende 1943 bis 2005*. Hamburg: Dölling und Galitz, 2007.
Thomsen, Helmuth, ed. *Hamburg*. Munich: Prestel, 1962.
Tormin, Walter. *Der schwere Weg zur Demokratie. Politischer Neuaufbau in Hamburg 1945/46*. Hamburg: Landeszentrale für politische Bildung, 1995.
Voigt, Wolfgang and Klaus Weinrich. *Hamburg ahoi. Der Schwule Lotse durch die Hansestadt*. Berlin: Rosa Winkel, 1981.
Wagner-Kyora, Georg, ed. *Wiederbau europäischer Städte. Rekonstruktionen, die Moderne und die lokale Identitätspolitik seit 1945*. Stuttgart: Steiner, 2014.
Wedermeier, Klaus. "Vorwort." In *Kriegsende in Bremen. Erinnerungen, Berichte, Dokumente*, edited by Hartmut Müller and Günther Rohdenburg, 7. Bremen: Temmen, 1995.
Weichmann, Herbert. *Von Freiheit und Pflicht. Auszüge aus Reden des Bürgermeisters der Freien und Hansestadt Hamburg*. Edited by Paul Vogel. Hamburg: Hans Christians, 1969.
Wohleb, Leo. *Humanist und Politiker*. Edited by Paul Ludwig-Weinacht and Hans Maier. Heidelberg: F.H. Kerle, 1969.

Part III
Transnational Communities

8 Restoring the Republic of Letters
Romain Rolland, Stefan Zweig and Transnational Community Building in Europe, 1914–34

Marleen Rensen

Introduction

After the First World War, many intellectuals were eager to contribute to the process of reconciliation and peacemaking in Europe. Although they held differing views on the future of the continent, they seemed to share a sense of urgency in dealing with the nationalist aggressions so clearly exposed by the catastrophe of war. Pacifist humanists most particularly made efforts to advocate communication and understanding among the nations previously at war with one another. A primary concern was the restoration of a transnational community of intellectuals. In this context, intellectuals revisited the 'Republic of Letters' as it had existed in earlier centuries as a model for community formation across frontiers.

The notion of a 'Republic of Letters' may not have been in as general use as it was during the periods of the Renaissance and the Enlightenment, but the concept circulated widely in the interwar period in Europe. Intellectuals were inspired by the idea of a transnational community of men of letters, a notion that dates back at least to the sixteenth century. The exchange of knowledge and opinions was at the heart of this imagined community, which had 'no borders, no capital and no government'.[1] The wish to restore the Republic of Letters during and after the First World War was a desire that spoke as much to the sense of community articulated by these intellectuals as it was an expression of the actual network that bound them together across frontiers.

This chapter will explore the revived interest in the Republic of Letters in the interwar years in order to gain insight into understandings of communities and community constructions as means to overcome strife and instability in post-war Europe.[2] It will focus on the French writer Romain Rolland and the Austrian Jewish writer Stefan Zweig, who together attempted to form a cross-border community in the spirit of the Republic of Letters. Looking at their actions and ideas, as expressed in letters, manifestos and other writings, I will argue that they primarily conceived this community to be a community of discourse, grounded in communication and exchange. This chapter will also illustrate that in response to the political circumstances of the years between 1914 and 1934, the form, composition and purpose of the community they imagined were subject to constant debate.

The Early Modern Republic of Letters

Historians have demonstrated that the concept of the Republic of Letters first appeared in the fifteenth century, in correspondence among Italian humanists who referred to the *Respublica literaria* in the sense of a 'scholarly community transcending frontiers and generations'.[3] At that time, humanists across Europe exchanged manuscripts in order to contribute to the common good of the academic world. Yet the term itself was not widespread until the turn of the sixteenth century. Erasmus was one of the leading intellectuals who contributed significantly to the emerging conception of a cosmopolitan community of learned men, connected by a shared quest for knowledge. This self-governing Republic was imagined to be independent, open to all and 'transnational in its affiliations and the nature of its scholarly exchanges'.[4] Latin, the lingua franca in Erasmus's day, was gradually replaced by French when the centre of the Republic moved from Italy to France over the course of the seventeenth century.

As scholars have noted, the Republic of Letters is a complex area of study because of its 'double character'.[5] On the one hand, the metaphor of the republic expresses the ideal of an egalitarian, inclusive community—a conception that often conflicted with reality. As historians have demonstrated in great detail, religious affiliations and nationalist prejudices often prevented members of this community from associating on an equal and fraternal basis. On the other hand, the Republic of Letters can also be regarded as a real-world entity that manifested itself in exchanges of letters, networks and face-to-face meetings. Dena Goodman argued in *The Republic of Letters: A Cultural History of the French Enlightenment* that it is hard to distinguish the real and the ideal, for, as she notes, the Republic had a culture 'constructed out of discursive practices and institutions that shaped the actions, verbal and otherwise, of the people to whose lives it gave structure, meaning, and purpose'.[6]

The concept of the Republic of Letters becomes even more complicated in light of its historical evolution. There are obvious differences between the sixteenth-century Republic of Letters and its successor during the Enlightenment. The earlier iteration of Republic was, for instance, characterised by the classical and Christian morals of Renaissance humanism, whereas the later Republic was predominantly a French phenomenon, and oriented to a much greater extent towards politics and the public utility of scholarship.[7]

Historians disagree about when and whether the Republic of Letters came to an end, but one can at least say that it experienced fundamental changes from 1800 onwards. The specialisation of scientific disciplines was one factor that shattered the community. Another, arguably more important factor was the rise of nationalism. The Republic, once united by language and culture, lost much of its universal appeal in an age when language and literature were increasingly considered to be expressions of the nation and were instrumental to nation-building. Science, moreover, became an endeavour largely organised under the auspices of national institutions. Nevertheless, scientists themselves still emphasised the universal aspects of science, and certain forms of international scientific exchange became institutionalised with the emergence of internationalism during the nineteenth century.[8] All in all, however, increasing nationalisation severely challenged the ideal of an all-encompassing, open and inclusive transnational intellectual community with shared traditions of scholarship.

Recent historical research has focused on the Republic of Letters as a communication system that is rooted in the sixteenth century but has continued to exist up through the present. Peter Burke, for example, highlights fundamental technological changes in the means of communication but argues nevertheless that the Republic of Letters is still a useful concept for the intellectual history of the twentieth and twenty-first centuries, an era in which communication and solidarity among intellectuals has survived.[9] This chapter, however, will focus on the way in which the concept was revived in the years between 1914 and 1934, a time when various transnational communities were imagined and constructed in an attempt to help Europe recover from the catastrophe of the First World War.

The Impact of the First World War

The war had a profound impact on cross-cultural contacts within Europe. The unofficial claim of the Republic of Letters that 'the sciences are never at war' was severely discredited.[10] Many writers and academics, both in Germany and the Allied countries, passionately supported their national causes, which included the publication of collective declarations that endorsed or even promoted the war. The best-known examples are the manifesto of British intellectuals, 'Why We Are at War', and the 'Aufruf an die Kulturwelt', signed by ninety-three German scientists and cultural figures (and thus also known as the 'Manifesto of the Ninety-Three'), which provoked much controversy in Europe. In this combative atmosphere, former friends and colleagues were suddenly considered enemies and many of the established networks of artists and academics were brusquely disrupted.[11]

After the war, intellectuals, keen to distance themselves from this large-scale intellectual 'betrayal', sought to improve international relations. The post-war era saw an impressive number of intellectual endeavours aiming to promote international cooperation and dialogue in science and the arts. As Akira Iriye and others have pointed out, cultural internationalism had its origins long before the First World War, but it flourished more than ever before in the 1920s.[12] Numerous internationalist associations and leagues were founded: the various associations of the Esperanto movement, the International Research Council, the Institute of Pacific Relations, the

League of Nations' International Committee on Intellectual Co-Operation and countless others. The early 1920s also saw a peak of newly established cultural journals with the purpose of providing a platform for international exchange: *The Criterion* of T.S. Eliot and the *Europäische Revue* of Karl Anton Rohan are but two examples of this trend.

Whatever variation there might have been in the form and aims of these initiatives, the intellectuals involved conceived their efforts as a means to uphold peace through cultural cooperation and international dialogue. Akira Iriye rightly notes that many of these groups cast themselves, implicitly or explicitly, as heirs to the Republic of Letters.[13] They used all sorts of variations of the term: 'société des esprits', 'league of minds', 'fraternity of letters'. Typifying the spirit of cultural internationalism as Iriye describes it, both Rolland and Zweig explored how intellectual elites of Europe might be brought closer together in order to advance cross-cultural understanding.

Ranking among similar initiatives in the arts and sciences, their endeavours can be regarded as distinct efforts to constitute a non-institutionalised community of discourse that would articulate practices of dialogue, tolerance and fraternity. Communication was at the heart of the community Rolland and Zweig dreamt of. Their plans were primarily, though not exclusively, focused on Europe and centred on the reconciliation of France and Germany. Although some of these plans had roots in the period prior to 1914, Rolland's and Zweig's intellectual undertakings were deeply marked by the First World War and should largely be understood as an antidote to the 'patriotic infection' each man abhorred.

Rolland, one of few intellectuals who openly opposed the madness of the war, tried with all his might to maintain relations across the frontlines. Just as he had done before the war, he mobilised friends and acquaintances across Europe to rally public opinion against the hostilities. Living in self-imposed exile, he drafted the pamphlet 'Au-dessus de la mêlée' and a series of other writings collected under the same title, in which he criticised the bellicose authorities and the nationalist fury of the crowd. He called upon Europe's intellectual elites to rise 'above the masses', and proposed the instalment of an international tribune of independent minds to 'watch and pass impartial judgement on any violations of the laws of nations'.[14] His pacifism provoked hostile reactions on both sides of the front: Germans considered him a French chauvinist, whereas most French people regarded him with deep suspicion.[15] They insulted him and called him a traitor for discouraging the war effort and refusing to be loyal to his own country, which was, in their view, only defending the cause of justice and civilisation.

Rolland remained a marginal voice, but he was not alone. Hermann Hesse, too, appealed to artists and intellectuals in the essay 'O Freunde, nicht diese Töne', published in November 1914, encouraging them to distance themselves from the war.[16] Moreover, with Albert Einstein, the German biologist Georg Nicolaï brought forth an 'Aufruf an die Europäer' as a counter-manifesto to the appeal of his ninety-three colleagues who had publicly legitimised the

Figure 8.1 Romain Rolland on the balcony of his home (162, boulevard de Montparnasse, Paris), 1914.
Source: Agence de presse Meurisse. CC-PD.

war effort. Signed by only four scientists, the manifesto intended to rescue and preserve the 'common bonds we once shared'. Nicolai's call to form an international union was addressed to 'educated and well-meaning Europeans [. . .] all those who hold European civilisation dear, in other words, those who in Goethe's prescient words can be called "*good Europeans*"'.[17]

The term "good Europeans" was well known in the period, partly because Nietzsche had used it to refer to Goethe and other 'free spirits' who were open to differences and could think beyond their national boundaries. Even if the relationship between Nietzsche and pacifism is far from evident, several of the war's critics recalled the notion of the 'good Europeans' as an honourable marker, indicating kindred spirits who criticised narrow nationalism. They considered themselves to be members of a European cultural community and heir to the European spirit that might not survive the war if they made no efforts to preserve it.[18] Goethe often served as the great symbol of this type of writer who possessed a European spirit, who saw himself as both German and world citizen. He represented the humanist, cosmopolitan ideal that characterised the imagined European community. Rolland, who approvingly quoted Nicolai's call to 'good Europeans',[19] realised that he would have to wait until the end of the war before he could actually

158 *Marleen Rensen*

start rebuilding this community. In the meantime, he tried to keep European thinking alive through his exchange of letters with Hesse, Einstein and many others. In the view of Zweig, Rolland did indeed facilitate the sustenance of European fraternity by this means: 'Many writers did not venture to give their names, merely wishing to send a message of sympathy and to inscribe themselves citizens of that invisible "republic of free souls"'.[20]

Pan-European Networks and Correspondence, 1914–18

Restoring the European community of intellectuals was a recurring theme in Rolland's correspondence with friends abroad. Their self-representation, as articulated in concepts like 'the brotherhood of free spirits of the world', expressed the sentiment that the war had not destroyed their communal bond.[21] The use of such terms can be considered performative acts of writing that bring about or reaffirm this community's very existence.

Of particular interest is Rolland's correspondence with Stefan Zweig (see Figure 8.2). Rolland and Zweig were friends for more than thirty years. The two writers maintained a lively exchange of letters and met on a regular basis. Their references to 'our Goethe' and 'our Tolstoi' expressed the feeling of belonging to an imagined community characterised by a shared cultural heritage and a cosmopolitan, European orientation.[22] The experience of war

Figure 8.2 Stefan Zweig at his desk in his house in Salzburg about 1928.
Source: Stefan Zweig Centre/University Salzburg.

reinforced a sense of urgency towards the preservation of bonds of international friendship and towards rapprochement among the intellectual elites of Europe. Although Zweig put out a number of patriotic writings in the first phase of the war,[23] he soon turned to pacifism and helped Rolland in his efforts to continue the cross-border dialogue. In the aftermath of the war, he published, among others, an admiring biography of his friend as a way to further promote the spirit of European fraternity.[24]

Although their imagined community was not bound to a particular place, Zweig locates an important centre when he discusses the circle of exiled artists and scientists formed around Rolland in neutral Switzerland: 'there was a sense of fellowship which has always characterised a religious community in the making'. This was not literally a religious group, of course, but it was a spiritual community, representing a faith in the union of Europe. According to Zweig, the group formed a 'little oasis of independence' in wartime, where it was possible to breathe 'a European air'.[25] It was most remarkable, he stressed, that 'enemy brethren were not excluded from spiritual fellowship'. In his description of the group of 'young writers, disciples and friends' who surrounded him, Zweig mentions only male artists and writers such as Frans Masereel and René Arcos. Even though it was a predominantly male community, a few women, like the German writer Annette Kolb, took part in the dialogue and exchange of ideas in the informal circle around Rolland. Zweig's idealised portrait of his French friend, presenting him as the 'conscience of Europe', can be read and understood as an attempt to legitimise the European community he identified with.[26]

Like the intellectuals of the Republic of Letters in earlier centuries, Zweig and Rolland expressed the ideal of an open transnational community and were, at the same time, at the centre of a real-world network of correspondents. Another similarity resides in the fact that their imagined community not only unified scientists and artists on an international scale, but was also a collective entity based on mutual assistance, service and reciprocity.[27] Even during the war, Rolland and Zweig shared books and knowledge among friends and acquaintances and made efforts to bring each other's works to the attention of a broader public. The character and aims of the Republic of Letters come even more explicitly to the fore in the letters in which they discuss an international alliance of intellectuals that could be established as soon as peace was declared.

Rolland's Republic of the Mind

Starting in the early months of 1918, Rolland actively renewed his attempts to unite intellectuals with a European or cosmopolitan spirit. In March, he publicly denounced the betrayal of intellectuals who had disseminated warmongering propaganda on behalf of their nations. 'To a considerable extent, this war was their war', he observed. Rolland nonetheless hoped that intellectuals of the younger generation, men 'permeated with the European spirit', would take up 'the mission of reconciling the thoughts of the enemy nations' and realise an 'intellectual communion'. A few leading minds had already been collaborating, he noted, and he believed that more would link up soon. Building on the discourse of the older Republic of Letters, he referred to the cherished community as both an 'International of the Mind' (*Internationale de l'esprit*) and a 'Republic of the mind' (*République de l'esprit*).[28]

Rolland most likely used the term 'mind' (*esprit*) instead of 'letters' so as to refer to a broad group of men of 'arts, letters and science' who could all be embraced by the Republic of the Mind. In his article, a reply to Gerhard Gran's plan for an 'Institute of the Nations', Rolland insisted on a wider scope of international collaboration that extended beyond political affairs: 'Let us form a worldwide Institute of Art, Letters and Science'. Such an organisation would foster the spread of cultural internationalism and, for example, promote the study of foreign literatures and languages among young Europeans.

In June 1919, shortly after the Treaty of Versailles was signed, Rolland published his 'Déclaration de l'indépendance de l'Esprit', an elaborate proposal to restore a 'union' among intellectual elites in Europe:

> Workers of the Mind, comrades scattered throughout the world, separated for five years by armies, censorship, and the hatred of nations at war, we address an Appeal to you at this hour when barriers are falling and frontiers are reopening, to revive our brotherly union, which shall be a new union, more robust, more stable than that which existed before.[29]

The 'Declaration' appeared simultaneously in France, Switzerland, England, Italy and Germany and was circulated across Central Europe. Although many had turned down Rolland's request for support, he received hundreds of signatures from eminent intellectuals such as Jane Addams, Benedetto Croce, Albert Einstein, Maxim Gorki, Hermann Hesse and Jules Romains.[30] Needless to say, Zweig signed too. That the name of the Indian poet and literary writer Rabindranath Tagore equally figures on the list illustrates Rolland's ambition to build a worldwide community that would 'extend to Asia, to the two Americas, and to the great islets of civilisation spread over the rest of the globe'.[31]

Rolland never attempted to define this Republic, but its meaning can be derived from the way he uses the term. In a letter he insisted that his dream of an 'International of the Mind' was based on 'a free search for truth'.[32] Independent thinking, fidelity to reason and the service of humanity were the core values that tied these people together; distinctions of nationality were ignored. Amid the official lies and misleading war propaganda, it is truth we need, Rolland emphasised. As opposed to the thinkers and artists who disseminated 'an incalculable measure of poisonous hate', he thus redefined the social role of intellectuals:

> Let us arise! [. . .] Our role, our duty, is to be a centre of stability, to point out the pole star, amid the whirlwind of passions in the night [. . .]

Truth only do we honour, truth that is free, frontierless, limitless: truth that knows no prejudices of race or caste . . . For humanity we work [. . .] for humanity as a whole.³³

This 'brotherly union' of independent minds reflects a desire to return to an older tradition of universal humanism and critical reason. After 'reason went bankrupt in 1914', as Rolland noted, he had held firm to a belief in intellect.³⁴ Considering himself heir to the French Enlightenment tradition, he worked to continue its legacy. In 'Au-dessus de la mêlée', he wrote: 'Let the free men of all the countries of Europe when this war is over to take up again the motto of Voltaire: "Écrasez l'infâme"'.³⁵ Rather than a search for pure knowledge, the quest for truth is pursued to serve the interests of humanity as a whole.

Elsewhere, in a letter to Zweig of 20 March 1919, Rolland argued that he considered the German scientist Nicolai, with whom he discussed the 'Declaration' before it was published, to be a member of the family of French encyclopedists, who possessed 'the optimism of pure, clear and active reason'.³⁶ In another letter to Zweig, he compares the pioneering role of their small elite to those of the seventeenth-century Huguenot exiles who fled to London and Holland, a loss for France but not for humankind.³⁷ Rolland also mentioned that he had discovered manuscripts by Voltaire and the encyclopedists in the archives of Geneva.³⁸ He even discussed the potential collective enterprise of a twentieth-century encyclopedia, an undertaking that aligned with the ambition of the fin-de-siècle scientific internationalists who aimed to integrate all global manifestations of knowledge.³⁹

Renaissance humanism was another heritage cherished by Rolland. During the war, he had been inspired by the 'free spirits' of Erasmus and Montaigne to operate beyond the realm of politics by holding firm to standards of scholarly impartiality and objective moderation. This was his form of engagement, Rolland stated in his journal of the war years.⁴⁰ And in a letter of 1919, in which he explained his position to be a stance of radical doubt and a ceaseless search for truth, he declared that he came from 'Montaigne's country'.⁴¹ Thus while Rolland affirmed his adherence to French intellectual traditions, he equally embraced the ideal of Europeanism and cosmopolitanism, and found no conflict in combining these identities, as did Hesse and Nicolai.

The intellectuals who signed Rolland's 'Declaration' had different backgrounds and adopted diverging perspectives regarding Europe's future. They nonetheless found common ground in the importance they attached to tolerance, peace and the central role of reason, defined in opposition to the passion and force of narrow nationalism. After 1919, Rolland and Zweig resumed and intensified their attempts to give this community a solid foundation and a more permanent character.

Journals and Periodicals

A recurrent idea in the correspondence of Rolland and Zweig is the gathering of an international group of intellectuals around a review, which would spread news, ideas and opinions across frontiers. Since they had to deal with competing languages, Rolland once suggested the use of Esperanto as a transnational language for all.[42] Zweig, for his part, envisaged a journal published in three languages: French, English and German.[43] Parallels with the Republic of Letters emerge implicitly in Rolland's war journal, in which he mentions the *Correspondance littéraire* of Grimm and Diderot as a model for the journal he wished for.[44] Like this cultural newsletter, produced and distributed across Europe in the latter half of the eighteenth century by Baron Friedrich Melchior Grimm, Rolland wanted to create a periodical that would inform the educated reader about the most significant ideas in Europe. It likewise had the purpose of stimulating cross-cultural dialogue and making critical voices heard that would influence or even constitute public opinion.

As historians have argued, journals like these were of crucial importance for the Republic of Letters. Often managing to avoid censorship, they disseminated news and opinions on an international scale. Moreover, they illustrate the ideal of a public sphere that took shape during the Age of Enlightenment.[45] Similarly, Rolland wanted to create a European channel of communication to rival the nationalist media that controlled and censored public opinion in many countries. The choice of *Correspondance littéraire* as an example is significant because Grimm mostly focused on German and French culture and contributed considerably to the spread of French culture across the continent. Likewise, although Rolland's journal was to embrace the whole of Europe, it was very much centred on 'the grand nations',[46] chiefly France and Germany.

As in the Republic of Letters of the Renaissance and Enlightenment, letter exchange and publication in periodicals were considered modes of communication that constituted the community as such. In these practices, the process of exchange seems to matter as much as the content or the thing exchanged. Anne Goldgar, who studied the functioning of the Republic of Letters in the years between 1680 and 1750, remarked that exchange served to establish or strengthen the community's social ties.[47] The meaning of this community of discourse thus rested not merely in the content of the writings of its members; another important motivation was the creation of a transnational space for the exchange of ideas, opinions and works.

Rolland's plan to launch an international review in fact predated the First World War. Between 1910 and 1913, he had already discussed the idea with Zweig, Rainer Maria Rilke, Emile Verhaeren and H. G. Wells. As he explained in a letter to Wells, he aimed to combat the 'lies of our nations'.[48] The war only increased the need for an international publication; it could help correct the lies of war propaganda and provide a platform for alternative voices to be heard. Rolland was aware that the plan could not be fully realised as long as the conflict lasted. Yet he did not give up on his goal to address a European public, thereby articulating and constituting a European public sphere. This, for example, is evident in his open letter to the German novelist Gerhart Hauptmann in 1914, in which he dares Hauptmann to speak out:

> In the name of our Europe [. . .] I challenge you, you and the intellectuals of Germany, amongst whom I reckon so many friends, to protest with all your energy against this crime [. . .] I am expecting an answer from you, Hauptmann, an answer that may be an act. The opinion of Europe awaits it as I do.[49]

Hauptmann, among the signers of the Manifesto of the Ninety-Three, accused Rolland of nationalist partiality, thereby confirming his support for the German cause. Stirring European dialogue was not a neutral operation, Rolland realised. Whereas he had moments of discouragement and occasionally stopped publishing, he kept insisting in letters to friends that the free circulation of thought was of utmost importance to Europe. In 1915, he wrote to the Dutch writer Frederik van Eeden: 'We must re-create European opinion. That is our first duty'.[50] For that reason, Rolland published in the neutral Dutch journal *De Amsterdammer* and he warmly welcomed the new journal *Das Werdende Europa*, founded in 1918 by Nicolai, then living in exile in Denmark.

After the war, Rolland played an important part in the founding of the periodical *Europe: Revue littéraire mensuelle*. This new monthly, first published in January 1923, was pacifist in orientation and intended primarily to stimulate European dialogue. Its publishing house and editorial board were based in Paris and, unlike what had initially been planned, articles were published exclusively in French. *Europe*, however, did pay attention to foreign languages and literatures and was open to contributors from across Europe and beyond. Contemporary critics have therefore emphasised its contribution to the creation of transnational networks and communication channels that expanded the process of Europeanisation 'in discourse and practice'.[51] Like many other cultural initiatives in post-war Europe, the community *Europe* represented was confronted with increasing political tensions in the 1930s that caused divide.

Ideological conflicts invaded all initiatives of community formation in the interwar years, most particularly in the newly founded intellectual institutions and associations. Rolland and Zweig were both involved in diverse attempts to give their imagined community a more concrete shape. While they discussed the establishment of formal groups that could organise conferences and other gatherings on a regular basis,[52] they were sceptical about any kind of institutionalisation and felt cautious about becoming involved. As Rolland had already declared in his *Journal* of the war years, 'I prefer to remain a European who fights alone, outside of any society'.[53] He and

Zweig thus illustrate the intellectual dilemma of wanting to remain independent while being committed to peace and European unity.

Intellectual Leagues and Associations

The realities of post-war Europe further complicated matters because political issues manifested themselves in almost every intellectual grouping. National and ideological divides severely tested the bonds between intellectuals, who found it difficult, if not impossible, to stay neutral in their orientations. Problems finding agreement among the community's members often caused fragmentation and disintegration.

Clarté, one of the new intellectual groups in post-war Europe, is an illustrative case. An international movement of left-wing pacifist writers and philosophers gathered by Henri Barbusse, it aimed to contribute to 'human enfranchisement and progress' through 'clear-thinking'. Many members of Clarté had signed Rolland's declaration of intellectual independence. At the launch of the review *Clarté* in October 1919, the movement was presented as a 'league of intellectual solidarity for the triumph of the international cause'. Yet Rolland soon disagreed with Barbusse on the 'composition and purpose' of Clarté, and he regretted to see the movement shift towards revolutionary communism from the end of 1919 onwards.[54] Although Rolland admired the Soviet experiment and ultimately became a communist fellow-traveller, in 1920 the Marxist politics of *Clarté* caused him to break with the movement.

Discussing the altered course of Clarté, Rolland insisted on the independence of the International of the Mind. Representing absolute values of truth and reason, the International should not get involved in political praxis.[55] In a public controversy with Barbusse that unfolded in 1921–22, he claimed that critical reason would ultimately be more effective than violence; in support of his case, he aligned himself with the eighteenth century *philosophes*, who had taken on the responsibility 'to ridicule, to castigate, to fling stones at abuses'. He aimed to emulate 'the mordant criticism, the embittered irony of Voltaire and the Encyclopedists who did more for the downfall of the monarchy than the handful of rash men who took the Bastille'.[56]

Zweig, a member of Clarté's steering committee, resigned as well from the organisation when he realised that Barbusse intended to transform the movement into 'an instrument for class struggle'. Unlike Barbusse, whom he described as 'a soldier of action', he understood himself to be someone who adhered to 'the idea'.[57] He had always been uneasy with attempts to give the intellectual alliance a formal character, as he remarked in a letter of 1919, referring to Clarté: 'What are groups, banquets and all that good for? There's only the intimate community of souls, the fraternity of comrades, the invisible ties'.[58]

Zweig and Rolland favoured the intellectual leagues and clubs that firmly emphasised their apolitical character: the P.E.N. Club (Poets, Playwrights,

Editors, Essayists and Novelists), for example. Founded in 1921 in London, this literary association aimed at fostering understanding among individuals of different nations. Rolland was invited as a guest of honour to the first international P.E.N. Conference in London in 1923, where he met H. G. Wells, George Bernard Shaw and others. In his account of the meeting, Rolland mentions the speech of the British writer Israël Zangwill, who recommended the foundation of 'a Republic of Letters that includes writers of all nations and races'.[59] The concept of the Republic of Letters was often referred to within the circles of the P.E.N. Club, mostly to evoke a sense of community in which international exchange and solidarity were of central importance.

In his account of the meeting in London, Rolland seems to approve of Zangwill's words. More explicit was his agreement with Thomas Hardy's statement that 'the exchange of international thought is the only possible salvation for the world'. This dictum, taken from a letter Hardy wrote to the P.E.N. Club's first president John Galsworthy, could have been a motto of the association, which propagated literature as an art that 'transcends national divisions'.[60] Exchange was a central concern for Rolland, too, as can be gathered from his speech, in which he referred to Goethe's concept of world literature in the sense of an endless circulation of literary texts and criticism that would eventually foster international understanding. Zweig was not present at that particular conference, but he actively promoted world literature for similar reasons.[61]

Although the P.E.N. Club embraced cosmopolitan ideals and insisted time and again that it was independent of any political party, it was very difficult to remain above the political fray. The French section, generally disapproving of Rolland's 'unpatriotic' position during the war, was not pleased to see him granted honourary membership.[62] Rolland, for his part, was critical towards P.E.N. policy concerning membership and invitation. At its 1923 meeting, he declared that he regretted that German writers had been excluded due to a protest by the Belgian delegation. No matter what their attitude to the war might have been, he stated, no one should be barred from the possibility of changing their opinions. Rolland felt that Galsworthy had not been clear enough in his refusal to allow any restrictions on those invited to the conference, whatever nation they hailed from. Defending his ideal of a borderless community, Rolland stressed 'the rights of international intellectual cooperation, without frontiers'.[63]

The P.E.N. Club's ideals began to come in greater conflict with nationalist and fascist tendencies as the 1930s progressed. After 1933, for instance, the association was unsure how to deal with German writers in exile who had been expelled from their country's official delegation. And Zweig, too, presented a difficult case. He had moved to England when his Jewish background began to cause him trouble in Austria. Officially Zweig no longer belonged to the Austrian delegation, but neither could he become a member of his local P.E.N. Club branch, for he was not (yet) a British citizen. In the end he was invited to conferences by the international staff. P.E.N.'s presidents, who aimed to express solidarity with exiled writers, but for the sake of unity they allowed Filippo Tommaso Marinetti and other members who supported the fascist Italian regime to speak at international conferences. This evidently caused much uneasiness among participants.

At P.E.N. meetings Zweig tended to avoid ideological confrontations. At the congress in Buenos Aires in 1936 he refused an offer of the presidency because he wanted to avoid public attention and remain unattached to any formal position or stance.[64] That Zweig continued to support the P.E.N. Club provoked discussion; friends criticised him for his affiliation with a literary society with fascist members.[65] Unlike Rolland, who realised that radical protest was needed in the fight against fascism, Zweig always refrained from engaging in politics. Valuing writing over active intervention, he committed himself to the remembrance of the ideal of an intellectual community that had once existed but had failed to materialise in his day.

Zweig, Erasmus and the Republic of Letters in the 1930s

In his lecture 'Der europäische Gedanke in seiner historischen Entwicklung', delivered at the Palazzo Vecchio in Florence in May 1932, Zweig evoked the Republic of Letters in the age of humanism. At that time, he said, students from Bologna to Paris and Prague shared a common way of reasoning, thinking and interacting. He argued that Erasmus, Giordano Bruno, Spinoza, Bacon, Leibniz and Descartes all felt themselves to be citizens of the same Republic of Letters. This characterisation of the Republic ignores certain ambiguities: Bruno and Spinoza for instance, might not have been accepted as members of the Republic of Letters by most intellectuals of the eighteenth century. For Zweig, though, it was most important to advance the argument that the very existence of this Republic proved that a common mode of European thought had once been shared among an international intellectual elite, going beyond national borders.

This community did not rest on purely intellectual grounds or on reason alone; it resided first and foremost within interpersonal relations and experiences. This may explain why, a little later, Zweig began working on a biographical study of Erasmus in order to depict this community through the portrayal of an individual. The first chapter of the book, published in 1934, presents the humanist as 'the first conscious European and cosmopolitan', a man who 'recognised no superiority of one nation over another' and aimed to unite 'the men of good will in every land' in one 'great league of the enlightened'.[66] By promoting Latin as the common language, Zweig argues, Erasmus formed a transnational community of intellectuals that was united by universal values of humanity, tolerance and peace:

> For the first time since the break-up of Roman civilization, an all-embracing European culture came into being mainly through the instrumentality of

Erasmus and his republic of letters; for the first time national vanity was eclipsed and the well-being of mankind as a whole was set up as the goal. And this desire of the educated to bind themselves together in the realm of the spiritual, this wish to create a language which should be a supranational tongue, this longing that peace should be brought to every land by means of an understanding that superseded the individual nations, this triumph of reason over unreason, was Erasmus' own triumph, was his own short and ephemeral but sacred hour in the tale of mankind's years.[67]

As in his biographical study of Rolland, Zweig locates the centre of the Republic in Switzerland, where Erasmus had lived. In fact, the purpose of his Erasmus biography is essentially similar to the aim of the earlier book on Rolland. Although Zweig does not hide the weaknesses of his subject, his study is nevertheless an idealised portrait in which he appropriates Erasmus for 'European culture' and for the European Republic of Letters that he personally endorsed. His representation is not entirely unjust, for historians have illustrated that Erasmus did indeed contribute significantly to the idea of a community of learning. He carefully constructed the (self-)image of 'the international man of letters' who was connected with other scholars and learned men across Western Europe. As Lisa Jardine claims, 'it is *because* of Erasmus that such a European intellectual community can be imagined at all [. . .] he put considerable effort into reinforcing this illusion of a cohesive world of learning'.[68]

In his private correspondence, Zweig pointed to the parallels between the 1930s and the age of Erasmus, when Europe had been riven by religious wars.[69] It seems as if Erasmus's letters were written for him and his contemporaries, Zweig notes, voicing the feeling that he belonged to a community of humanist intellectuals across nations and generations.

As he admitted, *Triumph und Tragik des Erasmus von Rotterdam* was 'his most personal, most intimate book'.[70] Touching on Erasmus's personal dilemma, he observes that the humanist from Rotterdam became a tragic figure who had hesitated and avoided conflict when faced with the power of Luther's Reformation. Like Erasmus, Zweig himself failed to make resolute decisions under the pressure of circumstances and remained noticeably silent when fascism began to dominate intellectual debates.

That Zweig always tried to remain moderate and understanding, even towards the first Nazi policies, stirred debate and made him almost suspect in the eyes of his fellow writers. In the summer of 1933, when Rolland asked why he did not publicly denounce anti-Semitism in the recently established Third Reich, Zweig responded: 'One day you will read it all in my Erasmus'.[71] It is telling that Rolland congratulated him on this biography when it appeared as being a timely book and proposed that he should complement it with a portrait of Voltaire, 'the independent spirit, who knew how to act'.[72]

Zweig's writing of Erasmus's life story was a way of dealing with the apparent collapse of his longed-for transnational community. As long as he could, he tried to be an Erasmian 'mediator in the middle of the fray' who attempted to stay connected to all people and parties and denounced fanaticism of any kind.[73] Ultimately, however, Zweig's endeavour to defend tolerance and to preserve a transnational cultural community in Europe met with little success. Therefore, he felt, he shared the tragic fate of Erasmus, who had lost the battle with Luther. Because Zweig was beset by the anxious presentiment that Europe, and all that Erasmus symbolised, had been lost, he intended to erect a 'monument' to the humanist by writing his biography.[74] The fraternal European community might be predestined to remain 'a spiritual and aristocratic dream', he realised, but writing Erasmus's life was his way of ensuring that the dream would not be consigned to oblivion.[75]

Conclusion

In the aftermath of the First World War, pacifist humanists sought to reconstruct the European community of intellectuals that had suddenly collapsed in 1914. The notion of a Republic of Letters—or variations of the term—re-emerged in this context as an exemplary community of independent scholars who exchanged knowledge and opinions for the good of humanity. Addressing the intellectual elites of Europe by making reference to the Republic was a means of articulating the existence of a community with a long historical tradition. Fixed and recalled in letters, manifestos and declarations, this self-representation expressed a collective entity that individuals could link up to and identify with. As the Republic of Letters had (and has) always been vaguely defined and its history constantly rewritten, the term derived new meaning in the context of post-war Europe: it became endowed with the pacifism and idealism of the early 1920s. Whereas some critics argue that the Early Modern Republic had its own 'vague but vital ideals of peace and tolerance', Rolland and Zweig undoubtedly reinforced the idealist dimension of this community.[76]

These two writers' ideas and actions are interesting for what they reveal about the attempts, amid the ruins of war, to restore and continue an older transnational community of intellectuals. Already during the conflict, both Rolland and Zweig had insisted that independence of the mind was essential to the interests of society and humankind at large. They came to identify the Republic with the central role of reason and the universal humanist values of tolerance, peace and justice. Their main concern was the construction of a 'discourse community' whose purpose was to serve humanity and truth through international exchange. Through their writings in private letters and public journals, they provided links that constituted a transnational 'space' for communication. In ways analogous to what Dena Goodman has shown for the citizens of the Enlightenment's Republic of Letters, Rolland and Zweig in their own time helped shape the intellectual community they considered themselves to be part of through discursive practices which gave 'structure, meaning and purpose' to their lives.[77]

They succeeded in building a supra-national community of intellectuals within their communal networks, based on friendship. Yet their cases also reveal that every time a new community took on concrete or formal shape, controversies arose about the purpose and meaning of the established alliance. The major difficulty seemed to be that politics and culture were nearly always intersecting; the cultural domain became almost completely politicised in the 1930s. As a result, the Republic of Letters further fragmented into separate communities. One can wonder the extent to which this situation was really different from what had happened in the Renaissance and the Enlightenment, when there was also continuous debate and contention among the citizens of the Republic. The Reformation and subsequent religious conflicts especially disrupted communication and caused deep ideological divides, thus damaging notions of community. Nevertheless, in the interwar period, intellectuals regarded the Republic of Letters as an imagined community from the past that could serve as a powerful model for a united Europe of the mind.

The relationship between Rolland and Zweig survived war and conflict, but these men had their differences of opinion, too. Although each possessed a historical understanding of this community and were equally inspired by 'free spirits' from the past, each represented a competing discourse: whereas Rolland most admired Diderot and Voltaire, whom he saw as embodying Enlightenment reason and active intellectual engagement, Zweig found a role model in Erasmus, who favoured reflection over action in all circumstances. The failure to create a resilient European community of independent intellectuals is reflected in Zweig's biography of Erasmus. Zweig apprehended that these intellectuals possibly represented an ideal of community that might never be fully realised, but he believed in the creative force that this sense of community engendered, thus inspiring and influencing younger generations.

Rather than merely reminding people of the ideals and values that had defined earlier manifestations of the Republic of Letters, Rolland and Zweig each tried to give practical shape to the fraternal community of European intellectuals in the interwar era. Working within the fragmented political realities of 1914–34, they revived and sustained cross-border communication and exchange, carrying forward to future generations a formal practice and ideal. As men who made early attempts to re-establish a European community of discourse, thereby constituting a European public and a public sphere, they are worthy of further attention.

Notes

1. Grafton, "A Sketch Map," 1.
2. There are some scholarly studies on the topic, for example Antoine Compagnon's edited volume *La "République des Lettres"*. However, the 'long history' of the Republic of Letters remains to be written.
3. Fumaroli, "Republic of Letters," 137.
4. Armitage, *Foundations*, 19.

5. Goodman, *Republic of Letters*, 15.
6. Ibid., 1.
7. Goldgar, *Impolite Learning*; Goodman, *Republic of Letters*.
8. Geyer and Paulmann, *Mechanics of Internationalism*, 4–5; Somsen, "History of Universalism".
9. Burke, "Republic of Letters".
10. For a general overview of intellectuals and writers in the First World War, see Prochasson, "Intellectuals". For the notion of 'the sciences are never at war', see Beer, "Sciences".
11. Schöttler, "French and German Historians' Networks," 119–20; Trebitsch, "Organisations Internationales," 51.
12. Iriye, *Cultural Internationalism*, 51. For studies on cultural internationalism in the interwar years, see also Laqua, "Internationalism".
13. Iriye, *Cultural Internationalism*, 61.
14. Rolland, "Au-dessus de la mêlée".
15. For example, in his reply to Rolland's open letter, Hauptmann insulted him on account of his partiality towards the French. For the French reactions, see Duchatelet, *Romain Rolland*, 175–6, 182–83.
16. Hermann Hesse, "O Freund, nicht diese Töne," *Neue Zürcher Zeitung*, 3 November 1914.
17. Nicolai, "Manifesto to the Europeans," mid-October 1914, in *Einstein on Politics*, 65–66.
18. Kaufmann, *Nietzsche*, 39, 44, 296, 314.
19. Rolland, "A Great European: G. F. Nicolai," 15 October 1917, and "A Call to Europeans," 20 October 1918, in *Forerunners*, 140–75, 195–204, respectively.
20. Zweig, *Rolland*, 318.
21. Rolland, "To Maxim Gorki," 30 January 1917, in *Forerunners*, 45–47.
22. See for example Rolland-Zweig, *Briefwechsel*, vol. 1, 243: 29 March 1916.
23. See for example Matuschek, *Three Lives*, 134–37.
24. Zweig, *Rolland*.
25. Ibid., 313.
26. Rensen, "Writing European Lives," 15.
27. Goldgar, *Impolite Learning*, 13.
28. Rolland, "On Behalf of the International of the Mind," March and April 1918, in *Forerunners*, 185–95. Rolland used the term frequently in his correspondence. See, for example, his letter to E. D. Morel, 30 March 1919. Cited in Fisher, *Romain Rolland*, 61; Hoock, *L'Europe des lettres*, 455.
29. Rolland, "Declaration of the Independence of the Mind," in *Forerunners*, 209–17.
30. Duchatelet, *Romain Rolland*, 226.
31. Rolland, "On Behalf of the International of the Mind," 185–95.
32. Rolland, *Journal*, 14 December 1919.
33. Rolland, "Declaration of the Independence of the Mind," in *Forerunners*, 209–17.
34. Rolland, "A Great European".
35. Rolland, *Au-dessus de la mêlée*, 12–13.
36. Rolland-Zweig, *Briefwechsel*, vol. 1, 439.
37. Ibid., 691.
38. Ibid., 285. The date of the letter is 24 June 1922.
39. See also Fisher, *Romain Rolland*, 52. See for example Rolland, "Letter to Zweig," 18 August 1919, in *Briefwechsel*, vol. 1, 468. For the wider context of encyclopedic enterprises in the period, see also Wright, *Cataloging the World*; Laqua, "Transnational Intellectual Cooperation," 22.

40. 'Moi, je suis avec Érasme et Montaigne, qui se sont retirés de l'action pour mieux combattre'. Cited in Duchatelet, *Romain Rolland*, 207.
41. Rolland, "Letter to Max Eastman," 5 December 1919, cited in Fisher, *Romain Rolland*, 71.
42. Fisher, *Romain Rolland*, 52.
43. Zweig, "Letter to Rolland," 14 [15?] August 1919, in *Briefwechsel*, vol. 1, 465.
44. Rolland characterised the envisioned periodical as 'une sorte de correspondence littéraire comme celle de Grimm et de Diderot qui rayonnerait sur l'Europe et grouperait en un faisceau les pensées les plus significatives des grands pays de l'Europe'. Cited in: Hoock, *L'Europe*, 448–9.
45. See, for example, Goodman, *Republic of Letters*, 158–59.
46. Cited in Hoock, *L'Europe des lettres*, 448–49.
47. Goldgar, *Impolite Learning*, 7.
48. Rolland, "Letter to H. G. Wells," 1 July 1911, cited in Fisher, *Romain Rolland*, 38.
49. Rolland, "Lettre ouverte à Gerhart Hauptman," 29 August 1914, published on 2 September 1914, in *Au-dessus de la mêlée*, 5–9.
50. Rolland, "Een brief van Romain Rolland," in *De Amsterdammer*, 13 September 1914.
51. Wardhaugh, "Intellectual Dissidents," 23; Racine, "Clarté".
52. Fisher, *Romain Rolland*, 51.
53. 'Un jeune Anglais, Lionel Wyon, a fondé en avril, en Berne, une *Europaische Gesellschaft zur Verständigung der Intellektuellen*. Les intentions sont généreuses, mais extrêmenent vagues [. . .] en ce moment je me méfie particulièrement des sociétés imprécises. J'aime mieux rester un Européen, qui combat seul, en dehors de toute *Gesellschaft*'. The translation is mine. Rolland-Hesse, *D'une rive*, 21.
54. Racine, "Clarté," 201.
55. Rolland, "Journal inédit," 197–98.
56. Cited in Fisher, *Romain Rolland*, 96.
57. Zweig, "Letter to Rolland," 17 January 1921, in *Briefwechsel*, vol. 1, 610.
58. The translation is mine. Zweig, "Letter to Duhamel," 28 November 1919, *Briefe*, 31. '[. . .] à quoi bon des groupements, les banquets et tout cela? Il n'y a que la communion intime des âmes, la fraternité des camarades, les liens invisibles [. . .]'.
59. Rolland, "Réunion".
60. Doherty, "Guardian," 140.
61. A prime example is his initiative to create *Bibliotheca Mundi*: a series of literary classics published by Insel Verlag between 1920 and 1923.
62. Vegesack, *De intellectuelen*, 90.
63. Rolland, "Letter to Zweig," 30 May 1923, in *Briefwechsel*, vol. 1, 745–46.
64. Buchinger, *Stefan Zweig*, 189, 275.
65. Hofman, *Joseph Roth*, 494–97.
66. Zweig, *Erasmus*, 1–5.
67. Ibid., 7.
68. Jardine, *Erasmus*, 11.
69. Zweig, "Letter to Rolland," 10 May 1933, in *Briefwechsel*, vol. 2, 516–17.
70. Zweig, *World of Yesterday*, 276.
71. Zweig, "Letter to Rolland," 3 August 1933, in *Briefwechsel*, vol. 2, 529.
72. 'der unabhängigen Geistes, der zu handeln wusste': Rolland, "Letter to Zweig," 3 September 1934, in *Briefwechsel*, vol. 2, 578. The translation is mine.
73. Zweig, *Erasmus*, 17. See also Golomb, "Erasmus," 11.
74. Zweig, "Letter to Rolland," 26 April 1933, in *Briefwechsel*, vol. 2, 510.

75. Zweig, *Erasmus*, 168.
76. Grafton, "A Sketch Map," 5.
77. Goodman, *Republic of Letters*, 1.

Bibliography

Armitage, David. *Foundations of Modern International Thought*. Cambridge: Cambridge University Press, 2013.

Buchinger, Susanne. *Stefan Zweig—Schriftsteller und literarische Agent. Die Beziehungen zu seinen deutschsprachigen Verlegern (1901–1942)*. Frankfurt am Main: Buchhändler Vereigingung GmbH, 1999.

Burke, Peter. "The Republic of Letters as a Communication System: An Essay in Periodization." *Media History* 18, no. 3–4 (2012): 1–14.

Compagnon, Antoine. *La République des lettres dans la tourmente (1919–1939). Actes du colloque international, Paris, les 27 et 28 novembre 2009, Collège de France*. Paris: CNRS/Alain Baudry, 2011.

de Beer, Gavin. *The Sciences Were Never at War*. New York: Nelson, 1960.

Doherty, Megan. "A Guardian to Literature and its Cousins: The Early Politics of the PEN Club." *Nederlandse Letterkunde—De internationale PEN* (2011): 132–51.

Duchatelet, Bernard. *Romain Rolland tel qu'en lui-même*. Paris: Albin Michel, 2002.

Eliot, T. S. *Notes Towards a Definition of Culture*. London: Faber and Faber Limited, 1948.

Fisher, David James. *Romain Rolland and the Politics of Intellectual Engagement*. Berkeley: University of California Press, 1986.

Fumaroli, M. "The Republic of Letters." *Diogenes* 36 (1988): 129–54.

Galsworthy, John. "International Thought." In *Castles in Spain and other Screeds*, edited by John Galsworthy, 43–61. London: W. Heinemannm Ltd., 1927.

Geyer, Martin H. and Johannes Paulmann. *The Mechanics of Internationalism: Culture, Society and Politics from the 1840s to the First World War*. Oxford: Oxford University Press, 2001.

Goldgar, Anne. *Impolite Learning: Conduct and Community in the Republic of Letters 1680–1750*. New Haven and London: Yale University Press, 1995.

Golomb, Jacob. "Erasmus: Stefan Zweig's Alter-Ego." In *Stefan Zweig Reconsidered: New Perspectives on his Biographical and Literary Writing*, edited by Mark Gelber, 7–21. Tübingen: Max Niemeyer Verlag, 2007.

Goodman, Dena. *The Republic of Letters: A Cultural History of the Enlightenment*. [1994] Ithaca and London: Cornell University Press, 1996.

Grafton, Anthony. "A Sketch Map of a Lost Continent: The Republic of Letters." *Republic of Letters: A Journal for the Study of Knowledge, Politics and the Arts* 1, no. 1 (2009): 1–18.

Hesse, Hermann and Romain Rolland. *D'une rive à l'autre. Correspondance et fragments du Journal*. Paris: Éditions Albin Michel, 1972.

Hofman, Michael. *Joseph Roth: A Life in Letters*. New York: W.W. Nortan & Company, 2012.

Hoock-Demarle, Marie-Claire. *L'Europe des lettres. Réseaux épistolaires et construction de l'espace européen*. Paris: Albin Michel, 2008.

Ifversen, Jan. "The Crisis of European Civilization after 1918." In *Ideas of Europe since 1914: The Legacy of the First World War*, edited by Menno Spiering and Michael Wintle, 14–32. Basingstoke: Palgrave Macmillan, 2002.

Iriye, Akira. *Cultural Internationalism and World Order.* Baltimore: Johns Hopkins University Press, 1997.
Jardine, Lisa. *Erasmus: Man of Letters: The Construction of Charisma in Print.* Princeton, NJ: Princeton University Press, 1993.
Kaufmann, Walter. *Nietzsche: Philosopher, Psychologist, Antichrist.* [1950] Princeton: Princeton University Press, 1974.
Kolasa, Jan. "A League of Minds: The International Intellectual Cooperation Organization of the League of Nations." Ph.D. diss. Princeton University, 1960.
Laqua, Daniel. *Internationalism Reconfigured: Transnational Ideas and Movements between the World Wars.* London: I.B. Tauris, 2011.
Matuschek, Oliver. *Stefan Zweig: Three Lives—A Biography of Stefan Zweig.* Translated by Allan Blunden. [2006] London: Pushkin Press, 2011.
Prochasson, Christophe. "Intellectuals and Writers." In: *A Companion to World War I*, edited by J. Horne, 323–37. Oxford: Wiley Blackwell, 2010.
Racine, Nicole. "The Clarté Movement in France, 1919–1921." *Journal of Contemporary History* 2, no. 2 (1967): 195–208.
Reijnen, Carlos and Marleen Rensen. "European Encounters: Intellectual Exchange and the Rethinking of Europe 1914–1945." *European Studies: An Interdisciplinary Series in European Culture, History and Politics* 32 (2014): 13–31.
Rensen, Marleen. "Exemplary Europeans: Romain Rolland and Stefan Zweig." *European Studies: An Interdisciplinary Series in European Culture, History and Politics* 32 (2014): 173–89.
Rensen, Marleen. "Writing European Lives: Stefan Zweig as a Biographer of Verhaeren, Rolland and Erasmus." *European Journal of Life Writing* 4 (2015): 1–29.
Rolland, R. "Une Réunion Internationale d'Écrivains à Londres." *Europe. Revue littéraire mensuelle* 2, no. 5 (1932): 102–6.
Rolland, Romain. *Au-dessus de la mêlée.* Paris: Ollendorf, 1915.
Rolland, Romain. *The Forerunners.* Translated by Eden and Cedar Paul. [1919] New York: Brace and Howe, 1920.
Rolland, Romain. "Journal inédit (1919–1920)." *Europe* 43, no. 439 (1965): 175–207.
Rolland, Romain and Stefan Zweig. *Briefwechsel 1910–1940.* Berlin: Rütten & Loening, 1987.
Rowe, David E. and Robert Schulmann, eds. *Einstein on Politics: His Private Thoughts and Public Stands on Nationalism, Zionism, War, Peace, and the Bomb.* Princeton: Princeton University Press, 2007.
Schöttler, Peter. "French and German Historians' Networks: The Case of the Early Annales." In *Transnational Intellectual Networks: Forms of Academic Knowledge and the Search for Cultural Identities*, edited by Christophe Charle and Jürgen Schriewer, 115–35. Frankfurt am Main: Campus Verlag, 2004.
Somsen, Geert. "A History of Universalism: Conceptions of the Universality of Science from the Enlightenment to the Cold War." *Minerva* 46, no. 3 (2008): 361–79.
Trebitsch, Michel. "Organisations internationales de cooperation intellectuelle dans l'entre-deux-guerres." In *Antifascisme et nation. Les gauches européennes au temps du Front populaire*, edited by Serge Wolikow and Annie Bleton-Ruget, 49–58. Dijon: Presses universitaires de Dijon, 1998.
Vanheste, Jeroen. *Guardians of the Humanist Legacy: The Classicism of T.S. Eliot's Criterion Network and Its Relevance to our Postmodern World.* Leiden: Brill, 2007.

von Vegesack, Thomas. *De intellectuelen. Een geschiedenis van het literaire engagement 1898–1968.* [1986] Amsterdam: Meulenhoff, 1989.

Wardhaugh, Jessica, Ruth Leiserowitz, and Christian Bailey. "Intellectual Dissidents and the Construction of European Spaces, 1918–1988." In *Europeanization in the Twentieth Century: Historical Approaches*, edited by Martin Conway and Kiran Klaus Patel, 21–44. Basingstoke: Palgrave Macmillan, 2010.

Wright, Alex. *Cataloging the World: Paul Otlet and the Birth of the Information Age.* Oxford: Oxford University Press, 2014.

Zweig, Stefan. *Romain Rolland: The Man and His Work.* Translated by Eden and Cedar Paul. New York: Thomas Seltzer, 1921.

Zweig, Stefan. *Erasmus of Rotterdam.* Translated by Eden and Cedar Paul. [1934] New York: Viking Press, 1965.

Zweig, Stefan. *Die schlaflose Welt. Aufsätze und Vorträge aus den Jahren 1909–1941.* Frankfurt am Main: S. Fischer Verlag, 1983.

Zweig, Stefan. *Briefe 1914–1919.* Edited by Knut Beck, Jeffrey B. Berlin, and Nastascha Weschenbach-Feggeler. Frankfurt am Main: S. Fischer Verlag, 1998.

Zweig, Stefan. *The World of Yesterday: Memoirs of a European.* Translated by Anthea Bell. [1942] London: Pushkin Press, 2014.

9 A Vatican Conspiracy?
Internationalism, Catholicism and the Quest for European Unification, 1945–50

Maarten van den Bos

On 5 May 1948, three years after the liberation of the Netherlands from its Nazi occupiers, eight people met in the third-class waiting area of Utrecht's Central Station. After participating in an 'international route' organised by Pax Christi in Kevelaer, a well-known Catholic pilgrimage site just across the German border, they decided to establish a Dutch branch of the international Catholic peace movement. Growing out of the desire for reconciliation between France and Germany among members of the French resistance during the war's final months, Pax Christi had quickly become a large, international movement of predominantly young believers who deemed that peace would best be served by the former enemies getting to know one another. What the group lacked in well-formulated goals and clear ideas about its organisational structure, it made up for in vigorous enthusiasm and a devout belief in the healing power of singing, praying, and worshipping together. The members of the new Dutch section shared such fervour, as well as a lack of a clear ideology or organisational structure. Although the eight co-founders had high hopes, they did not get much further than ordering a large number of envelopes adorned with the logo of the new Dutch section, which were to be used for correspondence with potential beneficiaries. Everything else remained vague until the early 1950s.[1]

This vagueness was not entirely the new movement's fault. Almost accidentally, these youngsters in several Western countries had stumbled upon a debate that had split Catholic religious, intellectual and political elites from the mid-1930s until the early 1950s. Sparked by the sense that modernity would eradicate the solid position of the Catholic Church in the life of the flock as well as in society as a whole, a wide range of intellectuals declared that there was an urgent need for religious renewal.[2] During and after the Second World War, this sense was connected with the feeling that the modern state as the basis for international relations had failed.[3] Instead of meeting in church, Catholics of different nationalities confronted one another on the battlefield; instead of acting as brothers in faith, they slaughtered one another in combat. Therefore, a new international Catholic community had to be built upon the ashes of decades of war. There was no consensus, however, about what the foundations of this community should be. Roughly two lines of argument were available. The first, advocated most compellingly by the Holy See, stipulated that the nation-state was obsolete and needed to be replaced by an international spiritual community under papal leadership. The second, popular among Catholic intellectuals—writers, theologians, scholars—consisted of the conviction that a new international moral community had to be built. This would only be possible, however, if people would be willing to overcome their prejudices towards one another and, overcoming national and religious differences, would take on an active role in the creation of a truly international community. The central difference between the 'moral' and 'spiritual' emphases in these respective visions was that the community imagined by the Holy See was merely a religious project that in itself had few political implications, whereas the moral community envisioned by various intellectuals was broader, possessed social as well as political connotations, and was more inclusive towards non-Catholics.

The new Pax Christi movement was one of the 'laboratories' in which these new positions on the future of Catholic internationalism were discussed and developed.[4] In an attempt to build a solid international organisation, leading figures within the movement attached themselves to one of the two competing internationalist positions. The same was true for members of other organisations as well as for Catholic politicians, who had to find some middle ground between both views in order to gain support from the Vatican, from local religious leadership, and from leading intellectuals and cultural elites. Eventually, the possibility of building a European political community that would supersede the nation-state and overcome national self-interest gained support from the Vatican as well as critical Catholic intellectuals. In this chapter, I will use the early years of Pax Christi to further investigate different outlooks on community, justice and peace among Catholics in the late 1940s and early 1950s. I will focus especially on its French and German branches, since these were the most important strongholds of the international movement, and the Dutch branch, which was founded a few years later and defined its position in relation to those of both leading sections.

After the atrocities of war, Catholic intellectuals were determined to redefine the concept of community by removing its spatial demarcations and exclusionary mechanisms. No longer would national outlooks on community be acceptable; national boundaries had to be transcended in order to overcome the differences that had made enemies of brothers in faith. There was no agreement, however, on what the nature of such a new community would be, whether it had to be conceptualised in a strictly spiritual, moral or political sense and if and how it could be used as a foundation for international cooperation without losing its moral and spiritual dimension. In order to capture this debate, community will be understood here as an essentially contested concept that had to be redefined after a crisis: namely the two World Wars, after which Europe was in need of new political and philosophical norms.[5]

The post-war debate on community, internationalism and peace has not yet been sufficiently incorporated into the historiography of European integration or studies on the history of modern Catholicism, because the dominant frameworks to understand the history of European integration and modern religious history have mainly been conceived from national perspectives.[6] Recent research has done much to contest these frameworks. This chapter builds particularly on the work of Wolfram Kaiser and Kiran Klaus Patel, who have introduced a transnational and network approach to the study of the history of European integration.

According to Kaiser, who differentiates among informal networks, international non-governmental organisations, agencies such as international administrative unions and formal international organisations, these transnational networks have played a triple role. First, they have acted as facilitators of political cooperation and integration by sharing information and building mutual trust. Second, these networks have helped to familiarise new members with European or international politics. Third, transnational forums and organisations were important vehicles in the defining of common policy objectives.[7] The German historian Kiran Klaus Patel, in turn, has argued that we would better understand the different stages in the integration process if integration history were embedded in the broader history of twentieth-century Europe. In a recent article, he stresses the need to move beyond the exploration of the integration process itself by also taking into account contesting narratives on European integration that have no direct political connotations.[8] The American historian Mark Greif has recently emphasised the substantial influence of theologians and other religious leaders on public and political discourse in the first post-war decade.[9] Following the research agenda of Kaiser and Patel, we should more fully integrate the ideas of these religious elites into the historiography of European integration.

Traditionally, the European project has been seen as the domain of technocrats. According to Mark Mazower, the Second World War left Europe with a deep antipathy towards ideological politics. Not only did mainstream politics steer away from polarised attitudes in favour of compromise, international cooperation was also perceived as being merely an economic necessity.[10] Recent studies, however, highlight the importance of ideology in early integration history. Within political parties as well as in public discourse, European integration was connected with and informed by ideas on community and solidarity and therefore should not be understood only through the lens of international relations theory or state interest.[11]

Progressive Catholics formed an important transnational network that contributed much to the desire to form a European political community. In post-war Europe as well as in the United States, there were signs of a Christian reawakening. In Britain, the late 1940s and 1950s witnessed the fastest growth in church membership since the mid-nineteenth century. The war had strengthened the sense of Christian national identity, and the connection between Christianity and moral revival was strengthened by emergence of the Cold War, waged against the atheist Soviet Union. In France and West Germany, similar reawakenings took place.[12] The tendency to talk about the division of Europe in religious terms was reinforced by a desire for a return to normalcy after the horrors of war. The restoration of traditional family life became a particularly important concern for religious and political elites. This emphasis had a huge influence on the general image of post-war religion, which in historical research has frequently been framed as conservative. Especially with regard to Catholicism in the early post-war period, historians have linked moral and theological traditionalism to political conservatism.[13]

Although this narrative is not untrue, it is one-sided. Already in the 1930s, several Catholic theologians and philosophers had criticised the Church and Catholic politicians for being traditionalist and dogmatic. After the war, drawing on the ideas of those individuals, there emerged a network of progressive Catholics who argued against the alliance of Catholicism and conservatism and advocated a connection between religious and political renewal. Their ideas became exceedingly important for the reconceptualisation of community within Catholic circles.[14] Furthermore, Christian Democrats, including the French minister of foreign affairs Robert Schuman or the long-serving German chancellor Konrad Adenauer, based their ideas on European integration at least partially on new narratives of community, internationalism and peace that had been generated by this international network of progressive Catholic intellectuals.[15]

The pivotal figure in this network was the French philosopher Jacques Maritain. Based on his deep knowledge of the philosophy of Thomas Aquinas, Maritain denounced the division of functions between politics and faith and affirmed the primacy of Catholic values in political and social action. These views gave him and other likeminded intellectuals some space to withdraw from predominantly right-wing Catholic politics during the interwar period, and to subject its exponents to critical analysis. Living and working in Canada and the United States during the war, Maritain began conceiving of human rights as the cornerstone of Catholic social and political philosophy. The concept of, and devotion to, the rights of the human person was the most significant ameliorative political development of modern times, he wrote in 1942. At the same time, he warned against the secularisation of human rights; if grounded in 'a godlike, infinite autonomy of human will', the concept would lead to nothing but catastrophe. Here, Maritain made clear that human rights and human dignity were best served not only within the framework of Catholic natural law, but also within a wider conception of community that superseded traditional political narratives.[16]

During the war, a range of Catholic theologians and scholars adapted their beliefs in the dignity of the human person and the core right to religious freedom to the conditions of a transformed political landscape. Democracy, which had long been seen as one of the Church's enemies, was now perceived as an important ally in the fight against secularism, materialism, National Socialism and communism. According to historian Samuel Moyn, Christian narratives on human rights therefore have to be understood not as principal ideas about 'the inclusion of the other' but as ways of 'policing the border and boundaries' of their faith communities against looming enemies.[17] By claiming that Christian narratives of human rights were solely defensive in nature, Moyn, however, falls into the trap of perceiving all Christian advocates for human rights as conservative. Adopting this framework does no justice to the way Maritain integrated his ideas on human rights and human dignity into a broader narrative of community and internationalism. He was convinced that 'the only way of regeneration for the human community [was] a rediscovery of the true image of man'. Therefore, ideas of community had to be built upon its individual members; community had to be reconceptualised as a moral collective made up of equal members. These ideas were opposed to more communitarian conceptions of community informing traditional Catholic ideas of society, in which everyone had a fixed place and role.[18]

Human Rights, Spiritual Reform and International Relations

In the summer of 1943, the year after the publication of his book on human rights and natural law, Maritain gave a talk at a public meeting of France Forever, an organisation of French exiles in the United States. There, he explicitly connected respect for the dignity of the individual person with the construction of an international community after the war. 'The nations must choose between the prospect of aggravated, irremediable chaos and strenuous effort at cooperation, working with patience and perseverance towards a progressive organisation of the world in a supranational community'.[19] Although Maritain was living in exile in Canada, his ideas rapidly spread to Europe. His work was reprinted and cited in Britain, France, Germany and Italy, and not only by Catholics.[20] In the Netherlands, Maritain's views were adopted in two slightly contrasting ways: as a plea for international judicial cooperation and as a call for the creation of an international moral community. The former position's most fervent advocate was Didymus Beaufort, a Franciscan legal scholar and long-term Catholic Party member of parliament. The latter stance was brought to the fore by his colleague Johannes van der Ven, a legal scholar who became a professor of law at the Universities of Utrecht and Nijmegen in 1947.[21]

Beaufort was among the members of the Dutch delegation who attended the United Nations Conference on International Organisation in March 1945.[22] There, in San Francisco, he participated in the commission responsible for the composition of the UN Charter. Although Beaufort saw the extraordinary importance of the work being done, he was utterly disappointed with the final result, in particular because the Charter was based on the idea that state sovereignty should remain the cornerstone of international relations. In his 1948 inaugural address as professor by special appointment in international law at the Catholic University of Nijmegen, Beaufort embedded his criticism in a narrative of the history of international law. According to Beaufort, the divine origins of man gave every individual inalienable rights that transcended the power of the state. When human beings were seen merely as citizens, they had no sufficient protection against violence by their own governments. Therefore, they had to be protected by international law, which in turn had to be enforced by a supranational institution that superseded the authority of the state. The Charter—according to Beaufort—did not really enable the establishment of such an institution.[23]

These thoughts on international law, politics and human rights had evolved within the Dutch Roman Catholic Peace Union, a small Catholic peace organisation established in 1925. Beaufort was its study-secretary and was editor of *Pro Pace*, a monthly published from 1929 until the German invasion of the Netherlands in May 1940.[24] In several articles, he argued for an actualisation of classical just-war theology. Dating back to Augustine of Hippo and Thomas Aquinas, just-war doctrine became the cornerstone of Catholic theology on war and peace. The doctrine did not totally forbid the waging of war—although Aquinas stipulated that members of the clergy should not take part in acts of violence—but strongly regulated it. From the sixteenth century onwards, legal scholars such as Hugo Grotius secularised just-war doctrine. Its theological background was rediscovered by Catholic theologians in the second half of the nineteenth century, against the backdrop of a general revival of Thomist theology.[25]

After the First World War, Catholic legal scholars colligated just-war theology with changing notions of human dignity and state relations.[26] Whereas in the early 1920s some leading Catholics—both in the Netherlands and elsewhere—saw just-war doctrine as a way of regulating state relations, Beaufort went one step further.[27] In several articles in *Pro Pace*, he argued for binding legal arrangements and permanent international institutions to prevent not only war but also infringements on the unalienable rights of every individual. He developed a narrative in which the papacy was defined as the central institution to watch over the global assertion of human dignity. When necessary, the pope could be trusted to preside as judge over interstate conflict as well as over tribunals to address atrocities committed by countries against its inhabitants.[28] In the post-war years, under the influence of Maritain among others, Beaufort silently gave the central role of the pope over to international institutions that had to be enabled to uphold and enforce international law.[29]

Instead of focusing on international law and human rights, Beaufort's colleague J.J.M. van der Ven emphasised notions of community and cooperation in Maritain's work. At the 1947 annual conference for alumni of the Catholic University of Nijmegen, van der Ven called upon his audience not to remain passive. After an apocalyptic overview of the state of affairs in post-war Europe, he proposed that the way forward was to be found in two interconnected developments. First, there had to be spiritual renewal, so that the religious life of all churchgoers could be reinvigorated. Second, an international network of men and women of faith had to be built to overcome national differences and reconcile the various constituencies of Europe. Eventually, this network should become the foundation of a new international community, which would consist of likeminded individuals of different national, ideological and religious backgrounds who had actively decided to become part of this new community.[30] Although these ideas were rather vague, they provided the ideological backbone for a Dutch association founded by van der Ven just after the war ended: the Catholic Association for Spiritual Renewal (Katholiek Genootschap voor Geestelijke Vernieuwing; see figure 9.1). Its main goal was to build an international network of high-placed Catholic intellectuals who could discuss ideas concerning community, peace and international cooperation. Van der Ven thus presented the formation of the Dutch association as only a first step.[31]

The association's primary initiatives focused on Germany, because of the 'spiritual vacuum' that followed the collapse of the Nazi regime. Via meetings, talks, lectures and articles, the German people would be reconnected with Christianity. The benefits of this initiative would be twofold. By engaging in the association's activities, Dutch participants would strengthen their

Figure 9.1 The first meeting of the Association for Spiritual Renewal (May 1946). On the left is J.M.M. van der Ven.

Source: Catholic Documentation Centre, Nijmegen.

own beliefs and become advocates for religious and political renewal at home as well as abroad. Moreover, their activity across the border would establish important contacts with leading German Catholics. In a lengthy radio address, van der Ven explained that the founders of the new association were striving for nothing less than a new form of global citizenship, a mission to be accomplished through religious and political renewal.[32] Although there was no substantive divergence between his ideas on international politics and those of Beaufort, their goals were diametrically opposed. Whereas Beaufort wanted to build an international judicial structure to prevent violence, the aim of the Catholic Association for Spiritual Renewal was to create an international community from the bottom up: in his view, to have people's prejudices towards one another be stripped away through their contact as brothers and sisters would be far more effective than the creation of new judicial or political institutions.[33]

'Modern Ideas' and Church Leadership

The line of reasoning developed by van der Ven and Beaufort was not unique in post-war Europe. In 1950, the American socio-democratic political monthly *Partisan Review* published an issue on 'Religion and the Intellectuals'. The editors ascertained a 'new turn toward religion among intellectuals and [a] growing disfavour with which secular attitudes and perspectives are regarded in not a few circles that lay claim to the leadership of culture'.[34] Fears of secularisation were informed not only by the threat of Soviet Communism but also by a growing number of publications on the demise of community and the rise of mass society in the Western world. As discussed more extensively in the introduction to this volume, academic and intellectual elites in both North America and Europe had become concerned with the modern individual's isolation and alienation from civic participation. Modern urban-industrial society was contrasted with traditional society composed of genuine communities. The rise of fascism in the 1930s and the war itself were seen as having represented important warning signs of the potentially devastating effects of individualisation inflicted by modern mass culture.[35]

While the debate on community, internationalism and religious renewal had a relatively low profile in the Netherlands, in France it was conducted with more vigour and visibility. In various theological study-centres, ideas about the future role of the church in modern society were discussed with great urgency and with a relative openness made possible by a generation of bishops who shared a belief in the necessity of such conversations.[36] A fine example is the French worker-priest movement, which flourished between 1945 and 1954. Living in tenements rather than their presbyteries, worker-priests took jobs in factories or construction sites. They mixed conventional forms of evangelism with engagement of fellow workers in religious discussions, inviting them to celebrations of Mass and performing baptisms, weddings, funerals and other religious rites. Sharing the political interests and convictions of their fellow workers, some became active in Communist-dominated trade unions. International relations and the prospect of a supranational community—along with religion's role in the lives of the working class and the French government's social policies—were among their main topics of interest. The movement discussed the links among European cooperation, religious renewal and the role of the Church in modern society, offering a vision akin to van der Ven's. People having their prejudices towards one another stripped away through their relations as brothers and sisters would be a first step towards perpetual peace and the building of a true international community.[37] The movement was reluctantly approved by Pope Pius XII in 1945 but due to its increasing participation in left-wing politics it fell out of favour with the Vatican at the end of the decade.[38]

At the same time, a strong agenda in the service of community and internationalism had been developed within the Vatican itself. In his first encyclical on 'the unity of human society', Pius XII had already warned against the idea that the state was 'something ultimate to which everything else should be subordinated'. The text, published only days after the German invasion of Poland in September 1939, warned of the 'idea which credits the State with unlimited authority'.[39] This line of argument was continued in his Christmas messages of 1942 and 1944: in the latter address the pope concluded that 'the state does not contain in itself and does not mechanically bring together in a given territory a shapeless mass of individuals'.[40] In all three texts, one can recognise a general outline of an international spiritual community under papal leadership that would transcend state borders as well as national politics. It remained rather vague whether this leadership would have not only spiritual implications but also political consequences. Whereas in his first encyclical and in the Christmas message of 1942 it seems as if the Pope's leadership was to extend beyond the spiritual realm, the message of 1944 clearly stipulated that the role of the Church was limited to being the guardian of humanity's true dignity and liberty.

Fundamental to this position was the idea that the social order was a given. The most important lesson to be learned after the war was that the growing power of the state could potentially endanger the social order and infringe upon the fundamental rights of humanity. Therefore, Catholic community had to be strengthened by the preservation of traditional religious life, the protection of traditional family values and continued adherence to the Church's classic social teachings. Unity and tradition remained powerful shibboleths, hence the Vatican's doubts towards Maritain's ideas on religious renewal. And although the Christmas message of 1944 recognised democracy as 'a postulate of nature imposed by reason itself', this did not imply that every individual's opinion was essentially of equal importance. Whereas the pope conceptualised the Catholic community as a fixed order transcending state borders and led spiritually by the Holy See, community was regarded as a gathering of equal individuals by Maritain, the worker-priest movement and van der Ven's Association for Spiritual Renewal.[41]

The leadership of the national churches responded in different ways. In post-war Britain, the traditional values of family, home and piety were back on the agenda. The churches benefited to the extent that during the late 1940s and the first half of the 1950s, Britain witnessed the largest per annum growth in church membership since the mid-nineteenth century, as church leaders—Protestant and Catholic alike—vigorously brought the importance of those values to the fore. In Germany the churches connected the evils of secularisation with the rise of Nazism and identified among their prime responsibilities not only the seeking of forgiveness for the German people, but also the discernment of ways to prevent such degeneration from ever happening again.[42] In the Netherlands, the Protestant churches reacted along similar lines. The Dutch Reformed Church launched a campaign to reinvent itself as a 'professing church at the heart of society'. A strong emphasis on the need to deepen the religious life of the individual churchgoer was combined with harsh criticism directed at Dutch society as a whole. All forms of sectarianism had to be rejected, for 'the Church chooses the unity of the whole nation called to the service of the Lord above the separation of the people in different worshipping communities'. Here, the church was explicitly presented as a community-promoting force within the countervailing setting of a society that was being corrupted by division, secularisation and the rise of mass culture.[43]

The Dutch Catholic Church acted in ways similar to those of British religious elites during the first post-war years and followed the pace set by the Vatican in its analysis of new narratives of community and internationalism. In its first post-war pastoral letter, the Dutch episcopacy called upon its flock not only to reinstate Catholic organisations and restore damaged churches, but also to uphold traditional family life and to view 'modern ideas' and 'ecumenical overstretch' with caution. The bishops unmasked the renewal of religious life as it had been promoted by the Reformed Church, as well as by several Catholic intellectuals including those affiliated with the Association for Spiritual Renewal, as secularisation in disguise. Beaufort escaped such criticism; his line of reasoning did not conflict so much with the policy of the episcopacy due to his efforts to address international relations in a more isolated manner. The bishops called upon all believers to be wary of those who argued that a new era in need of a renewed church had now arrived. Because there were serious repercussions for those who ignored these exhortations, a number of leading Catholic intellectuals turned to world politics in order to create a space of intellectual freedom for thinking about the future role of their church in modern society. In several small but influential cultural journals, new ideas on the role of religion in modern mass society were joined with new theological insights and changing narratives regarding community and internationalism.[44] The Catholic Association for Spiritual Renewal was one of the organisations that fostered discussion of these themes.

The Dutch episcopacy kept a close watch on the activities of the Association. When asked for financial support, Archbishop Johannes de Jong responded that the Association's financial needs could be met if it would simply concentrate its work on spreading the faith across national borders. At the same time, however, de Jong urged van der Ven to be reticent in revealing his ideas on religious renewal at home. Ideas on community building from below, spiritual renewal and human dignity did not fit into the bishops' central narrative, in which placidity would best serve the Catholic community.[45] Their vision of community was still informed by classic Catholic social teaching that consisted of a strong anti-pluralism and a communitarian conception of society in which social harmony was optimally served by everyone knowing their place. Ideas brought to the fore by Beaufort on building a new judicial structure to regulate international relations were more compatible with this worldview.[46]

Differences between the episcopacy and the Association were concealed by the promise of the Association's leadership to be restrained about religious renewal in public and to focus on their work abroad. The bishops trusted the leadership because it consisted of leading academics and members of religious orders who would not, it was thought, risk open conflict with the episcopacy. With the newly founded Dutch section of Pax Christi—which had personal ties with, as well as some ideological resemblance to, the Association for Spiritual Renewal—the level of trust was much lower. When the eight who had established the Dutch section in May 1948 asked for financial support, only two years after the Association for Spiritual Renewal was awarded ten thousand guilders, their request was denied.[47] Shortly afterwards, the National Centre of Dutch Catholic Action, which coordinated most of the laymen's initiatives in the Dutch Church Province, advised vicar-general of the Archdiocese J.M. Geerdink to be cautious towards the new movement. Participation in it, especially by young working-class Catholics, could 'threaten their religious life', because the new movement had 'an openness towards new theological and political ideas while lacking leadership that was able to keep those voices of renewal in their place'. Only after a profound restructuring of the section in 1952, when auxiliary-bishop of Utrecht Bernard Alfrink became chairman of Pax Christi Netherlands, did the Dutch episcopacy conclude that the new movement could be an asset rather than a threat to the network of Catholic organisations in the Netherlands.[48]

Through Prayer, Not Politics

Although, obviously, the vast majority of church leaders and theologians adhered to the Vatican's position, oppositional forces that argued for church renewal were nonetheless quite strong. Especially in France, and to a lesser extent in the Netherlands, a wave of theological renewal swept through important institutions; a new era, in need of a new Church, was proclaimed in theological journals and manuscripts. The exact ramifications of these urges for renewal remained unclear, but within organisations like the worker-priest movement and the Dutch Association for Spiritual Renewal, the relations between religious and political modes of renewal were discussed with great urgency, an urgency that shared some similarities with the way the Dutch Reformed Church was reassessing its societal role.

These discussions were particularly vivid within the newfound Pax Christi movement. Whereas the French section adopted the ideas of Maritain and others, the German section followed the Vatican line. The Dutch section, founded two years after the French and the German branches, chose an intermediary position.[49] Early in March 1945, a small network of Catholics that had emerged within the French resistance, led by the teacher Marthe Dortel-Claudot, met with Bishop Pierre-Marie Théas of Montauban. They wanted to organise a 'crusade of prayer' for the spiritual healing of the German people after twelve years of Nazism. The bishop gave his warm support, provided his Archbishop would approve. Théas—a fierce critic of the Vichy government—had been promoted to bishop of Tarbes-Lourdes soon after the liberation because of his steadfast attitude during the war. One of his basic principles was that in the post-war years, reconciliation between Germans and Frenchmen had to be the top priority for both the French and German episcopacies.[50] It was therefore no surprise that the group went to Théas for support. After the archbishop gave his blessing, a crusade of prayer for the former enemy was announced in the prominent Catholic newspaper *La Croix*.[51]

Pax Christi grew quickly, and before long bishops in Germany and France proffered their support. There were pilgrimages to Lourdes and other actions to promote Franco-German reconciliation. By the summer of 1950, eleven national sections had been founded, including one in the Netherlands. In late July 1951, the movement organised its fourth international conference in Lourdes. Over a period of four days, twenty-five thousand pilgrims from no fewer than twenty countries attended talks, masses and public lectures (see figure 9.2).[52] The movement's rapid growth and internationalisation urged its leadership to formalise its organisational structure. In line with the customary principles governing Catholic lay organisations, Pax Christi was organised under the strict hierarchical control of the bishops and its efforts rested mainly upon the activism of a small elite of laypersons. In 1950, its headquarters was moved to Paris, where Archbishop Maurice Feltin took over the leadership of Pax Christi International. He declared that a member of the episcopacy must preside over each section and proclaimed the triad of prayer, study and action to be the ideological and practical backbone of the organisation.[53]

Already in the late 1940s, Pax Christi was beginning to realise that its model of spirituality would guide the movement towards social and political action. From this moment on, there was some disagreement between the French and German sections about the movement's central goals. According to Father Manfred Hörhammer, intellectual leader of the German section, Pax Christi ought to be a purely spiritual movement, its work free from any

Figure 9.2 A Pax Christi hike near Altenberg, Germany (1953).
Source: Catholic Documentation Centre, Nijmegen.

political implications. Hörhammer wanted Pax Christi to be concerned with reconciliation through prayer, not politics.[54] According to Marcel Smits van Waesberghe, secretary of the Dutch section, this was simply impossible. In a world still shaped by the consequences of the war, a movement of reconciliation could never be strictly spiritual, he noted following a speech delivered by Hörhammer in the Netherlands. But Hörhammer believed his ideals to be fully in line with the vision of Pope Pius XII, who also propagated a strand of non-political Catholicism and was in favour of building an international spiritual community separate from politics. At its best, this community could be a beacon guiding political leaders towards a road of peace and justice.[55]

Within the French section, such ideas were thought to be outdated. The section's leadership consciously adhered to Maritain's distinction between politics and faith. Because the latter always had to inspire the former, in practice this gave Pax Christi some room to operate. Their religious inspirations compelled members of Pax Christi to speak their minds on political and social themes. So, paradoxically, the emergence of a more politically loaded vocabulary within the French section depended on taking a step backwards, away from the sphere of politics.[56] Already in 1948, when he was still Archbishop of Bordeaux, Feltin offered a plea for a more active and outspoken Pax Christi as a forerunner of a more active and outspoken Church. In his speech, he quoted the works of Maritain more than once. After being ordained as Archbishop of Paris one year later, Feltin was one of the driving forces behind a plea by the French episcopacy urging all Catholics to support European unification. One of the first outlines of an ideological foundation of Pax Christi International, made by Abbé Bernard Lalande, Feltin's personal secretary, mentioned European integration—conceived not only as a form of state cooperation but as a community of people—as the movement's primary interest. When all Catholics chose to transcend borders, the work undertaken by Catholic politicians to unite Europe would have a much better chance to succeed since the people of Europe would already be 'united in spirit'.[57]

The same ideas were brought to the fore within the Dutch section, still in its embryonic stage at the end of the 1940s. In one of the movement's first publications, an article in the local daily *De Gelderlander*, a pilgrimage was announced for the first Sunday of Advent in 1949 'in support of the work being done by Catholic politicians to reunite our continent'. From 1950 onwards, however, leadership of the Dutch section became more conscious of the dangers of the French position. In 1950, Pius XII published his encyclical *Humani Generis*, in which he explicitly rejected as heretical the theological renewal that had been undertaken in recent years, especially in France. Several leading theologians were removed from their positions at Catholic institutions and their ideas were condemned. Thereafter, the French section steered clear of discussions about community building and European unification and focused instead on national issues such as disarmament and resistance to France becoming a nuclear power.[58]

Within the Dutch section, the international theological climate forced its leadership to avoid making political statements. Building better relations with the episcopacy became even more important; its leadership began to follow the German section in its reluctance to speak out on political themes. Ideas about community and peace from then on were developed in a solely spiritual fashion until at least the mid-1950s. These differences became clear at an international conference in Lourdes in 1950, according to one attendee. Whereas the French section had been politicised in recent years, German and Dutch participants remained primarily interested in spiritual matters. For them, the building of a European community was exclusively a spiritual endeavour.[59]

A Vatican Conspiracy

These different perspectives on European integration and the building of international community came to some sort of synthesis in early 1950.[60] On 9 May, Robert Schuman, foreign minister of France, proposed to 'place Franco-German production of coal and steel under one common High Authority in an organisation open to participation of other countries in Europe'. Although the initiative at first glance seemed exclusively economic in nature, the speech given at the launch of the project suggested otherwise. In his talk, Schuman emphasised the creation of 'Europe' as a necessary safeguard for peace. In a speech delivered a year earlier in Strasbourg, Schuman had concluded that perpetual peace would best be served by the creation of a 'true European spirit', echoing the words used by Feltin round the same time. This spirit 'signifies being conscious of belonging to a cultural family and to have a willingness to serve that community in the spirit of total mutuality without any hidden motives or hegemony'. Here, Schuman opposed this new spirit explicitly with the 'national spirit' of 'the nineteenth century'.[61]

In the years before, during and after the war, Schuman had had intensive contacts with both Pius XII and Jacques Maritain. On the one hand, his ideas on human dignity and natural law were heavily influenced by Maritain, with whom he corresponded extensively. On the other hand, Schuman understood the importance of good relations with the Vatican. He visited the pope several times in the early post-war period and shared with him the vision of a spiritual community of Catholics that would transcend state borders.[62] But while the pope understood such a community in strictly spiritual terms, Schuman knew that it would need to become a political reality in order to really support enduring peace between France and Germany. Like a tightrope dancer, Schuman was able to find middle ground in the post-war debate on community and internationalism. Along with several Catholic intellectuals, he acknowledged the need for spiritual renewal without ever stepping over the boundaries drawn by the Roman Curia. In his essay 'On Europe', Schuman noted that it was Christianity that taught that all people were equal in their essence. This law, which was at the foundation of social relations in the Christian world, would have to inspire the creation of a new international community. The European project was the political consequence of these beliefs.[63]

The French initiative was scrupulously kept secret. Only German chancellor Konrad Adenauer had been informed of it. Many governments, including the Dutch, were taken by surprise when it was revealed.[64] Like those on the French political left, Dutch social-democratic prime minister Willem Drees rejected the plan out of hand, framing it as a 'Vatican conspiracy' to rebuild Europe in a Catholic fashion.[65] According to Schuman, such a claim was false: 'The "Vatican Europe" is a myth. The Europe we envisage is as profane in the ideas which form its foundation as in the men who are establishing it. They take from the Holy See neither their inspiration nor their orders'. On the other hand, Schuman, too, concluded there was 'a sort of predisposition, a similarity of preoccupations which renders Christians open to European ideas'. Although Europe was no 'theocracy', the inspiration of its leaders and the spirit of their followers were important.[66]

In Catholic communities in Western Europe, during and immediately following the Second World War, a broad discussion was conducted on peace and community. Intellectuals, clerics and politicians formed an important network whose members discussed the role of religious doctrines and Catholic social teachings in the building of a peaceful post-war world. Within a broad range of magazines and movements, they conceptualised an international Catholic community as a moral community of likeminded and equal individuals. They combined a principal openness towards non-Catholics with the feeling that both religious life and church politics were in urgent need of renewal. At the same time, the Holy See developed ideas on international Catholic community in a more traditional sense by emphasising traditional family values, a strong anti-pluralism and a communitarian conception of society in which social harmony was best served by everyone knowing their place. The ideas of both groups were important, forming as they did the intellectual context for politicians working at the origin of Europe's political and economic integration. Following the work of especially Kiran Klaus Patel, these narratives of Europe as a spiritual or moral community should be more fully integrated into the history of early European integration. This chapter has aimed to show the benefits of adopting a transnational approach in order to understand the importance of intellectual debates on community, religious renewal and internationalism and political ideas about internationalism and European cooperation.

Notes

1. Van den Bos, *Mensen van goede wil*, 19–39.
2. Schloesser, *Jazz Age Catholicism*; Gauvreau, *Catholic Origins*; van den Bos, *Verlangen naar vernieuwing*.
3. Cortright, *Peace*, 114–17; Moyn, *Last Utopia*, 44–83; Burleigh, *Sacred Causes*, 290–318.
4. I use the term 'laboratories' here following the Italian social scientist Alberto Melucci, who concluded that social movements can best be analysed as places where new ideas arise out of discussions on the role and position of the organisation amid the different societal spheres it has to deal with. Melucci, *Nomads*.
5. Cf. Hobsbawm, *Age of Extremes*, 22.
6. Kaiser, "Transnational Western Europe," 17–35; McLeod, *Religious Crisis*, 58–59.
7. Kaiser, "Transnational Networks," 15–16.
8. Patel, "Provincializing Europe," 649–73.
9. Greif, *The Age*, 204–5.
10. Mazower, *Dark Continent*, 194. Also, Conway downplays the importance of ideas in the early post-war period: Conway, *Sorrows of Belgium*, 24–25.
11. Ardanuy, van den Bos, and Sporleder, "Laboratories of Community," 284–93; de Bruin, *Elastisch Europa*; Van Middelaar, "Telling Another Story," 82–89.
12. Brown, *Death of Christian Britain*, 170; Lawson, *Church of England*, 11–15; McLeod, *Religion*, 132–35.
13. Mazower, "Success," 51; Conway, *Sorrows of Belgium*, 212–4.
14. Van Melis, "Strengthened and Purified," 241; Horn, "Left Catholicism," 13–44.
15. Kaiser, *Christian Democracy*, 152–53; Fimister, "Integral Humanism," 25–37.
16. Alfond, *Narrative, Nature*, 49–81; Moyn, "Personalismus," 63–91.
17. Moyn, *Christian Human Rights*.
18. Greif, *The Age*, 7; Keller, *Deutsch-französische Dritte-Weg-Diskurse*, 234–37.
19. Quoted from: Kaiser, *Christian Democracy*, 153.
20. Moyn, "Personalismus"; McLeod, *Religious Crisis*, 34.
21. Simons en Winkeler, *Verraad der Clercken*, 178, 186; *Te Elfder Ure* 3 (1955–56): 324.

22. Van Kleffens to Beaufort, 7 March 1945, folder 11, Dydimus Beaufort Papers: 82, Archive of the Dutch Province of the Order of the Friars Minor (hereafter cited as AOFM).
23. Beaufort, *Anarchie naar rechtsgemeenschap*; Beaufort, "Universele verklaring," 459–64; Beaufort, "Universele Verklaring, ii," 483–90.
24. De Haan to 'leden voorlopig comité', January 1925, inv.nr. 2, R. K. Vredesbond Archives, Catholic Documentation Centre, Nijmegen (hereafter cited as CDC); Beaufort to Nolens, 21 January 1926; Beaufort to Nolens, 29 January 1926, both inv.nr. 325, W.H. Nolens Papers (hereafter cited as NOLE), CDC.
25. Massaro sj and Shannon, *Catholic Perspectives*, 4–22; Bainton, *Christian Attitudes*, 10–110.
26. Cf. Moyn, "Surprising Origins," 19–33.
27. Aengenent, *God en het kwaad*, 9, 54–56; De Langen Wendels op, *De christelijke vredesgedachte*, 38–39.
28. *Pro Pace* 1, 1 (1929–30): 5–7, 11; Beaufort to Nolens, 10 October 1928, inv. nr. 325, NOLE, CDC.
29. In 1948, Beaufort became a member of the UN commission drafting the Universal Declaration of Human Rights. During debates on different versions of the text, he never mentioned a political or judicial role for the Holy See. Cf. Morsink, *Universal Declaration*, 288–9.
30. "Reünistencongres te Nijmegen," *De Tijd*, 21 March 1947; van der Ven, *Geestelijke; Te Elfder Ure* 1, no. 4 (1950).
31. Minutes of the first meeting of the Association for Spiritual Renewal, 29 November 1945; minutes of the second meeting of the Association for Spiritual Renewal, 18 January 1946, both inv.nr. 13, J.J.M. van der Ven Papers (hereafter cited as VENJ), CDC.
32. "Katholiek initiatief," *De Tijd*, 10 April 1946; "De toekomst van Duitsland," *De Tijd*, 20 January 1947; radio address by van der Ven on spiritual renewal in Germany, 4 January 1946, inv.nr. 24, VENJ, CDC.
33. Van der Ven, *Geestelijke vernieuwing*.
34. Quoted from: Silk, *Spiritual Politics*, 31.
35. Butsch, *Citizen Audience*, 110–11; Greif, *Age*, 258–60.
36. Cholvy and Hilaire, *Histoire*, iii, 121–25, 151–56; Potorowski, *Contemplation and Incarnation*.
37. Cole-Arnal, "*Témoignage*," 118–41.
38. Cholvy and Hilaire, *Histoire*, iii, 255.
39. *Summi Pontificatus*, no. 40 and 71.
40. *Democracy and a Lasting Peace: Christmas Message of His Holiness Pope Pius XII*, no. 21.
41. Chenaux, *Une Europe Vaticane*, 21–33; Fimister, *Robert Schuman*, 57–71.
42. Brown, *Death of Christian Britain*, 172; Burleigh, *Sacred Causes*, 304–5.
43. De Rooy, *Openbaring*, 44–52; Meijers, *Blanke broeders*, 126–46.
44. Van den Bos, "etHet Het sein?," 79–100.
45. De Jong to van der Ven, 26 September 1946; de Jong to van der Ven, 18 June 1947, both inv.nr. 20, VENJ, CDC.
46. Van den Bos, *Mensen van goede wil*, 53–58.
47. De Jong to Emmen, 29 April 1948, inv.nr. 1380, Archive of the Roman Catholic Archdiocese Utrecht, The Utrecht Archives; Emmen to Custos, 23 March 1948, folder 2, Aquilinus Emmen Papers: 217, AOFM.
48. Divendal to Geerdink, 30 August 1948, inv.nr. 828, Archive of the National Centre of Catholic Action, CDC; van den Bos, *Mensen van goede wil*, 48–49.
49. Van den Bos, *Mensen van goede wil*, 43.
50. Latreille, "Un évêque résistant," 284–321; Cholvy and Hilaire, *Histoire*, 95, 111.

51. Chenaux, *Une Europe Vaticane*, 112–18; Mabille, *Les Catholiques et la paix*, 19, 23–29.
52. Mabille, *Les Catholiques et la paix*, 31–39, 120; Ziemann, "A Quantum of Solace?" 359–61.
53. Speech by Maurice Feltin, International Council Pax Christi, Paris, 16 December 1950, inv.nr. 1268, Pax Christi International Archives (hereafter cited as PXI), CDC.
54. Hecke, "Katholische Friedensgrupen," 128–9; Hörhammer, "Pionierarbeit," 30–6.
55. Response by Father Smits van Waesberghe on a lecture by Father Hörhammer, undated, inv.nr. 820, Pax Christi Netherlands Archives, CDC; Cf. Gerster, *Friedensdialoge*, 81–83.
56. Kelly, "Catholicism and the Left," 148.
57. *Documentation Catholique* 30 (1948): 1224; Lalande, "Le mouvement Pax Christi," undated, inv.nr. 318, PXI, CDC; Kaiser, *Christian Democracy*, 181.
58. Sevegrand, *Vers une église*, 44–47; Mabille, *Les Catholiques et la paix*, 115–30, 205–7.
59. Van den Bos, *Mensen van goede wil*, 38–39, 43, 47–48, 50.
60. Fransen, *Supranational Politics*, 94; Fimister, *Robert Schuman*, 17, 186–92.
61. Robert Schuman, Speech at the Council of Europe, Strasbourg, 16 May 1949; Robert Schuman, Declaration on Europe, Paris, 9 May 1950. Both texts can be found in full at http://www.schuman.info [accessed 21 April 2015].
62. Fimister, *Robert Schuman*, 131; Lejeune, *Robert Schuman*, 37–38, 51–58.
63. Schuman, *Pour l'Europe*, 57–58.
64. Nasra and Segers, "Between Charlemagne and Atlantis," 185.
65. Brouwer, "Architect van de Europese gemeenschap?" 201; Daalder and Gaemers, *Willem Drees*, 239–44.
66. Schuman in November 1954, quoted from: Fimister, *Robert Schuman*, 227.

Bibliography

Aengenent, J. D. J. *God en het kwaad in de wereld*. The Hague: Roebert, 1928.
Alfond, Fred C. *Narrative, Nature and the Natural Law: From Aquinas to International Human Rights*. New York: Palgrave, 2010.
Ardanuy, Mariona C., Maarten van den Bos, and Caroline Sporleder. "Laboratories of Community: How Digital Humanities Can Further New European Integration History." In *Social Informatics: SocInfo 2014—International Workshops, Barcelona, Spain, November 11, 2014, Revised Selected Papers*, edited by L.M. Aiello and D. McFarland, 284–93. Cham: Springer, 2015.
Bainton, Ronald H. *Christian Attitudes Towards War and Peace: A Historical Survey and Critical Re-Evaluation*. Pasadena: Wipf and Stock, 2008.
Beaufort, D. *Van anarchie naar rechtsgemeenschap*. Nijmegen: Dekker & Van de Vegt, 1948.
Beaufort, D. "Universele verklaring van de rechten van de mens." *Katholiek Staatkundig Maandschrift* 1 (1949–1950): 459–64.
Beaufort, D. "Universele Verklaring van de Rechten van de Mens, ii." *Katholiek Staatkundig Maandschrift* 1 (1949–1950): 483–90.
Bos, Maarten van den. *Verlangen naar vernieuwing. Nederlands katholicisme, 1953–2003*. Amsterdam: Wereldbibliotheek, 2012.
Bos, Maarten van den. "etHet Het sein om te vertrekken? Nederlandse katholieken in debat over verleden, heden en toekomst." In *Achter de zuilen. Op zoek naar*

religie in naoorlogs Nederland, edited by P. van Dam, J. Kennedy, and F. Wielenga, 79–100. Amsterdam: Amsterdam University Press, 2014.
Bos, Maarten van den. *Mensen van goede wil. Pax Christi, 1948–2013*. Amsterdam: Wereldbibliotheek, 2015.
Brouwer, J. W. "Architect van de Europese Gemeenschap? Jan Willem Beyen (1952–1956)." In *De Nederlandse ministers van Buitenlandse Zaken in de twintigste eeuw*, edited by D. Hellema, B. Zeeman, and A.C. van der Zwan, 199–210. The Hague: sdu, 1999.
Brown, C. *The Death of Christian Britain: Understanding Secularization 1800–2000*. New York: Routledge, 2001.
Bruin, R. de. *Elastisch Europa. De integratie van Europa en de Nederlandse politiek, 1947–1968*. Amsterdam: Wereldbibliotheek, 2014.
Burleigh, M. *Sacred Causes: The Clash of Religion and Politics from the Great War to the War on Terror*. New York: Harper, 2006.
Butsch, R. *The Citizen Audience: Crowds, Publics and Individuals*. New York: Routledge, 2008.
Chenaux, P. *Une Europe Vaticane? Entre le plan Marshall et les traités de Rome*. Brussels: Éd. Ciaco, 1990.
Cholvy, G. and M. Hilaire. *Histoire religieuse de la France Contemporaine, iii, 1930–1988*. Toulouse: Privat, 1988.
Cole-Arnal, O. "The *Témoignage* of the Worker Priests: Contextual Layers of the Pioneer Epoch (1941–1955)." In *Catholics and Society in Western Europe at the Point of Liberation*, edited by E. Gerard and G.R. Horn, 118–41. Leuven: Leuven University Press, 2001.
Conway, Martin. *The Sorrows of Belgium: Liberation and Political Reconstruction, 1944–1947*. Oxford: Oxford University Press, 2012.
Cortright, David. *Peace: A History of Movements and Ideas*. Cambridge: Cambridge University Press, 2008.
Daalder, H. and J. Gaemers. *Willem Drees. Premier en elder statesman. De jaren 1948–1988*. Amsterdam: Balans, 2014.
Fimister, A. P. "Integral Humanism and the Re-Unification of Europe." In *Robert Schuman et les pères de l'Europe*, edited by S. Schirmann, 25–37. Brussels: Peter Lang, 2008.
Fimister, A. P. *Robert Schuman: Neo-Scholastic Humanism and the Reunification of Europe*. Brussels: Pieter Lang, 2008.
Fransen, F. J. *The Supranational Politics of Jean Monnet: Ideas and Origins of the European Community*. Westport: Greenwood Press, 2001.
Gauvreau, M. *The Catholic Origins of Quebec's Quiet Revolution, 1931–1970*. Montreal: McGill-Queens University Press, 2005.
Gerster, D. *Friedensdialoge im Kalten Krieg. Eine Geschichte der Katholiken in der Bundesrepublik 1957–1983*. Frankfurt: Campus Verlag, 2012.
Greif, M. *The Age of the Crisis of Man: Thought and Fiction in America, 1933–1973*. Princeton: Princeton University Press, 2015.
Hecke, B. "Katholische Friedensgrupen in Westdeutschland zwischen 1945–1955— Brüche, Kontinuitäten." In *75 Jahre katholische Friedensbewegung in Deutschland*, edited by Johannes Horstmann, 117–36. Idstein: Komzi, 1995.
Hörhammer, M. "Pionierarbeit in den ersten Jahren. Die Erfahrungen von Krieg und Gefangenschaft führten zur Idee von Pax Christi." In *Pax Christi. Friedensbewegung*

in der Katholischen Kirche, edited by H. Pfister, 30–36. Waldkirch: Waldkircher Verlagsgestellschaft, 1980.

Horn, G. R. "Left Catholicism in Western Europe in the 1940s." In *Left Catholicism: Catholics and Society in Western Europe at the Point of Liberation*, edited by G.R. Horn and E. Gerard, 13–44. Leuven: Leuven University Press, 2001.

Kaiser, W. "Transnational Western Europe Since 1945: Integration as Political Society Formation." In *Transnational European Union: Towards a Common Political Space*, edited by W. Kaiser and P. Starie, 17–35. London: Routledge, 2005.

Kaiser, W. *Christian Democracy and the Origins of European Union*. Cambridge: Cambridge University Press, 2007.

Kaiser, W. "Transnational Networks in European Governance: The Informal Politics of Integration." In *The History of the European Union: Origins of a Trans- and Supranational Polity 1950–1972*, edited by W. Kaiser, B. Leucht, and M. Rasmussen, 12–33. London: Routledge, 2009.

Keller, T. *Deutsch-französische Dritte-Weg-Diskurse. Personalistische Intellektuellendebatten in der Zwischenkriegszeit*. Munich: Fink, 2001.

Kelly, M. "Catholicism and the Left in Twentieth-Century France." In *Catholicism, Politics and Society in Twentieth-Century France*, edited by K. Chadwick, 142–74. Liverpool: Liverpool University Press, 2000.

Langen Wendels op, G. de. *De christelijke vredesgedachte. Rede uitgesproken ter viering van den eersten dies natalis der R.K. Universiteit*. Nijmegen: Dekker & Van de Vegt, 1925.

Latreille, A. "Un évêque résistant. Mgr. Pierre-Marie Théas, évêque de Montauban, 1940–1946." *Revue d'histoire ecclésiastique* 75 (1980): 284–321.

Lawson, T. *The Church of England and the Holocaust: Christianity, Memory and Nazism*. Woodbridge: The Boydell Press, 2006.

Lejeune, R. *Robert Schuman, Père de l'Europe*. Paris: Serge Domini, 2000.

Mabille, F. *Les Catholiques et la paix au temps de la guerre froide. Le mouvement Catholique international pour la paix Pax Christi*. Paris: Harmattan, 2004.

Massaro sj, Thomas J. and Thomas A. Shannon. *Catholic Perspectives on War and Peace*. Lanham: Sheed and Ward, 2004.

Mazower, M. *Dark Continent: Europe's Twentieth Century*. London: Penguin Books, 1998.

Mazower, M. "Success of a Belgian Political Elite." *Low Countries Historical Review* 129 (2014): 50–54.

McLeod, Hugh. *Religion and the People of Western Europe*. Oxford: Oxford University Press, 1997.

McLeod, Hugh. *The Religious Crisis of the 1960s*. Oxford: Oxford University Press, 2007.

Meijers, E. *Blanke broeders, zwarte vreemden. De Nederlandse Hervormde Kerk, de Gereformeerde Kerken in Nederland en de apartheid in Zuid Afrika 1948–1972*. Hilversum: Verloren, 2008.

Melis, D. van. "Strengthened and Purified through Ordeal by Fire: Ecclesiastical Triumphalism in the Ruins of Europe." In *Life after Death: Approaches to a Cultural and Social History of Europe during the 1940s and 1950s*, edited by R. Bessel and D. Schumann, 231–41. Cambridge: Cambridge University Press, 2003.

Melucci, A. *Nomads of the Present: Social Movements and Individual Needs in Contemporary Society*. New York: Temple University Press, 1989.

Middelaar, L. van. "Telling Another Story about Europe: A Reply in Favour of Politics." *Low Countries Historical Review* 125 (2010): 82–89.

Milward, A. S. *The European Rescue of the Nation-State*. London: Routledge, 1992.
Morsink, J. *The Universal Declaration of Human Rights: Origins, Drafting and Intent*. Philadelphia: University of Pennsylvania Press, 1999.
Moyn, Samuel. *The Last Utopia: Human Rights in History*. Cambridge: Cambridge University Press, 2008.
Moyn, Samuel. "Personalismus, Gemeinschaft und die Ursprunge der Menschenrechte." In *Moralpolitik. Geschichte der Menschenrechte im 20. Jahrhundert*, edited by Stefan-Ludwig Hoffmann, 63–91. Göttingen: Wallstein, 2010.
Moyn, Samuel. "The Surprising Origins of Human Dignity." In: *Human Rights and the Uses of History*, edited by Samuel Moyn, 19–33. New York: Verso, 2014.
Moyn, Samuel. *Christian Human Rights*. Philadelphia: University of Pennsylvania Press, 2015.
Nasra, S. and M. Segers. "Between Charlemagne and Atlantis: Belgium and the Netherlands during the First Stages of European Integration (1950–1966)." *Journal of European Integration History* 18 (2012): 183–206.
Patel, K. K. "Provincializing European Union: Co-Operation and Integration in Europe in a Historical Perspective." *Contemporary European History* 22 (2013): 649–73.
Potarowski, C. F. *Contemplation and Incarnation: The Theology of Marie-Dominque Chenu*. Montreal: McGill-Queens University Press, 2001.
Rooy, P. de. *Openbaring en openbaarheid*. Amsterdam: Wereldbibliotheek, 2009.
Rooy, P. de. *Ons stipje op de waereldkaart. De politieke cultuur van modern Nederland*. Amsterdam: Wereldbibliotheek, 2014.
Schloesser, S. *Jazz Age Catholicism: Mystic Modernism in Postwar Paris, 1919–1933*. Toronto: University of Toronto Press, 2005.
Schuman, R. *Pour l'Europe. Cinquième Édition*. Paris: Nagel, 2005.
Seidel, K. "From Pioneer Work to Refinement: Publication Trends." In *European Union History: Themes and Debates*, edited by W. Kaiser and A. Varsori, 26–44. Basingstoke: Palgrave, 2011.
Sevegrand, M. *Vers une Église sans prêtres. La crise du clergé seculier en France (1945–1978)*. Rennes: Presses Universitaires de Rennes, 2004.
Silk, M. *Spiritual Politics: Religion and America since World War ii*. New York: Touchstone, 1988.
Simons, E. and L. Winkeler. *Het verraad der clercken. Intellectuelen en hun rol in de ontwikkelingen van het Nederlandse katholicisme na 1945*. Baarn: Arbor, 1987.
Ven, J. J. M. van der. *Geestelijke vernieuwing in Europa*. Nijmegen: Geert Grote Genootschap, 1947.
Ven, J. J. M. van der. *Geestelijke vernieuwing van West-Europa*. 's-Hertogenbosch: Katholiek Genootschap voor Geestelijke Vernieuwing, 1947.
Ziemann, B. "A Quantum of Solace? European Peace Movements during the Cold War and Their Elective Affinities." *Archiv für Sozialgeschichte* 49 (2009): 351–89.

10 Piercing the Iron Curtain?
Competing Visions of Transnational Expert Community and the Question of International Order after 1945

Phillip Wagner

Recent scholarship has shown that alongside the superpowers' political and economic rivalry during the Cold War, the arms race and the ongoing rhetoric of confrontation throughout the conflict, there were various forms of cultural, humanitarian and expert internationalism that could pierce the Iron Curtain. Although movements across the East-West divide intersected with the aspirations of the superpowers, they were not fully determined by American or Soviet aims and were capable of following distinct agendas of their own.[1] This happened in an international arena in which the non-aligned nations of Europe in particular could pursue flexible strategies towards the United States and the Soviet Union, often sponsoring interactions between the two spheres.[2] Moreover, programmes of cultural exchange promoted dialogue between East and West, and sporting events provided sites for contact through competition.[3]

Besides conferences and sport tournaments, various forms of expert internationalism aimed to transcend Cold War cleavages.[4] Numerous commissions of the United Nations (UN) and the International Labour Organisation (ILO) became forums for East-West cooperation among professionals such as nuclear scientists and social experts. Moreover, researchers attempted to continue long-established forms of professional communication, maintaining contacts with their colleagues working abroad and resuming their engagement in specialist networks across the new divisions of post-war Europe. Both the desire to compete with the ideological enemy and the belief in the objectivity and impartiality of science fostered faith in transnational cooperation.[5]

Building on the scholarship on relations across the political divisions of the Cold War, my chapter argues that expert internationalism put forth ideas about transnational professional community that could question the predominant geopolitical context of the Cold War on a broader scale than previous studies on East-West cooperation have suggested. I will show how expert networks imagined conceptions of transnational community that not only challenged the rivalry between East and West but also called into question the cohesion of the Western alliance and offered alternatives to the internationalism of intergovernmental organisations such as the UN.

To study the many discourses on the scope of transnational professional communities during the Cold War, I use the International Federation for Housing and Town Planning (IFHTP) as a case study. In the first half of the twentieth century, the IFHTP was the largest non-state expert network devoted to urban, regional and national planning. Its mission was to investigate how societies could be made more cohesive through the control of spatial development.[6] Founded in 1913 as an outgrowth of the English garden cities movement, the network was transformed into an organisation for science-based spatial planning, attracting government officials, professors and leaders of national professional societies mainly from Europe and North America in the interwar years.[7] With its focus on seemingly objective and impartial expertise, it managed to manoeuvre through the many ideological conflicts of the interwar North Atlantic world. Against the background of the massive destructions of World War II and the prospect of a United Nations emerging as a global development agency, the IFHTP aspired to contribute to a worldwide discourse of urban planning after 1945.

My objective here is to present the IFHTP as a site for the discussion of various notions of transnational professional association. I argue that IFHTP officials contributed to the post-war establishment of the Federation by espousing distinct conceptions of professional community. From a larger perspective, I also argue that by envisioning transnational communities of urban planners, IFHTP functionaries always sought to negotiate the international order, whether this meant, for example, viewing the international system as a set of differing political regimes, conceiving it to be a hierarchical structure, or emphasising the role of non-state actors in it.

Like other non-governmental (and unofficial) international professional institutions, of course, the Federation could not determine the course or condition of international relations. Still, non-state international networks were in a position to shape transboundary connections among national professional groups that participated in its projects, and did so to forge new fields of expertise and to support their domestic lobbying.[8] Networks such as the IFHTP could at least exert a limited influence on the making of the international order in matters pertaining to their professional fields.

Addressing how a transnational community of experts was constructed during the Cold War, this study focuses on three interrelated areas that were central to many unofficial networks after 1945. First, drawing on proposals for East-West cooperation offered by the IFHTP's Polish members, I analyse how the network responded to growing hostilities between the United States and the Soviet Union. Second, this chapter is concerned with the way the IFHTP dealt with the legacy of a horrendous war, and concentrates on how Western European planners modelled their vision of a professional community against the backdrop of controversies around the readmission of German planners to their group. Third, this study scrutinises how the emergence of the United Nations made British IFHTP members rethink what a global expert community should look like.

By analysing these topics, my chapter approaches the notions of 'transnational community' and 'international order' from the perspective of modern cultural history as outlined in the introduction. It does not conceive 'community' and 'order' to be essentialist categories, but rather tries to discern the different languages and imageries of community in play during the Cold War and seeks to grasp their implications for the international order of this era.[9] Adopting the 'decentred approach' as outlined by Mark Bevir and Roderick A. W. Rhodes, my analysis is grounded in the view that various individual beliefs and actions construct transnational communities.[10] In contrast to studies that highlight the largely harmonious elements of 'global' and 'epistemic' communities, I seek to shed light on the interplay of inclusionary and exclusionary mechanisms, as well as the rivalries among conflicting visions of transnational association, that lies behind the different attempts to construct communities across national borders.[11]

Negotiating the Cold War

Among those envisioning a transnational community of urban planners after 1945 were the IFHTP's Polish members. Studies on the post-war history of Poland have long emphasised how swiftly the country was integrated into the Soviet bloc. They not only stress how the Soviet-sponsored Lublin Committee and United Workers' Party seized power but also emphasise that Polish scientists rapidly accepted the Russian biology of Lysenkoism and Warsaw authorities adopted Stalinist monumentalism in the rebuilding of the capital.[12] The example of the IFHTP, however, shows that Polish experts could question the terms of the bipolar international order after 1945. It also reveals how unofficial expert networks became forums in which different groups sought to challenge, from early on, the ideological divisions of the post-war period.

To understand how Polish IFHTP members sought to penetrate the Iron Curtain, we need to go back to the war years, when British IFHTP officials and experts from allied governments set up the Federation's so-called Free Section. After their nations were defeated by the Nazis, statesmen from France, the Netherlands, Belgium, Norway, Poland and Czechoslovakia set up exile governments in London to claim sovereignty over their German-occupied territories, to assist the Allied powers in fighting the Germans and their Axis allies, and to plan for post-war reconstruction. These administrations were also involved in the establishment of international forums, including international conferences for ministries of education and a committee for housing professionals.[13] The multifaceted ideological and strategic controversies among the exile authorities, however, often rendered intergovernmental cooperation cumbersome.[14] In this context, the British civil servant and long-serving IFHTP official George L. Pepler set up the Free Section (later called the Inter-Allied Committee for Physical Planning and Reconstruction) to study problems of post-war urban and regional planning together with delegates from governments-in-exile.[15] To avoid complicated negotiations in intergovernmental forums, Pepler sought to produce 'unofficial studies' to which planners could contribute as independent experts but not as delegates of their respective governments.[16]

Some of the keenest members of Pepler's committee came from a group of Polish architects and planners who moved in the orbit of their country's government-in-exile. Figures such as Henry Spiwak and Erwin Wieczorek had spent their formative years in the Western-oriented Second Republic (1918–1939), which had attempted to modernise the country under the influence of models from Germany, Great Britain, France and the United States. During this period, they experienced firsthand the prominent role played by architecture and planning in the process of Polish nation-building.[17] Both had been educated at the School of Architecture at the Warsaw Polytechnic, which had become a hub for science-based urban and regional planning.[18] In the Free Section, they performed housing studies, including comparative accounts of the shortage of shelter in Europe, and devised technocratic proposals to overcome the current crisis.[19]

In this context, Polish experts became vocal supporters of continuing cooperation even beyond the war and amid emerging East-West controversies. Spiwak was particularly active in defining the place of Poland in the post-war expert community of the IFHTP. An authority on modern building methods, he became head of the Free Section's subcommittee on housing. In this position, he championed a vision of a transnational community of planners that sought to integrate the whole of Europe. The Free Section reminded him of a 'green table', where planners could enjoy the 'golden opportunity to sit together [. . .] and look over their neighbour's shoulders', following 'the progress of new technique and new social and economic relations'.[20] This techno-diplomatic rhetoric suggests that Spiwak believed that rational planning could dampen emerging conflicts between East and West, uniting Europe in its desire to build itself anew after the war. Although Spiwak believed in a unified continent, he proposed that Western countries should take the lead since progressive ideas had allegedly originated in the West and then travelled eastwards. Thus, he conceived European planning to be 'a continuous line of humanely and scientifically conducted analysis [. . .] leading from [. . .] the pre-war plan of a city like Amsterdam to the Swedish war-time planning and to the post-war plan of Warsaw'.[21]

Spiwak's claim to define Poland's position in the IFHTP provoked the opposition of Polish planners such as Wacław Ostrowski. In contrast to Spiwak, Ostrowski had stayed in the largely destroyed capital of Warsaw after the defeat of the Polish army. He experienced how German authorities had banned reconstruction planning by domestic authorities. It is not certain whether he also knew of the secret German plans to eradicate Warsaw. During the German occupation, Ostrowski was in the orbit of an underground workshop devoted to Warsaw's post-war rebuilding led by prominent modernist planner Szymon Syrkus.[22] In 1945, Ostrowski was appointed to the urban planning section of the Biuro Odbudowy Stolicy (BOS, Bureau for the Reconstruction of the Capital) to draft a plan for the decentralisation of Warsaw.[23]

As a high-ranking BOS official, Ostrowski exerted an influence that rivalled Spiwak's attempt to define Poland's position in the IFHTP's transnational community of urban planners. He regarded Spiwak, who had refused to return home to pursue his patriotic duty to help rebuild his country, as a dubious figure. It is not certain whether he also knew that Spiwak had become a protégé of IFHTP president Pepler and his future wife Elizabeth Halton, who represented London's anti-communist and conservative establishment.[24] With the support of his colleague Stanisław Dziewulski, Ostrowski dismissed Spiwak as a Polish representative of the IFHTP in April 1946.[25]

Spiwak was discharged during a time when the status of the Polish government-in-exile was steadily decreasing. The communist Lublin Committee determinedly contested the aspirations of exile leaders in London. Moreover, the Western powers withdrew their recognition of the Western-oriented, anti-Soviet Polish exile administration after the Yalta Conference had determined that post-war Europe would be divided into two spheres of influence. The clash between Spiwak and Ostrowski demonstrates that the desire for a transnational community of urban planners across Cold War boundaries did not always result in harmonious transnational relations. Rather, envisioning a modus operandi for transnational collaboration could contribute to political rivalries that were shaped by the dynamics of the early Cold War.

Ostrowski and Spiwak espoused similar visions of an integral community of European planners, and this was another reason for the rivalry between the two Poles. Like Spiwak, Ostrowski belonged to the group of planners who had spent formative years in the Western-oriented Second Republic. Moreover, he had been a member of the IFHTP before the war. After 1945, he sought to continue the East-West dialogue he had pursued before the invasion of his home country. By attending IFHTP conferences, continuing to compare Polish and Western methods and eagerly lobbying on behalf of the Federation in Poland, he attempted to implement a vision of a European expert community that would help integrate the whole European continent despite increasing tensions between East and West.[26] Unlike Spiwak, he did not accept the supremacy of Western experts in an integral European community of planners; he believed that state-controlled urban and regional development in communist Poland offered superior prospects for comprehensive urban planning than Western Europe's liberal democracies, which had never comprehensively controlled the private building sector.[27]

Ostrowski's vision of a transnational community of urban planners crumbled as the rift between East and West gradually solidified after 1948. After the inauguration of the Marshall Plan and the establishment of a Stalinist regime in Poland, Western functionaries and Polish delegates gradually began to use the IFHTP as a platform to engage in Cold War conflict. For example, when Federation officials chose to discuss strategies for non-commercial housing during its 1950 international congress in Amsterdam, they framed the topic so that the discussion concerned only social housing in liberal Western societies. In turn, Polish delegates at the same conference session contested its terms, boldly declaring that in Poland the era of bourgeois social housing was over for good.[28] In addition, the transformation of Poland into a Stalinist Soviet satellite obstructed collaboration among planners from either side of the Iron Curtain. After the imposition of rigid restrictions on travel to capitalist countries in Poland, Polish membership in the IFHTP decreased from forty-one to four members in the 1950s.[29]

Still, the legacy of a transnational community of urban planners stretching across the Iron Curtain lived on. A later historical context gave this idea new life. As confrontation gradually gave way to détente starting in the 1960s, international organisations could again become sites for exchange across the Iron Curtain.[30] The example of the IFHTP indicates that expert dialogue between East and West was renewed not only through governmental institutions such as the ILO but also through unofficial expert networks. In this era, the Federation's standing commissions became forums for the reintegration of Polish planners who had advocated dialogue with Western planners in the years immediately after 1945.

During this period, Ostrowski, now a professor at the Warsaw Polytechnic, resurfaced on the international stage. From 1962 and 1974, he led an all-European committee on historic urban areas. He and his French colleagues from the Centre de Recherche d'Urbanisme (Center for Research in Urbanism) issued the commission's official report recommending the integration of modernist planning and the conservation of historical sites.[31] By collaborating with European colleagues on a topic of common concern, Ostrowski finally implemented a vision of a transnational expert community in which East and West could reciprocally learn from each other—a vision he had first encountered at the IFHTP's interwar conferences and had promoted during the initial stages of the East-West divide. This example suggests that the increase of professional communication across the Iron Curtain in the 1960s and 1970s needs to be explored in a wider historical perspective: some of the ideas for cooperation not only originated in the early Cold War but were also inspired by the experience of interwar expert internationalism.

Coming to Terms with the Legacies of World War II

German planners also helped create a transnational expert community through the IFHTP. The commonly accepted narrative emphasises how easily German planners, despite their former affiliations with the National Socialist regime, restored links to the professional discourse in the West after 1945.[32] Many planning officials who had mostly worked on an intermediate or local level during the Nazi reign, such as Rudolf Hillebrecht, became internationally respected experts for reconstruction after 1945. In addition, after adopting a more democratic and liberal vocabulary, major planning theorists such as Johannes Göderitz were able to adapt to the Western discussion. The experience of the IFHTP, which debated conceptions of a transnational community of planners that excluded German participation, runs counter to this accepted narrative. An examination of the Federation's activities indicates that the integration of German experts in the post-war West was a more contested and complex process than has been previously assumed.

To understand the troubled relationship between Germany and the IFHTP, again one must go back to the interwar years. German delegates, then at the forefront of urban planning, had left an important mark on the Federation during this era. Robert Schmidt, director of the Ruhr Planning Association, was an important voice at IFHTP conferences; Gustav Langen, head of the Archive for Urban Planning, Settlement Design and Housing, was a member of the IFHTP international town plan notation and glossary committees.[33] Even after the Nazi seizure of power in 1933, the German delegation was dedicated to continuing the international study of urban planning, at least at first. With the sanction of the Ministry for Propaganda, however, Nazi institutions such as the German Association of Local Authorities worked to co-opt the IFHTP, for example by installing Stuttgart mayor Karl Strölin as the organisation's president in 1938.[34] After the German invasion of Belgium in 1940, Strölin turned to more aggressive strategies—epitomized by the seizure of the IFHTP headquarters in Brussels.[35] This happened in the same context in which the German Congress Centre, operating under the Ministry of Propaganda, confiscated documents and other property from the well-known Union of International Associations to obtain intelligence against political opponents of the Nazi regime.[36] Strölin transferred the IFHTP headquarters to Stuttgart and began to use the organisation to disseminate propaganda about German urban planning to neutral, occupied and Axis countries. Appalled by their president's actions, members of the Federation from Allied countries established the Free Section to counter Nazi Germany's 'new order'.[37]

After the German surrender in 1945, memories of the Nazi capture of the Federation played a decisive part in shaping the ways that Western European IFHTP members imagined their transnational community of experts. The dismay and outrage over Strölin's coup worsened when the horrendous dimensions of the war waged by Germany became apparent. Formerly prosperous cities such as Coventry, Rotterdam and Warsaw lay in ruins. Dwellings and factories, farms and infrastructures had been razed throughout Europe, and millions of people had been murdered, enslaved and uprooted.[38]

These traumatic experiences led many of the IFHTP's planners, particularly those Western European planners who had endured Nazi occupation, to advocate a vision of a transnational expert community that deliberately excluded the involvement of Germans. Remembering that the majority of Germans in the IFHTP had been Nazis, the Amsterdam planning official Louis S.P. Scheffer was sceptical of German post-war ambitions: 'How can we possibly know for certain about these people?'[39] Similarly, the Belgian Institute for Habitation and Housing under Joseph Paquay blamed Germany for his nation's domestic housing crisis at the first post-war IFHTP exhibition and conference in Hastings in 1946. One of its posters showed families uprooted and towns destroyed by Nazis troops. Another poster charted the destruction of one hundred forty thousand housing units during the Belgian campaign and the complete failure of German occupation authorities to construct new homes (see Figure 10.1). Against this background, IFHTP officials debated whether to include in its official rules a section on the 'guilt of Germany in the War'.[40] Although they decided not to do so, they suspended Germans from IFHTP membership, refused to use the German language in any of its conferences and excluded past president Strölin. In establishing a transnational expert community that was deliberately anti-German, the IFHTP followed a concept of international order that was strikingly different from the official positions of the Western allies, which would use the soon-to-be-founded nation of West Germany as a bulwark against Soviet influence.

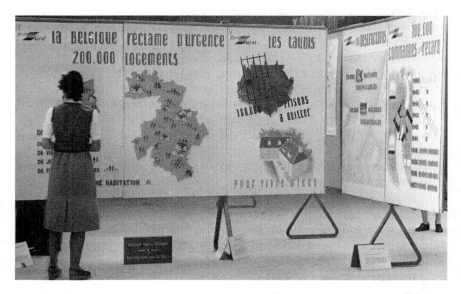

Figure 10.1 The Belgian section at the exhibition held during the 1946 IFHTP conference. The poster on the right represents the destruction committed by the German occupying forces and their shortcomings with regard to housing.

Source: IFHPA, box 9, courtesy of the International Federation of Housing and Planning, Copenhagen.

This vision was challenged by Paula Schäfer, a German who had cut her teeth as a secretary of the International Housing Association and the IFHTP in the 1930s. Fluent in English and French as well as her native language, she made her name as an organiser of international expert communication in the years leading up to the war. When Strölin assumed control over the Federation, she relocated to its new Stuttgart headquarters in 1940. Forced to resign from her post after the German surrender, she became secretary of the nascent professional organisation Deutscher Verband für Wohnungswesen, Städtebau und Raumordnung (DV, German Association for Housing, Urban and Spatial Planning).

In this position, Schäfer sought to regain access to the sphere of international professional communication. Challenging the prospect of a Federation that would exclude delegates from her native country, Schäfer envisioned the IFHTP as a transnational expert community that should also incorporate planners from a democratic Germany.[41] In countless letters to American and British IFHTP officials, she pursued different rhetorical strategies to advocate the readmission of German members to their organisation. First, she used every possibility to showcase her own internationalist credentials, emphasising the difficulties she had experienced because of her commitment to internationalism throughout the war, for instance when she secured 'the belongings of the IFHTP in the battles between US and German troops' in April 1945.[42] Like many other Germans after the surrender, she then presented her accidental conflicts with other institutions in Nazi Germany as signs of 'permanent opposition'.[43] Pointing to her membership in the Social Democratic Party before 1933, her rejection of National Socialism and her friends who had lost their lives 'opposing the fascist theory', Schäfer went to great lengths to refashion her image in terms of democratic respectability.[44] Finally, she stressed that the DV was similar to professional organisations in England and North America, all of which, she argued, conceived of planning as informing the policies of a modern, democratic and non-dictatorial welfare state.[45]

Schäfer supported her lobbying by investing considerable resources towards reintegrating the DV into the larger Western context. She forged links to well-known German émigrés in the United States, such as the modernist architectural pioneer Walter Gropius. In addition, she renewed connections with professionals in Austria and Switzerland (for example, the Viennese architect Franz Schuster) while attempting to prevent former Nazi collaborators (e.g., Ernst Neufert, an authority on architectural standardisation) from participating in international conferences.[46]

These strategies enabled Schäfer to earn respect and attention among those at the IFHTP headquarters. In 1948, the majority of Federation functionaries voted to include German reports in the proceedings of the next conference and to invite West Germany to send a delegation to a forthcoming conference in Zürich.[47] That year she also helped bring a group of famous English planners, including IFHTP officials Pepler and his wife

Elizabeth, to Germany to lecture about physical reconstruction. Two years later, Emile Vinck, the former mayor of Ixelles, Belgium, and at the time the grand seigneur of European municipalism who had favoured the readmission of Germans to the IFHTP after the First World War,[48] proposed that the DV be made the German section of the IFHTP and that German citizens from all zones of occupation be eligible for readmission to membership.[49] German planners, though feeling uneasy on the international stage due to their lack of international experience, were given full membership and representation in 1954.[50] In the year of her untimely death, Schäfer had achieved one of her greatest triumphs.

Historical conditions helped facilitate Schäfer's vision of German inclusion in the transnational community of the IFHTP. The implementation of the Marshall Plan, the blockade of Berlin and the foundation of the North Atlantic Treaty Organisation cemented the division between East and West in 1948–49 and assisted in making the Federal Republic of Germany a key nation in the so-called Free World. In addition, West German Chancellor Konrad Adenauer's policy of deliberate Westernization helped his country regain credibility beyond its borders, particularly with its neighbour to the west, France. However, it is important to note that these geopolitical realities did not fully determine the post-war reorganisation of professional institutions. As with Polish involvement in the IFHTP, the experience and attitudes of Scheffer, Paquay and Schäfer reveal that members in expert networks could envision a transnational community in a markedly different way than official diplomacy. Schäfer's example in particular contributes to our understanding that the westernization of Germany was a process not only controlled on the macro level but also shaped by individual internationalists on a non-state level.[51]

Competing Visions of the Global Division of Expert Labour

The discourses on the IFHTP professional community after 1945 revolved not only around topics of East-West cooperation and attitudes towards former World War II adversaries but also around the question how to engage with the nascent United Nations. The commonly accepted narrative argues that the UN, in becoming a dominant force that shaped global expert communication, sidelined professional networks and relegated them to the status of international non-governmental organisations (INGOs) in its consultative system.[52] The analysis of the Federation I offer here reveals, however, that focusing only on the marginalization of expert INGOs is too simplistic an approach. Unofficial networks such as the IFHTP could espouse alternative visions of a worldwide professional community that had consequences for the global division of expert labour in the UN.

In the early post-war years, it was not obvious that the UN could become instrumental in synthesising different professional fields within a relatively unified global development agenda. Although the nascent world organisation aspired to leadership in this field from early on, it did not at first possess the resources to conceive a programme of development and modernisation. For this reason, it depended on the cooperation of the official and unofficial expert organisations representing the professional spheres it wanted to combine in an integral scheme. For economic and financial policy, it could rely on experts from the recently disbanded League of Nations.[53] But urban planning—which had not been addressed by the League, but was now of immediate concern given the destruction wrought by World War II—was an area in which the UN was particularly attentive to suggestions from unofficial expert networks. Delegates from the International Congress of Modern Architecture, the renowned network of modernist architect-planners, and the International Union of Local Authorities, the principal municipalist organisation in Europe, found themselves lobbying the UN.[54]

In this context, the IFHTP also asserted itself. Having conducted a successful campaign for a new national planning system in Great Britain, which resulted in the 1946 New Towns Act and the 1947 Town and Country Planning Act, Federation officials George and Elizabeth Pepler were optimistic about repeating their success on a global scale, and felt that the UN could help achieve this aim. At the 1946 IFHTP conference, they passed a resolution that helped lead the UN to form a housing and planning section. In the following years, they advised a first series of UN housing studies.[55]

Against this backdrop, the Peplers sketched a vision of a global community of urban planners based on seemingly universal 'standards for the right homes in the right places'.[56] In this community, expert INGOs such as the IFHTP would be the principal forums for decision-making, with UN agencies being confined to executive action. As former League of Nations' functionaries such as Alexander Loveday had observed with regard to that global organisation, the Peplers believed that discussion of scientific and technical problems in UN meetings could not be impartial or objective: every delegate was bound by his or her government's instructions.[57] On the other hand, non-governmental networks could 'make decisions, [. . .] criticise methods, [. . .] support experiments' and 'advocate a course of action' because members participated in these organisations in a private capacity.[58] Thus, in conversation with high-ranking UN officials such as Maurice Milhaud and Alva Myrdal, Pepler proposed that INGOs would be ideal for the defining of global professional standards, which the UN could then transform into 'official' programmes.[59] In imagining a global community of urban planners, IFHTP officials also envisioned a worldwide division of labour in which transnational expert cooperation should determine intergovernmental policy norms.

The UN's reaction to the Federation's ideas largely depended on the liaison officers between the institutions. In the early post-war years, when the form of cooperation between the UN and INGOs had not yet been fully settled, these intermediaries exerted great influence in shaping the collaboration between governmental and non-governmental institutions. The

IFHTP's liaison was the American Charles S. Ascher, who had acted as treasurer for the American Society for Planning Officials and as the secretary of Julian Huxley at the United Nations Educational, Scientific and Cultural Organisation (UNESCO). Like the Peplers, he was aware of the important role of unofficial expert organisations in making 'free, professional, critical judgements'.[60] Still, he believed that the ultimate aim of expert networks was to influence state action. Because only the UN had direct access to governments, he advocated a subordination of its affiliated INGOs. He defined the Federation as a 'useful complement' to a UN that should exclusively define the profile of a global community of urban planners.[61] In such a context, transnational expert cooperation represented by institutions like the IFHTP would lend professional legitimacy to international policy norms sponsored by the UN.

Indubitably, IFHTP functionaries contested Ascher's notion of UN leadership in the global community of urban planners. The Peplers not only feared being superseded by better-equipped UN agencies. As George assumed the post of a planning consultant in Singapore during the era of 'welfare colonialism' in the 1950s, he also began to oppose the anti-imperial underpinnings of the UN's development agenda.[62] Calling attention to the Singapore Improvement Trust as 'one the most active and efficient housing authorities in East Asia', he believed that policies of colonial development could offer a model for modernisation in this region.[63] Pepler not only attempted to organise an IFHTP conference in Singapore together with British imperial institutions, he also opposed combining this congress with a UN regional seminar on housing and regional improvement in New Delhi, which was set to focus attention on India's post-colonial development after it won independence in 1947.[64]

In the end, George and Elizabeth Pepler did not succeed in building their global community of planners. To understand why, we should consider the IFHTP's weak financial position. Largely dependent on subsidies given by the hosts of its congresses, it used up its resources more than once in the time between these meetings.[65] Moreover, the institution failed to implement a new system for contributions, which would have had every nation represented commit to giving an annual sum of 10 pounds sterling per million of its population to the Federation. Consequently, the organisation's headquarters remained understaffed and secretaries were not appropriately remunerated, resulting in delays for many of its activities (such as the reissue of a glossary of terms used in planning and housing). IFHTP officials lamented that their institution was caught in a 'vicious circle': it was supposed to offer services, but membership fees were insufficient to finance its activities.[66] In a gesture that reflected the post-war geopolitical power shift from Europe to the United States, British IFHTP officials approached their American colleagues and asked for support, but were told that foundations, universities and professional organisations in the United States would be interested in the Federation only if it were willing to cooperate with the UN.[67]

In this context, opposition against the nascent world organisation gradually decreased. Moreover, Ascher and other American UN supporters played a decisive role in making George and Elizabeth Pepler resign from their respective posts as president and secretary in 1951 and 1952.[68] Thus the non-state IFHTP began to fully integrate itself into the global community of the UN that was dominated by a powerful secretariat and by governmental experts. For the first time, the Federation offered unofficial expert advice to a UN study, taking up the matter of urban land problems during its 1952 conference in Lisbon.[69] Two years later, it hosted a meeting during a UN-sponsored exhibition and seminar on housing and development aid in New Delhi.[70] Also in 1954, it founded the East Asia Regional Organisation for Housing and Planning so as to closely collaborate with the UN Economic Commission for Asia and the Far East, working, for instance, to transform abstract UN recommendations into 'specific programmes of action'.[71]

Although the UN ultimately integrated non-governmental organisations into its structures, the example of the IFHTP suggests that the process of finding a proper modus operandi for cooperation between official and unofficial institutions was highly contested. It would be too simplistic to view the subordination of non-state institutions to the UN as a teleological and one-dimensional process. Of course, INGOs such as the IFHTP failed to fully realise their vision of a worldwide expert community in which unofficial institutions occupied the upper echelons. Still, they were able to challenge the UN's claim to global leadership. Moreover, they championed a modus operandi for global work in which unofficial professional organisations acted as sources of seemingly impartial expertise—and this philosophy found its way into the UN's division of expert labour, albeit in a modified form.

Conclusion

In this chapter, I have argued that by espousing alternative conceptions of what a transnational professional community might be, unofficial expert organisations such as the IFHTP were able to challenge the terms of the post-war international order more extensively than previous studies have acknowledged. The IFHTP's example reveals that professional institutions could offer alternatives not only to the ideological rivalry of the Cold War but also to the Federal Republic of Germany's integration into Western Europe and to the UN's intergovernmental internationalism. In this light, I conclude that it would be simplistic to reduce post-war history to one-dimensional and teleological narratives such as those which highlight the 'natural' evolution of the Cold War, the direct Westernization of German experts and the inevitable rise of the UN. A 'decentred' take on the IFHTP, which emphasises the various forms of agency that contributed to the establishment of a transnational expert community, asks that we pay attention to tendencies that moved in the opposite direction. Here I have cast light on Poles who, believing that the challenge of reconstruction was a problem to be addressed by all Europeans, tried to forge an inclusive European network of professionals working in concert with one another. I have also revealed the plans of Western Europeans who, against the background of a horrendous world war and its aftermath, attempted to exclude West German participation in professional activity. Finally, this perspective uncovered the attempts of Britons who devised alternatives to the global expert community of the UN, efforts grounded in the belief that non-state experts were superior to what would emerge out of the UN's forums. Given this context, we should regard the post-1945 discourse on international order as a multifaceted wrangle in which different agents mapped out their plans against the backdrop of both their specific historical experiences and the evolving geopolitical scenario of the 1940s and 50s.

The case of the IFHTP also brings to light the fact that the discussion (and implementation) of ideas on a transnational expert community not only demonstrated the possibility of 'global interdependence' and 'shared interest', as argued by scholars such as Akira Iriye.[72] Visions of transnational community also created new grounds for political conflict. Spiwak and Ostrowski fought over the legitimacy to define the place of Poland in international professional communication; Schäfer challenged the vision of the IFHTP as an expert community that could exclude West Germany; and the Peplers argued with Ascher over the roles of INGOs and the UN within a global expert community. These examples show that the complex controversies of the post-war decade—e.g., the discussions on the growing hostilities between East and West, on the legacies of the war and on the emergence of global institutions—led to a proliferation of competing ideas about transnational community and international order that, in turn, contributed to prevailing international conflicts.

Further research should devote attention to the perplexing diversity and the conflictual nature of the discourse on transnational expert association after 1945. While my chapter is a provisional attempt in this direction, we need more studies on other institutions and agents to comprehensively make sense of the complex histories of the post-war international order.

Notes

1. Eschen, "Locating The Transnational"; I am indebted to Harm Kaal and Stefan Couperus for setting up a great conference, to the conference's attendees for much fruitful discussion, and to the reviewers at Routledge for useful suggestions. Julia Eichenberg and Seth Rogoff also provided helpful comments.
2. On the role of neutral countries, with a particular emphasis on Finland, compare contributions in Autio-Sarasmo and Miklóssy, *Reassessing Cold War Europe*.
3. Richmond, *Cultural Exchange*; Wagg and Andrews, *East Plays West*.
4. Due to the vagueness of terms such as 'expert' and 'internationalism', at least two provisional definitions seem necessary. Although experts seek to implement professional knowledge in public policy, their role in society is always subject to debate (Engstrom, Hess, and Thoms, "Figurationen des Experten").

Internationalism entails social reform through both transnational cooperation and the internationalization of ideas, goods and people (Geyer and Paulmann, "Introduction").
5. Iriye, *Global Community*, 60–95; Kott, "Par-delà la guerre froide"; Niederhut, *Wissenschaftsaustausch*; also see the contributions in Gestwa and Rohdewald, *Kooperation trotz Konfrontation*.
6. On the history of the IFHTP, see: Wagner, "Stadtplanung"; Geertse, "Defining the Universal City"; Riboldazzi, *Un' altra modernità*.
7. Government officials participated either in a private capacity or as delegates of their professional societies in the non-state IFHTP.
8. Kohlrausch, "Technologische Innovationen".
9. For similar approaches see Sluga, *Internationalism*; Mazower, *Governing*, and Herren, *Internationale Organisationen*.
10. Bevir and Rhodes, *State*.
11. Haas, "Introduction"; Iriye, *Global Community*. Sandrine Kott in particular has criticised the notion of 'epistemic communities' for obscuring the tensions between the conflicting priorities of transnational and national engagement that have prevailed in international organisations: Kott, "Une 'communautè èpistèmique' du social?".
12. Judt, *Post-War*, 135–36; DeJong-Lambert, "The New Biology"; Crowley, *Warsaw*.
13. Prost and Winter, *René Cassin*, 202–4; Ministry of Works. Post-War-Building Directorate—Allied Nations Committee, memorandum, n.d., file 102/65, Ministry of Health and Sucessors, National Archives, London (hereafter cited as HLG).
14. Cooperation and conflict among the exile governments and communities are studied in Conway and Gotovich, *Europe in Exile*.
15. George L. Pepler to Neal, 1 March 1943, file 102/65, HLG.
16. George L. Pepler, Town and Country Planning: Proposed International Study Group, *c*. May 1943, file 102/65, HLG.
17. Kohlrausch, "Houses of Glass".
18. Lesnikowski, "Functionalism," 211–12.
19. Report on a One-Day Conference Held at the Housing Centre on International Housing, memorandum, 1 March 1945, file H 14, Sir Frederic Osborn Archive, Hertfordshire Archives and Local Studies, Hertford (hereafter cited as FJO).
20. "Rehousing in Europe," 309.
21. Spiwak, "The Federation's Travelling Exhibition," 3.
22. Gutschow and Klain, *Vernichtung und Utopie*, 57–73.
23. Klain, "City Planning".
24. In the 1940s, Halton was a Tory member of London City Council (Russell and Pepler, "Obituary"). Pepler had anticommunist sentiments (George L. Pepler to Frederic J. Osborn, 27 September 1950, file H 7, FJO). As a refugee, Spiwak depended on both Halton and Pepler (Charles S. Ascher to Leon Steinig, 11 May 1953, box 91 (New Delhi Regional Conference), Charles S. Ascher Papers, Rare Book and Manuscript Library, Columbia University, New York (hereafter cited as Ascher Papers).
25. Diary of the IFHTP Secretariat, 23 April 1946, box 8, International Federation for Housing and Planning, Archive, formerly located in The Hague, now housed in Letchworth (hereafter cited as IFHPA).
26. Morris H. Hirsh, Report to the 3rd Meeting of the Bureau of the IFHTP, 1 May 1948, file 15, Papers of Sir George Pepler, section International Work, Strathclyde University Archives, Glasgow (hereafter cited as T-PEP).
27. Friedrich, "Modernitätsbegriff und Modernitätspropaganda," 317–18.
28. "Amsterdam 1950".

29. Analysis of Membership at 15th April, 1948 of the IFHTP, memorandum, box 7, IFHPA; Henk van der Weijde, "Where Does the Federation Stand Today? August 1957," file IFHTP-Bur.-65, box 84, Ascher Papers.
30. Kott, "Par-delà la guerre froide".
31. Ostrowski, *Les ensembles historiques*.
32. Continuities between the planning histories of Nazi Germany and the Federal Republic were first studied by Werner Durth: Durth, *Deutsche Architekten*.
33. George L. Pepler, Report of Notation Committee appointed by the Congress held at Gothenburg in 1923, 20 June 1924, file 3, box 70, John Nolen Papers, Cornell University Library, Ithaca; Charles B. Purdom, "The International Conference at New York," 194–98.
34. Beschluss des Magistrats der Stadt Frankfurt am Main Nr. 723, memorandum, 21 August 1933, and Beschluss des Magistrats der Stadt Frankfurt am Main Nr. 837, 11 September 1933, file MA 6340, Magistratsakten, Institut für Stadtgeschichte, Frankfurt am Main.
35. Nachtmann, *Karl Strölin*, 197–205, 278–95.
36. Herren, "Outwardly . . . an Innocuous Conference Authority".
37. George L. Pepler to Neal, 1 March 1943, file 102/65, HLG.
38. Judt, *Post-War*, 13–27.
39. Louis S.P. Scheffer to George L. Pepler, 11 June 1946, file 1, International Work, T-PEP.
40. Minutes of the 5th Meeting of the Provisional Committee, Hastings, 7 October 1946, file 1, International Work, T-PEP.
41. Paula Schäfer to Emile Vinck, paraphrased by Louis S.P. Scheffer to George L. Pepler, 11 June 1946, file 1, International Work, T-PEP.
42. Paula Schäfer to Coleman Woodbury, 9 September 1945, file 4, box 39, American Society for Planning Officials Records, Cornell University Library (hereafter cited as ASPO Records).
43. Ibid.
44. Paula Schäfer to Walter Blucher, 7 May 1947, file 8, box 39, ASPO Records.
45. Paula Schäfer to George L. Pepler, 9 February 1950, file 18, Personal Correspondence, T-PEP.
46. Paula Schäfer to Walter Gropius, 17 July 1947, file 164/1, Walter Gropius Papers, Bauhausarchiv, Berlin; Werner Hebebrand to Werner Taesler, 28 May 1948, file 951, Baukunstarchiv, Werner Hebebrand Archive, Akademie der Künste, Berlin; Paula Schäfer to Werner Moser, 10 August 1948, file Korrespondenz 1947–1948, Werner M. Moser Papers, gta Archiv, ETH Zurich.
47. Executive Committee, Agenda Item 4, c. March 1948, file 15, International Work, T-PEP.
48. Hermann Hecker to Minister of Works, 1 August 1922, file R 3901/21010, fol. 165–71, Reichsarbeitsministerium Records, Bundesarchiv, Berlin.
49. Minutes of the Eighth Meeting of the Bureau, Amsterdam, 20 January 1950, file 15, International Work, T-PEP.
50. Schäfer, "XXI. Internationaler Kongress."
51. On the role of cultural brokers in the Westernization of the Federal Republic, see Doering-Manteuffel, *Wie westlich*.
52. Herren, *Internationale Organisationen*, 92; on the relationship between INGOs and the UN in the realm of urban planning, see Saunier, "Sketches".
53. Clavin, *Securing*, 341–59.
54. Shoshkes, *Jaqueline Tyrwhitt*, 103–5; Louis Brownlow to William Benton, 15 April 1946, file 4, box 39, ASPO Records.
55. Recent literature on UN urban planning efforts often undervalues the IFHTP: Muzaffar, "The Periphery Within"; Harris, and Giles, "A Mixed Message".

56. What Is the International Federation?, brochure, c. 1946, file 1, International Work, T-PEP.
57. Elizabeth E. Halton and George L. Pepler, "The Future Policy of the Federation," 29 September 1946, file 15, International Work, T-PEP; Clavin, *Securing*, 353.
58. Elizabeth E. Pepler to White, 21 July 1948, file 10, box 39, ASPO Records.
59. George L. Pepler to Maurice Milhaud, 17 June 1947, paraphrased by Alva Myrdal to George L. Pepler, 2 June 1950, file 3, International Work, T-PEP.
60. Conference on Ways Increasing US Participation in International Housing and Town Planning, Washington, 6 June 1954, file 35, box 39, ASPO Records.
61. Charles S. Ascher, Interview with Ernest Weissmann, memorandum, 6 March 1951, box 90, folder IFHTP, Ascher Papers.
62. Home, *Of Planting*, 200–210; Particularly on Singapore: Kwak, "Selling".
63. George L. Pepler to Wilfred Blythe, 23 July 1952, file 7, International Work, T-PEP.
64. George L. Pepler to Henk van der Weijde, 28 March 1952, file 7, International Work, T-PEP.
65. Minutes of the 1st Meeting of the Executive Committee of the IFHTP, Paris, 7 June 1947, folder 15, International Work, T-PEP.
66. Charles S. Ascher to Morris H. Hirsh, 15 July 1947, file IFHP HQ, box 90, Ascher Papers.
67. Walter Blucher to Morris H. Hirsh, 2 March 1948, file 10, box 39, ASPO Records.
68. Charles S. Ascher to Walter Blucher, 23 July 1951, file 15, box 39, ASPO Records, box 39.
69. United Nations, *Urban Land Problems and Policies*.
70. International Federation for Housing and Town Planning, *Proceedings*.
71. East Asia Regional Organization for Housing and Planning, *Proceedings*, 62.
72. Iriye, *Global Community*, 94.

Bibliography

"Amsterdam 1950." *Town and Country Planning* 79 (1950): 447–51.

Autio-Sarasmo, Sari and Katalin Miklóssy, eds. *Reassessing Cold War Europe*. London: Routledge, 2011.

Clavin, Patricia. *Securing the World Economy: The Reinvention of the League of Nations, 1920–1946*. Oxford: Oxford University Press, 2013.

Conway, Martin and José Gotovich, eds. *Europe in Exile: European Exile Communities in Britain 1940–1945*. New York: Berghahn 2001.

DeJong-Lambert, William. "The New Biology in Poland after the Second World War: Polish Lysenkoism." *Paedagogica Historica* 3 (2009): 403–20.

Doering-Manteuffel, Anselm. *Wie westlich sind die Deutschen? Amerikanisierung und Westernisierung im 20. Jahrhundert*. Göttingen: Vandenhoeck & Ruprecht, 1999.

Durth, Werner. *Deutsche Architekten. Biographische Verflechtungen 1900–1970*. Braunschweig: Vieweg, 1986.

East Asian Regional Organization for Housing and Planning, ed. *Proceedings of the Second Regional Conference on Housing and Town Planning, Tokyo, Japan, 1958*. New Delhi: East Asian Regional Organization for Housing and Planning, 1958.

Engstrom, Eric J., Volker Hess, and Ulrike Thoms. "Figurationen des Experten: Ambivalenzen der wissenschaftlichen Expertise im ausgehenden 18. und frühen 19. Jahrhundert." In *Figurationen des Experten: Ambivalenzen der wissenschaftlichen Expertise im ausgehenden 18. und frühen 19. Jahrhundert*, edited by Eric J. Engstrom, Volker Hess, and Ulrike Thoms, 7–19. Frankfurt am Main: Peter Lang, 2005.

Eschen, Penny Von. "Locating the Transnational in the Cold War." In *The Oxford Handbook of the Cold War*, edited by Richard H. Immerman and Petra Goedde, 451–68. Oxford: Oxford University Press, 2013.

Friedrich, Jacek. "Modernitätsbegriff und Modernitätspropaganda im polnischen Architekturdiskurs der Jahre 1945–1949." In *Imaginationen des Urbanen. Konzeption, Reflexion und Fiktion von Stadt in Mittel- und Osteuropa*, edited by Arnold Bartetzky, Marina Dimitrieva, and Alfrun Kliems, 304–28. Berlin: Lukas Verlag, 2009.

Geertse, Michel. "Defining the Universal City: The International Federation for Housing and Town Planning and Transnational Planning Dialogue, 1913–1945." PhD Diss., Free University Amsterdam, 2012.

Gestwa, Klaus and Stefan Rohdewald, eds. *Kooperation trotz Konfrontation: Wissenschaft und Technik im Kalten Krieg*. Berlin: Deutsche Gesellschaft für Osteuropakunde, 2009.

Geyer, Martin H. and Johannes Paulmann. "Introduction: The Mechanics of Internationalism." In *The Mechanics of Internationalism: Culture, Society and Politics from the 1840s to the First World War*, edited by Martin H. Geyer and Johannes Paulmann, 1–25. Oxford: Oxford University Press, 2001.

Gutschow, Niels and Barbara Klain. *Vernichtung und Utopie: Stadtplanung Warschau 1939–1945*. Hamburg: Junius, 1994.

Haas, Peter M. "Introduction: Epistemic Communities and International Policy Coordination." *International Organization* 1 (1992): 1–35.

Harris, Richard and Ceinwein Giles. "A Mixed Message: The Agents and Forms of International Housing Policy." *Habitat International* 2 (2003): 167–91.

Herren, Madeleine. *Internationale Organisationen seit 1865. Eine Globalgeschichte der internationalen Ordnung*. Darmstadt: Wissenschaftliche Buchgesellschaft, 2009.

Herren, Madeleine. "Outwardly an Innocuous Conference Authority: National Socialism and the Logistics of International Information Management." *German History* 1 (2002): 67–92.

Home, Robert. *Of Planting and Planning: The Making of British Colonial Cities*. London: I.B. Tauris, 1997.

International Federation for Housing and Town Planning, ed. *Proceedings of the South East Asia Regional Conference, New Delhi, Febuary 1–7, 1954*. New Delhi: East Asian Regional Organization for Housing and Planning, 1957.

Iriye, Akira. *Global Community: The Role of International Organizations in the Making of the Contemporary World*. Berkeley: University of Berkeley Press, 2002.

Judt, Tony. *Post-War: A History of Europe Since 1945*. London: Penguin, 2005.

Klain, Barbara. "City Planning in Warsaw." In *Mastering the City: North European City Planning, 1900–2000*. Vol. 2, edited by Koos Bosma and Helma Hellinga, 112–27. Rotterdam: NAI, 1997.

Kohlrausch, Martin. "Technologische Innovationen und transnationale Netzwerke: Europa zwischen den Weltkriegen." *Journal for Modern European History* 2 (2008): 181–94.

Kohlrausch, Martin. "Houses of Glass: Modern Architecture and the Idea of Community in Poland." In *Making a New World? Architecture and Communities in Interwar Europe, Leuven: Leuven UP 2012*, edited by Tim Aevermate and Rajesh Heynickx, 93–103. Leuven: Leuven University Press, 2012.

Kott, Sandrine. "Une 'communautè èpistèmique' du social? Experts de l'OIT et l'internationalisation des politiques sociales dans l'entre-deux-guerres." *Genèses* 2 (2008): 26–46.

Kott, Sandrine. "Par-delà la guerre froide: Les organizations internationales et les circulations Est-Ouest (1947–1973)." *Vingtième Siècle* 109 (2011): 143–54.

Kwak, Nancy H. "Selling the City-State: Planning and Housing in Singapore, 1954–1990." In *Another Global City: Historical Explorations Into the Transnational Municipal Movement 1850–2000*, edited by Pierre-Yves Saunier and Shane Ewen, 85–100. New York: Palgrave Macmillan, 2008.

Lesnikowski, Wojciech. "Functionalism in Polish Architecture." In *East European Modernism. Architecture in Czechoslovakia, Hungary and Poland between the Wars, 1919–1939*, edited by Wojciech Lesnikowski, 203–85. New York: Rizzoli, 1996.

Mazower, Mark. *Governing the World: The History of an Idea*. London: Penguin, 2012.

Muzaffar, Ijal. "The Periphery Within: Modern Architecture and the Making of the Third World." PhD Diss. Massachusetts Institute of Technology, 2007.

Nachtmann, Walter. *Karl Strölin. Stuttgarter Oberbürgermeister im 'Führerstaat'*. Tübingen: Silberburg Verlag, 1995.

Niederhut, Jens. *Wissenschaftsaustausch im Kalten Krieg: Die ostdeutschen Naturwissenschaftler und der Westen*. Köln: Böhlau, 2007.

Ostrowski, Wacław. *Les ensembles historiques et l'urbanisme*. Paris: Centre d'Urbanisme, 1976.

Prost, Antoine and Jay Winter. *René Cassin et les droits de l'Homme. Le projet d'une generation*. Paris: Fayard, 2011.

"Rehousing in Europe." *Journal of the Royal Institute of British Architects* 10 (1944): 308–12.

Riboldazzi, Renzo. *Un' altra modernità. L'IFHTP e la cultura urbanistica tra le due guerre, 1923–1939*. Rome: Gangemi, 2009.

Richmond, Yale. *Cultural Exchange and the Cold War: Raising the Iron Curtain*. University Park: Penn State University Press, 2004.

Russell, Daniel and Pepler, Giles. "Obituary: Lady Pepler Hon MRTPI." *Planning for the Natural and Built Environment* 1263 (1998): 21.

Saunier, Pierre-Yves. "Sketches from the Urban Internationale, 1910–50: Voluntary Associations, International Institutions and US Philanthropic Foundations." *International Journal of Urban and Regional Research* 2 (2001): 380–403.

Schäfer, Paula. "XXI. Internationaler Kongress für Wohnungswesen und Städtebau, 21–27. Sept. 1952 in Lissabon." *Mitteilungen des deutschen Verbandes für Wohnungswesen, Städtebau und Raumplanung* 3–4 (1952): 1–10.

Shoshkes, Ellen. *Jaqueline Tyrwhitt: A Transnational Life in Urban Planning and Design*. Farnham: Ashgate, 2013.

Sluga, Glenda. *Internationalism in the Age of Nationalism*. Philadelphia: University of Pennsylvania Press, 2013.

Spiwak, Henry J. "The Federation's Travelling Exhibition: Hastings, Paris, London." *News Sheet of the International Federation for Housing and Town Planning* 5 (1947): 3–4.

United Nations, ed. *Urban Land Problems and Policies: Housing and Town and Country Planning Bulletin No. 7*. New York: United Nations, 1953.

Wagg, Stephen and David L. Andrews, eds. *East Plays West: Sport and the Cold War*. London: Routledge, 2007.

Wagner, Phillip. "Stadtplanung für die Welt? Die performative Konstruktion internationalen Expertenwissens in der ersten Hälfte des 20. Jahrhunderts." PhD Diss., Humboldt University Berlin, 2014.

Part IV
Nation, Class and Religion

11 Reconstructing Post-War Political Communities
Class, Religion and Political Identity-Formation in the Netherlands, 1945–68

Harm Kaal

In *The Principles of Representative Government* the French political scientist Bernard Manin argues that from the end of the nineteenth century onwards a new model or ideal type of representative government took shape, which he labels 'party democracy'. It was characterised by mass parties, which according to Manin emerged around shared social identities. People felt themselves to be represented by one of these parties, rather than by a particular individual, as had been the case before, and they tended to stay loyal to their chosen party throughout their lives. Support for a political party was based more on a 'feeling of belonging and sense of identification' than on a party's political agenda per se.[1] It thus seems to make sense to conceptualise a party's constituency in terms of a 'political community', at least in the era of party democracy, which lasted until the 1960s. In line with the purpose of this volume, this chapter interrogates the construction of these communities.

The controversial political theorist Carl Schmitt once argued that political representation had to be understood as the 'realization of the unity of an authentic community'. In a thought-provoking article on political representation, Michael Saward takes issue with Schmitt's reading of political community. Building on Bourdieu and Anderson, he contends that political '[c]onstituencies, like communities, have to be "imagined"' and that politicians are always engaged in the 'active constitution of constituencies'.[2] Moreover, the construction of political communities—to adopt this volume's vocabulary—should be seen as a process of *claim-making*: politicians assert that they represent a particular political community, which in fact comes into being only through the expression of this claim. If we want to understand the construction of political communities we should therefore study political communication. Through the political language they use, politicians define the nature and identity of the communities they claim to represent.[3]

For political historians, Saward's approach to political representation sounds familiar.[4] Since the 1980s, starting with Gareth Stedman Jones's work on the Chartist movement, the cultural and linguistic turns have informed a large body of scholarship on the formation of political identities and electoral constituencies through the language and culture of politics.[5]

Political constituencies, Jon Lawrence has argued, should not be treated as 'pre-established social blocs awaiting representation' but rather seen as 'painstakingly constructed . . . alliances'. Parties, in turn, were not the 'passive beneficiaries of structural divisions within society' but 'dynamic organizations actively involved in the definition of political interests and the construction of political alliances' through political discourse.⁶ The performative power of the language and culture of politics has also been taken up by German political historians such as Willibald Steinmetz and Thomas Mergel and the British political scientist Michael Freeden in explorations of both extremist and democratic politics.⁷

Building on these approaches, this chapter offers an investigation of the construction of political communities by two of the major Dutch political parties in the early post-war decades: the social-democratic Partij van de Arbeid (Labour Party: PvdA) and the Katholieke Volkspartij (Catholic People's Party: KVP).

How representative is the Netherlands in terms of the history of political representation as sketched by Manin? In the past, historians were keen to stress the idiosyncratic nature of Dutch politics.⁸ Their rather structuralist views on political representation centred on the concept of 'pillarisation' (in Dutch: *verzuiling*). From the late nineteenth century up until the 1960s, Dutch society was said to be dominated by the existence of three closely-knit communities or 'pillars' that were based on either a shared religion—the Catholic and Protestant pillars—or class—the socialist pillar. These pillars were characterised by a dense structure of associations that covered all spheres of life, from sports clubs to trade unions.⁹ Eventually, in the 1960s 'depillarisation' (*ontzuiling*) set in when the existing political communities evaporated under the pressure of secularisation and rising affluence. Recent studies, however, have convincingly dismantled the 'myth' of pillarisation by showing the generic nature of this mode of political representation, which was evident across Europe.¹⁰

What has, remarkably, remained uncontested is the nature of the political communities themselves in the Netherlands. Pillarisation historiography has mainly presented them as mirrors of existing cleavages in society: up until the 1960s political identities supposedly reflected the socio-religious structures in which voters were embedded.¹¹ Elections were characterised as censuses instead of true contests among parties fighting for popular support: parties were mainly concerned with mobilising 'their' supporters, not with the expansion of electoral support among 'other' groups. The cultural turn in political history has done much to improve our understanding of how this mobilisation was achieved. It has inspired research on party culture, showing how demonstrations, symbols and songs, among other manifestations of party loyalty, contributed to creating a sense of belonging and how party culture offered opportunities for popular engagement in politics.¹² What has, however, remained undervalued—particularly in comparison to Germany and Britain—is the importance of political discourse for the construction of political communities.¹³

Adopting a cultural and discursive approach to political communication, this chapter revisits the (re)construction of political communities by focusing on post-war Dutch general election campaigns up through the 1960s. It will do so by discussing the impact of social-scientific understandings of political identity-formation on the language of politics through which politicians expressed their representative claims. After the Second World War all major parties started to systematically use scholarly research on social stratification and voting behaviour. Studies from the fields of sociology and political science provided them with clues about how to classify the electorate and about the key characteristics of various groups in society, which resulted in the transfer of scientific concepts to the language of politics. Through this social-scientific frame, parties tried to fathom political identity-formation and the nature of their political communities. This chapter will narrate how a social-determinist approach to the construction of political communities became entrenched in Dutch party politics, but also met with increasing contestation from the 1950s onwards, eventually resulting in a fundamental reconceptualisation of political representation in the late 1960s.

National Community versus Political Division

During the German occupation of the Netherlands (1940–1945), the representation of the Dutch political landscape as consisting of distinct, self-contained political communities met heavy criticism. While incarcerated in German internment camps, politicians and intellectuals began to make plans for a fundamental reconstruction of the post-war political order in order to end the dominance of the pre-war *hokjesgeest*: the division of society along ideological and religious lines (the term *verzuiling* was not yet commonly used). Adopting Tönnies's binary of *Gesellschaft* and *Gemeinschaft*, the fragmented and divided pre-war society was contrasted with the organic people's community that would be constructed after the war. In anticipation of Germany's defeat, calls for the reconstruction of an inclusive *national* community and the advancement of 'community spirit' (*gemeenschapszin*) were widespread, particularly in progressive circles.[14] Intellectuals from various fields inside and outside the social sciences, ranging from sociology, psychology and pedagogy to theology, were deeply involved in shaping this perspective on the reconstruction of community.[15] In the political sphere the PvdA, a new, social-democratic political party that also included former members of progressive liberal and confessional political parties, invoked the concept of a cross-class, inclusive people's community as well. The PvdA accused the confessional parties, who had dominated Dutch politics in the interwar years, of creating division by politicising religion.[16]

The experience of war made this dichotomy, which set pre-war division or pillarisation against the conception of a post-war people's community, the basis of a very powerful discourse. The occupation of the Netherlands had resulted in the forced disbandment of the existing political parties and the establishment of 'national', non-national-socialist political movements that aimed to be inclusive, like the Nederlandsche Unie (Dutch Union) and the Nederlandsche Volksbeweging (Dutch People's Movement). Queen Wilhelmine, while in exile in London, had also nourished a sense of necessary change through national unity through her radio broadcasts.[17] Tapping into this sentiment, the newly established PvdA framed the war as a major caesura by associating itself with the dawn of a new era, symbolised in its publicity by repeated use of a sunrise coming over the horizon.[18] By identifying itself with post-war change and renewal, the PvdA framed the first post-war elections as a choice between a better future and a return to the horrors of recent history. Voters were warned that if they supported one of the other parties, they would risk the return of the pre-war situation of crisis, unemployment and instability.[19] This would take the Netherlands back to 'April 1940', to a situation of 'egoism, petty politics, narrow-minded conservatism and profit seeking'.[20]

The confessional political parties carefully negotiated their positions in the post-war order. They legitimised their resurrection after the Nazi occupation through a counter-discourse of 'unity in diversity', arguing that parliamentary democracy enabled the peaceful and harmonious coexistence—and the presence of political representation—of various communities in society.[21] Catholic Party leader Carl Romme accused the social democrats of trying to 'crush community life by imposing a national identity on the people from above'.[22] As such, Romme still perceived communities as distinct associations of people united by a common identity based on either class or religion. Simultaneously, the confessional parties were keen to demonstrate that they had adapted to the new post-war order. The Catholic Party renamed itself, embraced a progressive agenda of social reform and referred to itself as 'radically progressive' or even 'Christian socialist', a term that was also occasionally used by the orthodox-Protestant party ARP (Antirevolutionary Party).[23] Moreover, the social democrats of the PvdA (Labour Party) and the Catholic Party each labelled themselves 'people's parties'. Along with some of the other Dutch parties, they adopted this concept in order to show that they no longer catered to the interests of a particular section of the electorate but rather to the 'general interests' of the Dutch people at large.[24] More specifically, the notion evoked their ambition to construct a community that transcended the boundaries of class and religion.

The social democrats and the Catholics were mainly preoccupied with the political fate of the expanding social stratum of the *middengroepen* or *middenklasse* (the middle classes) and with the effects of secularisation on political communities. Sociological research on these issues attracted their attention and informed their reconceptualisation of their sense of political community. The following paragraph is dedicated to a discussion of the dominant conceptions of social structure and class in the sociological research of the era and will also explore the perceptions within the PvdA and KVP of the relations among class, religion and political identity-formation.

Social Structures and Political Identities

In the interwar years sociological research discussed the rise of a new middle class of civil servants and private-sector employees.[25] Political parties were thus faced with the question of how to approach this new category of voters. Moreover, they were concerned about what they perceived to be an increasing political resentment among the 'old' middle class of shopkeepers and farmers.[26] One of the developments that contributed to this perception was the emergence in the interwar years of a range of so-called *middenstandspartijen* (middle-class parties) at the local and national levels who tried to mobilise sections of the middle classes as a political force in their own right. The populist, anti-political and anti-statist rhetoric of the middle-class parties contributed to the perception among the established parties that the middle classes were a complex category: they seemed to be preoccupied with their own interests and immune to political principles.[27] In Marxist social theory the middle classes were characterised as being hostile towards the working class; such animosity came from a desire among the middle classes to obtain higher social status. Marxism, however, taught that the inevitable development of capitalism doomed the middle classes to sink into the proletariat.[28] In the early 1930s, socialist intellectuals began to argue that the new middle class was in fact a new section *within* the working class or proletariat. Members of the new middle class, however, wrongly perceived themselves to belong to a distinct social category by othering the working class.[29] Responding to this idea, the pre-war social democratic party SDAP (Sociaal-Democratische Arbeiderpartij) tried to convince members of the middle class that they were in fact on the same plane as the working class, as both groups were subjected to the mechanisms of capitalism.[30] The construction of a more inclusive socialist political community seemed a long way off, however, as long as members of the middle classes were still referred to, in the words of a 1934 social-democratic brochure on the 'middle class issue', as 'mentally instable' (*psychisch labiel*) and politically 'uneducated' (*ongeschoold*).[31] Suggestions to use the term *volkspartij* (people's party) instead of *arbeiderspartij* (workers' party) to express the more inclusive nature of the SDAP were at first turned down, because this might indicate that the party was abolishing its ideology of class struggle. Moreover, some social democrats associated a rapprochement with the middle classes with the propaganda of fascism and national socialism: a path the SDAP should not travel down.[32]

Eventually, however, those in favour of a more inclusive approach got the upper hand. In the mid-1930s, prompted by the rise of fascism and national socialism and the economic crisis of the 1930s, and after years of heated ideological debates, the SDAP finally shed much of its Marxist orientation. Towards the end of the 1930s the party rebranded itself as a cross-class people's party, and the PvdA continued in the same vein after the war.[33] The post-war rise of the welfare state gave added credence to the view that the middle classes were ever more important as the backbone of any party that aimed to be a 'people's party' (see Figure 11.1).

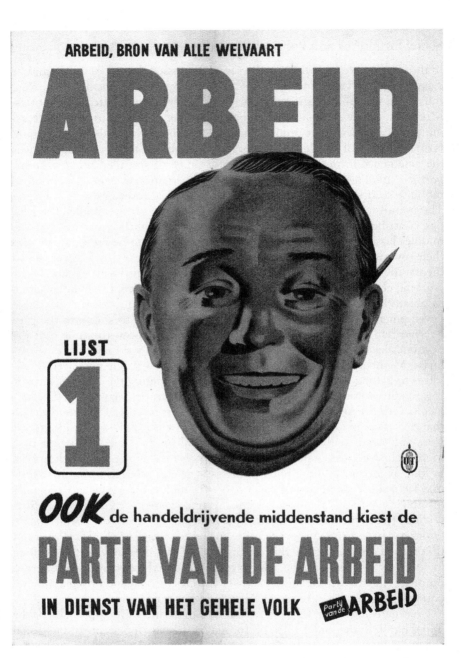

Figure 11.1 In the 1946 campaign the PvdA issued posters aimed at different groups of voters, such as women, intellectuals, farmers and tradespeople. The caption at the top of this poster reads 'Labour, the source of all affluence', followed at the bottom by 'Also tradespeople vote for the Labour Party. At the service of the whole of the people'. Poster, 79.5 × 53.5 cm. Design: Studio Uschi Torens.

Source: International Institute of Social History (IISH), Amsterdam.

Cross-class relations and the rise of a new middle class were also key areas of interests within the emerging field of political sociology. In 1947 the Amsterdam-based professor of sociology J.P. Kruijt dedicated his inaugural lecture to the relationship between workers and the new middle class.[34] Kruijt warned that social differentiation could result in communal disintegration: '[t]he lower ranks of manual workers and the higher ranks of brain workers have a different lifestyle. This is not only understandable, but also desirable, because this differentiation enriches our culture. But differentiation without integration results in the disintegration of community and in alienation'.[35] In another inaugural lecture Kruijt's Leiden colleague Frederik van Heek adopted a less normative approach, but also signalled that increasing differentiation would dispel the class system. Because of rising socio-economic and psychological differences among members of the working class, the borders between classes had become blurred. Sociologists such as Kruijt and van Heek, who both supported the social democrats, played a significant role in intraparty debates on political and electoral strategy with regard to the middle classes. They also contributed to the dominance of social-determinist interpretations of voting behaviour that linked voting preferences to social factors like class or religion.[36]

In the 1950s the social democrats of the PvdA became obsessed with the process of *embourgeoisement*, which threatened to hollow out their political community: people who could 'objectively' (based on their economic situation) be classified as working class increasingly perceived themselves as members of the middle classes and had embraced middle-class attitudes—that is, bourgeois norms, values and lifestyles. Dutch social democrats were particularly worried about the successive electoral defeats of the British Labour Party in the 1950s. In Britain, rising affluence had resulted in an increasing number of voters adopting a 'middle-class mentality' that had prevented them from supporting the social democrats, according to Joop den Uyl, the head of the social-democratic think tank WBS (Wiardi Beckman Stichting).[37] In an economic sense, differences between workers and members of the new middle class were rapidly diminishing, and this development, in turn, catalysed a defensive reflex among members of the new middle class, who feared absorption into the proletariat and therefore cultivated sociocultural differences that would distinguish themselves from those of the working class.[38] Den Uyl and others like him aimed to show that, when casting their ballots, middle-class voters were allowing their decisions to be dominated by emotions rather than reason. The rational choice would have been to support the social-democratic party, since that party defended their socio-economic interests. Instead, guided by emotional attachments, they used their votes in the service of constructing a distinctly middle-class identity for themselves.[39] When, in the latter half of the 1950s, support for the social democrats seemed to grow, den Uyl argued that the behaviour of voters was shedding its emotional biases and had become more rational.[40]

In its election campaigns, the PvdA looked for ways to broaden its appeal among the middle classes without alienating its 'core' working-class electorate. With concepts like 'the people' and 'the common man', the social democrats hoped to attract working- and middle-class voters alike, much as the British Labour party had done in the early post-war years.[41] 'Division and pillarisation' (*splitsing en verzuiling*) had to be replaced by a 'vivid, organic people's community'.[42] To that end, the party strategically moved away from a language of class in its appeals aimed at middle-class voters.[43] Where state intervention was deemed necessary, the PvdA preferred to speak of a 'task for the community', which sounded less statist.[44] The party also tapped into cross-class male pastimes like the Dutch football league, which turned professional in the mid-1950s. In a pamphlet used in the 1956 general-election campaign, the PvdA combined information about a match between GVAV (Groningen) and Willem II (Tilburg) with a call to vote for PvdA party leader Willem Drees: 'even if you support GVAV, vote for Willem (of list number) II'.[45]

Despite these attempts to construct a cross-class constituency, the public overtures of the social democrats still revealed their working-class bias. In 1952 the PvdA campaigned with a letter to managers calling for 'solidarity' and 'cooperation' but did not appeal to specific interests of this group of voters.[46] Shopkeepers were told that they would benefit from increasing 'affluence among the masses': '[a] shopkeeper will fare well, if workers prosper'.[47] Negative perceptions of the middle-class electorate persisted. In intraparty debates and election publicity middle-class voters were accused of having 'insufficient insight' (*geen voldoende inzicht*) into political issues, and were characterised as being self-centred and apathetic towards politics.[48] The ongoing discussions about the nature of the middle classes, their economic position and their relations with the working class reveal the continuation of a perception of the middle classes as 'the other' whose integration in the socialist constituency was desirable but far from easy to realise—as was illustrated by varying, often disappointing electoral results—and first and foremost required an effort on the part of the middle classes themselves: much like the working class in the early years of social democracy, middle-class voters needed to recognise that it was the social-democratic party alone that would defend their interests.[49]

Although the Catholic Party was much more concerned about the effects of secularisation on the nature of its political community, it also discussed the rise of the middle classes. The notion of *embourgeoisement*, however, did not worry the KVP as much as it did the PvdA. Its corporatist view of society fostered a perception of the middle classes as constituting a distinct social stratum (or *stand*, as Catholics would often call it) coexisting peacefully with other social strata. With its call for property accumulation and the loosening of wage controls, the Catholic Party was convinced it could keep middle-class voters on board.[50] The KVP—and other confessional political parties, for that matter—was far more concerned about another major social-structural development that forced it to reconceptualise its political community: the increasing number of people who no longer identified themselves as belonging to a particular denomination. The degree to which Dutch Catholics were preoccupied by secularisation is evident from the plethora of reports on religious affiliation published in the 1950s and 1960s. Research on religious decline was one of the main topics explored by KASKI (Catholic Institute for Social-Ecclesiastical Research), a new social-scientific research institute established in 1946.[51] Although KASKI was mainly oriented towards episcopal policymaking, from its early days it also developed intimate ties with the Catholic Party.[52] Its research was conducted in the Dutch tradition of sociography, a geographical approach to sociological issues established in the interwar years by Professor Sebald Steinmetz at the University of Amsterdam, which Liesbeth van de Grift discusses more extensively in her chapter elsewhere in this volume. KASKI reports often contained several maps which visualised the degree of secularisation across the country and showed where it was most urgent for the Church or party to mount a rapid response.[53]

The basic assumption behind the political studies carried out by KASKI was that an individual's political identity resulted from the degree to which one practised one's faith. KASKI sociologists introduced the concept of 'political orthodoxy' to qualify the correlation between being registered as a Catholic in the census and supporting the KVP at elections (see Figure 11.2).[54] A high degree of political orthodoxy indicated that the KVP could count on the support of almost all registered Catholics. Research showed that registered Catholics who did not support the KVP tended to disregard their religious duties. The Catholic political community was thus represented as the substrate of the Catholic religious community.[55] Although the Catholic party indeed in essence represented Catholics—its (neo-Thomist) intention to appeal to wider, non-Catholic sections of the electorate through its political programme never materialised—this focus on political orthodoxy resulted in a distorted image of voting behaviour.[56] Structural explanations prevailed: the lack of support for the Catholic Party was never related to the nature of the Catholic Party and parliamentary politics but instead was seen as the result of structural developments like urbanisation and industrialisation, which catalysed secularisation and thus resulted in the erosion of the Catholic community.

As such, politics hardly played a role in these sociological investigations, neither in those on the effects of *embourgeoisement* nor in studies on secularisation. Decreasing support for the PvdA and KVP was blamed not on a misguided political agenda but on distorted notions of belonging among the electorate itself. In the case of the Catholic Party, the main line of reasoning was that voters who no longer supported the party had been driven by opportunism and self-interest, which had made them vulnerable to socialist propaganda.[57] Such voters were first and foremost a *pastoreel* (pastoral) concern: the Church needed to revive their religious awareness. A lack of

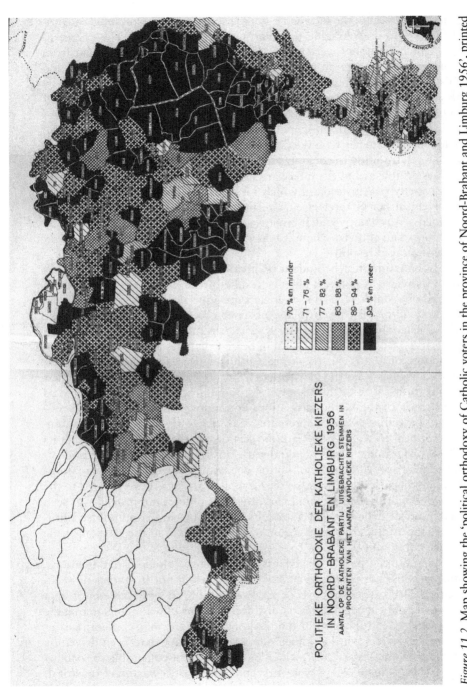

Figure 11.2 Map showing the 'political orthodoxy of Catholic voters in the province of Noord-Brabant and Limburg 1956', printed in *De politieke keuze der Nederlandse katolieken*, a report published by KASKI in 1957. The map shows that political orthodoxy was relatively low in the mining areas of southern Limburg and in the urban areas of Tilburg, Breda, 's-Hertogenbosch and Eindhoven.

knowledge of political programmes among these voters, so KAKSI sociologists argued, also indicated that their support for another party was not *politically* motivated in essence.[58] The key concern of post-war Catholic Party politics, therefore, was to keep reminding voters of the intimate ties between religion and politics.[59] The KVP did not hesitate to play on the conscience of voters by framing voting as a religious act through which an individual expressed one's religious identity, implicitly suggesting that those who did not support the party were not proper Catholics.[60] Religion was thus still perceived as the key marker of the Catholic Party's political community. When research in the 1960s showed that the ties between religion and political identity were rapidly becoming less self-evident, the Catholic Party was, however, forced to reconsider its self-understanding as a confessional political party.

Social Determinism Contested

The concept of (de)pillarisation was instrumental to the narrative of political and societal change in the 1960s. Declining church attendance, the emergence of a more libertarian attitude towards sex and gender relations, a rising number of floating voters and the existence of a 'cleavage' separating politicians and the people they claimed to represent—all these developments and more were linked to one another in scientific and public discourse through the concept of depillarisation. The term 'pillarisation' had been introduced by sociologists in the 1950s as a metaphor for the coexistence of various distinct socio-religious communities (pillars) united around shared notions of class or religion. In a context marked by depillarisation the concept of political communities, thus, seemed to lose much of its force as the key notion through which one could make sense of political representation and political engagement. The narrative of depillarisation was based on the perception that voters were autonomous individuals first, rather than members of a particular community.[61]

Who did parties claim to represent now that the notion of distinct political communities was being increasingly questioned? Part of the answer is that the parties were clueless. Strikingly, they began to discuss their political language—the social democrats, for instance, considered abandoning the concept of 'workers' because they believed that voters no longer treated it as a marker for political identity[62]—as they searched for a new way to address voters now that political identities no longer seemed self-evident. Parties were curious to know more about voters' motivations and choices made at the ballot box, and about their appreciation of particular political platforms and leaders. This new interest contributed to a boom in electoral and opinion research during the 1960s. Social scientists provided parties with a range of theories and approaches regarding voting behaviour and the popular appreciation of politics. Party committees on election strategy developed into forums of debate where engrained ideological approaches to political identity-formation clashed with the recent findings of social scientists and opinion researchers.[63]

Perceptions of political identity-formation among Dutch politicians showed the decline of social determinism. In the early 1960s Ed van Thijn, a social-democratic politician with a background in political science, argued against making a direct link between class and political affiliations and instead tried to show that the outcome of general elections depended on the *political* issues that happened to be at the centre of attention.[64] Van Thijn was inspired by a new approach in election studies promoted by the American political scientist V.O. Key and his Dutch colleague Hans Daudt, whose lectures van Thijn had attended while studying at the University of Amsterdam. In his 1961 study, *Floating Voters and the Floating Vote*, Daudt criticised the social determinism that dominated the analysis of electoral behaviour in the Anglo-Saxon world.[65] Instead he stressed the importance of the 'supply side' in explaining election results: a loss at the ballot box signalled a mismatch between a party's political agenda and the issues and demands on the minds of the electorate. Moreover, reflecting on Dutch politics, Daudt urged parties to place greater consideration on voters' self-representations and to appeal to them 'through their own language and images'.[66] Building on Daudt's work, other Dutch political scientists showed that the cleavages and issues highlighted by political parties in their election campaigns often did not coincide with how voters perceived reality, which resulted in political apathy or even hostility towards politicians and the political process among the electorate. Here the metaphor of a 'cleavage' (*kloof*) that separated the people from politicians first arose.[67]

Daudt's research also contributed to a reconceptualisation of floating voters among Dutch political parties, at first mainly among the social democrats. Parties used to perceive people who voted for different parties in consecutive elections as uninterested and politically ignorant. Apparently, these voters lacked the understanding to know which political community they actually belonged to. Daudt and Key, in contrast, argued that these voters were well aware of the issues at stake in an election and made a conscious choice for the party that served their interests best.[68] Opinion research further contributed to such new interpretations of the workings of political representation: opinion surveys provided social scientists and political parties with data on the *perceptions* of politics and the *motivations* behind the decisions made at the ballot box. Such research resulted in new categorisations of the electorate: voters were no longer chiefly grouped according to shared socio-religious or socio-economic characteristics, but also according to a shared preference for a certain political agenda or approach to politics, or they emerged in election studies as 'the electorate': an aggregated, non-categorised body of individual voters.[69] In its internal strategic discussions in the 1960s the PvdA, for instance, invented the group *cultuurgevoeligen* (people susceptible to cultural trends) as one of its 'target groups': voters whose behaviour at the ballot box was supposedly dictated by their desire to follow political trends.⁷⁰ The social democrats also repeatedly referred to 'the average voter' (*de gemiddelde kiezer*) and 'every Dutchman' (*elke Nederlander*) as a point of reference for their party publicity.⁷¹

What needs to be acknowledged, however, is that electoral research and the intraparty reflections on it did not result in a complete reset of party and electoral politics. On many occasions politicians and party strategists turned a blind eye to research findings that contradicted their convictions and instead preferred to rely on their own political antennae.⁷² Political parties had a strong sense of history and traditions connected to a distinct ideological profile that they cherished and protected. Such a culture was not easy to override since it also legitimised a party's continued existence: the imagined political community of the social democrats had been shaped through a common struggle against the plight of the working class. And how could one imagine a Catholic political community without religion as its backbone? These traditions had to be renegotiated when party strategists, campaigners and MPs discussed the approach to upcoming election campaigns. A fine illustration is the continuing prominence of an 'old-school' socialist language of class in the election campaigns of the PvdA during the late 1960s despite earlier attempts to develop a new approach towards the electorate. The social democrats feared that they would otherwise alienate themselves from what they still perceived to be their core, working-class electorate.⁷³

Political Communities beyond the 1960s

Manin has argued that from the 1960s onwards party democracy made way for 'audience democracy', a new mode of representative government. Its main feature was a personalisation of electoral choice, with parties developing into 'instruments in the service of a leader'. The use of mass media, particularly television, enhanced the opportunities for politicians to communicate directly with the people.⁷⁴ On the one hand, the notion of community seems to have less relevance here: according to Manin, compared to party democracy, audience democracy's political elite was in no position to 'inspire feelings of identification on the part of voters'.⁷⁵ On the other hand, recent studies on the 1960s have stressed that communities did not so much disappear but rather changed in nature and substance, a shift that has been conceptualised as a move from 'heavy' to 'light' communities. The latter were far more inclusive than the former and less concerned with the construction of a common identity.⁷⁶ To what extent does the conceptualisation of political representation by Dutch political parties meet this description? Did political constituencies lose their 'heavy' communal features?

It was evident that in the 1960s and 1970s parties no longer took the existence or reality of political communities for granted. Discussions about a 'crisis of party' abounded.⁷⁷ Ongoing discussions about political apathy among the electorate and discontent towards the behaviour of the political elite culminated in public and intraparty reflections on the state of political representation and subsequently in efforts to restore people's confidence in politicians and party politics. These efforts amounted to not so much a *reconstruction or reconfiguration* of political communities as an attempted *regeneration* of political representation, which ranged from calls for electoral reform and the popularisation of campaigning to the decentralisation of candidate selection.[78]

Changes in the party landscape also illustrate the emergence of new approaches to political representation. The new and surprisingly successful political party D'66—D for Democrats, established in 1966—did not hide its pragmatic rather than strictly ideological approach to politics and favoured individual freedom and development, unshackled from what it deemed oppressive forces, such as the Church. In addition, the party made a call for more direct democracy, for example advocating for the direct election of the prime minister.[79] The established parties also changed course. In the 1970s, after years of intense and faltering negotiations, the three major confessional parties (which included the KVP) joined hands and founded CDA (Christen-Democratisch Appèl, or Christian-Democratic Appeal), a new Christian-democratic political party. The new party abandoned the 'heavy' features of its predecessors: confessional politics was no longer inward-looking, endlessly trying to maintain denominational unity in politics. The Christian democrats, however, still tried to maintain some sense of community, projecting their communal rhetoric onto society at large. In response to the confrontational rhetoric of the social democrats, who had intensified their attacks on confessional party politics from the late 1960s onwards, the Christian democrats adopted an inclusive discourse centring on concepts like harmony and solidarity. They accused the social democrats of focusing on cleavages between different groups of people—progressive versus conservative, secular versus confessional—and stressed the need to work together on building a new society based on a shared set of values like 'love', 'justice' and 'solidarity' that could be derived, directly or indirectly, from the message of the Gospel.[80] In the end, this approach was successful, at least judging from the election results: from 1977 onwards the CDA managed to firmly establish itself as a Christian-democratic centre party. The social democrats had to acknowledge the failure of their aggressive 'polarisation' strategy: they toned down their confrontational rhetoric and assumed a less rigid profile in the 1980s.[81]

From the late 1960s onwards, then, without disappearing completely, the notion of community did lose many of its 'heavy' features. In his recent analysis of American public and academic debates in the 1970s, Daniel T. Rodgers identifies a disaggregation of the social and stresses the importance of the metaphor of the market in producing knowledge of society and social change. Although Rodgers might have overstated his claim, ignoring the persistence of a sense of 'community light', his argument does provide a useful perspective to make sense of new understandings of political representation among Dutch political parties in the 1970s.[82] Parties indeed began to make increasing use of experts and techniques from the world of marketing, public relations and advertising. Electoral research provided them with data on a (mis)match between 'supply' and 'demand' in the electoral marketplace. Not surprisingly, the jargon of marketing penetrated intraparty discussions on election strategies.[83] This novel language, however, did not bring the reward political parties hoped for. Through their development into catch-all parties, a 'heavy' communal understanding of political identity became obsolete, except for a couple of smaller, heavily orthodox-Protestant parties and new fringe parties with a strong ideological profile like the Maoist Socialist Party (Socialistische Partij: SP, established in 1972).[84] The dwindling of community accorded with a neoliberal, no-nonsense and managerial approach to politics that dominated the 1980s and 1990s. Towards the turn of the millennium, however, populist politicians started to attack this political culture. They constructed new cleavages around a notion of community that (again) became more political, the nation-state, and represented the people as a 'homogeneous whole'. Currently, a varying combination of anti-establishment, anti-immigration, anti-Islam and anti–European Union rhetoric has given them a wide and surprisingly stable following in various European countries, including the Netherlands. Although this does not implicate a return to the 'heavy' communities of the 1960s, it shows the political capital still inherent in highly exclusionary notions of community.[85]

Notes

1. This work was supported by a VENI-fellowship of the Netherlands Organisation for Scientific Research: "Constructing Constituencies: Dutch Political Parties and the Language of Politics, 1880 to the Present", under Grant number 275-52-009. Parts of this chapter are based on research that has resulted in the following publications: Kaal, "Constructing", and Wim de Jong and Harm Kaal, "Mapping the Demos: The Scientisation of the Political, Electoral Research and Dutch Political Parties, c. 1900–1980". Manin, *The Principles*, 210–11.
2. Saward, "The Representative," 313–14.
3. Ibid. See for a more extensive account also Saward, *The Representative*.
4. Saward does not seem to acknowledge this: he does not refer to any of the major historical studies on political representation mentioned in the notes below.
5. Stedman Jones, *Languages*.
6. Lawrence, "Class," 630–31.
7. Steinmetz, ed, *Political Languages*; Mergel, *Propaganda*; Freeden, *Liberal Languages*.
8. The first studies questioning idiosyncrasy were: Righart, *De katholieke*; Hellemans, *Strijd*.
9. Lijphart, *Verzuiling*.
10. Van Dam, *Staat*.
11. See the critical review by Peter van Rooden of several studies on Dutch pillarised society: van Rooden, "Studies".
12. Voerman, "De stand".
13. Cf. de Rooy, "Begeerten"; Rulof, "Selling".

14. Schuyt and Taverne, *1950*, 248; de Jong, *Van wie*, 42–43.
15. De Jong, *Van wie*, 48.
16. Kaal, "Constructing," 192–93.
17. Aerts et al., *Land*, 262.
18. Pamphlet "Kiest een nieuwe koers", inv.nr. 1494, KVP Archive, Catholic Documentation Centre Nijmegen (hereafter cited as KDC); Pamphlet "Wij boeren kunnen erover meepraten", inv.nr. 2087, PvdA Archive, International Institute of Social History (hereafter cited as IISH).
19. Kaal, "Constructing," 194.
20. Ibid.
21. De Jong, *Van wie*, 42–43.
22. Vertrouwen op gegrond beginsel, speech, 1946, inv.nr. 54, F.G.C.J.M. Teulings Archive, KDC.
23. Bornewasser, *Katholieke Volkspartij*, I, 149, 164, 469; Verkiezingsmateriaal ARP (Antirevolutionaire Partij) en enkele andere protestants-christelijke partijen (413), box 1, Historical Documentation Centre of Dutch Protestantism (hereafter cited as HDC).
24. Ontnuchterende en nuchtere feiten!, PvdA campaign brochure, 1948, inv.nr. 1494, KVP Archive, KDC; Voor heel het volk, KVP pamphlet, 1959, inv.nr. 1489, KVP Archive, KDC.
25. Wijmans, *Beeld*.
26. Hartmans, *Vijandige broeders*, 196–99.
27. Vossen, *Vrij vissen*, 130–31.
28. Wijmans, *Beeld*, 132–33.
29. Emanuel Boekman. "De beteekenis van de middengroepen in den strijd voor het socialisme," *De Socialistische Gids* 18 (1934): 703–15; Hartmans, *Vijandige broeders*, 196–99.
30. Boekman, "De beteekenis," 710.
31. B. Engelander, *Het middenstandsvraagstuk in een nieuw licht* (Amsterdam: Arbeiderspers, 1934), 3–4.
32. *Rapport van de Herzieningscommissie der SDAP* (Amsterdam: Arbeiderspers, 1933).
33. Kaal, "Constructing," 191.
34. Kruijt, *Arbeiders*.
35. Ibid., 23. 'De lagere rangen der handarbeiders en de hogere der hoofdarbeiders hebben een verschillende levensstijl. Dat is niet alleen begrijpelijk, maar ook wenselijk: deze differentiatie verrijkt onze gehele cultuur. Maar differentiatie zonder integratie veroorzaakt ontbinding van gemeenschap en vervreemding'.
36. Van Heek, "Klassen," 261 (this is the text of van Heek's 1948 inaugural lecture); Jonker, "Kruijt"; Jonker, "Heek".
37. J.M. den Uyl, "Om een eigentijds socialisme: Labours nederlaag," *Socialisme & Democratie* (hereafter cited as *S&D*) (1959): 714–21.
38. A. van Braam, "Misnoegen der middengroepen," *S&D* (1958): 510–35.
39. "Verkiezingen in Nederland," inv.nr. 38, WBS Archive, IISH; Van Braam, "Misnoegen". The same line of reasoning was used to explain the low level of unionisation among the middle classes: "NVV zoekt weg naar middengroepen," *Het Vrije Volk*, 13 October 1962.
40. J.M. den Uyl, "Politieke voorkeur en politieke wetenschap," *S&D* (1957): 344–55; den Uyl, "Krachtmeting zonder beslissing," *S&D* (1962): 321–29.
41. List of adverts, 1946, inv.nr. 2087, PvdA Archive, IISH; Ontnuchterende en nuchtere feiten!, PvdA campaign brochure, 1948, inv.nr. 1494, KVP Archive, KDC; "Middenstandspartij?" *Het Vrije Volk*, 27 March 1950.
42. Doorbraak springlevend, PvdA campaign brochure, 1956, inv.nr. 2089, PvdA Archive, IISH.

43. In 1948, the PvdA did not use the terminology of old and new middle classes in its electoral strategy. It aimed its publicity at communist voters, workers, shopkeepers, farmers, market gardeners, Roman Catholics and Protestants. Wim Thomassen, Evert Vermeer, and Kees Woudenberg, *Inzet verkiezingsactie 1948. Aan de Besturen van de Afdelingen van de Partij van de Arbeid*, December 1947, inv.nr. 2087, PvdA Archive, IISH.
44. Woorden van Dr. Drees, PvdA campaign material, 1946, inv.nr. 2089, PvdA Archive, IISH.
45. [no title], PvdA pamphlet, 1956, inv.nr. 1496, KVP Archive, KDC.
46. Letter to managers (*bedrijfsleiders*), 9 May 1946, inv.nr. 2087, PvdA Archive, IISH.
47. Wie verstandig is gaat op weg met de PvdA, PvdA campaign material, 1959, inv. nr. 1497, KVP Archive, KDC.
48. Van Praag, *Strategie*, 247.
49. J. Harmsen, "De doorbraak in het maatschappelijke vlak," *S&D* (1949): 285–91; van Braam, "Misnoegen," 527; "Partij van de Arbeid haalt 27 zetels," *Het Vrije Volk*, 8 July 1948; "Goede hoop," Ibid., 17 June 1949; "'Socialisten moeten hoofd- en handarbeiders verenigen,'" Ibid., 27 February 1950.
50. J. G. M. Delfgaauw and A. I. V. Massizzo, "De financiële positie van de middengroepen in loondienst," *Katholiek Staatkundig Maandschrift* (hereafter cited as KSM) [extra edition] (1952); Th. J. Platenburg, "De intellectuele positie van de midden-groepen in de Nederlandse samenleving," ibid.; Commissie voor de Middengroepen der Katholieke Volkspartij, "Verbetering van de positie der midden-groepen," ibid.
51. Ziemann and Dols, "Catholic Church," 295–97; Dols, *Fact Factory*.
52. The second report published by KASKI, in 1948, contained an analysis of the election results of 1937 and 1946: *Analyse van de uitslagen der verkiezingen voor de 2e Kamer der Staten-Generaal 1937 en 1946*. KASKI (The Hague: KASKI, 1948).
53. For a couple of examples see: Dols, *Fact Factory*, 251–53.
54. The concept was first used in the 1950s: *De politieke keuze der Nederlandse katolieken. Deel I. Kwantitatieve analyse van een aantal verkiezingen voor de Tweede Kamer der Staten-Generaal sedert 1933* (The Hague: KASKI, 1957); *Het stembusgedrag der katholieken van 1954–1959* (The Hague: KASKI, 1960).
55. *Analyse*, KASKI; *De politieke keuze*.
56. Bornewasser, *Katholieke Volkspartij*, I, 153.
57. L.A.H. Albering, "Na de verkiezingen van 1952," *KSM* 6 (1952): 136; Albering, "De verkiezingen," 179; Ibid., "De Kamerverkiezingen van 1959," *KSM* 13 (1959): 85–94.
58. *De katolieke arbeider en zijn politieke houding* (The Hague: KASKI, 1958).
59. A fine example is the 'You Campaign' (the 'Actie U') of the early 1960s: De 'Aktie U', 22 October 1962, inv.nr. 1504, KVP Archive, KDC.
60. Verklaring van het Hoogwaardig Episcopaat, inv.nr. 54, Teulings Archive, KDC; Vertrouwen op gegrond beginsel, KVP campaign material, 1946, inv.nr. 54, Teulings Archive, KDC.
61. Van Dam, "Constructing," 2.
62. Minutes of the Electoral Research Committee, 27 February 1962, inv.nr. 1366, PvdA Archive, IISH.
63. Ibid., 21 December 1965, inv.nr. 1367, PvdA Archive, IISH; C. de Galan, "Mogelijke oorzaken van het stemmenverlies," *S&D* (1963): 597–60; de Jong and Kaal, "Mapping".
64. E. van Thijn, "Kritische kanttekeningen bij een trek naar rechts," *Sociologische Gids* 10 (1963): 239–48; Ibid., "De lange golf kort en klein," *S&D* (1963): 54–63; ibid., "De Kamerverkiezingen van 1963," *S&D* (1963): 485–509.

65. Daudt, *Floating Voters*.
66. Gerda Brautigam, "Politiek in de televisie—het was allemaal zo abstract," *Opinie* 3, no. 6 (March 1967).
67. A. Hoogerwerf, "Sociaal-politieke strijdpunten: smeulend vuur," *Sociologische Gids* 10 (1963): 249–63; R. Kroes, "Ideologie en politiek in Nederland," *Sociologische Gids* (1964): 184–94; ter Hoeven, *Bedreigde democratie*.
68. Daudt, *Floating Voters*; Key, *The Responsible Electorate*.
69. *De Nederlandse kiezer: Zijn gedragingen en opvattingen* (The Hague, 1956), 34.
70. Van Praag, *Strategie*, 48–49.
71. Notitie centraal thema 'Den Uyl, een man om mee te werken', PvdA, 1967, inv. nr. 636, Den Uyl Archive, IISH. For a similar line of argument see: Igo, *The Averaged American*.
72. Minutes of the Commissie Kiezersonderzoek, 16 September 1963, inv.nr. 1366, PvdA Archive, IISH; de Jong and Kaal, "Mapping".
73. Van Praag, *Strategie*, 365, 388–89; Verkiezingszendtijd PvdA, 8 February 1967, inv.nr. 3553, KVP Archive, KDC; Notitie centraal thema 'Den Uyl, een man om mee te werken', PvdA, 1967, inv.nr. 636, Den Uyl Archive, IISH.
74. Manin, *The Principles*, 219–20.
75. Ibid., 233.
76. Van Dam, "Constructing"; Duyvendak and Hurenkamp, *Kiezen*.
77. Van den Berg and Molleman, *Crisis*; Wattenberg, *The Decline*.
78. Verslag van een 7-daags studiebezoek, report, 15 September 1965, inv.nr. 1367, PvdA Archive, IISH; Bornewasser, *KVP*, II, 220; "Verkiezingscampagne in Amerikaanse stijl: KVP-lijsttrekker Schmelzer op toernee door Limburg," *Limburgs Dagblad*, 31 December 1966; "Verkiezingskaravaan met Veringa twee dagen in Limburg," Ibid., 10 March 1971.
79. Te Velde, *Stijlen*, 209–12.
80. Werkgelegenheid, campaign flyer, inv.nr. 100, CDA Archive (1965–1980), National Archives, The Hague; Willem Aantjes, Liever vuile handen dan in onschuld gewassen handen, speech, inv.nr. 3, Documentation ARP, HDC; Een zaak van vertrouwen, ARP campaign material, 1972, inv.nr. 301, ARP Archive (850), HDC; speech by A.D.W. Tilanus, 9 September 1972, inv.nr. 642, Den Uyl Archive, IISH.
81. Van Praag, *Strategie*, 388–89.
82. Rodgers, *The Age*.
83. Chris Vos, "Politiek als koopwaar: De moderne verkiezingscampagne," *Intermediair* 14 (1978): 3–11, and "De Nederlandse verkiezingscampagne: De intrede van het 'mannetjes maken'," *Intermediair* 14 (1978): 23–29.
84. Voerman, "Van Mao".
85. Vossen, *Rondom*; Houwen, *Reclaiming*, 95–101.

Bibliography

Aerts, Remieg, et al. *Land van kleine gebaren. Een politieke geschiedenis van Nederland, 1780–2012*. Amsterdam: Boom, 2013.

Berg, J.Th.J. van den and H.A. Molleman. *Crisis in de Nederlandse politiek*. Alphen aan den Rijn, 1975.

Bornewasser, J. A. *Katholieke Volkspartij 1945–1980. Band I. Herkomst en groei (tot 1963)*. Nijmegen: Valkhof Pers, 1995.

Bornewasser, J. A. *Katholieke Volkspartij 1945–1980. Band II. Heroriëntatie en integratie (1963–1980)*. Nijmegen: Valkhof Pers, 2000.

Dam, Peter van. *Staat van verzuiling. Over een Nederlandse mythe*. Amsterdam: Wereldbibliotheek, 2011.

Dam, Peter van. "Constructing a Modern Society through 'Depillarization': Understanding Post-War History as Gradual Change." *Journal of Historical Sociology* 28, no. 3 (2015): 291–313.
Daudt, H. *Floating Voters and the Floating Vote: A Critical Analysis of American and English Election Studies*. Leiden: Stenfert Kroese, 1961.
Dols, Chris. *Fact Factory: Sociological Expertise and Episcopal Decision Making in The Netherlands, 1946–1972*. Nijmegen, 2014.
Duyvendak, Jan Willem and Menno Hurenkamp, eds. *Kiezen voor de kudde. Lichte gemeenschappen en de nieuwe meerderheid*. Amsterdam: Van Gennep, 2004.
Freeden, Michael. *Liberal Languages: Ideological Imaginations and 20th Century Progressive Thought*. Princeton: Princeton University Press, 2005.
Hartmans, Rob. *Vijandige broeders? De Nederlandse sociaal-democratie en het nationaal-socialisme, 1922–1940*. Amsterdam: Ambo, 2012.
Heek, F. van. "Klassen en standenstructuur als sociologische begrippen." In *Het sociale leven in al zijn facetten. Sleutel tot moderne maatschappelijke problematiek, I*, edited by S.J. Groenman, W.R. Heere, and E.V.W. Vercruijsse, 245–66. Assen: Van Gorcum, 1958.
Hellemans, Staf. *Strijd om de moderniteit. Sociale bewegingen en verzuiling in Europa sinds 1800*. Leuven: Universitaire Pers Leuven, 1990.
Hoeven, P. J. A. ter. *Bedreigde democratie*. Utrecht: Bijleveld, 1965.
Houwen, Tim. *Reclaiming Power for the People: Populism in Democracy*. Enschede, 2013.
Igo, Sarah E. *The Averaged American: Surveys, Citizens, and the Making of a Mass Public*. Cambridge, MA and London: Harvard University Press, 2007.
Jong, Wim de. *Van wie is de burger? Omstreden democratie in Nederland, 1945–1985*. Nijmegen, 2014.
Jong, Wim de and Harm Kaal. "Mapping the Demos: The Scientisation of the Political, Electoral Research and Dutch Political Parties c. 1900–1980." *Contemporary European History* 26 (2017).
Jonker, Ed. "Heek, Frederik van (1907–1987)." In *Biografisch Woordenboek van Nederland*. http://resources.huygens.knaw.nl/bwn1880-2000/lemmata/bwn4/heek
Jonker, Ed. "Kruijt, Jakob Pieter (1898–1975)." In *Biografisch Woordenboek van Nederland*. http://resources.huygens.knaw.nl/bwn1880-2000/lemmata/bwn4/kruijt
Kaal, Harm. "Constructing a Socialist Constituency: The Social-Democratic Language of Politics in the Netherlands, C. 1890–1950." *Archiv Für Sozialgeschichte* 53 (2013): 175–202.
Key, V. O. *The Responsible Electorate: Rationality in Presidential Voting, 1936–1960*. Cambridge, MA: Belknap Press of Harvard University Press, 1966.
Knegtmans, Peter Jan. "De jaren 1919–1946." In *Honderd jaar sociaal-democratie in Nederland, 1894–1994*, edited by Maarten Brinkman, Madelon de Keizer, and Maarten van Rossem, 62–117. Amsterdam: Bert Bakker, 1994.
Kruijt, J. P. *Arbeiders en nieuwe middenstand. Rede uitgesproken na de aanvaarding van het ambt van gewoon hoogleraar in de sociologie aan de Rijksuniversiteit te Utrecht*. Amsterdam: H.J. Paris, 1947.
Lawrence, Jon. "Class and Gender in the Making of Urban Toryism, 1880–1914." *English Historical Review* 108 (1993): 629–52.
Lawrence, Jon. *Speaking for the People: Party, Language and Popular Politics in England, 1867–1914*. Cambridge: Cambridge University Press, 1998.

Lawrence, Jon. "Labour and the Politics of Class, 1900–1940." In *Structures and Transformations in Modern British History: Essays for Gareth Stedman Jones*, edited by David Feldman and Jon Lawrence, 237–60. Cambridge: Cambridge University Press, 2011.

Lijphart, Arend. *Verzuiling, pacificatie en kentering in de Nederlandse politiek*. Amsterdam: De Bussy, 1968.

Manin, Bernard. *The Principles of Representative Government*. Cambridge: Cambridge University Press, 1997.

Mergel, Thomas. *Propaganda nach Hitler. Eine Kulturgeschichte des Wahlkampfs in der Bundesrepublik 1949–1990*. Göttingen: Wallstein Verlag, 2010.

Praag, Philip van, Jr. *Strategie en illusie. Elf jaar intern debat in de PvdA (1966–1977)*. Amsterdam: Het Spinhuis, 1990.

Righart, Hans. *De katholieke zuil in Europa. Een vergelijkend onderzoek naar het ontstaan van verzuiling onder katholieken in Oostenrijk, Zwitserland, Belgiëen Nederland*. Meppel: Boom, 1986.

Rodgers, Daniel T. *The Age of Fracture*. Cambridge, MA: The Belknap Press of Harvard University Press, 2011.

Rooden, Peter van. "Studies naar verzuiling als toegang tot de geschiedenis van de constructie van religieuze verschillen in Nederland." *Theoretische Geschiedenis* 20 (1993): 439–54.

Rooy, Piet de. "Begeerten en idealen. Een eeuw sociaal-democratie in Nederland." In *De rode droom. Een eeuw sociaal-democratie in Nederland. Een essay en een beeldverhaal*, edited by Piet de Rooy, Nico Markus, and Tom van der Meer et al., 8–77. Nijmegen: SUN, 1995.

Rulof, Bernard. *Een leger van priesters voor een heilige zaak. SDAP, politieke manifestaties en massapolitiek, 1918–1940*. Amsterdam: Wereldbibliotheek, 2007.

Rulof, Bernard. "Selling Social Democracy in the Netherlands: Activism and its Sources of Inspiration during the 1930s." *Contemporary European History* 18 (2009): 475–97.

Saward, Michael. "The Representative Claim." *Contemporary Political Theory* 5 (2006): 297–318.

Saward, Michael. *The Representative Claim*. Oxford: Oxford University Press, 2010.

Schuyt, Kees and Ed Taverne. *1950. Welvaart in zwart-wit*. Den Haag: Sdu Uitgevers, 2000.

Stedman Jones, Gareth. *Languages of Class: Studies in English Working Class History*. Cambridge: Cambridge University Press, 1983.

Steinmetz, Willibald, ed. *Political Languages in the Age of Extremes*. Oxford: Oxford University Press, 2011.

Velde, Henk te. *Stijlen van leiderschap. Persoon en politiek van Thorbecke tot Den Uyl*. Amsterdam: Wereldbibliotheek, 2002.

Voerman, Gerrit. "De stand van de geschiedschrijving van de Nederlandse politieke partijen." *BMGN* 120 (2005): 226–69.

Voerman, Gerrit. "Van Mao tot marketing. Over het populisme van de SP." *Socialisme & Democratie* 66 (2009): 26–32.

Vondeling, Anne. *Nasmaak en voorproef. Een handvol ervaringen en ideeën*. Amsterdam: De Arbeiderspers, 1968.

Vossen, Koen. *Vrij vissen in het Vondelpark. Kleine politieke partijen in Nederland 1918–1940*. Amsterdam: Wereldbibliotheek, 2003.

Vossen, Koen. *Rondom Wilders. Portret van de PVV*. Amsterdam: Boom, 2013.

Wattenberg, M. *The Decline of American Political Parties 1952–1984*. Cambridge, MA: Harvard University Press, 1984.
Wijmans, L. L. *Beeld en betekenis van het maatschappelijke midden. Oude en nieuwe middengroepen, 1850 tot heden*. Amsterdam: Van Gennep, 1987.
Wolinetz, Steven B. "Beyond the Catch-All Party: Approaches to the Study of Parties and Party Organization in Contemporary Democracies." In *Political Parties: Old Concepts and New Challenges*, edited by Richard Gunther, José Ramón Montero, and Juan J. Linz, 136–65. Oxford: Oxford University Press, 2002.
Ziemann, Benjamin and Chris Dols. "Catholic Church Reform and Organizations Research in the Netherlands and Germany, 1945–1980." In *Engineering Society*, 293–312.
Ziemann, Benjamin, Richard F. Wetzell, Dirk Schumann, and Kerstin Brückweh. "Introduction: The Scientization of the Social in Comparative Perspective." In *Engineering Society: The Role of the Human and Social Sciences in Modern Societies, 1880–1980*, edited by Benjamin Ziemann, Richard F. Wetzell, Dirk Schumann, and Kerstin Brückweh, 1–40. Basingstoke: Palgrave Macmillan, 2012.

12 Dialogues on Religion in a "Socialist Society" under Construction
Marxist Social Scientists and Czech Protestants, 1940s–60s

Ondřej Matějka

The book *Church in a Marxist Society: a Czechoslovak View*, published in 1970 by the prestigious American publishing house Harper & Row, caused a stir among Western Protestant intellectuals.[1] Instead of offering another variation on the classical theme of persecution of churches in Communist dictatorships, Jan Milíč Lochman (1922–2004), a well-known and respected Czech theologian,[2] proclaimed that at the end of the 1960s in Czechoslovakia, a model of society had emerged which might be considered 'a substantial step forward on the way of humanization'. It was a model of society, Lochman argued, which, on the one hand, had 'broken the basic bondage of economic inequality and oppressive financial power', and, on the other hand, was 'applying democratic brakes to the monopoly of political power'. Such a society, Lochman concluded, 'could correspond to some basic insights of the Biblical faith of the Old and New Testaments'.[3]

Lochman's main thesis on the fundamental compatibility of Christian and Marxist visions of an ideal 'socialist society', and his detailed account of the active collaboration of dialogically oriented Protestants and Communists in putting this ideal into practice, produced a mixture of shock, denial and curiosity among his English-speaking readers. Certain representatives of American Protestantism immediately labelled him a 'Communist agent',[4] the customarily anti-Communist reviewer for the influential Protestant magazine *Christianity Today* firmly stated that 'it would have been better for Dr. Lochman not to have written this book'[5] and the prestigious *Journal of Church and State* characterised his analysis as being 'profoundly annoying' yet 'strangely moving'.[6]

The goal of this chapter is to retrace how this conception, which for certain Western observers was particularly disturbing, of a joint Christian-Marxist venture of the (re)construction of a 'socialist society' came into being, and how it evolved in the Czech lands in the quarter-century following the end of the Second World War.[7] On the basis of archival sources of various state institutions, the Communist Party of Czechoslovakia (CPC) and the dominant Czech Protestant church—the Evangelical Church of Czech Brethren (ECCB)—and also of international organisations (in particular the World

Dialogues on Religion in a "Socialist Society" under Construction 239

Council of Churches [WCC]), as well as on interviews both published and unpublished, this chapter chronologically charts the interaction between two main groups of actors (most of them prolific authors of articles and books, constituting another important body of sources for this chapter) who 'co-constructed' these visions. These actors consist of Czech Marxist intellectuals and elite Protestant theologians whose at times intense contacts eventually led to the overcoming of ideological and political barriers and to the formation of a surprising coalition (evolving, of course, over time and in space) making their way towards a shared ideal of a 'socialist society'.

Given that the Czech language has no two terms to adequately cover the different semantic field(s) of the *Gemeinschaft/Gesellschaft* duality so strongly conceptualised in classical (German) sociological tradition,[8] one of this chapter's objectives is to clarify the particular mixture of elements connected with these two concepts in the discourses of Czech Marxists and Protestant theological elites. In fact, although all these actors used (almost consistently) the generic term 'socialist society' (*socialistická společnost*), the polarising issues along the *Gemeinschaft/Gesellschaft* continuum related to the production of social coherence, the reduction of alienation and the parameters of the scientific design of a 'modern' social order remained very much present in their lively exchanges, which we will follow in this chapter.

Burying the Old World

Even though contacts and first attempts at dialogue between Czech Marxists and Protestant intellectuals can be traced back to the interwar period,[9] the concrete basis for their cooperation on the definition and realisation of the socialist project of reconstructing Czech society should first be situated in the context of the Second World War. The devastating effects of two World Wars, as amply suggested in the present book, offered plenty of ruined sites—literally and figuratively—on which new communities were to be constructed.[10] Seen from a purely material perspective, the Czech lands survived the Second World War in rather good shape. In contrast, the predominantly Western-oriented political preferences of Czech intellectual elites, which were connected to the defining influence of the founding father of the Czechoslovak Republic, Tomáš Garrigue Masaryk, fell victim to the war storm. The shock of the Western powers' 'betrayal' in Munich in October 1938 indeed substantially shook the previously undisputed belief in liberal democracy among Czech intellectual elites of different generations and allowed for a radical (geo)political re-orientation towards the Soviet East.[11] The case of Josef Lukl Hromádka (1889–1969), professor of systematic theology at the Prague Protestant Theological Faculty and the most publicly influential Czech Protestant since the 1930s, is illustrative in this regard:[12] 'We will carry it to our graves, our children and grandchildren will feel it inside of them and will find no surgeon who can operate and remove it from their inner being'.[13] These impassioned words gave expression to

Figure 12.1 In January 1969 Josef Lukl Hromádka attended a conference on East-West relations at VU University Amsterdam.

Source: Fotocollectie Anefo, file 922–0174, 2.24.01.05, National Archive, the Netherlands. Photographer: Jac. de Nijs. Creative Commons License, CC-BY-SA.

Hromádka's perception of the Munich trauma. But in the early days following the Munich agreement, Hromádka, who after having studied in Basel, Heidelberg and Aberdeen considered himself to be an entirely 'Western man',[14] also framed this event in a global historical context by interpreting it to be the 'death sentence' for 'liberal Europe of the period 1789–1938'.[15]

Hromádka's visions resonated not only within the small Czech Protestant minority, which constituted around two to three per cent of the Czech population. In the interwar period his views were audible and respected at the national level thanks to his close relationship to the Czechoslovak YMCA, a mighty association in Czechoslovakia because of its close connections to leading political elites around Masaryk and Edvard Beneš. Furthermore, since the mid-1930s Hromádka had risen to become the undeniably best-known Czech Protestant in the Western world. His early attachment to dialectical theology and personal friendship with Karl Barth opened the door for him to move among the core of the rapidly expanding circle of the international ecumenical movement.[16] These networks enabled him to leave the Czech lands occupied by the German army in late March 1939:[17] his Western friends helped procure him an invitation to teach at Princeton Theological Seminary, where he became a popular professor of systematic theology while also being an active participant in the preparation of the WCC.[18]

During his American exile, Hromádka continued to develop his sociopolitical reflections on the precipitous evolution of the Western world, which he perceived in growingly apocalyptic terms. He presented these thoughts in a book significantly entitled *Doom and Resurrection*, in which he argued that 'the [European] civilization as it existed prior to 1914 and, in a way, until 1930, is gone. The cathedral of common norms and ideas, standards and hopes, disintegrated from within. The present world war manifests in an unparalleled way the destruction of the (certainly imperfect yet real) unity on which the community of the civilized nations had rested'. In his conclusions Hromádka insisted on the radical and even absolute nature of the threshold he believed the world had reached: 'We are living on the ruins of the old world, both morally and politically. [. . .] All is literally at stake. No one single norm and element of our civilization can possibly be taken for granted'.[19]

When looking into the future, Hromádka, who had stated in the days of the Munich shock that 'freedom, tolerance and human rights have to be secured, from now on, by alternative means',[20] always turned his attention more thoroughly towards the East than the West. In the early 1940s he stated that the 'hidden revolutionary forces' of Soviet Russia had opened the way 'towards real humanity, brotherhood, peace' and had created 'a reliable road towards a permanent overcoming of material iniquity, exploitation and social insecurity'.[21] In these war reflections, Hromádka thus outlined the fundamental elements of his ideal of a 'new society' (growing out of a profoundly changed social architecture and based on norms and values substantially differing from those of pre-war 'bourgeois' society), the goal he envisioned as well for the post-war reconstruction of Czechoslovakia. These elements undeniably connected his Christian background with his more recent interest in Marxist conceptions of revolutionary utopia and praxis.

Despite the thousands of kilometres that separated Hromádka from his home country, he used a discourse that was very similar to what could be heard from some of his most radical countrymen and women—teenagers and young adults then coming of age within the largest Protestant church in the Protectorate Bohemia-Moravia, the Evangelical Church of Czech Brethren. The ECCB constituted at that time, as we will see, a haven especially well equipped for the development of nonconformist thinking on social change. In fact, the Nazi authorities had progressively abolished and destroyed every institution that could serve as a gathering place for independently thinking Czech youth (an essential part of this policy was the closing of Czech universities in autumn 1939). During the second half of the war, churches and their youth associations, considered apolitical by the Nazis, remained the only exception to the occupation's clampdown. They were authorised to continue to offer youth-oriented activities outside of the Nazi-friendly *gleichgeschaltete* network. The ECCB, with its extensive experience and infrastructure regarding this type of work, began to attract the attention of radicalised young intellectuals who were desperately seeking spaces to get in touch with their likeminded peers. In the early 1940s the ECCB's 'youth clubs' thus became privileged (and relatively safe) spaces where young men and women were allowed to discuss all sorts of subversive political and social ideas despite the organisation's official line that it was exclusively dedicated 'to the study of the Bible' and 'parlour games in closed rooms'.[22]

The history of the Protestant youth group in the parish of Prague-Smíchov is the most fully documented example of a process of ideological radicalisation that we can partially reconstruct thanks to the correspondence and diaries of its key participants.[23] For teenagers with a Protestant background like Karel Hiršl (1922–1945) and his friends Václav Dobiáš (1921–1945) and Jiří Staněk (1921–1945), youth-club meetings in the Smíchov Protestant parish soon became the centre of their otherwise grey and boring existence in the Protectorate. Here, under the tolerant supervision of Pastor Jan Kučera (1894–1973), they took up risky and sensitive socio-political questions on the basis of Marxist literature that they began hungrily devouring. The concepts of 'society' and 'social change' represented two of the core issues in their debates.

The continuing Nazi terror and the 'always stronger wind blowing from the cradle of the sun'[24] led them inexorably towards ideological radicalisation. Hiršl and his friends thus rapidly moved away from John MacMurray's 'creative society' (the principal reference at the end of 1942), which integrated elements of Marxist thought into Christianity and emphasised the ideal of individual liberation from guilt, shame and fear through love and forgiveness,²⁵ and towards Marx, Engels and Lenin and their reflections on the revolutionary obligation 'to destroy actual social order, to rip away the tumour'.²⁶ In November 1943 this group felt quite clearly that their autodidactic reappropriation of Marxist thought provided them with the necessary tools for the construction of a 'new society', and this aim became the focal point of their discussions: 'We can discover the real laws of the evolution of human society only on the basis of materialism. [. . .] The sense of human life becomes very clear then: interiorise these laws of evolution and invest the energy into the acceleration of this evolution'.²⁷ These young men thus clearly evolved towards an always more rigid 'scientific' understanding of social change, constructed using the conceptual apparatus of dialectical materialism.

However, it is interesting to observe, mainly in their correspondence, that New Testament discourse (interpreted à la MacMurray), with its images of a community of brothers and sisters connected by non-exploitive, 'genuinely human' relationships, continued to form a background for these young people's reflections on revolutionary change. In this way their debates took shape as the domestic counterpart of Hromádka's thoughts formulated overseas.

In late 1943 radical Marxism unmistakably oriented Hiršl and his friends towards resistance against the Nazi occupiers: they launched the illegal journal *Předvoj* (Vanguard) and, simultaneously, they tenaciously tried to contact the underground Communist Party of Czechoslovakia (CPC). These activities eventually cost the lives of the founding fathers of the Vanguard movement, which, nevertheless, had developed into the largest resistance network in the Czech lands by the end of the war.²⁸

Those who survived, such as Radovan Richta (1924–1983) and Erika Kadlecová (b. 1924), sustained their visions and became the most dedicated builders of a new 'socialist society' in post-war Czechoslovakia.²⁹ The CPC offered itself as a powerful means for them to realise their dreams. At the same time, these young comrades, with their remarkable intellectual potential and determined energy, naturally represented a great resource for the CPC, which was haemorrhaged by war losses. The CPC adroitly instrumentalised them, particularly in the field of propaganda. In the late 1940s and early 1950s the likes of Richta and Kadlecová preached to the masses the good news about the construction of a socialist society that would offer 'a new joy of life, a new sense of life, a new style of life'.³⁰ In their texts from this period we can observe the symptomatic mixture of indomitable optimism ('we have all the necessary tools to transform the soul of the people', declared Kadlecová in 1949) and an underlying absolute certainty as to the right direction to adopt in their construction of a new social order. They considered dialectical materialism to be the science which 'precisely shows us how to build a new society'³¹ and people's democracies to be 'the only refuge of truly impartial scientific research, of the relentless search for truth'.³²

These statements from the beginning of the 1950s show another interesting transition in these young ex-resistants' conceptualisation of 'socialist society'. As simplified versions of Marxism-Leninism in East-Central European public and academic spaces enjoyed undisputed dominance, 'modern science' arose as the key element on the road towards this joyful community of the future. Not only did this line of thought sideline all Gospel-related elements in any reflections on a 'socialist society'. It also more rigidly associated religion and churches with the 'old world' and thus forged a more exclusionary image of the new society.

'Progressive Christians' versus 'Religious Prejudice' in the Construction of a Socialist Society

Despite this discursive turn and the fact that young, formerly Protestant Communist ideologues such as Kadlecová became atheists and accepted the thesis that religion would progressively disappear once its social roots were liquidated, they still kept up social bonds with their original milieu. In agreement with their senior comrades returning from exile in Moscow or London, they remained open until the early 1950s to the idea of (at least temporary) collaboration with 'progressive Christians' in their attempts to construct a new society.[33] Such a coalition was made possible by the presence of a number of enthusiastic partners on the Christian side who, as one of them said, 'were really eager to build a socialist society'.[34] Local state as well as parish archives in various regions of Bohemia and Moravia give evidence of the undeniable interpenetration of Communist and Protestant milieus during the late 1940s and early 1950s.[35] Numerous elders in Protestant parishes became active members of the CPC. One of them declared that 'a genuine Communist should be at the same time a genuine Christian as were the first Christians', a sentiment that probably expressed a relatively wide consensus.[36]

These local constellations both reflected and strengthened the discourse of the leading national representatives of the CPC and the ECCB. For instance, at the first post-war CPC congress held in March 1946, Václav Kopecký (1897–1961), the leading Czech communist ideologue after 1945, devoted an important passage of his programmatic statement to the subject of the CPC's relationship towards Christianity: 'We consider the so-called "culture war" to be a historically overcome phenomenon. [. . .] We have nothing against the interpretation of social progress as a way of approaching the Christian ideal of love towards neighbours. We also accept that socialism and communism be interpreted as a realisation of Christian equality and genuine Christian community'.[37] On the Protestant side, Kopecký's friend from the pre-war years, Josef L. Hromádka, who had returned from American exile and became the dean of Prague Protestant Theological Faculty, used a similar discourse. In 1946 he stated that communism could arise only on the 'land ploughed upon by Christian spiritual tradition and civilisation', adding that 'when one reads Marx and Lenin, one can hear resonance of what was announced by the Old Testament prophets and New Testament apostles'.³⁸ He insisted on a particularly important role for Christians in this 'enormous enterprise': the construction of a 'more just society'.³⁹

Hromádka exported this sort of ideas even internationally. For instance, at the WCC's opening assembly, held in August 1948 in Amsterdam, he caused quite a commotion by proclaiming, in his closely followed address 'The Church and the International Disorder', that 'Communism represents, although under an atheistic form, much of the social impetus of the living Church, from the Apostolic age down through the days of the monastic orders to the Reformation and liberal humanism'. In this way Hromádka responded to the previous speaker on the same subject, the American diplomat (and later secretary of state) John Foster Dulles (1888–1959), who had thundered against 'the coercive and terrorising nature of Marxian communism'. Hromádka concluded by outlining his conception of the right position to be taken by Christians in these complicated times: 'Free of illusion and of cheap optimism and equally free of hysteria, panic and despair, the Church of Christ summons all of her members [. . .] to make a new beginning, to start from the bottom and to work for a new society, a new order'.⁴⁰

Hromádka, elected to the governing bodies of the WCC, remained until the late 1960s the principal spokesperson for a Western Christian audience on this project of a religiously inflected construction of a 'socialist society'. On the basis of their experience inside the Czechoslovak Communist regime, Hromádka and his colleagues developed an elaborate view of the inevitable end of the 'Constantinian era' that had lasted for sixteen centuries and had been characterised by an intense and multilayered interconnectedness of Christian church(es) and state power.⁴¹ Czech Protestant elites insisted on the benefits of surpassing this post-Constantinian threshold and the necessary transformation of the Church into a '*communio viatorum*'. This concept (significantly presented in Latin even in Czech publications) referred to a 'community' bound to no political order that was always 'on the road' and, on this journey, faced new historical conditions 'without fear'.⁴² Furthermore, Hromádka ceaselessly reminded his Czech brothers and sisters of the specific task of Christians in the current context, which was to 'spiritually stabilise' what he labelled 'the colossal construction of a socialist society'⁴³ with its 'enormous emancipatory and liberating potential' and to defend 'its great conquests [. . .] even against the Communists themselves'.⁴⁴ Hromádka, who during his studies had been deeply influenced by his professor Ernst Troeltsch's historical approach to the interpretation of religious (and social) change, never stepped back from his conviction that the advent of a 'socialist society' represented an inevitable, irreversible step in the 'history of salvation'.⁴⁵ But from the early 1950s onwards he could not ignore the growing discrepancies between the discursive construction of Protestant-Communist proximity in the yet to be fully realised 'socialist society' and the complex political reality of Communist Czechoslovakia in the midst of the Cold War. His theologically sound arguments were being confronted ever more sharply with the political praxis of Czechoslovakia's

Communist dictatorship, which included a growing number of anti-religious measures. In fact, an influential group inside the Czech communist apparatus proposed as its ultimate goal an articulate vision of a 'socialist society' without religion.

This vision was most explicitly embodied in the programme of 'the termination of the cultural revolution', launched in the late 1950s, which contained pronounced anti-religious accents. The programme's orientation was taken up by local Party elites as a means to limit the sphere of public action for believers, and in particular for Christian teachers, a massive number of whom were expelled from their jobs on all levels of the school system. In response Protestant theologians, on the one hand, interpreted the progressive estrangement of state and church in the Czech version of the post-Constantinian era as the inevitable judgment upon the Church for its centuries-long involvement in the justification of an unjust social order.[46] On the other hand, they manifested their disagreement when confronted with outright discrimination against believers. Hromádka himself publicly expressed his opposition to this policy in a long letter to the Politburo of the Central Committee in May 1958, taking a position based largely on the consensual concept of a 'socialist society'. He thus first restated his 'total conviction on the historical and moral necessity of socialist reconstruction of our society', yet at the same time rejected the tendency to 'present believers as citizens of second or third rank' and criticised 'bureaucratic measures' for their destructive effects on the 'lively fellowship of builders of a socialist society'.[47]

His protest did not, however, lead to any immediate change in the prevailing political trends towards religion, which were the result of a complex mixture of both intra-national and international dynamics. In fact, in the late 1950s the Czechoslovak Communist leadership, always struggling for the prestigious position of being Moscow's best pupil, decided to 'accelerate the construction of a socialist society' so that they could proclaim Czechoslovakia the second socialist state in the world.[48] A successful attack on 'religious obscurantism' as a remnant of the 'old world' was to symbolise, in concert with a parallel outburst of anti-religious propaganda and anti-church measures in the USSR, the capacity of Czechoslovakia to attain this goal 'in a historically short period of time'.[49] This effort culminated in an upsurge of anti-religious propaganda in Czechoslovakia in the beginning of the 1960s. Religion was now excluded from the dominant conception of socialist society.

Restarting the Dialogue

It is important to underline that this particular anti-religious offensive, and the project of the 'termination of the cultural revolution' itself, constituted *in fine* only one aspect of a wider socio-political shift in the early 1960s. Czechoslovakia was witnessing the emergence of a pervasive discourse on the 'scientific management' of socialist society, supposedly based on 'the most advanced scientific interpretation of social reality'.[50] In this regard, Czechoslovakia's Communist dictatorship followed a European pattern of yet another phase of modernisation. In the era of 'planned modernisation' and 'social engineering', 'expert' solutions became fundamental sources of social and political legitimacy.[51] From the beginning of the 1960s, the Czechoslovak Communist leadership thus encouraged the creation of various expert committees focused on the analysis of all sorts of economic and political issues.[52]

The institutionalisation of the particular research field of 'scientific atheism' with the objective of orchestrating anti-religious campaigns was a part of this tendency. Nevertheless, as with those working in the spheres of economics and political science, 'experts' on atheism soon emancipated themselves from the original framework dictated by the CPC Politburo and, to the dismay of the conservative Party leadership, they began to produce an independent discourse on current social affairs whose unintended consequences included the re-emergence of Christian-Marxist dialogue.

The beginning of this enterprise is to be found precisely in the late 1950s, when several research groups were established in the field of 'scientific atheism' thanks to generous state funding. Progressively two centres acquired the dominant positions: the department of scientific atheism at the Academy of Sciences headed by Erika Kadlecová[53] and the department of philosophy at the Faculty of Arts of Charles University, where an assistant professor, Milan Machovec (1925–2003), began to produce numerous writings on 'methods of education towards atheism'.[54] These 'experts' also collaborated within the CPC apparatus, which substantially enlarged the social impact of their reflections.

What was their message? Even though Kadlecová and Machovec had each entered academia as rather dogmatic young Stalinists in the late 1940s, they were able to mature intellectually and to genuinely interiorise critical scientific perspectives through the possibility of continuing their studies in the early 1950s, the discovery of the writings of young Marx and closer encounters with seamy aspects of Soviet reality.[55] Thus when asked at the end of the 1950s to contribute to anti-religious propaganda, these researchers refused to simplify the matter and to merely repeat 'old anti-clerical diatribes against superstitious Christianity'.[56] Quite the contrary: Kadlecová, Machovec and their collaborators argued that if they were to remain faithful to the scientific perspectives of dialectical materialism, they had to interpret the persistence of religious beliefs as an important symptom that clearly marked insufficiencies in the construction of a Czechoslovak socialist society, which therefore called for serious philosophical and sociological analysis.

Several years later, during the economic and political crises of the early 1960s, Kadlecová finally persuaded the Party leadership that it was necessary to conduct a large-scale survey on religious practices: such knowledge would provide 'the key pre-condition for an effective transformation of society'.[57] Kadlecová's survey, carried out in 1963, attracted a great deal of attention even among Western sociologists of religion, for it remained the only serious source of data on religious life in Czechoslovakia for several decades.[58] It showed undeniably 'heavy losses' in religious adherence in the fifteen years following the Communist takeover, yet it did not hide ambiguities in the resulting situation: only thirty per cent of respondents could be considered committed atheists, another thirty per cent remained believers and forty per cent were labelled as 'religiously undetermined'.[59] The socio-political conclusions that Kadlecová inferred from her survey and offered to Czechoslovak Communist leaders centred on the continuing 'compensating function' of religion in Czechoslovakia, which had been proclaimed 'socialist' several years earlier.[60] She recommended, on the one hand, the continuation of social policies aimed at social improvement so that the need for 'illusory compensation' would disappear.[61] On the other hand, strikingly, she called for respectful dialogue with our 'sincere believing opponents',[62] arguing that in such a process 'there is no polarity of light and darkness' and 'both actors can educate each other' as long as each was motivated to improve their 'common socialist society'.[63] Kadlecová's study thus clearly marked the return of a more inclusive conception of socialist society—namely in relation to religion. A personal (post-1956) 'ideological' crisis and the economic recession of the early 1960s seem to explain this reversal.

The Christian-Marxist dialogue represents a particularly noteworthy dimension of this new trend. In the late 1950s, this enterprise was initiated, rather inconspicuously, by young Protestant intellectuals who had carefully watched the Czech Marxist scene even in the most critical years of anti-religious oppression in search of figures open to discussion like Milan Machovec.[64] This young philosopher attracted their attention because of his genuine interest in the Czech reformation and his 'independent reflection' on Marx and Lenin in connection to questions on the 'sense of life in a socialist society'.[65] When Machovec, elevated to the rank of a preeminent expert on scientific atheism, began to publicly criticise 'bureaucratic methods of intimidation of believers'[66] as being contrary to the spirit of 'genuine Marxism' in the late 1950s, two young pastors—Karel Trusina (1933–1978) and Milan Opočenský (1931–2007)—decided to attend his seminars at the Faculty of Arts. Soon afterwards, they proposed that Machovec discuss these issues with Professor Hromádka. Machovec agreed and never regretted it: 'I was thirty-three years old and, for the first time in my life, I met a Protestant who was not only deeply religious but also a remarkable intellectual. [. . .] I had never met someone like this before'.[67] Their relation then evolved from courteous watchfulness[68] to profound admiration: Machovec later called Hromádka the 'prophet of planetary dialogue'.[69]

It took several years before the dialogue became 'planetary', though. In the late 1950s it slowly developed in various Prague apartments, with the kitchen of Machovec's flat gradually becoming the chief meeting place. Profoundly spiritual debates were soon confronted with more earthly concerns. After the birth of Machovec's second child in 1963, Mrs Machovec gave her husband an ultimatum: either Machovec, Opočenský, Trusina, Hromádka, Lochman, Kadlecová and their growing circle of Christian and Marxist associates find an alternative space for their noisy encounters other than the Machovec family kitchen, or the meetings would have to stop.[70] At this critical moment, Machovec decided to transfer the site of these debates to academic territory (without asking for permission from Charles University authorities),[71] thus establishing their discussion sessions as a semi-official institution.

The dialogue could continue despite hostile reports of the secret police, who warned the CPC Politburo of 'social dangers' connected to the ongoing dialogue,[72] not least because it was attracting ever-growing international attention: one of the key issues of interest for Eastern European and Western Marxists alike and their Christian counterparts, which was making Western intellectuals from both sides of the ideological divide eager to come to Prague, was the 'humanisation of socialist society'.[73]

Talk about such 'humanisation' first sprung forth from passionate debates among Czech Marxists and Protestants in relation to questions concerning alienation in the socialist society in which they all lived. In their discussions they struggled with the challenge of how to 'protect the individual against all attempts to reduce him merely to a medium for the construction of a technologically over-rationalised future'.[74] The debate on the dangers of a nascent consumer society progressively appeared as a logical outgrowth of this subject. Participants at Machovec's seminar discovered and enthusiastically reappropriated the ideas of Erich Fromm (1900–1980) on 'humanist socialism', which emphasised the opposition between 'the spirit of socialist society as Marx visualised it' and 'the spirit of consumption'.[75] Fromm himself, together with Roger Garaudy (1913–2012), Herbert Marcuse (1898–1979), Jürgen Moltmann (b. 1926) and others, joined Prague debates on several occasions during the 1960s.[76]

Traces of these lively discussions on the alienated socialist form of *homo consumens*[77] can be found even in the files discussed by the Czechoslovak Politburo in the mid-1960s. Through texts prepared by Kadlecová and her colleagues (members of various expert commissions), the CPC's top representatives were told that 'the spirit of consumerism is foreign to authentic socialism' and that precisely in this aspect Christians represented valuable allies on the road towards a genuine 'socialist society'.[78] Kadlecová's ability to be persuasive on the importance of these points was rather impressive: she secured official authorisation for an international congress that gathered Christians and Marxists from both sides of the Iron Curtain in Marienbad for several days of discussions in 1967.[79]

Debates on the socially isolating and fragmenting effects of 'consumerism' provided Czech Protestant elites and their Marxist counterparts with another opportunity to explicitly express that there was common ground in their ideals of a 'socialist society'. This was the moment when its *'gemeinschaftliche'* traits came markedly to the forefront: Christians and Marxists were in perfect agreement on the 'close and sincere bonds' and the 'rich social net of absolutely transparent relationships' which were to connect men and women who shared 'constructive enthusiasm' for the constitution and betterment of a 'socialist society'.[80] The version of 'socialist society' which took shape via the process of Christian-Marxist dialogue had indeed a much more inclusive character. It opposed itself to images of a 'dehumanised' and 'bureaucratised' state (and/or Party) apparatus, associated with the 'arbitrary' exclusion of believers in the Stalinist period and, on a more general level, with the alienating aspects of modern-day *Gesellschaft*.[81]

The Common Struggle for 'Socialism with a Human Face'

From all these common endeavours and ventures a firm conviction grew, both among the Protestant elites and their Marxist discussion partners, of the uniqueness of this cooperation 'of people who are urged by the deepest motives of their convictions to challenge fatalism and indifference and to be concerned about historical and social responsibility'.[82] Jan Milíč Lochman, when trying to explain this surprising closeness, thus did not hesitate to write about dialogically oriented Czech Marxists and Protestants—'two minority sects in a sea of indifference' of consumer societies arising in both the West and the East—sharing a common vision of a 'humanised socialist society'.

The earthquake at the topmost level of the Czechoslovak Communist hierarchy in January 1968 and the ascension of the reformist team of Alexander Dubček (1921–1992) to the leading positions in the CPC and state administration opened unexpected opportunities for these two 'minority sects' to try to transform their visions into social reality. What forms did these efforts take in the moment that Lochman labelled the 'crucial year of Czechoslovak socialist society'?[83]

Church-state and church-CPC relations represented, of course, the most obvious area of this cooperation. In fact, some of the dialogue's most active participants on the Marxist side were called to serve in the highest stratum of the state apparatus for church affairs: in early spring 1968 Kadlecová became the head of the Secretariat for Church Affairs and she immediately named as her deputies Jaroslav Hranička and Ladislav Prokůpek (her closest collaborators from the Academy of Sciences and active participants in dialogical initiatives). Vítězslav Gardavský, professor of philosophy at the Army Academy in Brno and the author of *God Is Not Quite Dead*,[84] a best-seller that even attracted Western attention, frequently assisted this trio in the preparation of materials for the Central Committee. Machovec, in addition to his extensive lecture tours abroad, published frequently in the national media in the spring months of 1968.

On the national level, this dialogue-oriented, reform-minded team struggled to push through and make official a revised conception of the role of Christians in a 'socialist society'. Kadlecová succeeded in integrating their vision into the main political-programmatic document of the Prague Spring, the 'Action Programme', issued by the Central Committee in April 1968, which proclaimed, among its other declarations: 'We openly invite believing members of our society to participate as equals at all the difficult tasks in the construction of socialist society'.[85]

This explicit return to the rhetoric of the early post-war period was accompanied by various practical steps. The most striking manifestation of this new attitude on the central level was the official acceptance of Christian-Marxist dialogue. In April 1968 it unmistakably left private or academic ground and entered public space: several thousand spectators could watch exchanges among Machovec, Lochman, Hromádka and others in one of central Prague's largest halls (*Slovanský dům*); all these participants could also profit from the wider access to national media that had been recently authorised. On the local level, in a less spectacular manner, pastors and Protestant laymen became closely involved in the application of 'new church policy'.[86]

Moreover, during the Prague Spring, dialogically oriented Protestants and Marxists sensed and made use of opportunities to reach beyond the spheres of church policy and politics. It was Machovec, the principal champion of 'socialist humanism' à la Fromm in Czechoslovakia, who launched, in close collaboration with his Christian (principally Protestant) friends, the Association for Human Rights, intended to ensure the institutional basis for the spread of the ideals of a 'genuine socialist society' by 'educating its members in the spirit of socialist democracy and humanism'.[87]

The Association for Human Rights constituted the first platform created outside of the 'National Front' framework, which had delimited the sphere of authorised social bodies in Czechoslovakia after 1948. Presided over by Machovec (with prominent Christians in its Central Committee, such as J.B. Souček and the bishop of Prague Tomášek, and having numerous Protestants working at a growing number of local outposts[88]), it proclaimed its intention to fight against 'egoism, consumerism, indifference' and to try to strengthen 'humanism, democratic principles and altruism'.[89] Thousands of membership applications received in the spring months of 1968 attest to the genuine popularity of such an idea.[90]

Inside the ECCB, these initiatives launched a wave of genuine exultation: Souček, for instance, proclaimed in April 1968 that 'this attempt to connect socialism, freedom and democracy which for years seemed unattainable is worth all our support and efforts, energy and ardour'.[91] Such an enthusiastic attitude among Protestant elites was certainly important to the building of support at home for the Prague Spring, but their positions even had a noticeable global impact: Czech Protestants like Souček, Lochman and Hromádka, with their extensive networks in Western ecumenical milieus, effectively helped to spread the 'good news' about the Czechoslovak experiment and its 'epochal importance' throughout the world and, furthermore, opened the doors to the West for their Marxist counterparts and friends who were exporting the same message.[92]

Lochman was probably the most outspoken 'evangelist' for the Prague Spring in the Western Protestant world: we have already seen that the message he transmitted to his often sceptical Western audiences on Czechoslovak 'socialism with a human face' aimed to show the way towards 'a model of society [. . .] which could correspond to some basic insights of the Biblical faith of the Old and New Testaments'.[93] In his interventions at such prestigious fora as the General Assembly of the WCC in Uppsala (where he was elected to the organisation's Executive Committee),[94] or during his lectures in the United States, he emphasised the historical unicity of the Prague Spring constellation, which contributed to the construction of an idea of Czechoslovak exceptionalism: 'In the struggles in our country today [. . .] the future of democracy and socialism in Europe is at stake'.[95]

Lochman's Marxist colleagues (Machovec, Gardavský, Prokůpek) transmitted the same type of discourse during their lecture tours in the West. Together, they awakened enthusiasm in Western observers such as Paul Oestreicher, the secretary of the British Council of Churches, who in a published essay wrote of his 'tremendous encouragement' in seeing that 'in Czechoslovakia where, in difficult and discouraging times [of the late 1950s], the dialogue was carried on with fervour and intensity, the fruits have become evident'.[96]

Last but not least, Josef Hromádka, who in April 1968 presided over the All-Christian Peace Assembly that attracted more than six hundred participants from fifty-five countries to Prague,[97] shared with his Western and Eastern European colleagues and friends his conviction that the Prague Spring was indeed proof that 'living creative socialism' was being realised. He saw the events unfolding around him illustrating that 'in a socialist society there is much more personal initiative and responsibility, much greater room for personal decisions' than in 'the so-called "open society" [in the West, which was] in fact directed or manipulated by anonymous financial and economic forces'. Hromádka contributed to the image of uniqueness and exceptionality of the Czechoslovak enterprise as well: 'our people have attempted to make a synthesis of a real socialism and of real personal freedom and cultural maturity'.[98]

Conclusion

The liberal atmosphere of the Prague Spring thus allowed this particular combination of ideas from the Gospel, Marx and Fromm to shape the ideal of a 'socialist society' that emphasised 'genuine' relationships, a non-consumerist lifestyle and eschatological visions of Czechoslovak uniqueness to get out in the open and to become, at least for several months, a very visible part of the debates on 'socialism with a human face' both inside Czechoslovakia and internationally.

In this chapter we have followed, chronologically, the twists and turns on the road leading towards this consensual and influential version of the discourse on 'socialist society'. This analysis focused on one of the most dynamic and controversial elements in this process—the debate between Czech Marxist and Protestant intellectual elites on the inclusion of religious elements into this discourse, and the invitation extended to Christians to join the corresponding social enterprise. The inclusive and cooperative conception of a 'socialist society', which grew out of common wartime resistance engagements and the shared enthusiasm of the immediate post-war years, was substantially questioned in the late 1950s. The proponents of 'the termination of the cultural revolution' equated religion with backwardness and excluded believers from full participation in a 'socialist society'. From the early 1960s onwards, the crisis of the regime and the growing influence of 'experts' in the field of 'scientific atheism' prepared the way for another inclusive moment. In the mid-1960s, the confrontation with emerging consumer practices further cemented the Czech Christian-Marxist coalition and inspired its rich intellectual activity, which constituted an original contribution to discussions on issues concerning social cohesion in the era of high modernism that extended beyond a purely national context.

This transnational dimension of the Czech Christian-Marxist debate on 'socialist society' represented another important focus of this chapter. It first acquired global resonance through extensive international networks involving Czech Protestant elites in the late 1940s and, after the setback of the 1950s, it returned to the forefront of international attention in the mid-1960s. At that moment Prague became a favourite meeting point for Eastern European and Western Christian theologians and Marxists concerned with issues of alienation, consumerism and other high-modernist challenges to social cohesion.

After 1968, however, the intense interaction between Protestants and Marxists almost completely disappeared. The involvement of the main Czech proponents of this dialogue in the Prague Spring and their post-1968 expulsion from political and academic institutions only partially explain such a spectacular retreat. Generational change in connection with the wider shifts conceptualised by Daniel Rodgers in terms of an 'Age of Fracture' and the marginalisation of thinking in terms of 'society' seem to have been in effect on the eastern side of the Iron Curtain as well. Even among the Czech anti-normalisation dissenters around Charter '77 (in which, for instance, Machovec and Kadlecová actively participated), reflections on the ideal of a 'socialist society' ceased to attract interest. The post-1989 years only confirmed this development: when in the early 1990s some of the remaining proponents of the Christian-Marxist dialogue tried to resuscitate this initiative, they were rejected by the representatives of the dominant neoliberal discourse, who instead emphasised the notion of the 'individual' and firmly refused any attempts to reflect on alternatives that might achieve a stronger and more enduring sense of social cohesion.[99]

Notes

1. I am grateful for support by SCIEX funding (Geneva University), the FNS project—"Shared Modernities or Competing Modernities? Europe between West and East (1920s–1970s)" (Geneva University), the PRVOUK research framework at FSV UK (Charles University, Prague) and the UNCE project on collective memory (Charles University, Prague).
2. At the time of the book's publication he was appointed Karl Barth's successor at one of the most respected of theological chairs, the chair for Systematic Theology at the University of Basel. In 1968 he was also elected to a prestigious position as member of the Executive Committee of the World Council of Churches.
3. Lochman, *Church*, 197.
4. Ibid., 17.
5. Hruby, "An Example," 24.
6. Matchett, "Review of Church," 337–40.
7. The difference between the western (Czech) and eastern (Slovakia) parts of the Czechoslovak state in this particular domain is pronounced enough that the article will focus exclusively on the developments in the western part (the Czech lands).
8. Balík, "Politické společenství".
9. Matějka, "Správný komunista," 284–96.
10. See the introduction to this volume.
11. Abrams, *Struggle*.
12. Matějka, "A Generation?".
13. Hromádka and Odložilík, *S druhého břehu*, 122. All translations are by the author unless indicated otherwise.
14. 1st World Council of Chuches Assembly, Amsterdam 1948, 31.004/13, Section IV: Minutes, 26, World Council of Churches Archives (hereafter cited as WCC Archives), Geneva.
15. Hromádka, "Na prahu zítřka," 11.
16. Visser 't Hooft, *Memoirs*, 12.
17. He was one of the best-known anti-Nazi intellectuals in the Czech lands, closely following the struggles of the Confessing Church in Germany and reporting on it in the Czech press from the mid-1930s onwards.
18. Correspondance Visser 't Hooft-Hromádka 1938–1940, World Student Christian Federation, Europe: Czechoslovakia, Finland 1930–1945, 213.11.7.16, WCC Archives, Geneva.
19. Hromádka, *Doom and Resurrection*, 118–19.
20. Hromádka, "Na prahu zítřka," 11.
21. Hromádka, *Mezi Východem*, 67–69, 84.
22. Synodal Council to all the pastors of the Evangelical Church of Czech Brethren, 24 April 1942, fond SR, box XV/B/1, Central Archives of the Evangelical Church of Czech Brethren, Prague.
23. Wagnerová and Janovic, *Neohlížej se*.
24. Letter of Karel Hiršl from 17 February 1943, private archives of Alena Wagnerová, Prague.
25. This book from 1935 (*Creative Society: A Study of the Relation of Christianity to Communism*) was translated to Czech in 1936 by František Linhart, a professor at the Prague Protestant Theological Faculty.
26. Letter of Karel Hiršl, 21 January 1943, private archives of Alena Wagnerová, Prague.
27. Ibid., 4 November 1943, private archives of Alena Wagnerová, Prague.
28. Wagnerová and Janovic, *Neohlížej se*, 188.
29. Matějka, "We Are the Generation," 123–25.

30. Jindřichová-Kadlecová, *Úloha křesťanství*, 99.
31. Kadlecová, "Jak studovat," 2.
32. Richta, "Vědečtí advokáti," 94.
33. Jindřichová-Kadlecová, *Úloha křesťanství*, 90.
34. Jan Šimsa, interview with author, 5 April 2007.
35. Matějka, "Správný komunista," 284–96.
36. "To Members of the CPC and to Other Progressive Citizens" (by Eduard Kylar, Hněvkov u Zábřeha), fond ONV Zábřeh, IV.ref.—zn 292, Varia concerning churches 1949–1951, State Departmental Archives Šumperk.
37. Václav Kopecký, "O národní a státní ideologii nového Československa," *Rudé právo*, 31 March 1946.
38. Hromádka, *Komunismus*, 35.
39. Ibid., 34.
40. 1st World Council of Churches Assembly, Amsterdam 1948, 31.004/02, WCC Archives, Geneva.
41. Lochman, *Church*, 57–59.
42. Molnár et al., *Od reformace*, 226.
43. Hromádka, "Na prahu nové éry," 261.
44. Hromádka, *Křesťanství a komunismus*, 38.
45. Hromádka, *Looking History*.
46. Molnár et al., *Od reformace*, 268–69.
47. J. L. Hromádka to the Central Committee of the CPC, 5 May 1958, fond 1261/0/11, Politburo 1954–1962, f. 179, a.u. 243, point 15, National Archives Prague (hereafter cited as NA Prague).
48. 'Usnesení XI. sjezdu', *Rudé právo*, 23 July1958, 1.
49. For the Soviet context see Chumachenko, *Church and State*, 128, 145, 149; and Kopeček, *Hledání ztraceného*, 301.
50. The proposal of the Central Committee in relation to ideological issues, point 1, 10 September 1963, ÚV KSČ 1945–1989, Presidium 1962–1966, f. 34, a.u. 37, NA Prague.
51. Wagner and Wollmann, "Social Scientists," 601–5.
52. Mlynář, *Nightfrost*, 57; Voříšek, *Reform Generation*.
53. More details on this aspect in Matějka, "Between the Academy". See also Nešpor, *Ne/náboženské*, 239–313.
54. Machovec, "O metodách," 678–94.
55. Matějka, "Entre les sciences," 123–29.
56. Erika Kadlecová, interview with author, 15 January 2008.
57. Kadlecová, *Sociologický výzkum*, 9, 12.
58. Bruce, *God Is Dead*, xiii.
59. Kadlecová, *Sociologický výzkum*, 203.
60. In the Czechoslovak Constitution ratified in 1960.
61. Kadlecová, *Sociologický výzkum*, 157.
62. Kadlecová, ed, *Bozi a lidé*, 449.
63. Kadlecová, *Sociologický výzkum*, 159.
64. Balabán, "Panorama," 29; Šimsa, "Ježíš," 268–69.
65. Machovec, *O smyslu*.
66. Nytrová and Balabán, "Rozhovor," 176.
67. Ibid.
68. Machovec, *O takzvané*, 87–88.
69. Machovec, "Prorok planetárního," 38–45.
70. Pavel Žďárský, "Milan Machovec a jeho filosofická antropologie v 60. letech 20. století" (Doctoral Thesis, Charles University—Faculty of Pedagogy—Prague, 2011), 51.
71. Šiklová, "Dialogický seminář," 50, 56.

72. Report on the ecumenical seminar 3 February 1965, box C, file 77, ÚV KSČ, fond A. Novotný, NA Prague.
73. Machovec, "Dialog," 10–11.
74. "Christians and Marxists in Marianske Lazne," 10 July 1967, 300-8-3-13449, Records of Radio Free Europe/Radio Liberty Research Institute, Publications Department, Background Reports, Open Society Archives at the Central European University, Budapest.
75. Fromm, ed, *Socialist Humanism*, 214–15.
76. Šiklová, "Dialogický seminář," 51.
77. Fromm, ed, *Socialist humanism*, 214.
78. Questions of ecclesiastical policy and the development of scientific atheism in Czechoslovakia (12 November 1965), fond 1261/0/15 —Secretariat of the Central Committee 1962–1966, f. 46, a.u. 89, NA Prague.
79. "Christians and Marxists in Marianske Lazne," 10 July 1967, 300-8-3-13449, Open Society Archives at the Central European University, Budapest.
80. Lochman, *Church*, 12, 182, 193. Kadlecová, *Bozi a lidé*, 470–78.
81. Lochman, *Church*, 182ff.
82. Ibid., 192.
83. Ibid., 106.
84. Gardavský, *Bůh není*.
85. *Akční program*.
86. Erika Kadlecová, interview with author, 15 January 2008; Survey 1968 ECCB, box 17–18, fond Ministry of Culture—Secretariat for Church Affairs, NA Prague.
87. "Association for Human Rights, Statutes," 73.
88. Škarvan, *Vzpomínky*, 95.
89. Interview with the general secretary of the Association for Human Rights from April 1968, in *Občanská společnost*, 78.
90. Ibid., 77.
91. Souček, "K naší," 75.
92. Lochman, *Oč mi*, 152.
93. Lochman, *Church*, 197.
94. Lochman, *Oč mi*, 115–16.
95. Lochman, "Církev," 104; Lochman, "Dialog," 13.
96. Oestreicher, *The Christian Marxist Dialogue*, xiii.
97. Hromádka, *Save Man*.
98. Memorandum of the President of the Christian Peace Conference, October 1968, 42.3.036, Country files and correspondence—Czechoslovakia, WCC Archives, Geneva.
99. Matějka, "Uses," 277–78.

Bibliography

Abrams, Bradley F. *The Struggle for the Soul of the Nation: Czech Culture and the Rise of Communism*. Lanham: Rowman & Littlefield, 2005.
Akční program komunistické strany Československa. Prague: Svoboda, 1968.
"Association for Human Rights, Statutes (April 1968)." In *Občanská společnost 1967–1970*, edited by Josef Belda, Jindřich Pecka, and Jiří Hoppe, 73–75. Brno: Doplněk, 1998.
Balabán, Milan. "Panorama Machovec." *Křesťanská revue* 73 (2006): 29–32.
Balík, Stanislav. "Politické společenství a národ." *Revue Politika* 11 (2012): http://www.revuepolitika.cz/clanky/1755/politicke-spolecenstvi-a-narod

Dialogues on Religion in a "Socialist Society" under Construction 257

Belda, Josef, Jindřich Pecka, and Jiří Hoppe, eds. *Občanská společnost 1967–1970.* Brno: Doplněk, 1998.

Bruce, Steve. *God is Dead: Secularization in the West.* Malden, MA: Blackwell, 2002.

Chumachenko, Tatiana Aleksandrovna. *Church and State in Soviet Russia: Russian Orthodoxy from World War II to the Khrushchev Years.* Armonk: Sharpe, 2002.

Currier, Alvin C. "An Intimate, Non-Theological Report: Church in a Marxist Society by Jan Lochman." *Journal for the Scientific Study of Religion* 9, no. 4 (1970): 344–46.

Fromm, Erich, ed. *Socialist Humanism: An International Symposium.* New York: Doubleday, 1965.

Gardavský, Vítězslav. *Bůh není zcela mrtev: úvaha o křesťanském teismu a marxistickém ateismu.* Prague: Československý spisovatel, 1967.

Hromádka, Josef Lukl. "Na prahu zítřka." *Křesťanská revue* 12, no. 1 (1938): 8–12.

Hromádka, Josef Lukl. *Doom and Resurrection: Joseph L. Hromádka; With an Introduction by John A. Mackay.* London: SCM, 1945.

Hromádka, Josef Lukl. *Komunismus a křesťanství: o nápravu věcí lidských.* Hradec Králové: Evangelické dílo, 1946.

Hromádka, Josef Lukl. *Mezi Východem a Západem.* Prague: Kalich, 1946.

Hromádka, Josef Lukl. "Na prahu nové éry." *Křesťanská revue* 16 (1949): 261–62.

Hromádka, Josef Lukl. *The Church and Theology in Today's Troubled Times.* Prague: Ecumenical Council of Churches, 1956.

Hromádka, Josef Lukl. *Save Man, Peace is Possible.* Prague: Christian Peace Conference, 1968.

Hormádka, Josef Lukl. *Looking History in the Face.* Madras: Christian Literature Society, 1982.

Hromádka, Josef Lukl and Otakar Odložilík. *S druhého břehu: úvahy z amerického exilu 1940–1945.* Prague: Laichter, 1946.

Hruby, Blahoslav. "An Example of Limited Freedom: Church in a Marxist Society by Jan Milic Lochman." *Christianity Today* 14, August 1970: 24.

Jindřichová-Kadlecová, Erika. *Úloha křesťanství v historii třídních bojů. Rigorózní práce.* Prague: Filosofická fakulty Univerzity Karlovy, 1950.

Kadlecová, Erika. "Jak studovat marxismus leninismus." *Mladá fronta* 8 (1952): 2–3.

Kadlecová, Erika, ed. *Bozi a lidé.* Prague: Nakladatelství politické literatury, 1966.

Kadlecová, Erika. *Sociologický výzkum religiozity Severomoravského kraje.* Prague: Academia, 1967.

Kopeček, Michal. *Hledání ztraceného smyslu revoluce: zrod a počátky marxistického revizionismu ve střední Evropě 1953–1960.* Prague: Argo, 2009.

Lochman, Jan Milič. "Církev a obnova společnosti." *Křesťanská revue* 35 (1968): 102–6.

Lochman, Jan Milič. "Dialog překračuje meze." *Literární listy* 1, no. 14 (1968): 13.

Lochman, Jan Milič. *Church in a Marxist Society: A Czechoslovak View.* Evanston: Harper & Row, 1970.

Lochman, Jan Milič. *Oč mi v životě šlo: cesty českého teologa doma i do širého světa.* Prague: Kalich, 2000.

Machovec, Milan. *O smyslu lidského života.* Prague: Orbis, 1957.

Machovec, Milan. "O metodách ateistické výchovy." *Filosofický časopis* 5 (1959): 678–94.

Machovec, Milan. *O takzvané 'dialektické' teologii současného protestantismu.* Prague: Nakladatelství ČSAV, 1962.

Machovec, Milan. "Dialog v procesu humanizace člověka." *Osvětová práce* 15 (1965): 10–11.
Machovec, Milan. "Prorok planetárního dialogu." In *Jako blesk z oblohy. Sborník k výročí J.L. Hromádky (1889–1969)*, edited by Milan Opočenský, 38–45. Geneva: WARC, 1999.
Matchett, Kathleen. "Review of Church in a Marxist Society: A Czechoslovak View: By Jan Milic Lochman." *Journal of State and Church* 16, no. 2 (1974): 337–40.
Matějka, Ondřej. "Between the Academy and Power: Czech Marxist Sociology of Religion (1954–1970)." In *Sociology and Ethnography in East-Central and South-East Europe: Scientific Self-Description in States Socialist Countries*, edited by Ulf Brunnbauer, Claudia Kraft, and Martin Schulze Wessel, 107–33. Munich: Oldenbourg, 2011.
Matějka, Ondřej. "We are the Generation that Will Construct Socialism: The Czech 68ers between Manifest Destiny and Mark of Cain." In *Talkin' bout My Generation: Conflicts of Generation Building and Europe's 1968*, edited by Anna Von der Goltz, 118–39. Göttingen: Wallstein, 2011.
Matějka, Ondřej. "A Generation? A School? A Fraternity? An Army? Understanding the Roots of Josef Lukl Hromádka´s Influence in the Czech Protestant Milieu 1920–1948." *Communio Viatorum* 54, no. 3 (2012): 25–38.
Matějka, Ondřej, "Entre les sciences sociales et la construction de la 'société socialiste'. Une perspective générationnelle." In *Individus sous contrôle*, edited by Françoise Mayer and Ondřej Matějka, 105–53. Prague: CEFRES, 2012.
Matějka, Ondřej. "Správný komunista má také býti správným křesťanem, jako byli křesťané první. Vztah českobratrských evangelíků ke Komunistické straně Československa 1921–1970." In *Český a slovenský komunismus (1921–2011)*, edited by Jan Kalous and Jiří Kocian, 284–96. Prague: Ústav pro studium totalitních režimů, 2012.
Matějka, Ondřej. "Uses of a 'Generation': The Case of the Czech '68ers'." In *History by Generations: Generational Dynamics in Modern History*, edited by Hartmut Berghoff et al., 258–78. Göttingen: Wallstein, 2012.
Mlynář, Zdeněk. *Nightfrost in Prague: The End of Humane Socialism*. New York: Karz Publishers, 1980.
Mojzes, Paul. *Christian-Marxist Dialogue in Eastern Europe*. Minneapolis: Augsburg Publishing House, 1981.
Molnár, Amedeo, Bohuslav Pospíšil, Josef Bohumil Souček, Josef Lukl Hromádka, and Luděk Brož. *Od reformace k zítřku*. Prague: Ústřední církevní nakladatelství, 1956.
Nejedlý, Zdeněk. *Komunisté, dědici velikých tradic českého národa: výbor statí*. Prague: Práce, 1978.
Nešpor, Zdeněk R. *Ne/náboženské naděje intelektuálů: vývoj české sociologie náboženství v mezinárodním a interdisciplinárním kontextu*. Prague: Scriptorium, 2008.
Nytrová, Olga and Milan Balabán. "Rozhovor s profesorem Milanem Machovcem." *Křesťanská revue* 65, no. 7 (2000): 175–77.
Oestreicher, Paul. *The Christian Marxist Dialogue: An International Symposium*. London: Macmillan, 1969.
Richta, Radovan. "Vědečtí advokáti útočné války." *Tvorba* 4 (1951): 94–95.
Šiklová, Jiřina, "Dialogický seminář na Filozofické fakultě UK v 60.letech." In *Mistr dialogu Milan Machovec. Sborník k nedožitým osmdesátinám českého filosofa*, edited by Kamila Jindrová et al., 49–58. Prague: Akropolis, 2006.

Šimsa, Jan. "Ježíš pro Milana Machovce." In *Mistr dialogu Milan Machovec. Sborník k nedožitým osmdesátinám českého filosofa*, edited by Kamila Jindrová et al., 268–74. Prague: Akropolis, 2006.
Škarvan, František. *Vzpomínky. Sloužil jsem třem prezidentům, dělníkům a církvi*. Prague: Soukromé vydání, 1999.
Souček, Josef Bohumil. "K naší nynější politické situaci." *Český bratr* 44 (1968): 74–76.
Visser't Hooft, Willem Adolph. *Memoirs*. Geneva: WCC Publications, 1987.
Voříšek, Michael. *The Reform Generation: 1960s Czechoslovak Sociology from a Comparative Perspective*. Prague: Kalich, 2012.
Wagner Peter and Hellmut Wollmann. "Social Scientists in Policy Research and Consulting: Some Cross-National Comparisons." *International Social Science Journal* 38, no. 4 (1986): 601–17.
Wagnerová, Alena and Vladimír Janovic. *Neohlížej se, zkameníš*. Prague: Naše vojsko, 1968.

13 Languages of "National Community" and Its "Others" in Europe, 1918–68

Stefan Berger

The concept of a 'national community' was an integral part of national historical master narratives in modern Europe.[1] However, the content of what constituted that 'national community' was strongly contested among competing master narratives in virtually every existing or aspiring nation-state in Europe. An often somewhat elusive idea of 'national community' was related to a range of other spatial and non-spatial ideas of community, many of which have been examined in other chapters in this volume. They include conceptions of urban, rural and regional communities, of transnational communities as well as those based on ethnicity, class and religion. Languages of national community were interrelated with those other languages of community in manifold, often ambiguous and contradictory ways, but attempts to frame 'national communities' almost always sought to integrate, subsume and submerge other forms of community construction under the national frame.[2] Hence, the potential 'others' of a 'national community' became part and parcel of the very construction of the national. The national was often already inherent in them and they themselves formed important building blocks of what the 'national community' was imagined to be. In this brief essay, I would like to investigate the diverse and contested languages of national community in national historical master narratives in relation to those other languages of community, many of which are highlighted in other chapters of this book. I will adhere to this volume's historical framework, which ranges from the end of the First World War to the 1960s. After reviewing the impact of the First World War on concepts of national community, I will examine the role of contested borderlands in interwar Europe in re-forging notions of regional as well as national community. Subsequent ethnic, racial, social, religious and political constructions of national communities will be analysed with a view to demonstrating the complex layers of possible mixtures of the national with other spatial and non-spatial conceptions of community. I will argue that the alleged break with ideas of national community after 1945 is often overemphasised, as historians who have put forth this view have sought to reinvent conceptions of national community across the Cold War divide, often using very traditional tropes and narratives.

The experience of the First World War had a deep impact on the languages of 'national community' in many parts of interwar Europe, especially in those countries that had participated in the war. In Germany the construction of an alleged 'community of the trenches' contributed to attempts by a younger generation of historians to move away from the profession's strong statism (oriented towards the Prussian state and its mission to unify Germany) and historism.[3] They became champions of an ethnically and racially inflected 'people's history' (*Volksgeschichte*) that posited the *Volk* as the leading category for analysing and understanding the 'national community' through national histories.[4]

Understanding the 'national community' through the state or through the *Volk* were not the only options—culture (*Kultur*) was the other key concept brought front and centre by the First World War. Thomas Mann's espousal of cultural nationalism and his idea of a state-protected inwardness (*machtgeschützte Innerlichkeit*) which allowed true culture to blossom led to the juxtaposition between a purportedly deep and authentic German culture and a shallow Western 'civilisation' that Mann and others associated with the Western democracies, notably Britain, the United States and France.[5] Among historians, Friedrich Meinecke contrasted a 'German humanity' against the humanity of the West, connecting 'German humanity' to a sense of national community (*Gemeinschaft*) that was far superior to the Western concept of mere 'society' (*Gesellschaft*),[6] thereby falling back on a famous juxtaposition by the German sociologist Ferdinand Tönnies.[7] That discourse also underpinned a range of languages of 'national community' which were essentially anti-modern in different guises—representing an anti-capitalist or anti-consumerist stance, or an attack on the allegedly stuffy bourgeois world order.

Notions of 'national community' also figured strongly in the discourses surrounding the alliances between Imperial Germany and the Austro-Hungarian Empire. Time and again the community of the Nibelungen saga was invoked to emphasise the national togetherness of Germans and Austrians in the war.[8] Catholic historians in both empires were particularly vigorous in stressing that 1914 would heal and overcome the fateful division of 1866 and lead to the higher unity of a greater Germany. Greater Germany, however, remained as elusive in its practical outlook as it had been with the 'greater Germans' before the German civil war of 1866, which ultimately pushed Austria out of German nation-making.[9] As one of the leading German Catholic historians of the time put it: 'We stand anew on stable ground designated by history! It again bands us together with the Austrians in complete harmony [. . .] For the historian it has something of compelling magnificence that the stream of German history has flowed back into its mighty bed'.[10]

The reinvigoration of the languages of community during wartime was not restricted to Germany. If we look to Britain, we find that there are no shortages of examples of how the war was constructed in terms of a political 'national community' coming together to defend the specific political values of a civilised society against the expansionist, aggressive and authoritarian 'Hun', who threatened to overrun Europe.[11] This conception was accompanied by various other discourses on 'community', such as, for example, the 'community of the generations', used to justify the British war effort as well. As wrote Arthur Lionel Smith, historian and Master of Balliol College at the University of Oxford between 1916 and 1923: 'War is indeed a mighty creator. It is an intellectual awakener and a moral tonic. [. . .] It creates a conscious unity of feeling which is the atmosphere needed for a new start. It purges away old strife and sectional aims, and raises us for a while into higher and purer air. It helps us to recapture some of the lofty and intense patriotism of the ancient world. It reveals to us what constitutes a modern nation, the partnership between the living, the dead, and the yet unborn'.[12] And, as is underlined by Stefan Goebel's comparative study on medieval memory in Britain and Germany during the First World War, in both countries the war engendered a strong anti-modern discourse that glorified pre-modern forms of 'national community'.[13]

As the case of *Volksgeschichte* in Germany shows, the war had the power to ethnicise notions of 'national community'. It could, however, have the opposite effect. Henri Pirenne, the foremost national historian of Belgium, began to de-ethnicise his history of Belgium. The German occupiers had deported him to Germany because he refused to endorse the occupation regime and teach his classes in Flemish at the University of Ghent. As prisoner of war in Germany, he began to rethink his boundless admiration for German historical sciences before 1914. He returned to Belgium after the war convinced that German historism's combination of statism and a commitment to culture and ethnicity was a cul-de-sac for historians. Hence he called on fellow historians to 'un-learn' from Germany, and he did his best to keep German historians out of international meetings and conferences. He began to re-write his multi-volume history of Belgium, carefully eliminating references which constructed notions of ethnicity underpinning Belgian identity. Instead, he replaced notions of community with ideas about society and, together with the founders of the French Annales school, Marc Bloch and Lucien Febvre, sought to develop a new kind of history that was closer to the social sciences and to ethnology, interdisciplinary in nature and comparative in outlook. These efforts represented a deliberate attempt to learn from the mistakes of the methodological nationalism that had flourished before the war and move history away from the languages of 'national community'.[14]

In the interwar period, however, such de-ethnicisation of national histories was very much a minority undertaking. Given the significance of contested borderlands in East-Central and Eastern Europe following the dissolution, as a result of the war, of Imperial Germany and the Romanov, Habsburg and Ottoman empires, ethnicised languages of 'national community' loomed large over those borderlands. If we take the example of Germany, millions of ethnic Germans who found themselves outside the borders of the German Reich after 1919 employed this language of 'national community' in order to keep open the possibility of a future revision of borders. Many German historians aided the politically motivated efforts of the German Foreign Office to work towards such a revision of the Versailles Treaty.[15] The massive collection of documents concerning the outbreak of the war, financed and sponsored by the Foreign Office, had precisely this aim. And historians also rose to the challenge to research the communities of ethnic Germans living beyond Germany's borders, demonstrating how they had provided the 'cultural soil' (*Kulturboden*) on which civilisation and progress had developed.[16] These arguments were thinly veiled justifications of territorial expansionism.

We observe similar processes elsewhere in East-Central and Eastern Europe, especially in Hungary, which had lost two-thirds of its pre-war territories.[17] In the new borderlands with Romania and Slovakia there were massive history wars marked by fierce clashes of vying languages of 'national community' in rival attempts to incorporate those borderlands into one or the other nation-state.[18] With regard to the Romanians in Transylvania, Florian Kührer-Wielach has discussed the ways they reconceptualised regional belonging to fit with their new conception of national belonging, underscoring the strong proximity between regional and national senses of belonging. The situation, of course, was entirely different with Hungarians in Transylvania, who developed their own language of a diasporic 'national community'.[19] History wars justified alleged 'historical rights' over borderlands in many parts of interwar Europe: in Silesia and other new western territories of the newly reconstituted Poland, Polish and German narratives clashed; in the Sudetenland Czech and German constructions battled it out; in South Tyrol, rival claims were brought forth on behalf of Austrian and Italian 'national communities'; in Lower Styria, Carinthia and Carniola, Austrian and Slovene historical national master narratives competed; and Romanian and Hungarian rivalry could be found in not only Transylvania but also Bessarabia and Bukovina. Everywhere in the interwar period the nationalisation of borderlands aimed to eradicate multiculturalism and the nationalisation of newly acquired or recently lost territory through the languages of 'national community', which merged with diverse local/regional and non-spatial constructions of community.[20]

Similar battles between rival languages of 'national community' could be observed in many border cities or the major cities (often new capitals) of newly founded nation-states. In this volume Tanja Vahtikari has shown how the reconstruction of urban community life in Helsinki depended vitally on the construction of a continuous storyline that connected past, present and future. The languages of 'national community' at times loomed large over these constructions and intersected powerfully with local, urban and diverse non-spatial constructions of community in the city. This was especially the case in the wake of Finland's declaring its independence from Russia in

1917. The city became at times an extension or a *Brennglas* of the imagined 'national community', and, as Vahtikari's chapter shows, professional historians were very much at the forefront of attempts to link the 'urban community' to the national. Interwar borderland cities such as Gdansk, Poznan and Strasbourg witnessed veritable history wars as the urban became closely aligned with the national.[21]

The construction of 'national communities' was often combined with a sense of ethnic repression—especially in newly constituted nation-states during the interwar period. Whether it was the Finns deploring the repression of Finnish language and culture, first by the Swedes and then by the Russians,[22] or the Norwegians accusing first the Danes and then the Swedes of not allowing Norwegianness to emerge fully over the course of centuries of oppression,[23] a 'centuries of darkness' paradigm ruled supreme as new 'national communities' were ethnicised during the interwar period. The same is true in East-Central and Eastern Europe, for example in Bulgaria, where the Bulgarian nation had allegedly been held back by the Ottomans. The strong ethnic languages of 'national community' in Eastern Europe made it extremely difficult for composite states such as Yugoslavia, founded in 1929, to develop viable national historical master narratives. From early on, each of the diverse republics within Yugoslavia constructed its own ethnic language of 'national community', largely disassociated from Yugoslavia. In the Yugoslav civil wars of the 1990s these discourses erupted with a vengeance, underpinning much of that conflict's ethnic cleansing and other ethnic violence.[24]

However, languages of 'national community' in interwar Europe not only referred to ethnicity. Social distinctions were salient as well. A newly emergent Czech national historical master narrative, for example, actively constructed the Czech nation as a proletarian nation vis-à-vis the bourgeois Germans who occupied the same space but were not part of the Czech nation. The key marker of difference here was not merely ethnicity but rather an ethnicised class difference.[25] Similar processes can be observed in the Baltic states, where, for example, Latvian peasant communities were pitted against the aristocratic Baltic Germans in notions of 'national community' that merged ethnic and class elements.[26]

Peasants could form the backbone of liberal-democratic languages of community, for example in Sweden, Denmark and Norway, and they could also be the powerful representatives of an ethnicised and racialised 'national community', for example in National Socialist Germany. As Liesbeth van de Grift's chapter in this volume argues, the ideas of inner colonisation, under very different ideological circumstances, harked back to ideas of a healthier peasant life in comparison to the experience of urbanised modernity. Carrying anti-capitalist and anti-modern overtones, the colonisation of new land and the settling of peasants on such developments were projects that assigned important political and social roles in the 'national community' to rural workers and their families. This was also reflected in many national historical master narratives in the interwar period.[27]

Languages of "National Community" and Its "Others" in Europe 265

If the languages of national community could be inflected with the markers of social class, they could equally be religiously inflected. Ireland, Poland and Spain are three countries in which the 'national community' was strongly associated with Catholicism during the interwar period. Where religion was nationalised, the nation became a sacred object, and the national historical narratives became infused with religious meaning. In Hungary the close identification of the nation-state with the Catholic church found one of its most powerful expressions in the St Stephen cult, which signalled an anti-liberal, anti-socialist and hierarchical, authoritarian framing of the 'national community'.[28] The importance of religion to languages of community are stressed in this volume by Maarten van der Bos, who discusses the transnational Catholic group of post–Second World War intellectuals and their attempts to construct plans for a peaceful Europe that rested on religious values and norms. Looking at the other side of the Cold War divide in Europe, Ondřej Matějka draws our attention to the rival constructions of religious and class communities in post-war Czechoslovakia by the Communist regime, on the one hand, and the Protestant churches on the other.

Whether based on class or sacralised or racialised, the languages of 'national community' were invariably exclusive. Under diverse occupation regimes during the Second World War, illiberal languages of community blossomed. In France, for example, they could build on the work of historians associated with the Action Française, such as Jacques Bainville and Pierre Gaxotte. Few professional historians in France were affected by this particular discourse, however, so it ultimately fell to an outsider, George Montandon, to come up with a racial historical national master narrative for France. Both the cult of Joan of Arc and the invention of a 'national archaelogy' served to undermine the dominant republican historical master narrative.[29] In Slovakia, František Hrušovský wrote a *History of Slovakia* (1939) in which he ethnicised national history in line with the models provided by the Nazified German historical profession in the Third Reich.[30]

In interwar Europe the liberal-parliamentary and democratic constructions of 'national community' had looked increasingly beleaguered. The languages of class in the Soviet Union, of religion in nations such as Franco's Spain or Salazar's Portugal and of ethnicity/race in Fascist Italy and National Socialist Germany were hostile to such liberal constructions; and political regimes that were oriented toward liberal 'national communities' were toppled. In much of East-Central and Eastern Europe, new nation-states that in their beginnings bore vestiges of liberal democracy, complete with liberal national master narratives, had succumbed to various forms of authoritarianism during the interwar period. By the mid-1930s Great Britain was one of the few remaining bulwarks of the idea of 'national community' that had a predominantly liberal construction. As George Trevelyan put it in a speech he wrote for King George V for the opening of Parliament in 1935: 'It is to me a source of pride and thankfulness that the perfect harmony of our parliamentary system with our constitutional monarchy has survived the shocks that have in recent years destroyed other empires and other liberties [. . .] The complex forms and balanced spirit of our Constitution were not the discovery of a single era, still less of a single party or of a single person. They are the slow accretion of centuries, the outcome of patience, tradition and experience constantly finding outlets [. . .] for the impulse toward liberty, justice and social improvement inherent in our people down the ages'.[31] Such constructions of the 'national community' could also rely on the kind of localised constructions of community that are the subject of Jon Lawrence's chapter in this book. Lawrence argues that an inclusive politics of place in Bermondsey was, above all, created by a specific form of Labour politics that constructed 'community' as an achievement of ordinary folk. This 'discursive Bermondsey' was just one of many places in Britain that strengthened its liberal-democratic 'national community'.

Of course, a similar liberal-democratic orientation can be found outside Britain. Tomáš Garrigue Masaryk's writings provided the underpinnings for a very successful construction of a liberal-democratic Czechoslovakia after 1918.[32] And Swiss constructions of 'national community' harked back to narratives of freedom, justice and federalism that were highly compatible with liberal-democratic ideas.[33] Even in many nation-states where the liberal-democratic narratives were ultimately defeated we find attempts to contest the dominant Communist, Fascist or authoritarian constructions of 'national community'. In Hungary, for example, Oscar Jászi was a prominent critic of the increasingly authoritarian languages of community and promoted the search for a cosmopolitan and democratic Hungary, and he continued to do so even after 1925, when his voice could only be heard from exile.[34] In Fascist Italy, the voice of Benedetto Croce maintained a liberal discourse of the pre-Fascist Italian nation-state,[35] and from within the resistance to Fascism, historians such as Carlo and Nello Rosselli attempted to forge republican languages of the nation that would be more in line with social justice than the pre-war liberal languages.[36] Even for National Socialist Germany we find a distinguished exile tradition of historical writing that maintained rival national historical master narratives; these were to become the building blocks for post-war West German attempts to establish a more liberal-democratic version of the 'national community'.[37] These efforts could be related to highly localised efforts to recover the liberal political language of community that are discussed in Jeremy de Waal's chapter on the re-forging of local identities in the north German cities of Hamburg, Lübeck and Bremen. Whilst de Waal emphasises that the deliberate linking of Hanseatic traditions with the values of cosmopolitanism, democracy and tolerance was meant to be a refutation of a poisoned 'national community', the rival, alternative, liberal-democratic 'national communities' that had been in circulation in exile could pick up such localised constructions of community and integrate them into new national storylines.

After the Second World War there is no immediate break with national historical master narratives. Rather, we witness a variety of attempts in

Western Europe to stabilise traditional notions of 'national community' by making them acceptable to liberal-democratic languages of 'national community' and purifying them of any contamination from Fascism, National Socialism and authoritarianism. In many cases, languages of an alleged 'community of victims' were vitally important to achieve such stabilisation. Germans, Italians and, most famously, Austrians were constructed as victims of National Socialism and Fascism. Austria was now constructed as the 'first victim' of National Socialist aggression in Europe. Those countries occupied by German troops had been 'victims' of occupation. This was also the case for Italians, who could sometimes forget that they had had a Fascist regime of their own. Even the Germans constructed themselves, first and foremost, as 'victims' of Hitler and of war. And, furthermore, the languages of 'national resistance' underpinned notions of alternative 'national communities' that had successfully upheld the good national traditions even in the years of darkness. Rival narratives of resistance led to different constructions of the 'national community' in Italy and France, where Communist narratives competed with Gaullist and Catholic narratives of resistance. The Italian resistance was hailed as a kind of second Risorgimento, and even in West Germany, the resistance of 20 July 1944 was the saving grace of Germany in the post-war world. Traditional national master narratives were also stabilised with reference to the Communist 'other' in the post–Second World War West. Erstwhile Fascists, National Socialists and supporters of other right-wing authoritarian regimes had to learn that many of their former beliefs and definitions of the 'national community' had been mistaken, but they could rest assured that at least their anti-Communism had been justified all along.[38]

Reconstructions of traditional languages of 'national community' in the post-war Western European nation-states were also infused with heavy doses of transnational Atlanticist and European values.[39] This construction of a European intellectual community could also refer to notions of intellectual circles that had formed cross-border communities in the interwar period, the subject of Marleen Rensen's chapter in this volume. After 1945 there were many deliberate attempts to recuperate that spirit and build on it—sometimes with reference to its tragic failure in the interwar period. A European transnational dimension in the forging of 'national communities' involved not just intellectuals, writers and artists but a wide variety of different expert organisations and professional communities that combined Europeanisation with a commitment to the 'national community'. Philip Wagner's chapter in this book explores the activities of one such organisation, the International Federation of Housing and Town Planning, but there were many more, including groups that deliberately set out to introduce European storylines into constructions of 'national community', e.g. historians' associations, literary societies and organisations of social scientists all intent on writing the transnational into the nation, often with the deliberate intent of strengthening the national. New transnational 'communities' now sought positive affiliation with 'national communities', including the 'community of the Occident', the Atlanticist 'community of values', the community of anti-Communists and the anti-totalitarian community—these new transnational communities, often in line with traditional notions of 'national community', mobilised specific notions about antiquity, Christianity and humanism in order to underpin the merger of transnational with national communities historically.

If we examine Eastern Europe in the post–Second World War world, we can observe a comprehensive reconceptualisation of national historical master narratives under class auspices across the Communist world, resulting in various mergers of the languages of 'class community' and 'national community'.[40] The first such merger was attempted by the Soviet Union following the successful Bolshevik revolution of 1917, though we might even go further back, to the European labour movements of the nineteenth century that produced largely autodidactic attempts to write class into national histories that comprehensively nationalised class histories in Europe well before 1914. In the early Soviet Union it fell to Mikhail Nikolaevich Pokrovskii, dubbed the 'Supreme Commander of the Army of Red Historians', to restructure the historical profession, train a new generation of Marxist-Leninist historians and pioneer a new way of writing history that would befit the first Communist state in history. Pokrovskii was, by inclination and training, a comparative social and economic historian with an internationalist outlook. His writings had refuted the notion of a Russian special path in history and instead located Russian history within the mainstream of European history. Yet eventually even he, unable to escape the political pressure from the new Soviet rulers to provide a new national historical master narrative, penned a national history that sought to merge class and national perspectives.[41] The Bolshevik historian, so wrote his fellow historian A.E. Presniakov, was 'another step in the ongoing process of national unification',[42] and the Bolsheviks were building a new nation-state erected on the empowerment of workers and peasants, the two classes representing it. The strong class perspective in Soviet national history was replaced under Stalin with a renewed emphasis on Russian ethnic particularism. Under Stalin, very traditional tropes from Tsarist historiographical traditions were dusted off and brought into line with a schematic class interpretation. Thus, for example, both Ivan the Terrible and Peter the Great were celebrated by Stalinist historians as great nation-builders. Socialism and nationalism were frequently collapsed into a single concept,[43] for example in Vasil'evich Shestakov's notorious *Short Course in the History of the USSR*, first published in 1937: 'The USSR is the land of socialism. There is only one socialist country on the globe—it is our motherland. [. . .] We love our motherland and we must know her wonderful history well. Whoever knows history will better understand current life, will fight the enemies of our country better, and will consolidate socialism'.[44]

Traditional national histories painted red also became a popular genre in Communist Eastern Europe after 1945. Communist national histories often divided their 'national communities' in two—a positive and a negative line of tradition, one to be endorsed, the other to be condemned; one progressive, which had foreshadowed the new communist state, and the other reactionary, having attempted (ultimately always in vain) to hold it back. The Communists' commitment to the writing of national histories is highlighted by Stalin's famous dictum that history had to be 'socialist in content and national in form'.[45] The initial search for diverse national roads to socialism soon gave way to a prescribed one-size-fits-all model that usually followed the Soviet script. There were some notable exceptions, such as Romania, where the historical regime first prescribed strict internationalism, denouncing everything Romanian as reactionary and backward, then from the late 1960s onwards turned this prescribed view of history on its head, promoting until Ceaușescu's fall a hypernationalism in which all the world's progressive developments always had Romanians among their pioneers.[46] But most other national histories in Communist Eastern Europe stressed the impact of revolutions, the development of the working classes under industrialisation and the emergence of working-class parties; they celebrated the proletarian nation and its anti-capitalism and anti-fascism. National forces were often portrayed as progressive forces in history and Communist historians frequently adopted the nationalist language of their sources. They also constructed new national heroes and were prone to link national storylines not only to class but also to ethnic descent. Most newly created historical institutes at the Communist academies set themselves the task of producing new national histories that traced the eventual emergence of the 'socialist nation' as a 'nation of a higher type'.[47]

Throughout the Communist period alternative constructions of 'national community' existed in exile. As demonstrated by the example of Baltic history writing in exile, these constructions often used interpretative frameworks and notions of 'national community' that were frozen, as it were, in the pre-Communist era, and they maintained very traditional national historical master narratives that were not renowned for their methodological or narratological innovations. These exile historiographies from Communist Eastern Europe were also often enlisted by the West in the Cold War struggle, as the Ukranian and Polish exile historiographies powerfully underline.[48]

Yet a class perspective on national history was not the sole preserve of Communist Eastern Europe. Class became an important concept in national history writing in Western Europe in the 1960s and 1970s, when new social histories, still widely national in orientation, began to appear across Western Europe. In Sweden in particular, the Social Democrats forged a powerful notion of 'national community' around the 'people's home' idea.[49] The building of the people's home was a form of community building, in which social equality and the emancipation of the working classes were important elements. It involved stark doses of social engineering, mostly involving top-down state initiatives but also sometimes bottom-up efforts which were always aimed at creating and enforcing notions of community. The planning initiatives that Stefan Couperus discusses in post-war Coventry are rooted in similar notions taken up with building communities around languages of class, citizenship and democracy that were also at the heart of the 'people's home' idea and of many social-democratic attempts at local, regional, national and transnational community building from the interwar period to the 1970s, when this model reached an intellectual crisis. With regard to the Netherlands, Harm Kaal's chapter explores this crisis of the discursive construction of a social-democratic community that he charts back to the 1960s.

By way of conclusion, our attempt to trace diverse languages of 'national community' in national historical master narratives in Europe from the end of the First World War to the 1960s has revealed very different ways of constructing such 'national communities' across time and space. The First World War reshaped the national imaginary in many European countries in decisive but often contradictory ways. Thus it could lead either to a strong ethnicisation and racialisation of 'national community' or to their opposite—de-ethnicisation. However, especially in the contested borderlands of East-Central and Eastern Europe, we can observe a strong ethnicisation of the language of 'national community' in the interwar period. In that era, liberal languages of 'national community' often faltered before the vigorous forward march of right-wing authoritarian, Fascist, National Socialist and religious languages of 'national community' that were hostile to parliamentarism, constitutionalism and republicanism. At the end of the Second World War, in stark contrast to the impact of the First World War, there were no major attempts to refocus national historical master narratives. Instead, across Western Europe we have observed attempts to stabilise traditional master narratives. The prominent merging of 'class communities' with 'national communities' in Eastern European Communist national historical master narratives produced often facile and ideologically oriented national histories that only painted red very traditional national histories. The more convincing attempts to merge class communities with national communities were undertaken under social-democratic auspices in Western Europe, where in many states, notably Sweden, these efforts succeeded in capturing the imagination of what should constitute 'national community'. The vision put forth of a community socially engineered from above, reinforced by an active notion of citizenship that would lead to the self-empowerment of the working classes, reached a crisis point only towards the end of the period under investigation in this volume. Overall, our discussion has shown the persistence of languages of 'national community' but also their strong contestation. Hence we often have several competing versions of 'national community' promoted by different political and professional interest groups. Invariably notions of 'national community' have been very successful in accommodating other visions of community under their remit. Whether they were local, regional or transnational constructions of community, or whether they referred to communities of class, religion and ethnicity/race, the languages of 'national community' could frequently relate to these constructs and incorporate them into their national visions. Hence, in the period under discussion, the languages of 'national community' were by far the most important political languages in Europe.

Notes

1. For a comprehensive comparative overview of the development of national historical master narratives in modern Europe, see Berger and Conrad, *The Past as History*.
2. Berger and Lorenz, eds, *The Contested Nation*; Middell and Roura, eds, *Transnational Challenges*.
3. Whereas 'historism' (in German, *Historismus*), as associated with Leopold von Ranke, can be seen as an evolutionary, reformist concept which understands all political order as historically developed and grown, 'historicism' (in German, *Historizismus*), as defined and rejected by Karl Popper, is based on the notion that history develops according to predetermined laws moving towards a particular end. Hence, I would plead that we follow the German language and introduce two separate terms in English as well, in order to avoid confusion.
4. Haar and Fahlbusch, eds, *German Scholars*.
5. Mann, *Betrachtungen eines Unpolitischen*.
6. Meinecke, *Die deutsche Erhebung*.
7. Tönnies, *Gemeinschaft und Gesellschaft*.
8. Watson, *Ring of Steel*.
9. Sheehan, "What Is German History?".
10. Martin Spahn, "An den Pforten des Weltkrieges", in: *Hochland*, Oct. 1914, 20ff.
11. Wallace, *War and the Image of Germany*; Hawes, *Englanders and Huns*.
12. Cited in Wallace, *War*, 77.
13. Goebel, *The Great War*.
14. Schöttler, "After the Deluge," 412.
15. Herwig, "Clio Deceived".
16. One famous example is Werner Conze, whose dissertation was on one such German diasporic community, Hirschenhhof. See Werner Conze, *Hirschenhof. Die Geschichte einer deutschen Sprachinsel in Livland* (Berlin: Junker und Dünnhaupt, 1934); on Conze and his dissertation, see also Etzemüller, *Sozialgeschichte als politische Geschichte*, 272ff.; Dunkhase, *Werner Conze*, 31ff.
17. Von Klimó, *Nation, Konfession, Geschichte*.
18. Hudek, "Slovak Historiography".
19. Ludanyi, "The Legacy of Transylvania".
20. See many of the contributions in: Frank and Hadler, eds, *Disputed Territories*.
21. On the close relationship between urban and national identity constructions, see also Umbach, "A Tale of Second Cities".
22. Fewster, *Visions of Glory*.
23. Aronsson et al., "Nordic National Histories".
24. Brunnbauer, *(Re)Writing History*.
25. Heiss et al., "Habsburg"s Difficult Legacy".
26. Wendland, "The Russian Empire".
27. Berger and Conrad, *The Past as History*, 96ff.
28. Von Klimó, "St. Stephen's Day".
29. Gordon, "Right-Wing Historiographical Models".
30. Hudek, "Slovakia," 152ff.

31. Cited in Hernon Jr, "The Last Whig Historian," 86.
32. Řepa, "The Czechs, Germans and Sudetenland".
33. Marchal, *Schweizer Gebrauchsgeschichte*.
34. Litván, *A Twentieth-Century Prophet*.
35. Rizi, *Benedetto Croce*.
36. Morgan, "Reclaiming Italy?".
37. Lehmann and Sheehan, eds, *An Interrupted Past*.
38. Berger, "A Return to the National Paradigm?".
39. Jiménez and Rediker, "What Is Atlantic History?" http://marcusrediker.com/writings/atlantic-history.php [accessed 28 January 2016].
40. Antohi, Trencsényi, and Apor, eds, *Narratives Unbound*.
41. Enteen, *The Soviet Scholar-Bureaucrat*.
42. Rieber, "Introduction," quote on xxviii.
43. Powell, "The Nationalist Trend".
44. Cited in Mazour, *Modern Russian Historiography*, 204.
45. Von Klimó, "Helden, Völker, Freiheitskämpfe".
46. Durandin, "La function de l'histoire".
47. Hadler, "Drachen und Drachentöter".
48. Mandelíčková and Goddeeris, "Living in the Past".
49. Liljefors and Zander, "Der zweite Weltkrieg".

Bibliography

Antohi, Sorin, Balázs Trencsényi, and Péter Apor, eds. *Narratives Unbound: Historical Studies in Post-Communist Eastern Europe*. Budapest: CEU Press, 2008.

Aronsson, Peter, et al. "Nordic National Histories." In *The Contested Nation: Ethnicity, Class, Religion and Gender in National Histories*, edited by Stefan Berger and Chris Lorenz, 256–82. Basingstoke: Palgrave Macmillan, 2008.

Berger, Stefan. "A Return to the National Paradigm? National History Writing in Germany, Italy, France and Britain from 1945 to the Present." *Journal of Modern History* 77, no. 3 (2005): 629–78.

Berger, Stefan and Chris Lorenz, eds. *The Contested Nation: Ethnicity, Class, Religion and Gender in National Histories*. Basingstoke: Palgrave MacMillan, 2008.

Berger, Stefan and Christoph Conrad. *The Past as History: National Identity and Historical Consciousness in Modern Europe*. Basingstoke: Palgrave Macmillan, 2015.

Brunnbauer, Ulf. *(Re)Writing History: Historiography in Southeast Europe after Socialism*. Münster: Lit-Verlag, 2004.

Dunkhase, Jan Eike. *Werner Conze. Ein deutscher Historiker im 20. Jahrhundert*. Göttingen: Vandenhoeck & Ruprecht, 2010.

Durandin, Catherine. "La function de l'histoire et le statut de l'historien à l'époque du national-communisme en Roumanie." In *Enjeux de l'histoire en Europe Centrale*, edited by Marie-Élizabeth Ducreux and Antoine Marès, 103–12. Paris: L'Harmattan, 2002.

Enteen, George M. *The Soviet Scholar-Bureaucrat: M.N. Pokrovskii and the Society of Marxist Historians*. University Park, PA: Pennsylvania State University Press, 1978.

Etzemüller, Thomas. *Sozialgeschichte als politische Geschichte. Werner Conze und die Neuorientierung der westdeutschen Geschichtswissenschaft nach 1945*. Munich: R. Oldenbourg, 2001.

Fewster, Derek. *Visions of Glory: Nationalism and the Construction of Early Finnish History*. Helsinki: The Finnish Literature Society, 2006.

Goebel, Stefan. *The Great War and Medieval Memory: War, Remembrance and Medievalism in Britain and Germany, 1914–1940*. Cambridge: Cambridge University Press, 2007.

Gordon, Bertram M. "Right-Wing Historiographical Models in France, 1918–1945." In *Writing National Histories: Western Europe Since 1800*, edited by Stefan Berger, Mark Donovan, and Kevin Passmore, 163–75. London: Routledge, 1999.

Haar, Ingo and Michael Fahlbusch, eds. *German Scholars and Ethnic Cleansing, 1918–1945*. Oxford: Berghahn, 2005.

Hadler, Frank. "Drachen und Drachentöter. Das Problem der nationalgeschichtlichen Fixierung in den Historiographien Ostmitteleuoropas nach dem Zweiten Weltkrieg." In *Die Nation schreiben. Geschichtswissenschaft im internationalen Vergleich*, edited by Christoph Conrad and Sebastian Conrad, 137–64. Göttingen: Vandenhoeck & Ruprecht, 2002.

Hawes, James. *Englanders and Huns: The Culture Clash which Led to the First World War*. London: Simon and Schuster, 2014.

Heiss, Gernot, et al., "Habsburg's Difficult Legacy: Comparing and Relating Austrian, Czech, Magyar and Slovak National Historical Master Narratives." In *The Contested Nation: Ethnicity, Class, Religion and Gender in National Histories*, edited by Stefan Berger and Chris Lorenz, 367–404. Basingstoke: Palgrave Macmillan, 2008.

Hernon, J. M., Jr. "The Last Whig Historian and Consensus History." *American Historical Review* 81 (1976): 66–97.

Herwig, Holger. "Clio Deceived: Patriotic Self-Censorship in Germany after the Great War." In *Forging the Collective Memory: Government and International Historians through Two World Wars*, edited by Keith Wilson, 87–127. Oxford: Berghahn, 1996.

Hudek, Adam. "Slovak Historiography and Constructing the Slovak National Story up to 1948." *Human Affairs* 1 (2006): 51–65.

Hudek, Adam. "Slovakia." In *Atlas of European Historiography: The Making of a Profession 1800–2005*, edited by Ilaria Porciani and Lutz Raphael, 152–53. Basingstoke: Palgrave Macmillan, 2010.

Jiménez, Michael and Marcus Rediker, "What Is Atlantic History?" http://marcusrediker.com/writings/atlantic-history.php [accessed 28 January 2016].

Klimó, Árpád von. "St. Stephen's Day: Politics and Religion in Twentieth-Century Hungary." *East Central Europe* 26 (1999): 15–29.

Klimó, Árpád von. *Nation, Konfession, Geschichte. Zur nationalen Geschichtskultur Ungarns im europäischen Ausland (1860–1948)*. Munich: R. Oldenbourg, 2003.

Klimó, Árpád von. "Helden, Völker, Freiheitskämpfe. Zur Ästhetik stalinistischer Geschichtsschreibung in der Sowjetunion, der Volksrepublik Ungarn und der DDR." *Storia della Storiografia* 52 (2007): 83–112.

Lehmann, Hartmut and James J. Sheehan, eds. *An Interrupted Past: German-Speaking Refugee Historians in the United States after 1933*. Cambridge: Cambridge University Press, 1991.

Liljefors, Max and Ulf Zander. "Der zweite Weltkrieg und die schwedische Utopie." In *Mythen der Nationen–1945. Arena der Erinnerungen*. Vol. 2, edited by Monika Flacke, 569–92. Mainz: Philipp Zabern, 2004.

Litván, György. *A Twentieth-Century Prophet: Oscar Jászi*. Budapest: CEU Press, 2006.

Ludanyi, Andrew. "The Legacy of Transylvania in Romanian and Hungarian Historiography." In *Disputed Territories and Shared Pasts: Overlapping National Histories in Modern Europe*, edited by Tibor Frank and Frank Hadler, 247–72. Basingstoke: Palgrave Macmillan, 2011.

Mandelíčková, Monika and Idesbald Goddeeris. "Living in the Past: Historians in Exile." In *Setting the Standards: Institutions, Networks and Communities of National Historiography*, edited by Ilaria Porciani and Jo Tollebeek, 394–414. Basingstoke: Palgrave Macmillan, 2011.

Mann, Thomas. *Betrachtungen eines Unpolitischen*. Berlin: S. Fischer, 1918.

Marchal, Guy P. *Schweizer Gebrauchsgeschichte. Geschichtsbilder, Mythenbildung und nationale Identität*. Basel: Schwabe, 2006.

Mazour, Anatole G. *Modern Russian Historiography*. Princeton, NJ: Princeton University Press, 1958.

Meinecke, Friedrich. *Die deutsche Erhebung von 1914*. Stuttgart: Cotta, 1914.

Middell, Matthias and Lluis Roura, eds. *Transnational Challenges to National History Writing*. Basingstoke: Palgrave Macmillan, 2013.

Morgan, Philip. "Reclaiming Italy? Antifascist Historians and History in 'Justice and Liberty'." In *Writing National Histories: Western Europe Since 1800*, edited by Stefan Berger, Mark Donovan, and Kevin Passmore, 150–60. London: Routledge, 1999.

Powell, A. "The Nationalist Trend in Soviet Historiography." *Soviet Studies* 2, no. 4 (1951): 361–79.

Řepa, Milan. "The Czechs, Germans and Sudetenland: Historiographical Disputes in the 'Heart of Europe'." In *Disputed Territories and Shared Pasts: Overlapping National Histories in Modern Europe*, edited by Tibor Frank and Frank Hadler, 303–28. Basingstoke: Palgrave Macmillan, 2011.

Rieber, Alfred J. "Introduction." In *The Formation of the Great Russian State: A Study of Russian History in the Thirteenth to Fifteenth Centuries*, edited by A.E. Presniakov, vi–lix. Chicago: University of Chicago Press, 1970.

Rizi, Fabio Fernando. *Benedetto Croce and Italian Fascism*. Toronto: University of Toronto Press, 2003.

Schöttler, Peter. "After the Deluge: The Impact of the Two World Wars on the Historical Work of Henri Pirenne and Marc Bloch." In *Nationalizing the Past: Historians as Nation Builders in Modern Europe*, edited by Stefan Berger and Chris Lorenz, 404–25. Basingstoke: Palgrave Macmillan, 2010.

Sheehan, James J. "What Is German History? Reflections on the Role of the Nation in German History and Historiography." *Journal of Modern History* 53 (1981): 1–15.

Tönnies, Ferdinand. *Gemeinschaft und Gesellschaft*. Berlin: Fues, 1887.

Umbach, Maiken. "A Tale of Second Cities: Autonomy, Culture and the Law in Hamburg and Barcelona in the Long Nineteenth Century." *American Historical Review* 110, no. 3 (2005): 659–92.

Wallace, Stuart. *War and the Image of Germany: British Academics*. Edinburgh: John Donald, 1988.

Watson, Alexander. *Ring of Steel: Germany and Austro-Hungary at War 1914–1918*. London: Penguin, 2014.

Wendland, Anna Veronika. "The Russian Empire and Its Western Borderlands: National Historiographies and Their 'Others' in Russia, the Baltics and the Ukraine." In *The Contested Nation: Ethnicity, Class, Religion and Gender in National Histories*, edited by Stefan Berger and Chris Lorenz, 405–41. Basingstoke: Palgrave Macmillan, 2008.

Contributors

Stefan Berger is Director of the Institute for Social Movements and Professor of Social History at the Ruhr-University Bochum and Chairman of the Committee of the Library of the Ruhr Foundation.

Maarten van den Bos is a Postdoctoral Researcher at Utrecht University.

Stefan Couperus is Assistant Professor of European Politics and Society at the University of Groningen.

Jeremy DeWaal is a Postdoctoral Fellow at the Berlin Program for Advanced German and European Studies at the Freie Universität Berlin.

Liesbeth van de Grift is Assistant Professor of the History of International Relations at Utrecht University.

Harm Kaal is Assistant Professor of Political History at Radboud University Nijmegen.

Florian Kührer-Wielach is Director of the Institute for German Culture and History in South-Eastern Europe (IKGS) associated with the Ludwig-Maximilians-Universität München.

Jon Lawrence is Reader in Modern British History at the University of Cambridge and a Fellow of Emmanuel College.

Ondřej Matějka is Assistant Professor of Modern European History at the Faculty of Social Sciences of Charles University, Prague.

Marleen Rensen is Assistant Professor of Modern European Literature at the European Studies Department of the University of Amsterdam.

Tanja Vahtikari is a Postdoctoral Research Fellow at the University of Tampere.

Phillip Wagner is a Researcher at the Humboldt-Universität zu Berlin.

Index

Adenauer, Konrad 178, 189, 205
Alba Iulia 8, 87–93, 99–102
Amsterdam 113, 163, 199, 201, 203, 223, 225, 228, 245
Anderson, Benedict 1, 5–6, 71, 217
anti-modern 76, 261–2, 264
anti-Semitism 3, 167
Aquinas, Thomas 178, 180
architecture 4, 45, 47, 58, 199, 204, 206, 241
Asia 160, 207–8
Ascher, Charles S. 207–9
atheism 178, 244–5, 247–8; scientific atheism 247–8, 253
Austria 93, 153, 165, 204, 261, 263, 267
Austria-Hungary 96
authoritarianism 47, 265
Averescu, Alexandru 94, 100

Banat 88–9, *91*, 92, 101
Bauman, Zygmunt 110
Beaufort, Didymous 179–80, 182, 184–5
Belgium 132, 144, 165, 198, 202–3, 205, 262
Beneš, Edvard 241
Bermondsey 7–8, 19–37, 266
Bessarabia 88, 93, 101, 263
Bethnal Green 20, 25
Birmingham 46, 48–51
Bohemia-Moravia 242
Bourdieu, Pierre 217
Brauer, Max 136–7, 139
Bremen *134*, 136, 139, 142
Brubaker, Roger 102
Brussels 6, 202
Bucharest 87, 89–90, 93–8, 100–3
Bukovina 88, *91*, 93, 101, 263

Cambridge 5
Canada 23, 178–9; *see also* North America
Canley 48, 51–3, 55–6, 59
Carpathia 87, 92, 94–7, 103
Catholicism 10, 34, 90, 92, 111, 115, 175–190, 218, 220, 224–7, 229, 261, 265, 267: Catholic Association for Spiritual Renewal 10, 181–6; Catholic Church 175, 184, 265; Catholic Institute for Social-Ecclesiastical Research 225, *226*; Catholic Party (The Netherlands) 179, 220, 224–5, 227; Catholic United Church 90, 92, 99–100
Catholic People's Party *see* Catholic Party
Central Europe 88, 99, 160
China 23, 26, 28
Christianity 115, 154, 177–9, 181, 189, 238, 242, 244–53, 268: Christian Democrats 178, 230; Christian-Marxist dialogue 247–8, 250–1, 253
class 1–2, 4–5, 7, 10–11, 19–20, 23, 27–34, 37, 45, 47–9, 51, 54, 58–9, 66, 78–9, 90, 93, 164, 183, 185, 217–21, 223–4, 227–9, 260, 264–5, 268–71
Cluj 91, 96, 98–9
Cologne 131, 136, 138, 140
communism 11, 67, 79, 102, 164, 179, 182–3, 200, 238, 244–8, 250, 265–70; Communist Party of Czechoslovakia 238, 243–4, 247, 249–50
communitarianism 6
community: exclusion 1, 3–9, 11, 28, 31, 37, 66, 80, 144, 176, 198, 231, 244, 250; expert 197, 199–204,

208–9; imagined 5, 69, 132, 153, 158–9, 163, 169; local 9, 28, 73–4, 103, 130–3, 135–9, 141–2, 144–5; modern 9, 76, 115–18, 120, 122, 125, 138; reconstruction 1, 3, 8–9, 20, 45, 65, 69, 72, 80, 110, 131–2, 136–40, 143–5, 219, 230, 246, 263, 267; rural 9, 73, 109, 113–18, 120, 122, 125; sense of belonging 7–9, 21, 26, 28, 31, 66, 74, 80, 88, 91, 97, 115, 130, 142, 144, 158, 189, 217–18, 225, 263; transnational 2, 6, 9–11, 73, 140, 153–55, 159, 162, 166, 168, 196–205, 208–9, 260, 265, 267–8, 270–1; urban 4–5, 8, 45, 65–6, 69, 71–5, 77–80, 263–4; vernacular understandings of 2, 7–8, 22, 26, 31, 38
conservatism 37, 178, 220
Coventry 7–8, 46–53, 55–6, 58–9, 202, 270; Coventry Corporation 47–9, 59
CPC *see* Communist Party of Czechoslovakia
CPC Politburo *see* Czechoslovak Politburo
Croce, Benedetto 160, 266
Czechoslovakia 11, 91, 93, 198, 238–9, 241–53, 263–6; Czechoslovak Politburo 246–7, 249; Czech Protestant Church 238

Dacians 92, 96–7; Daco-Romanian 92
democracy 1, 6, 47, 50, 87, 89, 90, 96, 102, 110, 131, 138–41, 202, 204, 218, 238, 251, 265; democratisation 50, 96, 130; undemocratic 48, 97, 144
Denmark 163, 264
Deutscher Verband für Wohnungswesen, Städtebau und Raumordnung 204–5
Drees, Willem 189, 224
Dubček, Alexander 250
Dudley Report 45, 48, 53, 56, 58
Dulles, John Foster 245
Dutch Reformed Church 184, 186
DV *see* Deutscher Verband für Wohnungswesen, Städtebau und Raumordnung

ECCB *see* Evangelical Church of Czech Brethren
economic crisis 108, 111, 125, 221
Engels, Friedrich 243

England 7, 19, 21, 25, 27, 29, 56, 160, 162, 165, 197, 204, 238
Enlightenment 122, 153–4, 161–2, 166, 168–9
Erasmus, Desiderius 154, 161, 166–9
Etzioni, Amitai 6
European integration 177–8, 188, 190
Evangelical Church of Czech Brethren 238, 242, 244, 251
expert network 10, 196–8, 201, 205–7

family 3–4, 6, 23–9, 32, 34, 36, 52, 54, 71, 112, 116–17, 141, 178, 183–4, 190
fascism 67, 73, 165–7, 182, 204, 221, 265–7, 269–70
Federal Republic of Germany *see* West Germany
Feltin, Maurice 186–9
Finland 7, 66–76, 78–9, 263–4
First World War 8, 87–8, 90, 92, 97, 110–12, 153, 155–6, 162, 168, 180, 205, 260–2, 270
Firth, Raymond 20–4, 26–8, 30–2, 37
Foucault, Michel 5
France 4, 10, 111, 153–4, 156, 159–63, 165, 175–6, 178–9, 182–3, 185–9, 198–9, 201, 204–5, 217, 261–2, 265, 267
Freedman, Maurice 26
Fromm, Erich 249, 251–2

generation 5, 25, 36, 92, 109–10, 114, 125, 159, 182, 261, 268
Goethe, Johan Wolfgang von 157–8, 165
Goga, Octavian 92, 98
Granovetter, Mark 32, 36
Great Britain 199, 206, 265
Greenhalgh, James 46
Gropius, Walter 204
Guinness Trust Buildings 20, 21; Guinness Trust 21, 29

Haarlemmermeer 113, 117–18
Habsburg Empire 92–3, 95
Habsburg-Cisleithania *see* Bukovina
Hamburg 9, 131, 133, 135–43, 266
Hanseatic 9, 131–4, 136–44, 266
Hauptmann, Gerhart 163
Heimat 73–4, 130–2, 135–43
Helsinki 7–8, 65–80, 144, 263
Hesse, Hermann 156, 158, 160–1
high modernity 75, 253

Hiršl, Karl 242–3
Hitler, Adolf 1, 267
Hobsbawm, Eric 5
Holy See 176, 183, 189–90
Hörhammer, Manfred 186–7
housing shortage 26–7, 47, 54
Hromádka, Josef Lukl 239, 240, 241–6, 248–9, 251–2
humanist 10, 153–4, 157, 161, 166–8, 245, 249–51, 268
human rights 178–80, 241; Association for Human Rights 251
Hungary 87, 89, 91–4, 96, 98–100, 261, 263, 265–6

IFHTP *see* International Federation for Housing and Town Planning
ILO *see* International Labour Organisation
industrialization 32, 79, 111, 125, 225, 269
Institute for Social Research on the Dutch People 113–14
International Federation for Housing and Town Planning 10, 197–209
International Labour Organisation 196, 201
internationalism 132, 140, 143, 155–6, 160–1, 176–9, 182–4, 186, 189–90, 196, 201, 204–5, 208, 268–9
International of the Mind 160, 164
interwar 2, 4, 9–10, 34, 45, 69, 72, 79, 89, 94, 103, 108–9, 111, 117, 123, 125, 144, 153, 163, 169, 178, 197, 201–2, 219, 221, 225, 239, 241, 260–5, 267, 270
Iriye, Akira 6, 155–6, 209
ISONEVO *see* Institute for Social Research on the Dutch People
Italy 124, 154, 160, 179, 265–7

Jacobs, Jane 5
Jephcott, Pearl 19
Jew 28, 91, 101, 143, 153, 165

Kadlecová, Erika 243–4, 247–51, 253
Kaisen, Wilhelm 137, 139
KASKI *see* Catholic Institute for Social-Ecclesiastical Research
Karelia 73–5, 80
Katholiek Genootschap voor Geestelijke Vernieuwing *see* Catholic Association for Spiritual Renewal
Katholieke Volkspartij *see* Catholic Party

kinship 20–3, 26, 37
Kopecký, Václav 244
Kuper, Leo 51–9

Labour 8, 22, 31–2, 34, 36, 38, 47–9, 218, 220, 222, 223–4, 266; Labour Government 20, 34, 46
League of Nations 156, 206
Lenin, V.I. 243–4, 248
liberal democracy 31, 110, 200, 239, 264–7
liberalism 2, 6, 111, 114, 143, 201–2, 219, 241, 245, 252, 265, 270
Lisbon 208
Lochman, Jan Milíč 238, 249–52
London 7, 19–20, 23, 25–31, 34, 37, 46, 66, 161, 165, 198, 200, 220, 244; London County Council 23; London School of Economics 19, 28, 37
Lübeck 9, 130–1, 134, 135, 136, 138–40, 142, 266
Lublin Committee 198, 200

Machovec, Milan 247–53
MacIver, Robert Morrison 3, 20
MacMurray, John 242–3
Madge, Charles 20, 50
Maier, Charles S. 1
Manin, Bernard 217–18, 229
Maniu, Iului 92–4, 98, 100
Mann, Heinrich 136
Mann, Thomas 136, 261
Mannerheim, C.G.E. 71
Mannheim, Karl 1–2, 123
Marinetti, Filippo Tommaso 166
Maritain, Jacques 10, 178–80, 183, 186–7, 189
Marx, Karl 243–4, 247–9, 252
Marxism 164, 221, 238–9, 242–4, 247–53, 268
Masaryk, Tomáš Garrigue 239, 241, 266
Mass Observation 51
Mazower, Mark 144, 177
memory 8, 34, 65–6, 68–72, 75, 77–80, 96, 131, 137, 139–40, 262
modernisation 3–4, 65, 75–6, 87, 96, 102–3, 108, 111–12, 114, 199, 206–7, 247; modernist planning 5, 47, 69, 75, 199, 201, 204, 206; modernity 1, 3, 65, 76, 80, 138, 175, 264
Moscow 66–7, 244, 246
Moyn, Samuel 179
Munich 239, 241

280 Index

nationalism 1–6, 71, 98, 102, 132, 137, 140–1, 143, 153–7, 161–3, 165, 261–3, 265, 268–9
National Party *see* Romanian National Party of Transylvania and the Banat
National Peasants' Party 88, 100–2
National Socialism 3, 130, 137, 141, 179, 184, 186, 201, 204, 221, 264–7, 270
nation-state 4, 8–9, 92–3, 176, 231, 260, 263–8
Nazi Germany 130, 155, 202–4, 219, 264–6
Nazism *see* National Socialism
neoliberalism 231, 253
Netherlands 9–10, 23, 108–14, *115*, 116, 119, 123, 132, 144, 163, 175, 179–82, 184–9, 198, 218–20, 224–5, 231, 270; Dutch episcopacy 184–5; Dutch politics 11, 108, 111–12, 189, 218–20, 223, 228–9, 231
New Delhi 207–8
new towns 4, 29
Nicolaï, Georg 156–7, 161, 163
Nisbet, Robert 3–4, 6
Noordoostpolder 108–9, *115*, *118*, 119–20, *121*, 125
North America 3, 182, 197, 204
Norway 198, 264

Opočenský, Milan 248–9
orthodox Protestant 120
Oslo 66
Ostrowski, Waclaw 199–201, 209
Ottoman empire 262

Parent Teacher Association 23
Paris 67, 87, *157*, 163, 166, 186–7
Partium 88, 92
Pax Christi 10, 175–6, 185–8
Peasants' Party 88, 90, 99–102
P.E.N. Club 164–6
Pepler, Elizabeth 206–9
Pepler, George L. 198–200, 204, 206–9
Poland *91*, 183, 198–201, 209, 263, 265
Politburo of the Central Committee *see* Czechoslovak Politburo
political orthodoxy 225, *226*
political science 11, 19, 217–19, 228, 247
Pius XII 183, 187–9
Prague 166, 239, 242, 244, 248–9, 251–3; Prague Spring 251–3

race 5, 7, 11, 28, 89, 161, 196, 260–1, 264–5, 270–1
Rawls, John 6
Regat 87–8, 90, 94, 96–9, 101–2
Reilly, Charles 53
religious renewal 175, 182–3, 185, 188, 190
Republic of Letters 9–10, 153–6, 159–60, 162, 165–9
Republic of the Mind 159
Rhineland 139, 141, 143
Richards, Audrey 20, 23, 25, 27–8
Richta, Radovan 243
Rodgers, Daniel 230, 253
Rolland, Romain 10, 153, 156–69
Romania 8–9, 87–103, 263, 269: Greater Romania 87–90, 98–102
Romanian National Party of Transylvania and the Banat 89, 90, 93–6, 98–101
Rotterdam 167, 202
Russia 73, 79, 88, *91*, 92–3, 198, 241, 263–4, 268

Salter, Alfred 19, 31–3, 36–8
Schäfer, Paula 204–5, 209
Scheffer, Louis S.P. 203, 205
Schuman, Robert 178, 188–9
Second World War 10–11, 20, 25, 65, 68, 70–1, 73, 79, 109, 111, 114, 119, 124, 175, 177, 189
secularisation 11, 178–80, 182, 184, 218, 220, 224–5
segregation 5
Sibiu *91*, 93, 99
Singapore 207
Social Democrats 67, 78–9, 90, 111, 204, 220–1, 223–4, 227–30
social engineering 2, 109–10, 112, 114, 117, 123, 125, 247, 269
social experts 110, 114, 125, 196
social geography 108, 113–14, 116, 120
socialism 11, 19–20, 33–4, 47, 90, 132, 218, 220–1, 224–5, 229, 231, 238–9, 243–53, 268–9; humanist socialism 249
social planning *see* social engineering
sociology 2–5, 8, 11, 19–20, 22, 32, 46, 48–51, 53, 55–6, 58–60, 74, 108–9, 111–14, 116–17, 119–20, 122–3, 125, 219–21, 223, 225, 227, 239, 247–8, 261
South Africa 23, 51

Soviet-Union 3, 67, 70, 73, 79, 91, 110, 134, 144, 164, 178, 182, 196–8, 201, 203, 239, 241, 247, 265, 268–9
Spiwak, Henry 199–200, 209
spiritual renewal *see* religious renewal
Stedman Jones, Gareth 5, 217
Stockholm 66, 72
Strasbourg 189, 264
Strölin, Karl 202–4
Stuttgart 202, 204
suburbs 26, 32, 47
Suolahti, Eino E. 69, 71, 75
Sweden 68, 79, 199, 264, 269–70
Switzerland 159–60, 167, 204, 266

Théas, Pierre-Marie 186
theological renewal *see* religious renewal
Third Reich *see* Nazi Germany
Tile Hill 48, 56, 57
Tönnies, Ferdinand 3, 110, 116, 125, 219, 261
town planning 10, 53, 56, 58, 197
transnational networks 6, 154–5, 158, 162–3, 169, 177, 196–7, 201, 205–7, 241, 251, 253; *see also* community: transnational
Transylvania 88–97, 99–101, 144, 263
Trusina, Karel 248–9

UNESCO *see* United Nations Educational, Scientific and Cultural Organisation
United Church *see* Catholic United Church
United Nations 124, 179, 196–7, 207–9; United Nations Educational, Scientific and Cultural Organisation 207
United States of America 3, 5, 19, 23, 25, 27, 45, 139, 160, 177, 182, 196, 204, 207–8, 228, 230, 238, 241, 244–5; *see also* North America
urban governance 48–50
urbanisation 1, 3–4, 9, 32, 46–7, 111, 114, 125, 143, 201, 225, 264
urban planning 5, 45–6, 50, 54, 58, 60, 75, 197, 200, 202, 206
urban renewal 47, 75

Vaida-Voievod, Alexandru 92–5, 98
Vaterstädtische Vereinigung 136, 138, 142
Veen, Henri Nicolaas ter 109, 113–20, 122–5
Ven, J.J.M. van der 179–82, 185
vernacular sense of place *see* community: vernacular understandings
Vienna 91, 96, 204

Ward, Barbara 25–6, 28
Warsaw 198–202
WCC *see* World Council of Churches
Weimar Republic 92, 102, 110–11, 156, 160, 162, 199, 202, 261–3
Wells, H.G. 162, 165
Western Europe 7, 167, 189, 197, 200, 202, 208–9, 267, 269–70
West Germany 9, 73, 103, 130–45, 175, 178–9, 181, 184, 186, 189, 203–5, 208–9, 267
Wieringermeer 108–9, 113, 117, 120, 122, 124–5
World Council of Churches 238–9, 241, 245, 252

Young, Michael 20, 25
Yugoslavia 93, 264

Zweig, Stefan 10, 153, 156, 158–69